Immigration, nationality & refugee law handbook

A USER'S GUIDE

1997 edition

Sue Shutter

Joint Council for the Welfare of Immigrants

The Joint Council for the Welfare of Immigrants is the only national independent organisation working solely in the areas of immigration, nationality and refugee law and practice. Through the 30 years of its existence it has remained entirely independent of central government funding, and thus is free to speak out on behalf of people directly affected by immigration and asylum laws and policy and to campaign for justice.

JCWI advises and represents individuals and families with problems caused by these laws, lobbies and campaigns for changes in the law and practice, produces written information and campaigning material and trains advisers, lawyers and others in all aspects of these laws.

© JCWI 1997

The forms and notices in Appendix 5 are Crown copyright and are reproduced with the permission of the Controller of Her Majesty's Stationery Office.

ISBN 1 874010 04 8

Design: Pat Kahn
Typesetting: Boldface, 17A Clerkenwell Road, London EC1M 5RD
Printing: Unwin Brothers, Woking

JCWI, 115 Old Street, London EC1V 9JR
tel 0171 251 8708, fax 0171 251 8707
email JCWI@mcr1.poptel.org.uk

Preface and acknowledgements

Many people have helped in the preparation and research for this third edition of the *JCWI Handbook*. It has been extensively revised, updated and expanded and reflects changes in law and practice up to mid-February 1997.

JCWI is very grateful to the people who have read all or part of the manuscript in draft and have made helpful corrections and suggestions. Thanks are due to Hilary Belchak, Eileen Bye, Don Flynn, Laurens Fransman, Ayodele Gansallo, Neil Gaskin, Olivia Goulden, Belayeth Hussain, Beth Lakhani, Duncan Lane (twice!), Fiona Lindsley, John McCarthy, Jennifer Osborne, Robert Phillips, Nirmala Rajasingam and Richard Towle. Anne Owers' work is still the basis of the nationality chapters. Readers of previous editions have made helpful suggestions and discussions with colleagues at JCWI have been ongoing and valuable.

JCWI gratefully acknowledges financial support towards the production of the book from the British Council and the European Commission which has generously supported JCWI through its European Year against Racism funding.

JCWI's clients and others who come to us for advice and information are as always an invaluable source of ideas and knowledge of how the system works and resilience in dealing with it. We are grateful for their confidence in us to help with areas of vital importance in their lives and we hope that this book is of use to them in understanding the immigration and asylum system which affects them.

Finally, it is important to remember that law and practice frequently change. Keep abreast of developments by joining JCWI and receiving our quarterly *Bulletin* and details of other publications.

February 1997

Contents

Full contents listing   vi

Introduction   1

1   The background to British immigration, nationality and refugee law   1

Section 1   FAMILY
2   Spouses and fiancé(e)s   9
3   Children   43
4   Relatives other than children and spouses   70

Section 2   REFUGEES
5   Refugees and asylum-seekers   79

Section 3   THE EEA
6   The European Economic Area   111

Section 4   NON-EEA WORKERS
7   Workers and business people   128

Section 5   TEMPORARY PURPOSES
8   Visitors   148
9   Students   159

Section 6   BENEFITS
10   Immigration, benefits and other state provisions   180

Section 7   TRAVEL

11   Coming, going and staying:
      the practicalities of travel   215

12   Problems and emergencies   242

13   Passport stamps and codes   254

Section 8   ENFORCEMENT OF CONTROLS

14   Deportation, illegal entry and removal   264

15   Detention   284

Section 9   APPEALS

16   The immigration and asylum
      appeals systems   292

Section 10   NATIONALITY

17   British nationality   317

18   How to become British   338

Section 11   USEFUL INFORMATION

19   Useful addresses and telephone numbers   346

      Glossary   356

Appendices   1 Relevant Acts and rules   364
                  2 Delays   365
                  3 Selected fees   365
                  4 Designated posts   366
                  5 Standard forms and letters   369

      Index   392

Full contents

Chapter 1
THE LEGAL BACKGROUND 1
Immigration, nationality and the right of entry to the UK 1
   European freedom of movement
   Refugee law
The structure of immigration control 3
The system of immigration control 5
The basis and history of British immigration control 6
   Towards the future

Chapter 2
SPOUSES AND FIANCÉ(E)S 9
People who do not have to fit into the rules 10
People coming to the UK as spouses or fiancé(e)s 11
The rules 11
   Spouse or fiancé(e)
   Present in the UK
   Entry clearance
   The 'primary purpose' rule
   Intention to stay together permanently
   The couple have met each other
   Support and accommodation
How to apply abroad 15
   Documents needed for an interview
   Information needed specifically for spouses and fiancé(e)s
When an application is successful 16
When an application is refused 17
People who marry or become engaged in the UK 18
People who apply when they are legally in the UK 18
The rules 18
   A person with limited leave married to a person settled here
   Tests of the marriage
   How to apply

   Some problems which may arise
When an application is successful 20
When an application is refused 21
People who apply when they are in the UK without permission 21
The rules 21
   Home Office policy and enforcement action
   How to apply
   Some important points to consider
People admitted or given leave to remain as spouses 25
The initial 12-month period 25
   Claiming benefits
   Travelling into and out of the UK
Applying for settlement (indefinite leave to remain) 26
The rules 26
   Making the application
   Documents required for the application
Spouses coming to the UK for temporary purposes 27
Workers and business people 27
Students 28
Refugees and people with exceptional leave 29
   Asylum-seekers
Other partnerships 30
Non-marital relationships 30
Gay and lesbian relationships 31
Polygamous marriages 32
Marriages and divorces in other countries 32
Marriage breakdown and immigration consequences 34
   Access to children
ANNEX: The primary purpose rule 36
Criteria used in primary purpose refusals 37
   Religious or cultural traditions

Previous migration
Discussion between the couple
Previous marital status
Depth of relationship
Women applying to come to the UK 38
Questioning by British officials 38
Case law 39
Points to consider 42

Chapter 3
CHILDREN 43

People who do not have to fit into the rules 44

Children under 18 joining both parents 45
The rules 45
  Parents
  Under 18 and unmarried
  Both parents are settled in the UK
  Support and accommodation

Children applying overseas to join their parents 47
  Evidence that may be required
  Box on DNA fingerprinting 48
  If the application is successful 49
  Applying for settlement after one year 49
  If the application overseas is refused 50

Children joining lone parents in the UK 50
The rules 50
  The 'sole responsibility' rule
  'Exclusion undesirable'
  The 'under-12 concession'
  Joining a relative who is not a parent

Children applying to come to join parents in the UK for temporary purposes 53
  Children of workers and business people
  Children of students
  Children of working holidaymakers
  Children of refugees and people with exceptional leave

Applying in the UK 55
Children over 18 56
  Special quota voucher scheme

Adopted children 58
Children who have already been adopted 58
The rules 58
  Legal adoptions
  Reasons for adoption
  Nationality of adopted children
Children coming to the UK for adoption 61
  When the application is successful
  Adoption proceedings

Children in the UK without their parents 64

Fostering of children/children in care 64
Other legal procedures 65
Children at school 66

Children born in the UK 67
  Children born in the UK in or after 1983: immigration status
  Children born in the UK before 1 January 1983
  Children whose parents are forced to leave the UK

Chapter 4
RELATIVES OTHER THAN CHILDREN AND SPOUSES 70

People who may not have to fit into the rules 70

Parents and grandparents 71
The rules 71
  Age requirement
  Previous financial support
  No other relatives to turn to
  Emotional dependence
  Support and accommodation
How to apply 75
  Applying abroad
  Applying in the UK
  Parents joining young children

Relatives other than parents and grandparents 77
The rules 77
  More distant relatives

Chapter 5
REFUGEES AND ASYLUM-SEEKERS 79

The UN Convention relating to the Status of Refugees 80
Interpretation of the Convention and Protocol 80
  European definitions
  Well-founded fear
  Persecution
  Reason for fear of persecution
  Outside the country of nationality
  Criminal convictions
Deciding if people qualify for asylum 84

Policies to discourage asylum-seekers 84
Visas and carriers' liability 84
Detention of asylum-seekers 86
Definition of a claim for asylum 86

How the Home Office deals with asylum applications 87
Decision-making criteria 87
  Connections with another country

viii • JCWI immigration, nationality and refugee law handbook

How to apply for asylum 91
Applying overseas 91
Applying on entry to the UK 91
   The short procedure
   'Third country cases'
   Fingerprinting
   Other applications
Applying after entry to the UK 95
Asylum interviews 96
Sources of information 98
While an application is pending 99
   Welfare benefits
   Working
Special groups of asylum-seekers 101
   Unaccompanied child asylum-seekers
   Detained asylum-seekers
Refusal of applications 102
   Curtailment of leave
Rights of appeal 103
   People refused asylum before 26 July 1993
   People refused asylum on or after 26 July 1993

When applications are successful 105
If refugee status is granted 105
Exceptional leave to remain 106
Family reunion 107
Other rights connected with asylum 109
Transfer of asylum 109
Loss of asylum 109

Chapter 6
THE EUROPEAN ECONOMIC AREA 111

European institutions 112
Box on background to the EEA 112
Freedom of movement 114
   Entry procedures
   Residence permits
   Appeals for EEA citizens
   Deportation of EEA citizens
Family members 118
   Dual British/EEA nationals
Public funds 121
EU nationals: the UK's definition 122
Association and Co-operation Agreements 123
The removal of internal frontiers 124
   The Schengen group
Third country nationals as service providers 125
Future developments 126

Chapter 7
WORKERS AND BUSINESS PEOPLE 128

Workers 128
The work permit scheme 128
How the work permit scheme operates
Applying when the worker is abroad
Applying in the UK
When a permit is granted
Extending a permit
Families of work permit holders
Settlement
Permit-free employment 134
Short-term workers 137
People allowed to work outside the immigration rules 137
   Voluntary work
   Academic work
   Domestic workers
Exemption from control 139
   Diplomatic work
Training and work experience 140
   Student nurses
Other ways of being able to work in the UK 142
   British-born grandparents
   Working holidaymakers
   Au pairs
   Unauthorised workers

Business people, the self-employed and persons of independent means 145
Business people 145
Self-employed people 146
   Writers, composers and artists
Investors 147
Retired people of independent means 147

Chapter 8
VISITORS 148

The rules 148
   The intention test
   The support and accommodation test
   Meeting the cost of the return journey
   Length of time for visits
Medical visitors 151
Working holidaymakers 152
Applying for entry clearance 152
Arrival in the UK 153
   Leave to enter
   Transit passengers
   Work and business
   Refusal of entry
Applying for extensions 155
The rules 155
   How to apply for an extension
Visitors as carers 156
Visitors changing their status 157
Travel outside the UK 158
   Frequent visits
   Visa nationals

Chapter 9
STUDENTS 159
The rules 159
    Education institutions
    Full-time studies
    Financial support
    Ability to follow the course
    Intention to leave the UK
Students not yet accepted on a course: prospective students 162
Arrival in the UK 163
    Leave to enter
    Refusal of entry
Families of students and prospective students 164
Applying for extensions 166
The rules 166
    Full time studies; maintenance and accommodation
    Regular attendance
    Satisfactory progress
    Short courses
How to apply for an extension 168
    Permission to work
Fees and grants 170
Studies including training 172
    Nursing and medical students
    Training and work experience
    Applying for extensions
EEA students 175
Becoming a student when already in the UK 176
Students changing their status 176
Temporary stay 177
Working after studies 177
    Work experience, Academics
Travel outside the UK 178

Chapter 10
IMMIGRATION, BENEFITS AND OTHER STATE PROVISIONS 180
Box on public funds 180
Who is not affected by the public funds requirement? 181
Who is affected by the public funds requirement? 181
Sponsorship 182
Undertakings 183
Possible effects of claiming 184
    Home Office practice
Eligibility to claim 186
The 'habitual residence' test 187
    Commissioners' decisions
    Benefits Agency guidelines
EEA nationals 189

    Requirement to leave
    Habitual residence
    Rights of residence directives
'Public funds' benefits 191
Income support and income-based jobseeker's allowance 191
    Benefit regulations
    Urgent cases rate
    Benefits Agency practice
    Asylum-seekers
    Immigration consequences
Box on entitlement to income support/JSA(IB) 192
Housing benefit and council tax benefit 196
    Benefit regulations
    Immigration consequences
National Assistance Act 1948 and Children Act 1989 197
Family credit 198
    Benefit regulations
    Immigration consequences
Disability benefits 199
    Benefit regulations
    Immigration consequences
Child benefit 199
    Benefit regulations
    Immigration consequences
Council housing and homeless persons' accommodation 200
    Housing regulations
    Local authority housing departments
    Immigration consequences
    The Housing Act 1996
Deciding whether to claim 203
Benefits which are not 'public funds' 205
    Residence requirements
National Health Service 205
    Exemptions from charges
    Liability for charges
    Procedures
    Private medical treatment
    General practitioners
    People with AIDS or HIV infection
    Carers
State education 210
Status checking 211
    Home Office efficiency scrutiny
    Home Office aims
    Access to benefits
    Information-gathering and sharing
    National Insurance numbers
    Register offices
    Opposition to status checking

Chapter 11
COMING, GOING AND STAYING:
THE PRACTICALITIES OF TRAVEL 215
Entry clearance 215
　People who need entry clearance
　How to apply for entry clearance 216
　Applications for settlement 216
　　Documents required
　Applications to work 220
　Applications for temporary stay 220
　Advantages and disadvantages of applying for optional entry clearance 221
　If the application is successful 221
　Box on general grounds for refusal of entry clearance/leave to enter 222
　If the application is refused 222
Arrival in the UK 223
　Illegible passport stamps
　Entry through Ireland 224
Travelling in and out of the UK 226
　People who always qualify to re-enter 226
　　People with the right of abode
　　British Visitor's passports
　　Certificates of entitlement to the right of abode
　People with leave to enter/remain for six months or less 227
　People with leave to enter/remain for more than six months but with a time limit 228
　People who have indefinite leave to enter/remain: the returning residents rule 229
　The rules 229
　　Returning for the purpose of settlement
　　Indefinite leave when they last left the country
　　Not had assistance from public funds to leave
　　Not been away for more than two years
　　If the application is successful
　　If the application is refused
Applying to the Home Office 232
　Applying in time: valid applications and application forms
　The application forms
　Applying after leave to enter or remain has expired
　General grounds for refusal of leave to remain 234
　Box on general grounds for refusal of leave to remain 235
　Dealing with the Home Office 236
　Box on changes of status 237
　　Home Office discretion
　　The 'ten-year concession'
　　The 'fourteen-year concession'
　Requesting return of passports 239
　　Variation of Leave Order
　　Travelling before an application is decided

Chapter 12
PROBLEMS AND EMERGENCIES 242
　Refusal of entry clearance overseas 242
　　When there is no right of appeal
　Problems on arrival in the UK 244
　Late applications to the Home Office 248
　Refusals without right of appeal 249
　Arrest and threatened deportation or removal 251
　Appealing to the courts 253

Chapter 13
PASSPORT STAMPS AND CODES 254
　Interpreting passports 254
　Entry clearance 254
　Certificates of entitlement to the right of abode 255
　Passport stamps at ports of entry 255
　　Visitors 256
　　Students 256
　　Workers and business people 257
　　Refugees and those granted exceptional leave 258
　　Registration with the police 258
　　Family members 259
　Re-entering the UK 259
　　Section 3(3)(b)
　　Multiple-entry visas and visa exemption
　Leave to remain 260
　Settled status 260
　Leaving the UK 262
　Refusals and problems 262
　British passports 263

Chapter 14
DEPORTATION, ILLEGAL ENTRY AND REMOVAL 264
　How people are traced 264
Deportation – through the criminal courts 266
　Criminal offences under immigration law 266
　　Overstaying, Breach of conditions
　　Criminal convictions for non-immigration matters
　The court process 268
　Recommendations for deportation 269
Deportation – Home Office administrative powers 270

The deportation process 271
Decisions to deport 271
Rights of appeal against decisions to deport 273
  People who have been in the UK less than seven years
  People who have been in the UK for more than seven years
  When a deportation order has been signed
Alternatives to deportation 275
  Leaving the country quickly
  Supervised departure
Enforcement of deportation 276
Returning to the UK 277
  Revocation of deportation orders
  After supervised or voluntary departure
Illegal entry – Home Office administrative powers 278
Entering without leave 279
  Without seeing an immigration officer
  Without obtaining leave from an immigration officer
  Entry through Ireland
In breach of a deportation order 280
'Deception' of an immigration officer 280
Establishing illegal entry 281
  Advising alleged illegal entrants
Removal 282
Returning to the UK 283
Repatriation 283

**Chapter 15
DETENTION** 284

Reasons for detention 284
Conditions of detention 286
Places of detention and visit facilities 287
Getting people out of detention 288
  Bail
  Temporary release
  Habeas corpus and other legal remedies
  Resistance

**Chapter 16
THE IMMIGRATION AND ASYLUM APPEALS SYSTEMS** 292

Box on immigration appeals and time limits 293
Powers of adjudicators 294
Recommendations 294
When people can appeal: immigration refusals 295
  Appeals from abroad
  Appeals against refusal of entry

Appeals against refusal to vary stay in the UK
Appeals against deportation and removal
Mixed appeals
When people can apply to the Tribunal 296
When there is no right of appeal 296
Box on when there is no right of appeal 297
How to appeal 298
  Forms and time limits
  Grounds of appeal
  Appealing 'out of time'
Waiting for an appeal hearing 301
The appeal process 301
  Appeals listed 'for mention'
How to prepare for an appeal 303
  Withdrawal of appeals
  Appeals on the papers
  Oral hearings: at the appeal
Appeals to the Tribunal 306
Appeals in the courts 307
When people can appeal: asylum 308
Box on asylum appeals and time limits 308
Appeals procedure and time limits 310
Claims 'certified' by the Home Secretary 310
  People who have only this short form of appeal
Appeals from abroad 312
Refused claims which are not 'certified' 313
Asylum appeal hearings 313
  Deciding asylum appeals
  Standard of proof
Applications to the Tribunal 315

**Chapter 17
BRITISH NATIONALITY** 317

The historical background 317
  Before 1948
  1948–1962
  1962–1981
  The British Nationality Act 1981
Chart on the development of British nationality and immigration law 318
Establishing citizenship 321
  Passports issued before 1 January 1983
  Passports issued on/after 1 January 1983
British citizens 323
Checking for British citizenship 323
Children born or adopted in the UK 323
  Before 1983
  Since 1983
Box: who is a British citizen? 324
People born overseas 326
  People born before 1 January 1983 with a British parent

xii • JCWI immigration, nationality and refugee law handbook

People born overseas *continued*
    People born on or after 1 January 1983 with a British parent
    People without a British parent
British citizenship by descent 328
Box on citizenship by descent 329
Citizenship through Crown or designated service 330

British nationals who are not British citizens 330
Right of readmission 331
Passing on nationality to children 331
British nationals with an East African connection 332
The special quota voucher scheme 332
    Qualifications for obtaining a special quota voucher
    Admission of dependants
    How to apply for a voucher
    People who do not have vouchers
British nationals from Malaysia 334
British nationals from Hong Kong 335
British Nationals (Overseas): the Hong Kong Act 1985 335
British citizenship: the British Nationality (Hong Kong) Act 1990 336
People from Hong Kong who are living in the UK 337

Chapter 18
HOW TO BECOME BRITISH 338
Naturalisation 339
Requirements for naturalisation 339
    Residence and settlement
    Language
    Good character
    Intention to live in the UK
The process of application 340

Refusals of applications 341
Crown service 341
Registration 342
Registration of adults 342
    British nationals who are not British citizens
    The process of application
Registration of children 342
Children with a right to register 342
Children who can apply to register at discretion 343
    The process of application
Passports and travel documents 344
Deprivation of citizenship 345

Chapter 19
USEFUL ADDRESSES AND TELEPHONE NUMBERS 346
Home Office, ports of entry, immigration service and detention centres 346
Immigration appeals offices 349
Passport Agency offices 350
Some other government departments 350
Some British high commissions and embassies abroad 351
Some agencies working on immigration and nationality matters 353

Glossary 356

Appendices 364
1 Relevant Acts and rules 364
2 Delays 365
3 Selected fees 365
4 Designated posts 366
5 Standard forms and letters 369

Index 392

This book went to press as a general election was expected. The Labour Party has made some commitments to change, such as the abolition of the primary purpose rule. The Conservatives have promised another review of the asylum and immigration appeals systems. Thus changes in law and practice can be expected, and the book will inevitably soon become out-of-date in parts. JCWI urges readers to become members of JCWI, and thus receive our updating *Bulletins* and other information from us. Fill in and return the form at the back of the book for more details.

INTRODUCTION

1 The background to British immigration, nationality and refugee law

Immigration, nationality and the right of entry to the UK

Immigration and nationality law are often talked about together, as though they were synonymous: this causes great confusion, as people often talk about 'citizenship' when they mean 'right of residence'. In fact, immigration and nationality are two separate areas of law, each with its own major primary legislation: the Immigration Act 1971 (as amended by the Immigration Act 1988, the Asylum and Immigration Appeals Act 1993 and the Asylum and Immigration Act 1996) and the British Nationality Act 1981.

Nationality simply defines the country of which people are citizens, and which usually issues them with passports. Nationality law sets out the ways in which people can become citizens (usually by being born in a country, being born abroad to parents who are citizens of the country, or taking out citizenship by naturalisation after a period of residence in a country).

Immigration is the system of laws and rules by which each country decides who shall be able to live in that country and under what conditions. Immigration law sets out the categories of people who are allowed in automatically (usually citizens of the country) and the mechanisms and officials who decide whether and on what conditions others may enter and enforce the departure of people who are not supposed to be in the country.

In Britain the simple distinction between nationality and immigration is complicated by the fact that not all those who have British nationality are automatically able to enter Britain as citizens. There are six categories of British nationality (described in detail in chapter 17) of which only one, British citizens, has an absolute right to enter Britain. The other five are people originating from British dependencies or ex-colonies who had their right of entry to Britain taken away in 1962 or 1968, even though they travel on British passports. **The British Nationality Act 1981** (which needs to be read with the Immigration Act 1971) sets out the conditions for acquiring five of those nationalities (British citizenship, British Dependent Territories citizenship, British Overseas citizenship, British subject status and British Protected Person status). It was slightly amended, for Falklanders, by the **British Nationality (Falkland Islands) Act 1983**. The sixth kind of British nationality, British National (Overseas) status, was created for people from Hong Kong in the **Hong Kong Act 1985** and the **Hong Kong (British Nationality) Order 1986**.

At the same time, a small number of people who do not have British nationality, but are citizens of independent Commonwealth countries, do have an automatic right of entry and are therefore free from immigration control. They are people who have the **right of abode** in the UK. Right of abode does not mean the same as the right to live in the UK, which many foreign nationals have. It is a special status, available only to Commonwealth citizens born before 1 January 1983 who had a parent born in the UK; and to women who were Commonwealth citizens on 31 December 1982 and who were married before 1 January 1983 to a man who was a British citizen or had the right of abode in the UK. Right of abode is defined in the **Immigration Act 1971** (the cut-off date of 1 January 1983 is found in the British Nationality Act 1981) and it has been slightly amended, as regards polygamous wives, by the **Immigration Act 1988**.

European freedom of movement

On 1 January 1973 the UK joined what was then called the European Economic Community, or Common Market. Since that date, there have been two different and contradictory systems of law on migration in force in the UK. Nationals of EC countries have the right to travel between EC countries and the law says that this should be 'facilitated'. Nationals of all other countries have no rights, and British immigration law has consistently whittled away their possibilities of coming to or staying in the UK. When larger numbers of people have travelled from a particular country, or for a particular purpose, immigration laws and rules have been changed in order to restrict and frustrate them.

One of the objects of the European Community was to reduce barriers to the **free movement of goods, capital, services and workers** between the countries concerned. The EEC is now called the European Union (EU) and has joined with three other European countries to form the European Economic Area (EEA).

Nationals of other EEA countries are not restricted by British immigration law. Their rights are found in the 1957 **Treaty of Rome** as amended by the 1986 **Single European Act** and the 1993 **Maastricht Treaty on European Union** and by binding Regulations and Directives issued by the European Council. All EEA nationals who are workers or who are seeking work, or who are providing or receiving services, have an absolute right of entry. The families and dependants of such people, whether or not they themselves are EEA nationals, also have an absolute right of entry (ironically, this puts the families of other EEA nationals resident in the UK in a much better position than families of British citizens resident in the UK, who have no such absolute right of entry). In addition, EEA students, pensioners and those without employment have had rights of entry from July 1992, provided that they can maintain themselves without needing social security.

Irish nationals are also EEA nationals. But in addition, there is no immigration control between the UK and the Republic of Ireland; this territory, together with the Isle of Man and the Channel Islands, is called the Common Travel Area and is defined in the Immigration Act 1971. This means that Irish and British citizens are exempt from any immigration control when they pass between the two countries (however, nationals of other non-EEA countries are not).

Refugee law

A separate but related area of law is refugee law. This is based on an international convention, the 1951 **United Nations Convention Relating to the Status of Refugees**, which the UK has signed. This Convention defines a refugee, as a person who has fled from persecution for particular reasons, and the treatment which must be accorded to refugees, but leaves it to each country to determine whether individuals fit into the definition and therefore must be granted asylum in that country. In the UK this power is carried out by the same officials who decide on other immigration matters.

Until the late 1980s, there was little development in refugee law. As more people from the South began to seek asylum in Western and Northern countries, procedures which were intended for displaced persons in Europe at the end of the second world war were adapted to the new situation. In 1985, there were 4389 applications for asylum in the UK; in 1995, there were 43,965. This reflects greater insecurity in the world and possibilities of travel abroad. Governments however have alleged that people are seeking asylum because immigration laws have become more restrictive and they have been unable to travel for economic betterment in any other way. In general, the response of governments has been to try to restrict the numbers of people coming and to interpret the terms of the UN Convention more strictly.

Refugee communities and others have resisted these trends, both legally and practically. The British courts have not always interpreted laws as the government would wish. Other international agreements which the UK has signed, such as the European Convention on Human Rights, or the UN Convention against Torture, have restricted some government intentions. There are constant conflicts between Britain's international obligations and government desires to restrict numbers of immigrants, migrants and refugees.

The structure of immigration control

Most of this book concerns people who are subject to the full requirements of immigration control: people who are not nationals of EEA countries and who do not have the right of abode in the UK. The

BRITISH IMMIGRATION CONTROL

Not subject to control	Subject to limited control	Subject to full control
British citizens	EEA nationals	Aliens (non-Commonwealth citizens)
Irish citizens		Other Commonwealth citizens
Commonwealth citizens with right of abode		Other types of British nationals

Immigration Act 1971 sets out the structure of immigration control, including the duties and powers of immigration officers, the system for appealing against decisions to refuse entry or stay in the UK and the mechanisms for deporting or removing people who are alleged to be in the UK illegally. The Asylum and Immigration Appeals Act 1993, amended by the Asylum and Immigration Act 1996, sets up a separate system for dealing with asylum-seekers.

The Immigration Act 1971 also gives the Home Secretary the power to make **immigration rules**. The immigration rules are in practice what decide whether and how someone can enter or stay in the UK. They set out in detail the categories of people (for example, families, visitors, refugees, students) who may enter and the criteria they must fulfil. They can be made and changed without needing to change the law: they are simply presented to Parliament, which may or may not decide to have a short debate (usually one and a half hours, often in a Committee rather than in the whole House of Commons) on them, and which cannot amend them, but can only accept or reject them in total. Immigration rules have only once been rejected in the past 15 years, when right-wing Conservatives felt the marriage rules were too lax and the opposition parties felt they were too restrictive. They were tightened up and then passed through Parliament in 1983. When changes are made to the immigration rules (for example, new visa requirements which have become at least an annual event) the Home Office usually publishes only the amendment, and does not reissue the whole of the rules. The most recent consolidated immigration rules (called, confusingly, *Statement of Changes in Immigration Rules*) were issued on 23 May 1994 (HC 395) and came into force on 1 October 1994. Several changes in the rules for dealing with asylum-seekers came into force on 1 September 1996, implementing parts of the Asylum and Immigration Act.

As well as the published immigration rules there are also secret internal instructions to immigration officials on the practical details of how they should deal with applications and how they should exercise their discretion. These are classified as confidential documents and all efforts to persuade the Home Office to publish them as a whole have failed. Some excerpts have been officially released or leaked and are useful in explaining how the Home Office uses its discretion in interpreting the law and rules.

The immigration appeals system has its own rules, the **Immigration Appeals (Procedure) Rules** and the **Asylum Appeals (Procedure) Rules**, which are now issued by the Lord Chancellor's Department. They set out the deadlines and the procedures for appealing to adjudicators, special adjudicators, the Immigration Appeal Tribunal and the courts.

The system of immigration control

There are three types of immigration control, which occur in different places and are run by three separate departments or groups of officials.

Before-entry control happens at British embassies, high commissions or consulates overseas when people apply for entry clearance (often called a visa) before they travel to the UK. Some people must apply for permission in this way: they are people who are visa nationals (listed in the immigration rules) who always need permission in advance, for whatever reason they are travelling; people coming intending permanent settlement (usually to join family members); or people coming for work. Other people may choose to apply for entry clearance because it will reduce problems on arrival in the UK. Before-entry control is administered by officials working for the Foreign and Commonwealth Office, although increasingly these are immigration officers working on secondment.

On-entry control happens at designated ports of entry to the UK (major airports and seaports). It is carried out by immigration officers, a separate branch of the civil service. They have the power to grant or refuse entry, to detain, to search people and their luggage, to read papers and letters and to require people to submit to medical examination (like the notorious 'virginity test' in the 1970s). They stamp passengers' passports to show how long they can stay and under what conditions, for example restrictions or prohibitions on working, or a requirement to maintain and accommodate themselves without recourse to public funds. Although they interview people seeking asylum in the UK, the decision on whether to grant refugee status is not made by them but by specialist civil servants at the Home Office Asylum Directorate in Croydon.

After-entry control happens within the UK. People may want to extend their stay or change their status (for example, a student who has married a British citizen). Applications to do this are administered by Home Office civil servants working in the Immigration and Nationality Directorate at Lunar House, in Croydon. They also deal with asylum applications and with preparatory work for immigration and asylum appeals. The second type of after-entry control is called enforcement: tracing people who are allegedly in the country illegally and enforcing their departure. This is done by immigration officers, from Becket House and Hounslow in London, and from major ports and airports throughout the country, who work closely with the police.

The basis and history of British immigration control

The present system of British immigration control began in 1905. Before this, the entry of people who were not British subjects was technically part of the royal prerogative, and the monarch could also make decisions to expel individuals or groups of people. **The Aliens Act 1905** was passed, after two decades of intermittent agitation, in order to prevent refugees, mainly Jewish, poor and fleeing from eastern Europe, from seeking refuge in Britain. The Act only applied to boats with more than 20 passengers and to those travelling steerage class who could be excluded if 'undesirable' – defined mainly as being unable to support themselves and their dependants. The Act only applied to 'aliens' – people not from any part of the British empire – but it set up the first rudimentary machinery for checking entry which was expanded and developed through the rest of the century.

However, it was not until 1962 that any attempt was made to control the entry of people who were subjects of the British crown by being born in a country which was, or which had been, part of the British empire. The **Commonwealth Immigrants Act 1962** was passed against a background of racist agitation and pressure. The Act and the subsequent laws passed in 1968 and 1971 were designed primarily to prevent the entry of black British subjects (Commonwealth and UK citizens); hence the invention of 'right of abode' (initially called 'patriality') and of preferential treatment for Commonwealth citizens with a UK-born grandparent, in order to ensure that many Australians, New Zealanders and Canadians were not excluded by the legislation.

These laws led to some British nationals (almost all black) being excluded from Britain while some foreign nationals (mostly white) from other Commonwealth countries were free to enter at any time. Britain's entry into the Common Market on 1 January 1973 (a date which coincided with the coming into force of the Immigration Act 1971) gave new rights to enter and work to hundreds of millions of European nationals.

The **Immigration Act 1971** and the **British Nationality Act 1981** codified British immigration and nationality law (and perpetuated the divisions described above). Since then, new laws, rules and practices have imposed increasing restrictions on people coming from countries of the South. The only right to family reunion in UK law (for long-settled Commonwealth men) was repealed in the Immigration Act 1988; meanwhile, the primary purpose marriage rule and the support and accommodation requirements meant that, in 1990, nearly 70% of husbands from the Indian sub-continent were refused entry. Deportation was made easier and swifter by the **Immigration Act 1988** and new Home Office practices which followed it. The numbers of people being allowed to settle in the UK has remained at about 55,000 for the past few years, around 26,000 from Asia, 12,000 from Africa, 8000 from the Americas.

Towards the future

The Home Office, together with other government departments, is also developing internal immigration controls. Different authorities, such as the Benefits Agency, local authorities, employers, colleges, the National Health Service and others have worked together in order to exchange information about the immigration status of people seeking to use them, or applying for jobs. Entitlements to many benefits and services are becoming ever-more-closely intertwined with people's immigration status. Many people who look or sound 'foreign' may be checked by all these authorities to try to determine their entitlements.

The **Asylum and Immigration Act 1996** and the process of an interdepartmental 'Efficiency Scrutiny' have developed these processes. The government's stated intention was to 'examine ways in which the government as a whole could work more effectively to strengthen immigration control and to prevent those temporarily or illegally in this country from receiving state benefits to which they should not be entitled'. It is doing this by reducing entitlements to benefits to those settled here.

Home Office practice with regard to asylum-seekers became more restrictive after the arrival of Tamils from Sri Lanka in the mid-1980s. Visas were imposed on more countries as more asylum-seekers fled from them. Next the **Immigration (Carriers' Liability) Act 1987** enlisted airlines in immigration control. They are fined £2000 per passenger they bring in to the country without the correct documents, as an incentive to stop people without visas from being able to board planes to travel. Other new laws, the **Asylum and Immigration Appeals Act 1993** and the **Asylum and Immigration Act 1996**, provided processes for dealing with applications for asylum and gave refused asylum-seekers limited rights of appeal but removed other rights, and new immigration rules limited the discretion of officers. Increasing visa restrictions, the loss of appeal rights and the decisions of immigration officers at ports have also made family visits more difficult for all the main ethnic minority communities in the UK.

At the same time, developments in Europe have continued to remove barriers to travel and work for nationals of European countries while raising them for people from outside. The process of European harmonisation under the **Single European Act** and the **Maastricht Treaty on European Union** and the increasing co-operation between ministers and civil servants from different European countries have resulted in ever-tighter controls on non-European nationals attempting to enter. The enlargement of the European Union, and its joining with three other countries to form the **European Economic Area** in 1994, all of whose nationals have free movement rights within the whole area, and the removal of internal frontier controls between 13 of the EU countries, under the Schengen agreement, continued this trend towards higher external barriers and more checks.

Throughout Europe, countries are strengthening their common external border (by increased visa controls, common visa procedures, fines on airlines and the automatic refusal of entry by one country to anyone previously refused entry, or deported, by another member state). They are also anxious to improve internal controls (by checks on people within a country to find out whether they have the right to be there, and by linking immigration status to access to work, benefits and services). Governments of all countries are debating their response to refugees and asylum-seekers coming to their borders, to try to ensure uniformity in dealing with applications and that asylum-seekers should not be drawn to particular countries, where they think it might be easier to remain. Britain is fully involved in these decisions and the two recent British Acts implement European decisions.

But on the other hand, European harmonisation provides opportunities for co-operation between non-governmental organisations in different countries. This may include attempts to use European freedom of movement legislation for European nationals and for nationals of countries which have formal association or co-operation agreements with the EC, or trying to use the European Convention on Human Rights more creatively to support family unity rights. At the time of writing, a UK general election must take place within a few months and parts of the Asylum and Immigration Act 1996 are widely seen as an electoral ploy by the government to gain votes from people opposed to migration. Opposition parties have some different policies, but support the main areas of control. It remains hard to stop the drift towards ever tighter controls, targeted against people from poorer countries of the South.

SECTION 1: FAMILY

2 Spouses and fiancé(e)s

It is often very difficult to explain the provisions and the purposes of the immigration rules on marriage. It is widely believed that being married to a British citizen gives a person a 'right' to enter or remain in the UK with his or her spouse. This is not correct; British immigration law gives no automatic rights to any family members. The spouses of certain people may be able to come to join them, but only if they satisfy the requirements of the immigration rules. This chapter covers five different sets of circumstances. These are:

- people who wish to enter the UK as spouses or fiancé(e)s of British citizens or people settled in the UK and who intend to settle permanently in the UK. They need to make applications for entry clearance before travelling to the UK (▶see page 11).
- people who entered the UK for a temporary purpose (for example, as visitors or students) and have married British citizens or people settled in the UK. They can make applications to stay in the UK on the basis of marriage, and remain in the country while they do so (▶see page 18).
- people who are accompanying, or coming to join, spouses who are in the UK for temporary purposes (for example as students, work permit holders, business people). They sometimes need to get entry clearance before they travel and sometimes can apply when they arrive (▶see page 27).
- people who want to come to, or remain in, the UK with a partner, but for whom there is no provision in the immigration rules – for example, spouses of refugees and those granted exceptional leave, couples who are not married or planning to marry, and gay and lesbian couples (▶see page 29).
- people whose marriages break down in the UK and any immigration consequences of this (▶see page 34).

REMEMBER:
- people abroad wanting to settle in the UK must get entry clearance before they travel
- people applying in the UK must use the official Home Office application forms to make a valid application
- BUT some family members may be British citizens
- AND some people may not have to fit into the immigration rules; see below

People who do not have to fit into the rules

Some people have stronger claims to enter the UK as spouses or fiancé(e)s because they can qualify under other parts of the immigration rules, or under Community legislation.

a) **EEA nationals** (▶see glossary for list of countries) who are living or working or studying in the UK have the right under Community legislation to be joined by a spouse, whether or not he or she is an EEA citizen and their partners do not have to meet the requirements of British immigration rules. There are full details of the procedures in chapter 6 on EEA citizens. Remember Ireland is also an EEA country, so foreign spouses of Irish citizens who have come to live in the UK may benefit.

Also remember the decision in the European Court of Justice case of *Surinder Singh* of 7 July 1992 ▶see pages 41–2 for more details. This confirmed that British citizens who have exercised their right of free movement within the EU, that is, who have lived in another EU country with their spouse and who later wish to return to the UK, are entitled to do so under the provisions of Community legislation, rather than under British immigration law. This is discussed further in chapter 6.

b) **Commonwealth citizens with a parent born in the UK** have the right of abode (▶see glossary for definition: this is more than merely being settled in the UK) in the UK and are therefore not subject to immigration control at all and are free to travel to the UK. They must have been Commonwealth citizens on 31 December 1982, the day before the British Nationality Act 1981 came into force. They must also obtain certificates of entitlement to the right of abode before travelling ▶see below and page 227. If the parents are not married, only the mother's status counts. See glossary for list of Commonwealth countries.

c) **Some Commonwealth citizen women** have the right of abode and are not subject to immigration control. They are women who were Commonwealth citizens on 31 December 1982, the day before the British Nationality Act 1981 came into force, and who were married on or before that date to British citizen men, or men with the right of abode (▶see glossary for definition). Such a marriage before this date meant that the woman automatically gained the right of abode in the UK herself, and therefore is no longer subject to immigration control. However, this fact needs to be proved before she travels, and she must apply to the British high commission for a 'certificate of entitlement to the right of abode' and pay a fee. There are special shorter queues for people with a claim to the right of abode in the Indian subcontinent countries.

In order to get the certificate, the woman will need her original marriage certificate, to show the date of the marriage, and proof that her husband was either a British citizen, or a Commonwealth citizen with the right of abode, at the time of the marriage. When the certificate of entitlement is granted, it is valid for the same length of time as the passport and she is free to travel to the UK and to return at any time during the validity of the passport. The returning resident rules (▶see pages 229–32) do not apply to her. When the passport expires, the Home Office or the British high commission will give a new certificate of entitlement in a new passport, on production of the same evidence.

NB This provision does not apply to men, or to non-Commonwealth citizen women. Cameroonian, Mozambican, Namibian, Pakistani and South African citizen women cannot benefit from this because these countries were not members of the Commonwealth in 1982.

People coming to the UK as spouses or fiancé(e)s

WHAT THE RULES SAY

The rules state that the requirements to be met by people seeking entry to the UK for marriage are that:

- they have entry clearance
- they are married to a person who is present and settled in the UK or who is on the same occasion being admitted for settlement
- they did not enter into the marriage primarily to obtain settlement in the UK
- they and their spouse intend to live together permanently as husband and wife and the marriage is subsisting
- they have met the other party to the marriage
- they will be able to maintain and accommodate themselves adequately, together with any dependants, in accommodation they own or occupy exclusively, without recourse to public funds
- none of the general grounds for refusal (▶see pages 222–3) apply to them.

The rules for fiancé(e)s are similar, but with a distinction made in the provisions for support and accommodation before and after the marriage, as the couple may not be living together until after they are married.

WHAT THE RULES MEAN

Spouse or fiancé(e)

A spouse means someone who is legally married, in a way recognised by UK law. The term does not cover common-law spouses, or same-sex relationships. A fiancé(e) must be someone who is legally free to marry under UK law. This excludes people under 16 even if they have been legally married, or are legally free to marry, in the countries from which they come. It also excludes people who are not yet divorced, even if divorce proceedings are under way. It can, however, include wives in polygamous marriages, as long as they were validly married in a country which permits polygamy and as long as they are the only wife in that relationship who has ever entered the UK as a spouse. If one wife of the relationship has already been admitted to join the husband, this marriage will have to be ended by divorce before another wife can qualify to enter.

Present in the UK

The other partner must be 'present and settled' in the UK or 'on the same occasion be admitted for settlement'. This applies even if the partner is a British citizen, who cannot have conditions placed on his or her stay in the UK and therefore is always settled. It means that the British or settled spouse must be in the UK at the time the application is made, or will be travelling to the UK, for settlement, with the non-settled spouse.

Entry clearance

All spouses and fiancé(e)s must obtain entry clearance before travelling to the UK, if they are planning to remain permanently. Spouses and fiancé(e)s who are visa nationals (▶see glossary) must obtain entry clearance even if they are only planning to stay for a short time. It is possible for a spouse to plan to come simply to visit the partner in the UK, or for a fiancé(e) to come simply for the marriage ceremony, after which the couple plan to live permanently elsewhere. However, it can sometimes be difficult to persuade immigration and entry clearance officers of this. They may suspect that a spouse or fiancé(e) is trying to avoid either the queues or the detailed interview they would face if they were to apply from abroad.

However the Tribunal in *Dela Vina Corte* (12708) held that a Filipino woman with a visit visa, whose British fiancé's divorce had been finalised since the visa was issued, still qualified to enter: 'Approaching it on a commonsense view we do not think that because the couple decided to get married during their visit to this country meant that the basis of the appellant's admission was removed. All that she was then seeking was limited leave to enter.'

The 'primary purpose rule'

- the non-settled person must not have married primarily to obtain settlement in the UK

The immigration rules require officials to be satisfied that the marriage was not entered into primarily so that a person from overseas could gain settlement in the UK. This is known as the primary purpose rule. It means that the couple have to show that they did not marry mainly for immigration reasons. The immigration officials use their subjective judgement, as well as the instructions they are given, to decide if they are satisfied.

It is quite clear that the procedures and practice vary enormously in different countries. In discussions with people who have come to the UK as spouses from Australia, for example, it is clear that no questions were asked on this point at all; it was simply assumed by the immigration official that this requirement was satisfied. For young men in the Indian subcontinent, eighty or ninety questions may be asked around this requirement, the questions being repeated again and again in slightly different forms to see if any 'admission' is made as to the primary purpose of the marriage. In 1990, 69% of husbands and fiancés from the countries of the subcontinent were refused under this rule, and it caused great hardship. In response to criticism from the courts and from other organisations, on 30 June 1992 the Home Office issued a statement on how it would operate the rule in future. It stated that primary purpose would no longer be used as a reason for refusal when either

- the marriage has subsisted for more than five years; or
- there is a child of the marriage with the right of abode in the UK.

Married couples kept apart for many years by the operation of the rule were therefore able to be reunited and the statistics of husbands granted entry clearance from the Asian subcontinent rose appreciably in the third quarter of 1992. However this improvement was not maintained and in 1995 the refusal rate had risen again to 58% for husbands and 69% for fiancés. Also the statement does not help engaged couples, or those who do not want or have not been able to have children, and there is no justification for having to wait five years before being able to live with a partner in the UK. This statement of practice has not been incorporated into the immigration rules, which means that couples considering applying to live in the UK may not be aware of it.

It is therefore very important that couples should understand the reasoning behind the questioning at the British high commission or embassy and be prepared in advance for the kind of questions they may be asked. Often people feel that they have been tricked or pressurised into giving answers to immigration officials which do not actually reflect their true feelings or intentions. The Annex at the end of this chapter explains this rule in more detail.

Intention to stay together permanently

The couple have to satisfy the official that they intend to stay together permanently as husband and wife. As with the primary purpose rule, this is also impossible to prove; questions may be asked about the purpose of the marriage and about where the couple intend to live after marriage. If it appears that the couple may have competing commitments in different countries this could be a reason for refusal. If a couple have been married for some time but have not been together for much of it, this could also be a problem. Where there is inadequate accommodation in the UK, this could also be used to argue that the couple will not be staying together permanently.

The couple have met each other

The meeting does not have to take place before an application for entry clearance is made but the couple must have met before the applicant spouse or fiancé(e) is interviewed about his or her application. This requirement was intended to place an extra hurdle in the way of some arranged marriages, where the couple may not meet before the wedding day, or, rarely, the wedding may be by proxy. It is only likely to be a problem for fiancé(e)s, as a married couple will almost certainly have met at the wedding but may entail the extra cost of a journey abroad or to the UK before the marriage.

The Immigration Appeal Tribunal has held, in the case of *Meharban* (6073), that a meeting does not have to take place in the context of a marriage; it is acceptable if the couple met each other as children, as long as they both have clear recollections of the meeting and know each other as individuals. The fact of meeting can be proved by photographs of the couple together, by the recollections of both parties, by passport stamps showing that both were in the same country at the same time, by corroborative statements from relatives or friends who know of the meeting.

Support and accommodation

The immigration rules say that the couple must be able to support and accommodate themselves and any dependants without recourse to public funds (▶see box on page 180). It may be possible for other family members, or friends, to show that they will support the couple; the immigration authorities require a letter to confirm the support as well as evidence such as recent pay slips or bank statements to prove ability to support. The important thing is to show that, when the spouse or fiancé(e) from abroad comes to the UK, the family will not need to have recourse to public funds.

The Home Office interprets this to mean that no *additional* public funds must be necessary for the support of the spouse coming in to the UK. If the settled or British spouse is living in homeless persons' accommodation, for example, this does not prohibit a partner from abroad from coming to the UK because no additional accommodation is required. If the partner in the UK is on benefit, but the partner abroad has the offer of a job in the UK when he or she arrives, this should be sufficient. But it is important to be aware that any job offer or work plans that were made before the marriage could be used by entry clearance officers to claim that the primary purpose of the marriage was to be able to work in the UK.

It is often more difficult for British or settled women than men to show that their partners can be supported in the UK. A woman looking after young children may not be able to work and therefore may rely on benefits. If she is living with other members of her family, for example her own parents, in their accommodation, she will have to show either that this will be an adequate long-term arrangement and that the couple will be paying their own way, or that they have realistic plans and expectations of having their own home soon. A Tribunal decision in August 1991, *Kausar* (8025), suggested that it was easier to satisfy this requirement when a couple live in a separate family unit, rather than joint family living arrangements. However, the cases of *Saghir Ahmed* (8260) and *Iftikhar Ahmed* (CO/2443/91) and subsequent correspondence from the Home Office confirmed that having a bedroom of their own in a joint house was adequate.

Since 1 October 1994, the immigration rules have stated that accommodation must be owned or occupied 'exclusively' by the sponsor for the use of the family, not merely that there must be accommodation 'of their own', but Home Office practice does not appear to have changed. ▶See chapter 11 for further details about evidence needed to satisfy the support and accommodation requirement.

How to apply abroad

Spouses and fiancé(e)s must apply for permission to enter at the British embassy or high commission in the country where they are living. They will almost certainly be interviewed by an official at the British post. In some countries, particularly those of the Indian subcontinent, the Philippines, Thailand and Jamaica, there are substantial delays before applications will be considered. Inadequate numbers of staff have been sent to the posts and they carry out extremely long interviews and checks on people, which are very time consuming. The Home Office publishes details of the waiting times in the countries of the Indian subcontinent in its twice-yearly *Statistical Bulletin: control of immigration: statistics* and the Foreign Office may give information about other countries when asked; the appendix gives details of some waiting periods near the time of writing. It is very difficult to bring forward an interview date unless there are exceptional compassionate circumstances, for example the severe illness of either partner. The fact that a couple want to be together for the birth of a child, for example, is not normally considered a strong enough reason.

Because of these delays, it is sensible to advise people to make applications well in advance of the time they hope to travel. For example, if a man in the UK seeks advice about his proposed marriage in India and is planning to travel for the wedding in several months' time, it is sensible for his fiancée to apply straight away to the British high commission, explaining when her wedding is planned and when her fiancé will be in India, to ask that an interview for them both can be fixed after the wedding while he is in India. The more notice that is given, the higher the chance that the high commission will be able to arrange this. If a couple marry while one is waiting in the queue for interview for a fiancé(e) entry clearance, they should inform the British high commission but they will not have to start the application again. If they have been able to live together after the marriage, outside the UK, this may also help in relation to satisfying the primary purpose rule.

It may be helpful for the British or settled spouse to be present at the interview, so that he or she is available if the British authorities want to check anything about the situation in the UK. The Foreign Office has confirmed in a letter to JCWI of 26 September 1996 that 'it is still policy to allow requests from MPs, solicitors and other representatives to attend an applicant's interview as an observer...provided that the representative clearly understands that, as an observer, he/she must not intervene while the interview is taking place. But at the end of the interview, the observer may then make comments on the case to the ECO.'

Documents needed for an interview

At the interview, the official will need evidence of the legal status of the spouse in the UK and of the support and accommodation available. ▶Chapter 11 gives details of the documents which may be required by the entry clearance officer.

Information needed specifically for spouses and fiancé(e)s

- **proof of the marriage**. If the original copy of the marriage certificate is in the UK, it should be sent to the spouse abroad to take to the British high commission or embassy for interview, with a certified photocopy being kept by the partner in the UK. If there is no such certificate in existence, the spouse abroad should explain this. In India, for example, if there is no marriage certificate there may be a declaration under the Hindu Marriage Act that the wedding has taken place. If it is a customary marriage, for example in West Africa, the British post may require statutory declarations from members of the family of both sides to confirm that the correct procedures took place.
- **proof that the couple were or are free to marry**. If either party has been married before, the British post will need to see evidence that the previous marriage(s) have ended, by death, divorce or annulment. The evidence could be original divorce certificates or statutory declarations to prove a customary divorce, or the original death certificate of a previous spouse who has died.
- **proof that the couple are over 16**. Their passports are normally adequate proof of this.

When an application is successful

If the application is successful, the spouse or fiancé(e) will be given a visa or entry clearance, which will confirm that the person is coming for marriage. The person must travel within six months; if people are unable to travel within this time, they should apply to the British high commission or embassy to explain the reasons for the delay and ask for the entry clearance to be extended.

Fiancé(e)s will be admitted for six months, with a prohibition on employment and business, on arrival at a British port or airport. People who arrived after 8 November 1996 may also have a condition requiring them to maintain and accommodate themselves and any dependants without recourse to public funds. They are expected to get married within that six months and should then apply to the Home Office, on the official application form FLR(M), for permission to remain for a year as a spouse. While the application is under consideration, the prohibition on work and business continues. If there are reasons why the marriage has to be delayed, the fiancé(e) should still apply to the Home Office, within the six months' leave granted, for an extension of the time, explaining why the marriage has not yet taken place.

Spouses will be admitted for one year. The stamp placed on their passports before 8 November 1996 stated 'given leave to enter the UK for twelve months', with no other restriction, which means that they are free to take employment, run a business or do anything else. After 8 November 1996, the stamp will normally include a condition requiring them to maintain and accommodate themselves and any dependants without recourse to public funds (see chapter 13 for example of this passport stamp). They are not normally given any further information about their rights and status by the immigration officers. Shortly before the year is over, they should apply to the Home Office, on the official application form SET(M), for permission to remain permanently; see below for details of making this application.

When an application is refused

If an application for entry clearance is refused, the British embassy or high commission has to give the spouse or fiancé(e) a formal letter stating that the application has been refused, with brief reasons for the refusal and information about the right to appeal against the refusal, and a form to fill in to appeal. Any appeal has to reach the British high commission or embassy within three months of the date of refusal. There are more details about the appeals processes in chapter 16.

If the appeal is lost, the couple can make representations to the Home Office to reconsider the case. Unless there is new information which was not available at the appeal, it is unlikely that representations will be successful. The person abroad may make a fresh application to come to the UK; if the couple are married, events since the marriage will be considered ▶see pages 12–13 and 39–42. When one of the couple is a British citizen, and therefore an EEA national, Community legislation may also be helpful; see chapter 6 for more information.

People who marry or become engaged in the UK

People already in the UK, for example as visitors or students, may apply to the Home Office, on the official application form FLR(M), to remain because they have married a British citizen or a person settled in the UK. They do not need to leave the UK in order to apply.

People who are in the UK illegally or whose leave to remain has already run out may also apply to stay on the basis of marriage, but this may be problematic. The rules state that the person applying to remain must not have been in the UK 'in breach of the immigration laws' before the marriage. Thus an overstayer applying to remain with a spouse is making an application for exceptional treatment, outside the immigration rules. Instructions to Home Office staff give examples of the rare occasions when an exception should be made ▶ see pages 21–23.

People who are on temporary admission, for example many asylum-seekers, may marry and then apply for leave to enter on grounds of the marriage. Because they have not formally been allowed into the country, the rules under which the application is considered are the rules for seeking entry, which state that people must have entry clearance for the purpose of marriage. This is impossible, so the application is always made outside the rules.

People who apply when they are legally in the UK

WHAT THE RULES SAY

The rules state the requirements for an extension of stay as the spouse of a settled person. These are that:

- the marriage must not have been entered into primarily to obtain settlement in the UK
- the couple must have met
- the person applying must have limited leave to remain and not have remained in breach of the immigration laws; and
- not be subject to deportation action; and
- be married to a person present and settled in the UK; and
- intend to stay permanently with his or her spouse, and the marriage must be subsisting; and
- there must be adequate accommodation, owned or occupied exclusively by the sponsor, for the couple and any dependants
- the couple will be able to maintain themselves and any dependants without recourse to public funds;
- the applicant must not be a person to whom the general grounds for refusal apply ▶see pages 234–5.

… Spouses and fiancé(e)s • 19

WHAT THE RULES MEAN

A person with limited leave to remain married to a person settled here

This phrase means that the person applying to remain on the grounds of marriage must have valid immigration leave to remain, for example as a visitor, a student or a work permit holder, and must apply to the Home Office before the end of the time limit on that leave (►see chapter 11 on how to apply). The person whom she or he is marrying must be a British citizen or have indefinite leave to remain in the UK. The rules and the way in which the application is considered are different if one partner is in the UK without permission (in breach of the immigration laws); ►see page 21.

Tests of the marriage

- 'primarily to obtain settlement'
- the couple have met
- intention to live together permanently
- support and accommodation ►see pages 14–15 and 218–220.

►see discussion of these points on pages 12–14

How to apply

Applications may be made in writing or in person at the Home Office, before the person's leave to remain runs out, on the official application form FLR(M). The person is legally in the UK while the application is being considered and the conditions attached to the original leave to remain, for example a prohibition on working, are still valid until the application is decided. The application may take a long time; for more information about the situation while applications are pending, see chapter 11.

The Home Office does not often subject such couples to the detailed questioning which happens in some countries abroad. The application form asks the couple a long list of questions about their relationship, when and how they met, why they married and their plans for the future. It also requests a list of documents ►see chapter 11 for details. The documents specifically required for marriage applications are the civil marriage certificate and, if either person had been married before, evidence of how that marriage had ended, such as a divorce or death certificate. The application form also requests proof to show that the already-settled spouse has lived in the UK for the past three years. The intention behind this is to show that the person is settled, but there is no legal justification for this to be for three years. For the application to be valid, it is necessary to send all the documents, or an explanation of why any documents are not being sent.

Both the person applying and the already-settled spouse have to sign declarations to confirm that the marriage has not been terminated, they are still living together and plan to do so permanently. However, if the person is legally in the UK at the time of marriage and at the time of application, and if the couple are able to support and accommodate themselves without recourse to public funds, there is a good chance that the application to remain will be granted.

Some problems which may arise

The Home Office may be suspicious of people who marry soon after gaining entry for another purpose. For example, if a person gained a visa as a visitor stating that he would be going back to his job in the Gambia after three weeks and then gets married after being in Britain for a fortnight and applies to stay as a spouse, the Home Office may suspect that this was his intention from the beginning, but that he wanted to avoid the problems of applying for a fiancé entry clearance. The Home Office may therefore treat the person as an illegal entrant who entered the UK by deception; ▶ see chapter 14 for further details on illegal entry. It is therefore important to explain in such applications how and why the person's plans changed after arrival in the UK, as well as showing how he or she fits into the rest of the immigration rules on marriage.

The Home Office may also be suspicious of people who marry very shortly before their leave to remain runs out, and may believe that the marriage was entered into primarily to enable the person to stay in the UK. Evidence of the length of relationship and of the reasons why the marriage was planned for that particular date may be helpful in this situation.

There are no provisions in the immigration rules for people who have been allowed into the country on some other basis to apply to remain as fiancé(e)s. A person who is in the UK for a temporary purpose may have plans to marry which cannot be achieved while his or her leave to remain is still current, for example because the British or settled partner is awaiting a divorce. It may be worth making an application as a fiancé(e) outside the rules, at the discretion of the Home Office, using the form FLR(O). The application should explain the reasons for the delay in marrying. As the Home Office is often very slow in replying to applications, the couple may well be able to marry while waiting for the Home Office to respond. After the marriage, they should continue the application for leave to remain to the Home Office, by filling in form FLR(M), together with the evidence requested and ask for leave to remain as a spouse.

When an application is successful

If an application is successful, a spouse will be given permission to remain for twelve months initially, without any restrictions on employment. After 8 November 1996, the passport stamp may also include a condition that the person maintains and accommodates him- or herself without recourse to public funds (see chapter 13 for examples of these passport stamps). The Home Office sends a standard, detailed two-page letter explaining other rights in the UK (▶see copy in appendix). During this year the person is free to do any kind of work or business without needing any permission. Shortly before the end of the twelve-month period, the person should apply to the Home Office for settlement; see below for the procedure.

When an application is refused

If the application was made while the spouse or fiancé(e) from abroad had leave to remain, there is the right to appeal against a refusal. The Home Office must give the person a letter explaining the reason for refusal and the right to appeal, and forms to fill in to appeal. The forms must be returned to the Home Office within fourteen days of the date of refusal. The spouse may remain legally in the UK while the appeal is going on. There is more information about appealing in chapter 16.

People who apply when they are in the UK without permission

WHAT THE RULES SAY

The immigration rules state that the Secretary of State must be satisfied that:

- the applicant has limited leave to remain in the UK
- the applicant has not remained in the UK in breach of the immigration laws
- the marriage has not taken place after a decision has been made to deport him or he has been recommended for deportation or been given notice under section 6(2) of the Immigration Act 1971.

WHAT THE RULES MEAN

Any application from a spouse who is an overstayer, or who has already been refused permission to stay on other grounds but is still in the country appealing against the refusal and therefore does not have leave to remain, is made outside the immigration rules, at the discretion of the Home Office. It is therefore possible for an application to be refused solely on the grounds that a person was in the UK without leave; it is not necessary for the Home Office to interview the couple or even to look into all the circumstances of their case.

When people have not remained illegally, for example if they are appealing against a refusal of further leave to remain, the Home Office may consider the application in a similar way to those made under the immigration rules.

Home Office policy and enforcement action

If people are in the UK illegally, the Home Office policy became much stricter from 13 March 1996, when it published new internal 'secret instructions' on marriage, to apply to marriages which 'came to the notice' of the Home Office after that date.

Since 13 March 1996, these instructions state that 'where the subject has a genuine and subsisting marriage with someone settled here and the couple have lived together in this country continuously since their marriage for at least 2 years before the commencement of enforcement action and it is unreasonable to expect the settled spouse to accompany his/her spouse on removal' action to force the person to leave should not be started. This 'enforcement action' is defined as either:

- a specific instruction to leave with a warning of liability to deportation if the person fails to do so (the standard letter that people receive after an appeal has been dismissed, or an out-of-time application has been refused); or
- service of a notice of intention to deport or of illegal entry papers; or
- a court recommendation for deportation.

If any of these actions have started, they 'stop the clock' and the person does not gain any more time by making representations or appealing.

Even if the marriage has subsisted for two years before action started, the Home Office must also believe that it is 'unreasonable' to expect the settled spouse to live abroad to continue the marriage. It is up to the couple to make sure that the Home Office has all the information on which to make a decision; the Home Office will not ask for it. The instructions say that the Home Office will consider whether the person:

- has very strong and close family ties with the UK, such as older children from a previous relationship who form part of the family unit; or
- has been settled and living in the UK for at least 10 years; or
- has medical reasons for remaining and medical evidence which conclusively shows that his or her life would be significantly impaired or endangered if he or she had to leave.

Any other matters which are put to the Home Office could also be considered. But the instructions stress that 'each case is to be decided on its individual merits and, for instance, a particularly poor immigration history may warrant the offender's enforced departure from the UK notwithstanding the factors referred to above.' Thus it is important that all the background and history of the couple's relationship should be explained to the Home Office at the time of application, rather than waiting for any further questionnaire. People should not rely on the application form alone, as it does not provide space for all the exceptional or compassionate factors, so it should be accompanied by a further covering letter of explanation.

Where there are children of the marriage with the right of abode, this is not enough in itself. The Home Office believes that 'a child of 10 or younger could reasonably be expected to adapt to life abroad' but if the child suffers from 'serious ill-health for which treatment is not available in the country to which the family is going' this should be considered.

These instructions state that 'where a person marries *after* the commencement of enforcement action removal should normally be enforced' and that 'detailed enquiries in order to ascertain whether the marriage is genuine and subsisting should *not* normally be undertaken'. Thus people who marry after they have had immigration problems cannot expect to be allowed to remain.

It is difficult to know how to advise people in this situation. They may wish to try to persuade the Home Office that their situation is so exceptional as to warrant being granted leave to remain, and thus run a serious risk of a deportation order being signed against them while they contest a refusal. Or they may leave the country and apply for entry clearance to return, but no guarantee can be given that this will be granted, as people can be refused under rule 320(11) for a 'failure to observe the time limit or conditions attached to any grant of leave to enter or remain in the UK'. This has not yet been used frequently, but could be. There are likely to be delays in the application being considered, as the British high commission or embassy will refer it to the Home Office for instructions. The couple may therefore be separated for months while the case is considered.

How to apply

When an overstayer or someone who has been treated as an illegal entrant gets married and wants to apply for leave to remain with his or her spouse, it is still important that the couple should seek detailed advice before deciding when or whether to make an application to the Home Office. The application must be made to the Home Office in writing, putting forward as full and detailed case as possible at the outset, and using the application form FLR(M).

There may be practical problems in getting married for people who are unwilling to produce their passports. The marriage registrar must by law be satisfied as to the identity, age and freedom to marry of couples requesting marriage. If the registrar is satisfied by what couples say, no further evidence may be requested. If not, instructions to registrars from the General Register Office state that the best evidence from a person from abroad is a passport. When people have lost their passports, or do not wish to show them, they may have difficulty in fixing a wedding. Birth certificates may be acceptable, but will not show whether people have been married, or whether they still hold their nationality of birth. Registrars state that a passport, issued more recently and which will have a photograph of its holder, is more useful, and the passports issued by many countries state whether the holder is married or single. Other evidence, such as driving licences, may be acceptable at the discretion of the registrar.

There have been reports of people being unable to book a wedding because the registrar has not accepted other evidence of their identity. There have also been cases where a registrar, suspicious about a particular person, has alerted the Registrar-General's office (now the Office of

National Statistics), which in turn has alerted the immigration authorities, to the date fixed for a wedding, or the immigration authorities have requested information from the registrar, and people have been arrested as overstayers before they are able to marry. In the first six months of 1996, 309 such reports were made and information about 232 people passed on to the Home Office, the vast majority from the London boroughs of Brent, Hackney, Lewisham and Tower Hamlets.

Some important points to consider

- **how long the person has been in the UK**. If this is less than seven years, there will be no full right of appeal against deportation, should the Home Office refuse the application (▶see chapter 16 for more details). If the person has been in the UK for nearly seven years, it may be worth waiting before making the application.
- **how long the relationship has subsisted** before enforcement action and any evidence to show this, for example, children of the relationship, joint purchase of property, evidence the couple have been together for a long time. When there is a child or children involved, particularly if they are nearly 10 years old, it is worth reminding the Home Office of the internal instructions ▶see above.
- **the person's previous immigration history** and any problems he or she has had with the Home Office in the past. When a marriage takes place at the end of a long series of applications or other immigration problems the Home Office will be particularly suspicious of the intentions of the person from abroad.
- **whether a deportation decision has already been made**. If so, it is important to urge that the decision be reversed or the deportation order be revoked. ▶See chapter 14 for details of the factors the Home Office must consider in deciding to deport a person and of how to counter them.

If the Home Office considers the application it may send out a further questionnaire, or may interview couples when the partner applying to remain is an overstayer or has had other immigration problems. They may be asked to go to the Home Office or to an immigration office, where they will be interviewed separately, but both may be asked the same questions about their meeting and relationship, to see if they give the same answers. Occasionally, the immigration service may come to a couple's home, unannounced, in order to see whether they are living together and whether there is any evidence that a couple live at that address.

In general, it is easier to get permission to stay as spouses outside the rules for women, and for people who come from countries other than those where the Home Office considers there is 'pressure to emigrate' (for example, the Indian subcontinent or North or West Africa). There is little point in an overstayer making an application to remain as a fiancé(e) unless there are very strong reasons why the marriage cannot take place before making an application to the Home Office.

When an application was made when the spouse or fiancé(e) from abroad did not have leave to remain, there is no formal right of appeal against refusal. The refusal letter states that the person should leave the UK without delay and the Home Office might make a decision to deport him or her at the same time. It is still possible to make further representations to the Home Office on the person's behalf, explaining or reiterating any compassionate or other circumstances why an exception to the rules should be made, as well as lodging an appeal against the deportation decision. If the application is successful, the person will be given twelve months' leave to remain, with no restrictions on taking employment.

People admitted or given leave to remain as spouses
The initial twelve-month period
Claiming benefits

It is expected that the couple will not have recourse to public funds (►see box on page 180) but if this is financially necessary it is possible for the settled spouse to claim certain benefits. See chapter 10 for more details about claiming.

The Home Office has stated that if a couple need to claim public funds for a short period during the twelve-month period, but are mainly able to support themselves, this will not automatically lead to a refusal. 'We would not use this power [to refuse] if a person had become dependent on public funds for a short time through no fault of his own. Moreover, if a sponsor here is dependent on public funds the relevant question will be whether extra funds were necessary to support the applicant.' (letter from David Waddington MP to Max Madden MP, December 1985) This was confirmed by Nicholas Baker MP in a letter to Sir Giles Shaw MP of 5 October 1994: 'there is no objection to other residents in the same household receiving public funds to which they are entitled in their own right. The question is whether additional recourse to public funds would be necessary on the applicant's arrival here.' Thus the British or settled partner may claim for his or her individual needs, but not for the spouse from abroad.

A couple asking about entitlements to benefit during this first year should therefore be informed if either of them has an entitlement to claim. However it is important they know of possible immigration consequences should they need to claim for a prolonged period, or should they still be claiming at the time of the settlement application. Since 1 November 1996 people may be admitted on condition they can maintain and accommodate themselves without recourse to public funds. Breach of this condition is a criminal offence and also could lead to a refusal. If a refusal is made solely on the grounds that a couple cannot show that they can support themselves, there is a right of appeal provided the application is made in time. During the appeal period, the spouse from abroad may be allowed to work, so if one of them could then find work and they no longer needed to claim benefits, a fresh application to the Home Office could be made, which would be granted.

Travelling into and out of the UK

During the initial twelve-month period, spouses from abroad are free to travel into and out of the UK and will be allowed in again until the end of the twelve months previously given. Visa nationals do not need visas to re-enter. When they return, the immigration officer may question them, and the already-settled spouse, to be sure that the couple are still together and the marriage is still continuing. If the officers are satisfied, leave to enter to the same date will be granted, usually with a stamp stating 'given leave to enter, section 3(3)(b) until date'. This refers to section 3(3)(b) of the Immigration Act 1971, which provides for people to be readmitted within a period of leave already granted.

Applying for settlement (indefinite leave to remain)

WHAT THE RULES SAY

The immigration rules state that the requirements for indefinite leave to remain are:
- the person was admitted, or was given an extension of stay, for 12 months and has completed a period of 12 months as a spouse of a settled person
- the person is still the spouse of the same person and the marriage is subsisting
- the couple intend to live together permanently as husband and wife
- the couple can support and accommodate themselves without recourse to public funds
- the person is not one to whom any of the general grounds of refusal apply ▶see pages 234–5.

Making the application

Before the one year's permission has expired, the spouse from abroad must apply to the Home Office for settlement (indefinite leave to remain) on form SET(M). The spouse who is British or settled should be in the UK at the time the application is made and must confirm the marriage is still subsisting. If he or she is temporarily abroad, this should be explained to the Home Office and it should be informed when he or she returns.

Documents required for the application

- applicant's passport
- husband's or wife's passport or, if a British citizen without a passport,

other evidence of settlement such as the full birth certificate and evidence of the person's residence in the UK for the past three years, such as a driving licence, income tax coding, building society or bank statement or national insurance or NHS number. The application form requests evidence for three years but there is no legal justification for this period.
- original marriage certificate
- passport-sized photos of both spouses
- if either partner had been married before, evidence of how that marriage ended
- proof that the couple have lived together during the previous 12 months. The forms request 'five items of correspondence addressed to you during the past year from the following sources if they clearly show that you and your spouse live at the same address'. These include correspondence from the local authority, from such organisations as British Telecom, a gas, electricity or water company, or a bank, building society or credit card company. For couples living in rented accommodation, or in joint family accommodation where the bills and official documents come to another family member, this could cause serious difficulties.
- evidence of financial support, for example bank statements for the past six months or pay slips for the past three months, to show that the couple can be supported without recourse to public funds.

It is usual for this application to be granted routinely if the Home Office has no reason to suspect any problems. If the Home Office has been informed, either by the couple or anyone else, that they have separated or there have been marital problems, or if they have claimed public funds during the year, it is likely that the Home Office will ask more detailed questions or want to interview the couple to be sure that the immigration rules are met.

Spouses coming to the UK for temporary purposes
Workers and business people

The immigration rules state the requirements that must be met by spouses of people coming for work which may eventually lead to settlement. The rules cover specific groups: workers with work permits, business people, investors, retired persons of independent means, representatives of overseas newspapers, news agencies and broadcasting organisations, and of overseas firms, employees of governments and international organisations, private servants of diplomats, ministers of religion and missionaries, operational ground staff of overseas airlines, Commonwealth citizens with UK-born grandparents, writers, composers and artists, trainees and exchange language teachers. The requirements are:
- they must intend to live together with their spouse as husband and wife in the UK, and the marriage must still be subsisting

- there will be adequate support and accommodation for them without recourse to public funds
- they must not intend to stay in the UK beyond their spouse's period of leave
- if seeking leave to enter, they must have entry clearance, or if seeking leave to remain they must have had entry clearance for this purpose
- they are not people to whom any of the general grounds for refusal apply ▶see pages 222–3.

Proof of their identity, and having adequate support and accommodation without recourse to public funds (▶see box on page 180) are the main requirements that these spouses have to fulfil. The 'primary purpose rule' and the requirement that the couple must have met do not apply.

Spouses who are abroad must apply for entry clearance at the British embassy or high commission in the country in which they are living. The British post will require evidence of identity and of the status of the spouse in the UK, usually attested photocopies of the passport to show his or her immigration leave. There is more information about making entry clearance applications in chapter 11 and in chapter 7 on workers and business people.

People with leave to enter or remain in the UK for some other temporary purpose who marry people who are in the UK in any of these categories may apply to the Home Office for leave to remain with their spouse. They do not have to leave the country to apply for entry clearance. The form they should use is FLR(O), which does not have a specific part for them, but they can qualify under 'other'. The form assumes that the worker and his or her spouse are applying together for an extension of stay, rather than that the spouse might be applying independently when, for example, she had permission to remain on a different basis before the marriage.

If the application is successful, leave to enter or remain will be granted for the same length of time as the spouse who is a worker, business person etc. The rules state that the spouses of retired persons of independent means will not be allowed to work but nothing is said about any employment conditions to be imposed on others. Home Office practice is not to restrict employment, so spouses of workers and business people are normally free to work. They will normally have a public funds condition stamped on their passports.

Students

Since 1 October 1994 the husbands as well as the wives of overseas students have been permitted to join them; previously only wives had been allowed. Spouses have to show that they can be maintained and accommodated without recourse to public funds, that they intend to leave the UK at the end of any period granted and are not people to whom any of the general grounds for refusal apply ▶see pages 222–3. If they are visa nationals they need visas, but non-visa nationals do not need to have entry clearance. If they are allowed in, they will be given permission for the same length of time as the student spouse. If this period is less than 12 months, the spouse will be prohibited from working. If it is 12 months or over, nothing is stated about working but Home Office practice is not to restrict the spouse from working.

▶Chapter 9 on students gives more information. Students' spouses should use application form FLR(O) if they are applying separately from the student spouse, FLR(S) if the student and spouse are applying together.

Refugees and people with exceptional leave

There is nothing in the immigration rules about families of refugees. It is Home Office practice to allow the spouse and the children under 18 of a person granted refugee status permission to stay for the same period as the refugee. If they apply to join the refugee later, they will be granted visas or entry clearance to do so, simply on establishing the relationship; there is no visa fee. It is not necessary for refugees to prove that they can support and accommodate their family. However it is Home Office practice not to make this exception when a refugee marries abroad after being granted asylum. The spouse would need to apply for entry clearance and meet all the other requirements of the immigration rules.

There is no right for a person granted exceptional leave to enter or remain to be joined by any family members. The Home Office has stated that family reunion will not normally be allowed until the person with exceptional leave has had that leave for four years, and the other criteria of the immigration rules on families, most importantly that there is adequate support and accommodation for the family, are met. The spouses of asylum-seekers, that is, people whose asylum applications have not yet been decided, have no right to come to the UK to join them. ▶See pages 107–8 for more information.

Asylum-seekers

Asylum-seekers often have to wait for long periods either for a decision on their cases, or for an appeal against refusal of asylum. If the asylum application was made on entry to the country, people may remain on temporary admission ▶see glossary for a long time. Because no decision has been made to recognise them as refugees or to grant exceptional leave, they have not formally been allowed into the UK. Thus, if they marry and apply to remain with their spouse, this application comes under the rules for seeking entry to the country ▶see above, not the rules for applying for leave to remain in the country. The practical effect of this is that because they do not have prior entry clearance for marriage, the application is outside the rules. If the asylum application has already been refused, the immigration authorities may see no reason why the person cannot return to seek entry clearance.

The Home Office does not normally deal with any application to remain on the grounds of marriage unless and until the asylum application is refused or withdrawn. This may then put people in great difficulties; they will not know for a long time what will happen about their future, but if they withdraw the asylum claim this may mean that they are immediately in the country without authority and not protected against deportation or removal (because the new application is made at a time when they do not have leave to remain).

Other partnerships

Non-marital relationships

There is no provision in the immigration rules for couples to be together in the UK if they are not married and not planning to marry. The formal provision for common-law wives was abolished in the 1985 immigration rule changes, on the grounds that it was sex discriminatory. However, in practice, permission was sometimes granted to couples who had a stable relationship and were from a culture where marriage is less important. There was a recognised unofficial practice to allow couples who had been together for over two years to be treated as though they were married, both for entry clearance and for further leave to remain. However, with no warning, the Home Office Minister Timothy Kirkhope announced on 22 February 1996, in debate on the Asylum and Immigration Bill, that 'foreign nationals who apply to enter or remain on the basis of a common-law relationship can, with immediate effect, expect to have their applications refused.' The reason given for this was that the numbers of people applying on that basis had gone up from 400 in 1991 to 900 in 1996. He said that 'it is not our intention to apply these new requirements retrospectively'. Thus people who had already been granted a year's leave to enter or remain on the basis of a common-law relationship may still be granted settlement if they apply near the end of the year and the relationship is still continuing and they have adequate support and accommodation.

The change means that people who are not married should not expect to be allowed to remain with a partner here. The Home Office has refused to give any indication if exceptions might be made. People who had been granted leave to remain for a limited period in the past, on some other basis, will be refused if they apply for extensions as common-law spouses after 22 February 1996.

Entry clearance as a fiancé(e) is not granted to anyone when both parties are not free to marry. Thus when people live in a country where divorce is very difficult, or impossible, for example the Philippines, there is no provision for them to come to the UK as fiancé(e)s in order to continue with divorce proceedings. They may be treated exceptionally, outside the rules, if the relationship is long-standing or if there are children involved, but an individual, detailed case will have to be made out in each instance. If people married abroad are already in the UK, living in a common-law relationship, it may be possible to apply for an extension of stay in order for the divorce to take place. Even if the application is not successful, people may be able to remain long enough to get divorced, and then remarried, because of Home Office delays in dealing with applications.

Gay and lesbian relationships

There is no provision in the rules for a gay or lesbian couple to remain together in the UK. Applications are entirely at the discretion of the Home Office and they are very rarely granted. The first couple to try to argue their case through the courts were a Swedish man, Lars Olaf Wirdestedt, and his British partner; they were unsuccessful but after their case had been heard by the Court of Appeal the Home Office decided to give in and to allow him to stay. The case was heard in 1984 but is reported in the 1990 Immigration Appeals reports, page 20.

The Tribunal case of *Webb* (5387), an Australian man fighting against deportation away from his British partner, refers to his gay relationship as 'permanent, and had it been contracted with a woman, would have been in the nature of a marriage'. His appeal was allowed, but this was also stated to be because of his responsible job and the support he gave to his partner's widowed mother, who had cancer. However, it is possible to ask that discretion should be exercised for a lesbian or gay couple, by stressing the length of the relationship, the difficulties there would be for the couple in living in the other person's country, or the particular reasons why it is necessary for the settled partner to remain in the UK. In some cases, the Home Office has treated the application as one for settlement with a close relative, and refused because the settled partner is not a relative. The Immigration Appeal Tribunal has held in two 1994 cases, *Lizarzaburu* (10848) and *Livingstone* (10964), that the Home Office should instead consider these applications on a similar basis to applications on the grounds of marriage. By the autumn of 1996, the Stonewall Immigration Group, set up to support couples and to campaign for a change in the law, ▶see chapter 19 for address knew of 17 men who had been allowed to remain on the basis of a gay relationship.

In a debate in the House of Commons on 4 May 1994 concerning a particular gay couple, Charles Wardle, then Home Office Minister, stated, 'Each application is considered carefully on its individual merits. Discretion will not normally be exercised in an applicant's favour unless compelling compassionate circumstances are present.' The factors which the Home Office states it takes into account 'in assessing whether compelling compassionate circumstances are present are the health of the settled partner and the length and stability of the relationship.' In a conversation with JCWI in 1992, the Home Office confirmed that discretion is less likely to be exercised in favour of a gay or lesbian couple than for an unmarried heterosexual couple, and that this reflects the fact that a common-law heterosexual relationship is recognised in English family law but a gay or lesbian one is not. The immigration rules, and now Home Office practice, recognise neither.

Community legislation may be helpful to gay and lesbian couples. Gay or lesbian relationships are recognised in the immigration regulations of Denmark, Finland, the Netherlands, Norway and Sweden. British citizens may therefore travel to these EEA countries and be joined there by a same-sex partner. As Community legislation gives free movement rights to 'spouses' of EEA citizens it may be possible to try to extend this to gay and lesbian marriages. For example, a British and Ghanaian gay couple might travel to Denmark, marry and live together there if the British man is engaged in any economic activity there. Stonewall (▶see chapter 19 for address) knows of couples who have been able to do this successfully in the Netherlands. Australia, Canada, New Zealand and South Africa also give some recognition to same-sex relationships.

Polygamous marriages

Since the Immigration Act 1988 came into force on 1 August 1988, it has not been possible for a woman who is a partner in a polygamous marriage and whose husband has previously brought another woman to the UK as his wife to come here on this basis. This applies irrespective of the legality of the marriage or of whether the wife concerned is the first wife of the marriage; if one wife has come to the UK as a wife, a second polygamous wife will not be recognised under British immigration law. This applies also to Commonwealth women who have gained the right of abode through marriage; a woman who has the right of abode because of a polygamous marriage cannot exercise that right if another wife has already come to the UK on that basis. Section 2 of the Immigration Act 1988 is the most tortuous part of the immigration law, drafted in order to try to express the concept of a right of abode which cannot be exercised.

Even if a polygamous marriage is not recognised for immigration purposes, it may be recognised for nationality purposes. The children from a legally contracted polygamous marriage are British citizens by descent from a British father, even if the marriage will not allow their mother to come to the UK (▶see chapter 3 for more details on children).

Marriages and divorces in other countries

There is often confusion with regard to marriages which took place abroad, in countries with very different marriage laws. Many people believe that, for example, a Ghanaian customary marriage is 'not recognised' in the UK, or that after seven years' separation, a marriage in the Philippines is 'automatically' ended. Couples may then marry, in the UK or abroad, in good faith, but then the Home Office may investigate past statements and allege that the marriage is bigamous. The police may be asked to investigate with a view to prosecution for bigamy. The whole subject is very complicated, as it involves the relationship between different countries' laws which may be constructed on entirely different bases. It is not proposed to go into all the details here.

Broadly, however, if a marriage is legally recognised and valid in the country in which it took place, it will be recognised as a valid marriage under UK marriage law. The validity of certain forms of marriage may depend on the country in which they took place and the domicile (which means more than simple residence in a country; ▶see glossary) of both parties involved. For example, a Nigerian customary marriage, where there is no documentation and the ceremony is an exchange of gifts between the families, will be valid if it takes place in Nigeria and both parties were domiciled in Nigeria at the time of the marriage. It will not be valid if it takes place in Britain or any other country which does not recognise this form of marriage.

Similarly, a customary divorce will also be valid if it took place in the prescribed forms in a country which recognises customary divorce and in which both parties were domiciled. When a person living in the UK performs a customary divorce abroad, and then marries again, the Home Office may argue that a divorce should take place in the UK before the person is free to marry again in a way that is valid in the UK.

Immigration status, nationality and the country where the marriage took place do not affect people's ability to divorce in the UK; the process is the same as for anyone else wishing to divorce. There may be extra delays in that papers may have to be sent to a spouse abroad, who may be difficult to contact and unwilling to co-operate, particularly when divorce is more difficult, or impossible, in that country. There is no need for specialist information about the divorce laws of the country in which the marriage took place if the divorce is taking place in the UK.

If a person has gained entry to the UK on the basis of a marriage which is later found to be invalid, the person can be treated as an illegal entrant. For example, a Filipino woman married a British man in Hong Kong when they were both working there. She had believed that because she had been separated from her husband in the Philippines (where divorce did not exist) for more than seven years, she was free to marry again, and later came to Britain. She was treated as an illegal entrant when she later tried to bring her children from her first marriage from the Philippines to join her, and it was discovered that there had been no divorce. She was able to obtain a divorce in the UK and then marry her British husband again, in order to secure her status.

Marriage breakdown and immigration consequences

Since 1 August 1988, both men and women entering the UK as spouses are given a year's initial stay. If marriages break down during that year, for whatever reason, and couples are no longer living together at the end of it, the partners from abroad no longer have any claim under the immigration rules to remain because of the marriage. Either they will have to show that they fit into some other part of the immigration rules, for example as students, or that there are strong exceptional compassionate reasons to permit them to stay. Unless the settled or British partner has died during the first year, it is unusual for this to be granted. The Home Office states that 896 applications for settlement on the grounds of marriage were refused in 1995 on the grounds that the couple did not intend to stay together.

This provision is seen at its worst when there is violence within the marriage. A woman may have to decide whether to remain in a violent and dangerous relationship for a longer period, and be granted settlement in the UK after a year, or whether to leave the marital home for her and her children's safety, and risk being refused permission to stay, deportation and possible family disgrace. Advice can only depend on the individual situation and the priorities for the person concerned.

If a marriage has broken down, an application outside the rules may be made to the Home Office and all the compassionate features can be argued. But the case is entirely discretionary and the Home Office will have to be persuaded of its truly exceptional nature. In the past, the presence of children of the marriage was considered significant, but since 13 March 1996, the Home Office has stated that 'the general presumption is that a child who has spent less than 10 years in the UK would be able to adapt to life abroad' and therefore is not a strong consideration. ▶See chapter 3 for more details on the policy on children. Any other compassionate points should be put to the Home Office with the application. When the marriage has ended, the person cannot use application form SET(M) but should use SET(O), and also send a more detailed covering letter as there is unlikely to be room on the form to explain her circumstances. The situation that she would face in her country of origin may also be relevant, if it can be argued that the discrimination and harassment there could amount to persecution. ▶See pages 82–83 for more information.

Thus it may be worth arguing that the person should be able to remain after a marriage breakdown. Even when there are no children involved, the Home Office may consider 'the respective strength of a woman's ties with the UK and her own country and whether she would suffer any hardship if she was to return to her own country.' The Home Office has stated in relation to a judicial review case '...leave to remain is not normally granted unless there are the most exceptional compelling or compassionate circumstances. The factors to be considered would include: the length of time the applicant was married before the breakdown; the length of time the applicant has been resident in the UK; the applicant's age and the proportion of time spent abroad before entering the UK; whether there are children of the marriage and the applicant's close family and other ties both in the UK and abroad.' In a letter to JCWI of 22 November 1996, the Home Office stated only, 'Cases where violence is the reason for the breakdown are considered sympathetically but domestic violence cannot automatically override the requirements of the immigration rules.'

This consideration is entirely discretionary and since the Immigration Act 1988 there has been no effective right of appeal against a decision to deport someone in these circumstances. Compassionate aspects can no longer be raised at an appeal against deportation for a person who has been in the UK for less than seven years. Only if the woman's circumstances in her country of origin would be so terrible as to give her a claim for asylum would the full facts be considered.

There have been some successful immigration campaigns for individual women threatened with deportation after leaving violent husbands within their first probationary year. Groups such as Southall Black Sisters (▶see chapter 19 for address) have taken up the issue as one of principle, in campaigning against the one-year rule.

If a marriage breaks down after the person has been granted settlement, this does not affect his or her immigration position. The person remains settled even if she or he is divorced or separated from his or her partner. When the separation has been difficult, it is not uncommon for the spouse who is British or was settled first to threaten the other partner with deportation. This is an idle threat if settlement has already been granted. The only exception to this is when the Home Office believes, and can prove, that settlement was granted through deception – that a couple had already separated at the time settlement was granted but had agreed at that stage not to inform the Home Office, or that the couple had never intended to remain together. It is theoretically possible then for the Home Office to initiate deportation proceedings on the grounds that the person's deportation would be conducive to the public good, because of the deception practised, but this is very rare.

Since 1 October 1996, under section 4 of the Asylum and Immigration Act, a person commits a criminal offence 'if, by means which include deception by him, he obtains or seeks to obtain leave to enter or remain in the UK.' This could be used against people granted settlement when the Home Office was not informed of the true situation of their marriage.

Access to children

From 1 October 1994, the immigration rules provide for 'persons exercising rights of access to a child resident in the UK'. This applies only to people who:

- are divorced or legally separated from the child's other parent
- do not intend to work or do business in the UK and can support themselves for the period requested without recourse to public funds
- have evidence that a court has granted them access to the child and are coming to the UK for that purpose
- intend to leave the UK at the end of this time
- have entry clearance for this purpose.

People may then be admitted for up to 12 months, with a prohibition on employment. The intention of this rule must be to attempt to comply with the European Court of Human Rights ruling in the case of *Berrehab* (1988 11 EHRR 322). This concerned a Moroccan man who was deported away from his Dutch ex-wife and their child, with whom he had kept up a very close connection, and it was held that this was an infringement of the child's right to respect for family life, under Article 8 of the European Convention on Human Rights. This Article guarantees the right to respect for family and private life and that any interference with this must, *inter alia*, be 'in accordance with the law'. Repeated decisions of the Commission and Court state that the law must be 'accessible' and 'foreseeable', which may be a reason for putting this restrictive provision in the published rules, rather than in internal instructions. It is unlikely that it complies with Article 8 because the British rules are clearly more restrictive in that couples must have been married, and must have court documents granting them access, rather than merely wishing to keep in contact with a child. It will be of very little use to most parents.

ANNEX: THE PRIMARY PURPOSE RULE

The 'primary purpose rule' is the basis for many refusals of couples, mainly from the Indian subcontinent and other Asian countries. The Labour Party is publicly committed to abolishing the rule if it comes to power but the rule is still in force at the time of writing. It is worth considering it in detail, to advise people whose partners are applying abroad to come to join them, so that they understand the rule and its implications and are therefore able to satisfy officials about their primary purpose in marrying. It is important that people reply truthfully to questions; an understanding of the process will help them to do so.

There are various areas of questioning which entry clearance officials use to try to establish people's motives in marrying. However, the main problem with the primary purpose rule is that, if rigidly applied, it is almost impossible for an applicant to prove a negative intention – that a marriage did not take place primarily for immigration reasons – when the foreign spouse is in fact applying to enter the UK and comes from a country with a lower per capita income than the UK, or a community with a history of emigration to the UK. This means the majority of people from Britain's black and ethnic minority communities.

Criteria used in primary purpose refusals

Religious or cultural traditions

Entry clearance officers may use their views or (often limited) knowledge about different religions and cultures. For example, a Pakistani Muslim man may be asked if he believes in Islamic traditions and follows them, and if he says he does, he may then be asked why he will be joining his wife, rather than she joining him, as this is contrary to 'Muslim tradition'. Officials may use such a statement to attempt to show that the primary purpose of the marriage is immigration since it goes against their views of the person's normal activities and plans.

Previous migration

Entry clearance officers may believe that people's past history shows that immigration is the primary purpose of marriage. For example, a man who has worked on contract in the Middle East, returned to Bangladesh when the contract came to an end and married a women resident in the UK may be assumed to have married in order to help him to work abroad again, his first venture having ended or been unsuccessful. The intention to work abroad may also be considered a strong motive for a man who is unemployed at home, or who has been unable to find work commensurate with his educational qualifications, who may be assumed to be seeking greater opportunities elsewhere. Although the Immigration Appeal Tribunal has stated that these should not be relevant considerations, they still appear to be so for entry clearance officers.

Discussion between the couple

Questions may be asked about what discussion the couple had before marriage as to where they would live. If it is alleged that the partner abroad did not know that the spouse came from the UK, or that no discussion took place, this is unlikely to be believed and officials will think that there is deliberate evasion. Often there are very strong reasons why the partner in Britain does not want to leave the country and it can be important for all these to be spelled out: not wanting to leave family or friends or job (although it must then be explained why the partner from abroad is more ready to do this), having family responsibilities in the UK (for example, having children from a previous marriage whose education should not be disrupted, or other dependent relatives who need physical care) or other reasons why it would be difficult. The authorities are becoming suspicious of UK-based women who say that the heat of a country in the subcontinent makes them ill, particularly when they or their family have come from a country with a similar climate.

Previous marital status

The position of the partner in the UK is also considered. If a woman in the UK has previously been married and divorced, and has then chosen a new husband from abroad, crude stereotypes about the prejudices against women who have been previously married may be brought into play. It may be suggested, directly or indirectly, that a pay-off for a man in getting married to a previously-married woman was that the marriage would enable him to go to the UK. This may also be used when the woman has a child or children from a previous marriage.

Depth of relationship

Entry clearance officers can demand any evidence they wish to show further details of the relationship. The case of *Arun Kumar* (1986 Imm AR 446) decided that if a couple who have been kept apart for some time can show there is 'intervening devotion' between them, this may show that the primary purpose of the marriage is no longer immigration. Often couples will show their letters to each other, in the hope that this will confirm an ongoing and genuine relationship. Officials are mainly interested in letters that were exchanged before the application to come to the UK was made, or any other evidence of a relationship continuing for some time. This may also lead to insinuations about a woman's physical attractiveness. If the woman has a physical disability, is older than the man or suffers from ill-health, entry clearance officers may insinuate that she was chosen because she lives in the UK.

Women applying to come to the UK

The primary purpose rule is also increasingly being used against women applying to join husbands and fiancés. This has been seen both in the Indian subcontinent and in other Asian countries, particularly Thailand and the Philippines. It is often assumed that women who have married British men who were on short holidays in those countries have done so because of the closing of doors on immigration to work in many Western countries and that the primary motivation for the marriage was to be able to work abroad and to support existing family members. This is particularly so if the couple had not known each other for long, or had been introduced by a marriage agency. British men separated from their wives in this way have joined together to form APART ▶see chapter 19 for address, a group set up to campaign for the abolition of the primary purpose rule and to provide mutual support.

Questioning by British officials

When a husband or wife is refused entry clearance and appeals against the refusal, it is now the practice of officials at the British post to give a full question-and-answer record of the interview as part of their statement of their reasons for refusal.

The following questions come from an explanatory statement and show how officials build up their case.

Did you meet Himat by prior arrangement?
Did you meet him specifically with a view to marriage?
Why did Mr P pick on you to show to the young man?
Did he invite other girls to see the man also?
So then why did he pick on you?
Yes, but of all the other single girls in the village, why you?
But how could your husband know he likes you if he hasn't met you yet?
But why did Mr P show you in the first place?
Was it possibly because your father had asked him to find someone suitable for you?
What requirements did your father have in a future son-in-law?
What do you mean, working out?
Do you mean your father wanted someone from London?
Why did your father want that?
Why was that important to your father?
Had your father or Mr P asked you to look at any other young men?
Was it essential to your father that he find someone from London for you?
Why was it essential from your father's point of view?
Just now you said it was important to your father that you live there so that you would be happy. Does that mean you would not be happy marrying someone and staying here?
Would you have even looked at this boy if he had not been from London?
Did you agree to marry him so that you could go to London like your brother?
Did you agree to marry him straight away after that five-minute meeting?
Did anyone tell you anything about the boy before you met other than that he was from London?
Other than the fact that he's from London I can't see any other convincing reason for you agreeing to marry him. Can you suggest any?
I've asked you at least twice but you haven't been able to tell me what you liked about him. Do you want to suggest anything now?
Anything else?
I'm sorry, I'm left with the overall impression that this marriage was arranged and undertaken by you and your family to enable you to go to the UK. I don't think it would have been contemplated if your husband had been resident here.

These questions are taken from a report of 86 questions a British high commission asked a 21-year-old Indian village woman who had recently married. She repeatedly stressed that she liked her husband and that the marriage would have been considered if he had been resident in India. She was refused entry clearance to join him. Entry clearance officers have expressed surprise at the readiness with which young girls in the sub-continent state that their families arranged their marriage in order for them to have a better life overseas.

Case law

A large body of case law, in the Immigration Appeal Tribunal and the courts, has now grown up around the interpretation of the primary purpose rule. Some frequently quoted cases are summarised below; most are reported in the quarterly Immigration Appeals Reports (Imm AR), known as the 'green books'; ►see chapter 16 for more details on appeals.

Arun Kumar (1986 Imm AR 446) established that entry clearance officers should differentiate between applications from husbands and from fiancés. In the case of a fiancé, the motives of the parties at the time of application have to be considered, while in the case of a husband, events since the marriage may be considered to show what its primary purpose is. Evidence of the 'intervening devotion' of the couple to each other in the period since the marriage, for example, time spent together outside the UK, is important. Although the primary purpose of the marriage and the couple's intention to stay together permanently are separate points, if the second is proved, this will 'often cast a flood of light' on the first.

Hoque and Singh (1988 Imm AR 216) provided a list of ten propositions which should be considered in marriage cases. These include a reminder that the burden of proof is on the person applying to come to the UK to show that the primary purpose of the marriage is not immigration; that the official dealing with the case may make his or her own inquiries into the marriage and is not limited to information given by the applicants; and that the reasons of anyone involved in organising the marriage may be relevant as to its primary purpose. It also stressed that the fact that the marriage is an arranged marriage 'though a circumstance which the entry clearance officer is entitled to take into consideration, does not show that its purpose is or was to obtain admission to the UK'.

Shameem Wali (1989 Imm AR 86) decided that it was reasonable for a woman living in the UK to make it a condition of her marriage that she and her husband should continue to live in the UK, and that this in itself was not enough to show that the primary purpose was immigration.

Najma Rafique (1990 Imm AR 235) decided that where an applicant had appeared uncertain as to whether he was coming to the UK permanently or temporarily for marriage, the application should be treated as one for settlement, because this, unlike a visit application, could encompass a person who was undecided as to his or her long-term intentions. Najma Rafique's fiancé, Abid Hussain, had applied to come to the UK to marry her, but had said it would depend on discussions with her after marriage whether they would settle in the UK or Pakistan.

Kandiya and Khan (1990 Imm AR 377) confirmed that it was generally helpful, though not necessary, that the entry clearance officer should make a decision on whether the couple intend to stay together permanently as well as on the primary purpose of the marriage. The officer should give reasons for believing that the primary purpose is immigration, and his or her understanding of customs and tradition may be used.

Mohammed Saftar (1992 Imm AR 1) decided that even though a Pakistani fiancé had stated that the primary purpose of his marriage was settlement and that he wanted to leave Pakistan, these answers were 'not fatal' to his case, because his later answers did not support this conclusion, and insufficient weight had been given to the British fiancée's intentions.

Sumeina Masood (1992 Imm AR 69) came to an opposite conclusion, deciding that because the wife did not want to live in Pakistan, and this had not been discussed before marriage, the marriage intention was only 'conditional' on the couple being able to live in the UK. The husband made it clear he wanted to come to the UK and was thought to be less concerned about breaking with some Muslim traditions than others when this would enable him to carry out this plan; the primary purpose of the marriage must be immigration.

Victoria Hansford (1992 Imm AR 407), a Filipino woman who married a British man after being pen-pals, was refused on primary purpose grounds although she was never specifically asked about the purpose of her marriage. She was successful in her application for judicial review, the judge stating: 'It is all too easy for those of us regularly engaged in poring over the entrails of these marriages to assume that the primary purpose of marrying an Englishman is to obtain admission to the UK. To jump to that conclusion, as I confess I did in the course of argument, in the absence of any other evidence and without the point ever having been put to Victoria is not fair to her and not fair to Mark (the husband).'

Raja Zafar Zia (1993 Imm AR 404), a successful case, urged adjudicators to consider carefully all the evidence with relation to the primary purpose of a marriage and to start with an open mind, rather than assuming that a couple have to rebut the presumption that theirs is a marriage primarily for immigration purposes. This time, the court thought that a conditional intention to live together was quite rational and acceptable.

Iram Iqbal (1993 Imm AR 270) decided that the adjudicator in an appeal should consider all aspects of the evidence in deciding on the person's credibility, not just rely on the entry clearance officer's assessment. The case had taken six years to come to this decision; it also contains a useful reminder of the absurdity of the primary purpose rule:

'...whilst the existence of a passionate love between a UK citizen and her foreign husband can help persuade the authorities that it is not the primary purpose of the marriage to obtain admission to the UK, in the context of an arranged marriage in Muslim society, the absence of such a passionate relationship or indeed 'being in love' is not in itself indicative of it being the primary purpose of a marriage to obtain for one of the spouses admission to the UK... To draw an analogy with English society at the turn of the century, the fact that an American heiress was so keen to be a duchess that she was prepared to marry an Englishman whom she did not love, would not lead one to suppose that the primary purpose of the marriage was for her to obtain admission to the UK. She may have been after his title and he after her money. Marie Antoinette married Louis XVI for dynastic reasons rather than as a love match but no one would regard that fact as indicating that the primary purpose of the marriage was to secure admission for Marie Antoinette into France.'

Surinder Singh (C-370/90, European Court of Justice, July 1992) decided that when a person from abroad is married to an EU citizen who has exercised his or her EC Treaty rights to free movement, the Home Office must consider any Community law aspects of the case. Mr Singh was an Indian citizen married to a British woman; they had lived and worked together in Germany, but their marriage broke down soon after they came to the UK. Because his wife had exercised her EU free movement rights, this gave Mr Singh rights under Community legislation, so it was decided that the British immigration rules could not be applied to him. Although the case was not specifically about primary purpose, it is important for advising couples who have been kept apart by the primary purpose rule. If they are able to live together for some time in another EU country, with the British partner working or carrying out any other activity there, they will then be able to return together to the UK under the wider provisions of Community law ►see page 118.

Bagdadi (1994 Imm AR 431) confirmed that a fiancé application and a husband application are different and must be considered separately. An adjudicator was wrong not to consider the appeal of a husband refused on primary purpose grounds because four years earlier he had been refused, and lost his appeal, as a fiancé.

Points to consider

- **is the marriage an arranged marriage or a 'love' marriage?** It is important for the couple to be clear and straightforward about the circumstances of the marriage. The fact that a marriage was arranged, that is, discussed and agreed by other members of the families concerned as well as, or largely instead of, the couple themselves, does not mean that the primary purpose was immigration.
- **customs and tradition:** entry clearance officers may have an out-of-date view of the customs and traditions of a particular area; the couple can explain how things have developed.
- **living together:** the fact that couples have spent prolonged periods together, outside the UK, and have proved their 'intervening devotion' is important in showing that the primary purpose is to be together, not to be in the UK.
- **children of the relationship:** although the birth of children does not affect the purpose at the time of the marriage, the Home Office has recognised in its June 1992 announcement (►see page 13) that keeping families apart solely for this reason cannot be justified. The European Court of Human Rights decision in the case of *Berrehab* (►see page 69) confirms children's right to be in contact with both of their parents and to live in the country of their nationality, but this has been diluted by the later case of *Poku* (►see page 69).

SECTION 1: FAMILY

3 Children

This chapter covers the immigration rules about children coming to the UK to join adults, usually their parents. It also covers children who may qualify to come to the UK in their own right, for example as students. There are four main sets of circumstances in which children may come to join their parents, or other guardian, in the UK. These are:

- children coming to join parents who are British or settled in the UK, or accompanying parents coming for settlement. They must obtain entry clearance from the British embassy or high commission before travelling.
- children who are accompanying, or coming to join, parents who are in the UK for temporary purposes, for example students or work permit holders. They sometimes need to have entry clearance before they travel and sometimes can apply at the port of entry. The rules about this are also discussed in the chapters which relate to their parents' status.
- children who are already in the UK for a temporary purpose, for example as visitors, and who then apply to remain in the UK with their parents or guardians. They can make applications to the Home Office while they are in the UK, and remain in the country while they do so.
- children of refugees and people granted exceptional leave to remain. There are no rules covering them, but the Home Office has established practices.

There are also provisions for children to join a lone parent in the UK (see page 50), or join a relative other than a parent (see page 53), for adopted children (see page 58), for some children over 18 (see page 56) and for children born in the UK but not born British citizens (see page 67) to come to or remain in the UK, but these are generally more restrictive and it is more difficult to convince the immigration officers that children qualify.

The Home Office interprets the immigration rules on children without reference to other childcare legislation such as the Children Act or the Child Protection Act. The Children Act 1989, in force from October 1991, states that when a court determines any question about a child, the child's welfare must be the paramount consideration, and also operates on the assumption that delay is prejudicial to the child, and that children should remain within their families wherever possible. Immigration law and rules state no such priorities. The case of *in re Fleur Matondo* (1993 Imm AR

541) was an application for a residence order for a child who had been ill-treated by her father, whose asylum application had been refused and they were both faced with removal. The judge held 'although the welfare of the child in such an application was paramount there had to be a balancing exercise with the requirements of public policy. The court could not ignore the immigration law and rely in isolation on issues of welfare. Due attention had to be paid to immigration law and the court had to be satisfied that an application was not designed to circumvent those laws. To grant the order there had to be "some extraordinary circumstances which take the case out of the normal considerations of welfare" '. In this instance, there were and the application was granted. This area of law may therefore be developed further.

REMEMBER:
- people abroad wanting to settle in the UK must get entry clearance before they travel
- applications to the Home Office must be made on the appropriate Home Office form
- BUT some family members may be British citizens
- AND some people may not have to fit into the immigration rules; see below.

People who do not have to fit into the rules

Some people have stronger claims to come to the UK in their own right and therefore do not have to fit into the rules.

a) **Children who are British citizens:** all children born in the UK before 1 January 1983 are British citizens and have the right of abode in the UK. Most children born abroad before 1983 to British citizen fathers are automatically British citizens and are not subject to immigration control. Children born in the UK from 1 January 1983 onwards are automatically British citizens if either parent was a British citizen or was settled ▶see glossary in the UK at the time of the child's birth. Most children born abroad from 1 January 1983 onwards are automatically British citizens if at the time of the birth either parent was a British citizen who was born, adopted, registered or naturalised in the UK. In all cases, the father's status counts only if the parents are married. See chapter 17 on nationality to check on the nationality status of children born in the UK or children with British parents.

b) **Other children with the right of abode:** a child who is a Commonwealth citizen and who was born before 1 January 1983 to a parent who was born in the UK has the right of abode in the UK and does not have to prove anything more than these facts to obtain a certificate of entitlement to the right of abode. If the parent is the father, the parents have to be married (which would normally make the child a British citizen as well).

The children need to have their position confirmed abroad before travelling by applying to the British high commission or embassy. If they are British citizens they may obtain British passports. If they are Commonwealth citizens they have to obtain a certificate of entitlement to the right of abode (see chapter 13 for example). They will need the birth certificate of the parent born in the UK, the marriage certificate of their parents if the parent concerned is their father, and their own birth certificate, to show that they are descended from that person. If these certificates are not available, or not accepted as genuine, it may be difficult to satisfy the British authorities about the relationship (see below).

c) **Children of EEA nationals:** nationals of any EEA country (►see glossary for list) other than the UK, who are engaged in any kind of economic activity or who are studying in the UK have the right under Community legislation to be joined by their children and grandchildren, automatically up to the age of 21, and beyond that age if the children are still dependent. There is no further definition of dependent, so it may mean emotionally or physically dependent as well as financially. If the children are visa nationals they have to obtain EEA family permits in advance. They must not be charged for these visas and the authorities must not delay the applications. Nothing other than the relationship and the ability of the EEA nationals to support themselves and their families has to be proved. See chapter 6 on EEA citizens for more details.

Children under 18 joining both parents

WHAT THE RULES SAY

The rules for children coming to join settled parents state that they must:

- have entry clearance
- be under 18
- be unmarried and not have formed an independent family unit and not be leading an independent life
- be supported and accommodated, in accommodation owned or occupied exclusively by their parent(s) without recourse to public funds ►see box on page 180
- not be people to whom any of the general grounds for refusal apply ►see pages 222–3.

If both parents are alive, they must both be settled in the UK, or be admitted for settlement on the same occasion as the child, or one must be settled and the other coming with the child for settlement. If one parent is dead, the other must be settled or coming with the child for settlement. If the child is from a polygamous marriage, and his or her mother does not qualify to enter because another wife has previously entered in that capacity, the child does not qualify to come under the immigration rules. But if a parent is a British citizen, the child may be a British citizen by descent; ▶see chapter 17.

If both parents are alive but one parent is not living in the UK and does not intend to live there, more tests must be satisfied; ▶see page 50 for further information. If the children have passed the age of 18, entry is much more difficult; ▶see page 56.

The rules are similar for a child accompanying, or coming to join, a parent who has been admitted for a year with a view to settlement.

WHAT THE RULES MEAN

Parents

In the immigration rules, the word 'parent' includes the stepfather of a child whose father is dead; the stepmother of a child whose mother is dead; and the father as well as the mother of a non-marital child. Thus a child should be able to join a step-parent if the other requirements of the rules are satisfied. It can also include an adoptive parent, but there are other restrictions on the entry of adopted children, discussed further on pages 58–64.

Under 18 and unmarried

Children must be under 18 on the date of application to come to or remain in the UK. An application from abroad is considered to be made on the day the application forms and the fee are received by the British post. An application in the UK is made on the date it is posted. To be valid, applications have to be made on the correct Home Office application form, and to be accompanied by all the documents specified on the form, or explanations of why any documents are not available and when they will be sent. It is therefore very important that the application be made, correctly, before the child is 18; it does not matter if the child becomes 18 while the application, or any appeal against refusal, is pending, as long as he or she was still under 18 when it was made.

A child who is married is not eligible for permission to come to or remain in the UK to join parents, even if he or she is still under 18. Marriage means that the child has formed a closer family link with his or her spouse and no longer qualifies to join his or her parent(s).

Since 1 October 1994, children who are not married but who are coming up to adulthood can be refused if immigration officials believe they have formed an independent family unit or are leading an independent life. This is not further defined: might it include a child who has a child of his or her own, even if not married to or living with the other parent of the child, or a child who has been at boarding school and has not returned to the parent(s) for every holiday, or who has spent time with other relatives after the parent(s) had emigrated? The Home Office has not explained the term further and there have been no Tribunal cases on the point.

Both parents are settled in the UK

This means that at the time the application is decided the child's parents must be in the UK and either be British citizens or have the right of abode or have indefinite leave to enter or remain. If they are outside the country, they must have British citizenship or right of abode, or be eligible to come back to the UK as returning residents ▶see page 229 and intend to travel with the child back to the UK when the child's entry clearance is granted. If only one parent is British or has indefinite leave and the child is applying with the other parent to come to join the settled parent, the child's status will depend on the parent he or she is accompanying. If the parent is granted entry clearance or leave to enter or remain, the child will be granted permission in line with this parent. If the child travels to the UK ahead of the parent, he or she will not be granted permission to enter unless the parent comes to the UK for settlement.

Support and accommodation

▶See details of this general requirement in chapter 11.

Children applying overseas to join their parents

▶See chapter 11 for general details of entry clearance applications.

The children have to satisfy the entry clearance officers at the British embassy or high commission that they qualify. They will be interviewed (unless they are under 10) and the person who has been caring for them abroad will be interviewed. In a letter to JCWI of 26 September 1996, the Foreign and Commonwealth Office confirmed that children between 10 and 14 years should be interviewed only in the presence of a responsible adult e.g. parent or guardian. Questions should be confined to relatively simple matters and details of immediate family. Older children may be questioned on their own and in more depth. All children will need to show evidence about their relationship to their parent(s) and of the support and accommodation available in the UK. If the child is from a polygamous marriage he or she will not qualify to come if the mother does not qualify.

Up-to-date evidence to support the application will be necessary when the child and/or guardians are interviewed. The interview may take place immediately, but long queues have built up in some British posts (see appendix for some of the delays near the time of writing). Where there is a long delay before interview, this evidence is not needed at the time of application but should be available at the interview.

Evidence that may be required

- **proof of the child's relationship to the parents.** If the child has a birth certificate showing the names of both the parents, this is very helpful.

However registration of births is not universal or compulsory in some countries and a birth certificate may not exist. Also British officials are often suspicious of documents that are produced by third world governments, refusing to rely on them. If the document does not exist, it is much safer to explain this and to provide any alternative evidence.

Examples of alternative evidence which could be helpful, if there is no birth certificate, include:

- records from the school the child is attending to show what that institution has been told about the child's age and parentage
- records from the hospital where the child was born
- information from the midwife or anyone else who knows about the birth
- affidavits from people, preferably not related to the child and parents, confirming their knowledge of the birth and relationship
- a scientific report of a DNA fingerprinting test (►see box below)

DNA FINGERPRINTING

DNA fingerprinting techniques, first used commercially in 1985, can prove conclusively that children are related to their parents. The test involves taking a small blood sample from the child and the parents and testing this for the DNA in the blood, to see that all the child's DNA corresponds to that of the parents. This is a much higher standard of proof than asking family members detailed questions. However it can show that, for example, a father is not the father of a child whom he has always accepted and believed to be his.

In January 1991 the immigration authorities set up a system for providing DNA tests for families applying to come to the UK *for the first time* 'where the relevant relationships cannot be demonstrated easily by other means' to the entry clearance officer, who would otherwise be likely to refuse the application. If families agree to take the test, arrangements will be made by the immigration authorities, at no extra cost to the family. If they refuse, this should not be a reason in itself for refusal of the application.

The scheme does not apply to reapplicants: people who have been refused once and who are applying again. Families not included in the scheme may still have tests done privately. They must get in touch with one of the companies which the Home Office has approved to carry out DNA testing and follow the company's procedures. The Home Office has approved only two companies, Cellmark Diagnostics and University Diagnostics ►see chapter 19 for addresses. From 1 May 1994, University Diagnostics has held the contract to do all the government tests. There are standard charges; ►see appendix for details. If the family want the test done before application or refusal, they will have to pay. If the application has been refused and there is an immigration appeal pending, and the family qualifies for legal aid for advice and assistance (green form), it is possible for the expenses of the test to be met under a green form extension or as a recoverable disbursement under a legal aid franchise.

- **proof of the parent(s)' status in the UK** e.g. certified photocopies of his, her or their passports (▶see information on applying for entry clearance in chapter 11)
- **the parents' birth certificates** if either of them was born in the UK
- **evidence of financial support** available to the children (▶see information on applying for entry clearance in chapter 11)
- **evidence of accommodation** available to the children (▶see information on applying for entry clearance in chapter 11)

If the application is successful

If the entry clearance officers are satisfied, they will grant entry clearance to the children. This is a blue and orange sticker in the passport, called a 'vignette' (see chapter 13 for example) and will usually state 'settlement – to join parents, valid for presentation at a UK port within six months of date of issue'. This means that the child must travel to the UK within six months of being granted entry clearance. If travel is delayed, the child has to apply again for the validity of the entry clearance to be extended, explaining the reasons for the delay in travelling.

When the child arrives at a UK port or airport he or she will be admitted until the same date as the parent if either parent is only allowed to stay for a year, or for an indefinite period if both parents already have this settled status. If the child is coming to join a lone parent in the UK, he or she will be given the same length of time to stay as that parent, which may be an indefinite period (settlement) (see chapter 13 for examples of these passport stamps). The child is free to remain for the period given and is immediately entitled to state education, National Health Service medical treatment and some non-contributory benefits. The settled parent can claim child benefit as soon as the child or one of the parents has been in the UK for six months, or immediately if a parent is working.

When a child has been admitted only for a year, because the parent who he or she was accompanying or joining was only allowed to remain for a year, he or she will not be eligible for most means-tested benefits (▶see chapter 10 for further details).

Applying for settlement after one year

If the child has been granted admission only for a limited period, it is important that an application is made to the Home Office before that period finishes, on the official application form SET(F), for permission to stay permanently. If a parent is applying for settlement at the same time, on form SET(M), the child should be added to this form. The Home Office will need the passports of the parents and the child, a photo of the child, the child's birth certificate and evidence that the family is able to support and accommodate itself without recourse to public funds, before settlement is granted. It is extremely rare for a child to be refused at this stage, unless the parent he or she accompanied or came to join has been refused.

The rules state that the child applying for settlement must be under 18, or was given previous leave to enter or remain on the basis of being a dependent child. Thus a child aged 17 on arrival in the UK who has had another birthday would still qualify for settlement.

If the application overseas is refused

The British embassy or high commission has to give a letter explaining why the application was refused, stating the child's right to appeal against the refusal, and sending forms to fill in to appeal. The appeal forms have to be returned to the British post which refused within three months of the date of refusal. It does not matter if a child becomes 18 while the appeal is pending; the important date is the date of application. If the appeal is successful two years later, when a child is 19 or 20, he or she will be granted entry clearance. However, if the appeal fails, but a child later produces fresh evidence, for example a DNA test result, and applies again, the application is considered to be made on the date of the second application.

Children joining lone parents in the UK

WHAT THE RULES SAY

If the other parent is dead, there are no other specific requirements the child has to meet apart from proving the death. If the other parent is still alive but will not be coming to the UK, the immigration authorities must be satisfied that either:

- the parent settled in the UK or on the same occasion admitted for settlement has had the *sole responsibility* for the child's upbringing; or
- the parent or a relative other than a parent is settled or accepted for settlement in the UK and there are serious and compelling family or other considerations in the child's own country which make the child's *exclusion undesirable* – for example, where the other parent is physically or mentally incapable of looking after the child – and suitable arrangements have been made for the child's care.

WHAT THE RULES MEAN

A substantial amount of case law has grown up around these definitions. The first cannot ever be wholly true when a parent has been living in a different country from the child and the second is difficult to quantify. The immigration authorities consider each case in detail, to weigh up where responsibility for the child's upbringing lies or the difficulties of his or her circumstances abroad. It is therefore important that full details of the child's circumstances, and any evidence showing the continued support, direction and concern of the parent in the UK should be provided at the time of application.

The sole responsibility rule

The sole responsibility rule was first promulgated in 1969. The government's stated intention was to prevent the growth of all-male Pakistani families, where men who had come to work in the UK were sending for their sons, but not their wives and daughters, and it was felt that this was not in the best interests of the children. The result was that whole families then applied to come.

The communities which have suffered most from the sole responsibility rule are people from the Caribbean and West Africa. Many women migrated in search of work, leaving young children in the care of an older relative, commonly a grandmother, for what was intended to be a short period until they could make a home for them in the UK. Money was sent for their support and close contact was maintained, but it was often not possible to say that the sole responsibility was with the mother. British high commissions also asked the children many questions about contact with their fathers, who may well have remained abroad but separated from partners and children. It was clearly hard for children or grandparents to admit that they had been abandoned – but if the father's contact had been kept up, even sporadically or at a very low level, this could be a reason for refusing entry clearance for the child.

The Immigration Appeal Tribunal decided in the case of *Rudolph* (1984 Imm AR 84) what should be proved in order for a child to qualify under the 'sole responsibility' rule. In this case, the parents were separated and the child had been brought up in a convent in Sri Lanka while her mother was in the UK. It stated 'we need therefore to be satisfied not only that essential financial support was provided by Mrs Rudolph but also that she was regularly consulted about and expressed a continuing and positive concern for Dilkish. We agree... we should not necessarily rule out 'sole responsibility' if for a limited time during childhood it cannot be proved. It is a matter of looking at the childhood as a whole and all the actions of the mother.'

Another case, *Ramos* (1989 Imm AR 148), gave a further definition of 'sole responsibility'. A Filipino mother, abandoned by her husband, had left her daughter with her own mother when she came to the UK to work to support them; the child's aunt and uncle lived nearby. 'Obviously there are matters of day-to-day decision in the upbringing of a child which are bound to be decided on the spot by whoever is looking after the child in the absence of the parents settled here, such as getting the child to school safely and on time, or putting the child to bed... and so forth. In the present case it is not in doubt that money was provided by the mother here to support the child, and indeed the grandmother, but that again is not *per se* conclusive of sole responsibility... The suggestion is of course not that the father has had any responsibility or that the mother has abandoned all responsibility, but that the true conclusion on the facts is that responsibility has been shared between the mother and the grandmother and possibly also the uncle and aunt.' The girl was not allowed to come to join her mother.

'Exclusion undesirable'

In general, proving that a child qualifies under any part of this rule can be very hard, and detailed representations have to be made to the relevant British high commission or the Home Office or in representing an appeal against refusal. It has been decided that the considerations making the child's exclusion undesirable are to do with the child's situation in the country of origin, and this must be exceptionally hard. For example, in one case where it was accepted that a father in Trinidad had sexually abused his daughter, but there was no evidence he had done anything other than beat his twin sons, the girl's appeal was allowed but her brothers' dismissed. In the case of *Rudolph*, the Tribunal stated, 'we are of the opinion that such [family and other] considerations must be applied to the country in which the appellant lives and not to those pertaining in the UK... The specific example of when the general requirements will be met [is] the inability of the parent in the foreign country to look after the child. It is strongly arguable that once we have found as a fact that Mr Rudolph is incapable of looking after Dilkish the appellant's case is made.' It has to be shown that the other parent is incapable of, as well as unwilling to, look after the child. The girl was allowed to join her mother.

However, the Divisional Court in *Iqbal Ali* (1994 Imm AR 295) held that a child's appeal should be reconsidered. He had applied to accompany his mother to join his father, but DNA testing showed that the man who had always believed he was his father was not, so the application was refused. However, Iqbal had always been accepted as a child of the family and had never been involved in any deception. The court accepted that these facts and the presence in the UK of both *de facto* parents amounted to serious family considerations making the child's exclusion undesirable.

The 'under-12 concession'

If children are under 12 at the time of application, they may satisfy this second criterion of the rule, that there are family or other considerations making their exclusion (from their mother) undesirable. Because of the very great difficulty of satisfying the sole responsibility rule, and because of the complaints and campaigning against it, the Home Office stated in 1975 that the full rigours of the rule would not be used against children who were under 11 when they applied to join a lone parent. They would 'fairly freely' be allowed to join a parent settled in the UK 'provided there is suitable accommodation and, if the parent is the father, there is a female relative resident in the household who is willing to look after the child and is capable of doing so'. This assurance was given in reply to a

Parliamentary question from Helene Hayman MP on 28 July 1975, and the terms of the concession were repeated on several subsequent occasions. In 1976 it was extended to children under 12 at the time of application. However the Home Office has refused to write it into the immigration rules and has made little attempt to publicise it. Officials at British high commissions overseas do not always carry it out unless reminded about it.

Joining a relative who is not a parent

Children may be able to join an older relative who is not a parent, if they are living in extremely difficult circumstances overseas. This is usually only possible if the child's parents are dead and if it can be shown that there are no other relatives in the country of the child's origin who could look after him or her instead. An adult sibling, for example, married and settled in the UK, might be the only relative to care for a child after their parents had died. Grandparents settled in the UK might wish to care for a grandchild abandoned by his or her parents. Any application for a child to join a relative other than a parent should be made in great detail, explaining the exceptional circumstances why the child needs to come to, or remain in, the UK and why no other arrangements could be made in the country of origin.

Children applying to join parents in the UK for temporary purposes

Children may be given permission to come to join their parents when the parents are not settled in the UK or British citizens. If they are allowed to come, they are given permission to stay for the same length of time as their parent(s). If the parent is prohibited from working (as, for example, persons of independent means are prohibited) the child will be as well. If the parent has a restriction on working, that is, may work only with the consent of the Department for Education and Employment, the child will be given no restrictions on working.

Children of workers and business people

They must apply for entry clearance abroad. The immigration rules state that the unmarried children under 18 of people admitted as work permit holders, for permit-free employment, as business people, writers, composers and artists and as self-employed people ▶see chapter 7 should be granted entry clearance to come to join them. They have to prove that they have not formed an independent family unit or led an independent life and that there will be adequate support and accommodation for them, in accommodation exclusively occupied by their parents, without recourse to public funds, and that none of the general grounds for refusal (▶see pages 222–3) apply to them. If only one parent is in the UK and the other is still alive, the more restrictive rules about children joining lone parents apply to them; see above for details.

Children who have come into the UK as visitors or students and whose parent(s) later come in to work may apply to the Home Office for permission to vary their leave to remain, on the official Home Office application form FLR(O), so that they can stay with their parents.

When the parents apply to extend their permission to remain, on the same FLR(O) form, they should also apply on behalf of the children. This application will normally be granted if the parents' is, but if the children are not formally mentioned in the application to the Home Office they may become overstayers while the parents' application is under consideration. When the parents apply for settlement, they must apply for the children as well, using form SET(O). It does not matter if the children have become 18 during the years they have been living here; they will still be granted settlement in line with their parent(s) if they have had leave to remain on this basis.

Children of students

Children of students may be allowed to come to join them. If they are visa nationals, they must obtain a visa from the British post overseas. If they are not, they do not need entry clearance and can apply for leave to enter at a sea- or airport. In most other respects, the rules are similar to those for the children of workers. Children of students also have to show that they will not remain in the UK after any period of leave granted to their parent(s). The accommodation for them, however, does not have to be exclusively occupied by the family; the Home Office has recognised that students are likely to live in shared or college accommodation. They will be admitted for the same length of time as the student. If this is for less than a year, they will be prohibited from working. They are entitled to state education and to NHS medical treatment.

In the past, it has been more difficult for female than for male students to have their children with them. Until 1 October 1994 husbands of students had no claim under the rules to join them while they studied and consequently they had to fulfil the more restrictive requirements of the rules for children joining lone parents; see above for details.

Children of working holidaymakers

Working holidaymakers are young Commonwealth-country citizens coming to the UK for an extended holiday but intending to work to help pay for their holiday ▶see pages 142–3 for more information. Before 1 October 1994, there were no specific rules for their children, but in practice they were normally admitted in line with their parent(s). From 1 October 1994, they need to have entry clearance, and only children who are under five, and who will still be under five when their parent(s)' two years as working holidaymakers are over, are permitted to come. Thus people with children of three or over do not qualify as working holidaymakers.

Children of refugees and people with exceptional leave

The immigration rules state nothing about the families of refugees but it is Home Office practice to grant them leave to enter or remain in line with the refugee. If children under 18 of a person granted refugee status travelled to the UK together with the parent when he or she sought asylum, they will be granted permission to stay for the same period as the refugee. If they apply to join the refugee later, they have the right to do so. If they require visas, these should be granted simply on establishing the relationship; there is no visa fee. Refugees do not need to prove that they can support and accommodate their children.

People granted exceptional leave to remain have no right to be joined by any family members. The Home Office has stated that family reunion will not normally be allowed until the person with exceptional leave has had that leave for four years, and the other criteria of the immigration rules, particularly on support and accommodation, are met. Children may make applications for entry clearance to join someone with exceptional leave earlier than this, but the Home Office will only grant the application if it can be shown that there are 'compelling compassionate circumstances'. Children of asylum-seekers, that is, people whose asylum applications have not yet been decided, have no right to come to the UK to join them.
▶See chapter 5 for more information.

Applying in the UK

If a child has already come to the UK for some other purpose, for example as a visitor, it is possible for an application to be made on his or her behalf to the Home Office, on the appropriate Home Office application form, for permission to remain permanently or in line with the parent(s)' stay unless the parents are working holidaymakers, when entry clearance is compulsory (▶see chapter 11 on making applications to the Home Office). The same requirements of the rules, apart from the need for entry clearance, have to be satisfied by convincing the Home Office, rather than officials at the British post abroad, that the child qualifies. Because it is possible for such applications to be made in the UK, entry clearance officers are often loath to grant entry clearance to children to visit their parent or parents in the UK. It can be very hard to satisfy them that the child intends to leave the UK at the end of the visit.

When children who are in the UK apply to the Home Office to settle or to remain temporarily with their parents it is important that the application should explain why the decision for them to settle was made. Any changes in their circumstances – for example, the death or incapacity of the relative who had been caring for them, the parent in the UK finding out from the child about the shortcomings of care abroad, the parent obtaining adequate accommodation in the UK – should be explained to the Home Office, with evidence if possible, to show why a decision was made during the child's visit that he or she should settle. It is also important that both parents intend to settle in the UK. If, for example, one parent has brought the child in and intends to leave him or her with the other parent and return abroad, the child may not qualify to stay unless the parent in the UK can show that the rules for children joining lone parents are satisfied.

Children over 18

There is no specific provision for children over 18 to join their parents in the UK. They have to meet the requirements of the immigration rules for 'other dependent relatives', see below and chapter 4 for more details.

There is a particular controversy about children, mainly from Pakistan and Bangladesh, who applied to come to join their parents before they were 18 but who were refused as the authorities were not then satisfied that they were related to their parents as they claimed to be. They were later able to use the DNA fingerprinting technique (▶see box on page 48) accepted by the immigration authorities since 1989 as conclusive proof of those disputed relationships but do not now fit into the immigration rules as children as they are over 18.

The only provision in the rules for such people is that for 'other relatives'. The rules state that they have to show they are financially dependent on the relatives in the UK, that they are living on their own with no other close relatives to whom they could turn for support and that they can be supported and accommodated in the UK without recourse to public funds in accommodation which the sponsor owns or occupies exclusively. They also have to show that they are living alone in the most exceptional compassionate circumstances.

The Home Office has stated that it will consider these people's cases individually to see if there are any exceptional compassionate circumstances involved. These have to be over and above the basic injustice of wrongly separating a family for many years. The young people also have to show that they have remained 'necessarily' dependent on their parents rather than dependent 'by choice' and that they are unmarried. It seems that there is no chance of people over 23 being allowed to come. The refusal rate is very high. By July 1991, the last time the Home Office released figures, 570 young people's cases had been decided; only 116 had been allowed to come and 454 refused.

Before 1 October 1994, the immigration rules provided that unmarried daughters between the ages of 18 and 21 might be given 'special consideration' in coming to the UK to join their parents for settlement. They had to show they were financially dependent on their parents, they formed part of the family unit overseas, they would be left entirely on their own in the country in which they were living, without any other close relatives to turn to for help and they could be supported and accommodated in the UK without recourse to public funds.

When a family is applying to join a parent in the UK and the eldest daughter is over 18, it may be possible for her to accompany the rest of the family provided the application was made before 1 October 1994. However it is likely that entry clearance officers will ask more questions about her than other members of the family and more checks will be made to be sure that she has needed to remain financially dependent, rather than has done so for immigration purposes.

Another common situation where children over 18 apply to settle with their parents is if the parents are granted settlement after the child has become an adult. If a family has come to the UK together as a family, for example if either parent was given a work permit, its members will all have been granted initial permission to stay for the same period. If a child becomes 18 during the four-year period, the rules allow for that child to be granted settlement in line with the rest of the family. When a child has been in the UK in his or her own right, for example as a student, and the rest of the family has come later, it may be more difficult to show that the child has remained part of this family unit and has not become independent and therefore should be allowed to settle, but it may still be worth making the application.

Special quota voucher scheme

An exception to the rules is usually made for children aged up to 25 of special quota voucher applicants, if they are not themselves British nationals and therefore will not qualify for vouchers in their own right. ▶See chapter 17 for an explanation of the special quota voucher scheme, which permits some British nationals who are not British citizens and who have a connection with East Africa to come to the UK. Because of the long waiting period for people applying in India, which has reached eight years in the past, and which meant that many children became adults while they and their parents were waiting in the queue, children up to the age of 25 have been considered as dependants.

Such people have to show that they can be supported and accommodated in the UK by the special voucher holder and have remained financially dependent on their parents, have not been working and are not married. These requirements have led to detailed inquiries being made, particularly into young women in their early twenties, as to whether they are married and therefore would not qualify as dependants. The British authorities appear to be particularly worried about allowing in young women who may get married soon after their arrival and then try to bring in their husbands to join them in the UK. If a woman gets married shortly after coming to the UK for settlement, it is likely that her husband's entry clearance interview will concentrate on his intentions in getting married. He will stand a high chance of refusal under the primary purpose rule.

Adopted children

Children who have already been adopted

WHAT THE RULES SAY

The immigration rules do not provide for adopted children to be treated in the same way as other children, even though British law provides for this in nearly all other circumstances. The rules state that adopted children will only be allowed to come to join their adoptive parents if in addition to the other requirements of the rules it can be shown:

- that an adoption 'in accordance with a decision taken by the competent administrative authority or court of his country of origin or the country in which he is resident' has taken place
- that the adoption took place either when both adoptive parents were living together in a third country or when either or both were settled in the UK and the child has 'the same rights and obligations as any other child of the marriage'
- that the adoption took place because of the inability of the birth parents or current carers to care for the child and there has been a genuine transfer of parental responsibility
- that the child has lost or broken ties with the family of origin and the adoption was not one of convenience arranged to facilitate the child's admission or remaining in the UK.

The Home Office has a detailed standard letter, RON 117, explaining the practicalities involved in a couple wanting to bring an adopted child, or a child they want to adopt, into the UK. These include providing detailed medical and social reports about both the child and the adoptive parents. The letter lists other documents not mentioned in the rules but required in practice.

WHAT THE RULES MEAN

Legal adoptions

Adoption laws are very different in different countries. An adoption that takes place overseas is only recognised in the UK as a valid adoption under the Adoption (Designation of Overseas Adoptions) Order if it takes place in one of a specified list of countries whose laws are considered to have similar safeguards for the child's welfare as British laws.

These countries are: Anguilla, Australia, Austria, Bahamas, Barbados, Belgium, Belize, Bermuda, Botswana, British Virgin Islands, Canada, Cayman Islands, China, Cyprus, Denmark, Dominica, Fiji, Finland, France, Germany, Ghana, Gibraltar, Greece, Guyana, Hong Kong, Iceland, Ireland, Israel, Italy, Jamaica, Kenya, Lesotho, Luxembourg, Malawi, Malaysia,

Malta, Mauritius, Montserrat, Namibia, the Netherlands, New Zealand, Nigeria, Norway, Pitcairn Island, Portugal, St Kitts and Nevis, St Vincent, Seychelles, Singapore, South Africa, Spain, Sri Lanka, Surinam, Swaziland, Sweden, Switzerland, Tanzania, Tonga, Trinidad and Tobago, Turkey, Uganda, United States of America, Yugoslavia (before the civil war and formation of new countries), Zambia and Zimbabwe.

If an adoption takes place in one of these countries, the child may apply for entry clearance to come to the UK to join his or her adoptive parents. If the other requirements of the immigration rules are met (see above), the child is recognised as an adopted child and will be granted entry clearance for settlement. The parents do not need to adopt again under British law.

If an adoption took place in a country not on this list, it can still be recognised for immigration purposes, provided it was valid under the law of the country in which it took place. This depends both on the procedures carried out and whether the adopter was domiciled (see glossary for definition) in the country where the adoption took place.

The wording of the rules about adoptions being in accordance with administrative authorities or courts and about the child having 'the same rights and obligations as any other child of the marriage', which were new in HC 395, appear to be aimed against adoptions of Muslim children. A series of court cases about a Pakistani child called Tohur Ali (culminating in the Court of Appeal, reported in 1988 Imm AR 237) had established that a *de facto* adoption could qualify a child for admission. There is no official adoption procedure under Islamic law and although it is comparatively common for a child to be brought up by another close relative, such as an uncle, there will be no formal legal process and the child may not be considered a full child of the marriage for inheritance purposes. Thus the change in the rules was intended to negate court decisions and to enable the Home Office to continue to exclude a small number of children from the UK. In countries where adoption is not recognised as a legal change of status, but where informal adoptions take place, often within the family, the facts of each case will be considered in deciding if the adoption could be recognised.

Thus when a child applies for entry clearance to join adoptive parents, the first consideration is whether the adoption can be recognised as valid. Even when it is, this does not qualify a child for admission unless the reasons for the adoption and the circumstances of the child's birth family are those stated in the immigration rules. When the child has been adopted by relatives, the alternative provisions in the rules for children joining relatives 'other than a parent' when their 'exclusion is undesirable' (▶see above) may be easier to satisfy.

Reasons for adoption

The rules state that there must be a 'genuine transfer' of parental responsibility for the adopted child, and that the adoption must not have taken place to 'facilitate' the child's entry to or remaining in the UK. When an adoption takes place mainly because a couple in the UK are unable to have children, this in itself is not a reason which will permit the child to enter. If the birth parents abroad are still physically able to care for the child, or are still caring for their other children, the child will not qualify under the immigration rules. It is quite common for a childless couple to wish to adopt a relative's child, for example a nephew or niece, and for this to be agreed within the family while other siblings of the adopted child remain abroad, but it is very hard to bring a child to the UK in these circumstances. The debate in the UK about inter-familial adoption may also make it less likely that an adoption order will be granted in a UK court.

The adopted child needs to apply for entry clearance to come to join the adoptive parents; if at that stage the child is living with its birth parents, they will be involved in the application and therefore will show that they are still concerned about the child and may still be caring for it. It will then be necessary to show why these arrangements cannot continue and why coming to the UK is the only solution for the child's care. The British post requires a social report about the child's current circumstances abroad and the reasons for the adoption, as well as the child's and adoptive parents' passports, the adoption order, and a photo of the child.

Poverty of the family abroad is not normally accepted as an adequate reason for adoption, as entry clearance officers may allege that family in the UK can send financial support which would enable the child to continue to stay with its birth family. Entry clearance officers may also claim that arrangements have been made within a family to send a child to the UK for educational or other purposes, rather than for a genuine adoption and may refuse entry clearance.

If it is impossible for the birth parents to care for the child, for example if the parent(s) are physically or mentally ill, medical evidence should be obtained to show that they cannot take responsibility for the child. If a child has been adopted from an orphanage or other agency caring for children, the entry clearance officers will require evidence that the child was genuinely available for adoption.

Adopted children also have to prove that there is adequate support and accommodation for them in the UK, without recourse to public funds. ▶See chapter 11 for details of these requirements and how to meet them.

Children adopted in countries where the adoption is not recognised in the UK may apply for entry clearance for adoption, outside the immigration rules. Because it is outside the rules, if the application is refused, there is no chance of winning any appeal. If the application is successful, they will probably be admitted for a year initially and must apply to the Home Office, on the appropriate application form, for an extension of this time. During the year, the parents can begin the process of adoption under

British law. They should keep the Home Office informed of its progress; if it is very slow, the Home Office may grant a further extension of stay. When the adoption is granted, this gives the child the right to settle in the UK and British citizenship if either adoptive parent is a British citizen.

Nationality of adopted children

At present, an adoption which takes place outside the UK does not affect the nationality of the adopted child. The proposed Adoption Bill would provide that a recognised overseas adoption by a British citizen would make the adopted child a British citizen too.

An adoption which takes place in the UK, when either adoptive parent is a British citizen, automatically gives the child British citizenship. An adoption which takes place in the UK when neither parent is a British citizen, but either parent is settled in the UK automatically gives the child settlement. Children adopted before 1 January 1983 only became British citizens if the adoptive father was British. See chapter 18 for further information about applying to register children to become British citizens.

Children coming to the UK for adoption

No immigration rule deals with this situation, which includes a *de facto* adoption which took place before the parents came to the UK. Therefore, if no adoption has taken place abroad, an application must be made outside the immigration rules to bring a child to the UK for adoption, to join its adoptive parents. Applications are dealt with exceptionally outside the rules.

The Home Office has worked out a long and complicated process which must be gone through in order that detailed checks can be made on the child's and the prospective adoptive parents' circumstances to see whether it is likely that the proposed adoption would be approved by a British court. The Home Office sends a detailed standard letter, RON 117, to inquirers, which gives full information about the process. This includes obtaining detailed medical and social reports on the child and on the prospective adoptive parents from official sources such as the Department of Health in the UK, and the social services department where the child is. This should give details of the child's parentage, the circumstances of the birth parents and the current carers, the degree of contact with the birth parents, the reasons for adoption, the date and reason for the child's entry to an institution or going to foster carers and how this was arranged.

Written consent to adoption from the child's birth parents, or those legally responsible for the child, done 'freely' after the child is at least six weeks old, is required. This needs to be done before starting the entry clearance application. Both parents must have visited the child before applying for entry clearance. It is likely that the application will be referred to the Home Office, to check that the immigration requirements are met. The Home

Office states this should 'normally' take not more than three weeks, but it does. The Home Office, if satisfied, refers the case to the Department of Health to check that health requirements are met. Some local social services departments refuse to cooperate because of their own policies discouraging inter-country adoption. In practice therefore it is very difficult to bring a child to the UK for adoption.

In May 1991 the Department of Health announced that new procedures would be set up to facilitate bringing adoptive children to the UK. A lengthy review of adoption procedures has been taking place but it was expedited in view of public concern about difficulties in adopting children from Romanian orphanages. In fact the vast majority of applications to bring children from Romania for adoption were successful; by December 1991, 330 children had been allowed to come and 12 refused. In March 1992, an agreement between the Romanian and British governments provided for closer checks on children leaving Romania; ten were allowed to leave for the UK in the first year of the agreement. The Department of Health's White Paper of November 1993, *Adoption: the future*, was strongly angled towards creating greater safeguards for the adoption of unrelated children from overseas, rather than facilitating inter-family adoption, and the mutual recognition of formal adoption procedures. The aims were stated to be greater clarity and reliability of the process, a more streamlined relationship between adoption and immigration processes and new protections against abuses such as ignoring the overseas parents' wishes or any payment made for adoption. These proposals were followed through in the March 1996 Department of Health and Welsh Office discussion document and draft new Adoption Bill, *Adoption: a service for children*, but this was dropped from the government's legislative programme in November.

When the application is successful

If entry clearance is granted for the child to come to the UK for adoption the child must travel within six months. He or she will be admitted initially for a year. During that time it should be possible to begin the legal process of adoption in the UK and to apply to the Home Office, on the appropriate application form, before the end of the year, to extend the child's permitted stay while the process goes on. If a child is legally adopted in the UK, the adoption automatically gives him or her the right to remain indefinitely; if either of the adopters is a British citizen, the child automatically gains British citizenship. A child who has been *de facto* adopted abroad, and whose relationship is recognised, will be admitted for an indefinite period on arrival. The child is not a British citizen. The parents could apply to register him or her to become British ▶see chapter 18, or, if they go through another adoption in the British courts, and one of the adoptive parents is British, that would make the child a British citizen.

Because of the delays and complications of this procedure, British or settled parents have sometimes circumvented it by travelling abroad and bringing babies or young children back with them, without entry clearance. The Home Office and adoption agencies discourage this practice, because it is effectively impossible to refuse entry to young children and to return them abroad on their own and because the detailed checks necessary to ensure the suitability of the adoption have not been done. The draft Adoption Bill proposes a new criminal offence for anyone other than a child's parent bringing a child in for adoption without prior authorisation from the Department of Health or an adoption agency. It also proposes that people who bring in a child without entry clearance should be liable for costs if the local authority has to take the child into care. However, in some inter-family adoptions (see above), adoptive parents may see this as the only way of being able to bring in a child. Visa national children cannot normally be brought in in this way, as most airlines will not carry them without visas.

If children do arrive without prior permission, they may be admitted for six months on arrival. The adoptive parents are then expected to begin the process of a British adoption and to apply to the Home Office, before the child's leave to enter has expired, for permission for the child to remain while the adoption takes place.

The government states it intends to ratify the 1993 Hague Convention on intercountry adoption and that in future adoptions taking place in other countries which have ratified this Convention will be recognised in UK law as granting British nationality to the child. There will be a new Adoption (Designation of Overseas Adoptions) Order, which will list only British dependent territories and countries with which the UK has a bilateral agreement; the intention being to restrict recognition of overseas adoptions to those in countries which have ratified the Hague Convention. These proposals had not come into force at the time of writing.

Adoption proceedings

It is possible for prospective adoptive parents to apply to adopt children admitted for another purpose, for example as visitors or students, and to apply to the Home Office for an extension of their stay while the adoption takes place. When the adoption case is heard in court, the court has to consider, among other things, whether the main purpose of the adoption was to keep a child in the UK, if he or she would not qualify to remain in any other way, rather than the lack of other arrangements for his or her care. If so, the application for adoption can be refused.

The internal instructions to immigration officials (DP4/96) also refer to adoption. They confirm the Home Office's views about adoptions for immigration purposes and its intention to combat them. The instructions state:

'The Family Court will generally attach much more weight to the child's welfare than to irregularities surrounding the immigration status of the child or a parent. Where however it is clear that the court proceedings are designed purely to enable the child or the parent to evade immigration control consideration may be given to instructing the Treasury Solicitor with a view to intervention in the proceedings. *There must be evidence, not just a suspicion, that there has been a serious attempt to circumvent the immigration control* and decisions to intervene must be taken at not less than SEO [Senior Executive Officer] level. Where intervention has been agreed the papers should be copied to the Treasury Solicitor's office as soon as possible. Their normal practice is then to apply for the Secretary of State to be joined as a respondent, and to file an affidavit setting out the child's and/or parents' immigration history and the Secretary of State's objections.'

Thus, when it is proposed to adopt a child subject to immigration control, the court will inform the Home Office Immigration Directorate and it will then decide whether to attempt to intervene in the adoption proceedings. It is therefore important that social services departments and solicitors dealing with adoption are aware of such possibilities. The internal instructions state specifically that 'where an order has been made under the Children Act this cannot in itself deprive the Secretary of State of the power conferred by the Immigration Act 1971 to remove or deport any party to the proceedings...' The immigration rules are therefore more powerful than the Children Act principles. This was shown in a case which received much publicity in April-May 1996 of a 10-year-old South African boy, Sifiso Mahlangu, who was not able to remain with his British adoptive mother, although he had lived with her here since 1992. The child did not want to return, but his birth parents did not want to give him up permanently, as they had thought he was coming to the UK mainly for education.

Children in the UK without their parents

Fostering of children/children in care

Families from abroad may want to make arrangements for their children's care in the UK, even if they themselves are unable to stay. A comparatively common situation is for a couple to come to the UK to study and decide they are unable adequately to concentrate on their studies while caring for the children. They therefore make private fostering arrangements. The children of overseas students are able to be with them in the UK under the immigration rules so there is often no reason to inform the Home Office about these arrangements while the whole family is still in the UK.

There are no provisions in the immigration rules for the children to stay if the parents leave and want the child to remain with the foster parents, so as not to disrupt their education, for example. If an application is made to the Home Office for the child to remain exceptionally, it should be done with great care and the plans for the child to rejoin his or her parents abroad should be explained. In some cases, the foster parents are unaware of any immigration implications and the children may inadvertently become overstayers. Specialist independent advice should be sought for any attempt to regularise the child's position.

If there are problems with the fostering, or if for any other reason the care for a child from abroad is inadequate or the child is in danger, the local social services department has the same statutory responsibility to care for the welfare of the children as for others in their jurisdiction. It is therefore possible for a child who is not settled in the UK to be taken into the care of the local authority. The local authority is then *in loco parentis* and will have to make arrangements for the child. This may be attempting to trace the parents in order to return the child to them abroad, or it may be applying to the Home Office for permission for the child to remain here exceptionally when there seems to be no prospect of the family being reunited abroad, or of the parents returning.

There is no authoritative statement about the immigration consequences of a child being taken into the care of the local authority. For a child who is not a British citizen, being taken into care does not in itself alter the child's immigration status. However, the local authority then has responsibility for the child and it is important that it should receive correct legal advice before making any approach to the Home Office. If it appears clear that there will not be further contact with the family and that the child's long-term future will be in the UK, and the authority applies to the Home Office for settlement on behalf of the child, with full details of the circumstances, it is likely that the application will be granted. However, when children have merely been 'accommodated' by the local authority, a more temporary arrangement, this is less likely to affect a Home Office decision. It is extremely important that any such application should be made to the Home Office before the child is 18, on form SET(O). Once children have become 18 and the local authority no longer has a legal responsibility towards them it is much more difficult to secure leave to remain.

Other legal procedures

The internal instruction on deportation refers to other procedures which may be taken by relatives or friends to attempt to safeguard children's welfare, such as custodianship, wardship, contact orders and residence orders. It confirms that while adoption in the UK gives a child definite immigration and nationality rights, the others do not affect a child's immigration status but merely mean that the leave of a court must be obtained before a child can be removed from the UK. However, 'the Family Court will generally attach much more weight to the child's welfare than to irregularities surrounding the immigration status of the child or a parent', so the implication is that Home Office officials should proceed with care when other court orders have been obtained.

The enforced departure of children is still possible, but the internal instructions state that it should only be carried out against children under 16 on their own here 'when the child's voluntary departure cannot be arranged'. Thus the Home Office may put pressure on those caring for children to return them and start deportation action if they do not, provided it is satisfied about the care arrangements in the country of destination. Only if there is 'evidence, not just a suspicion' that the care arrangements are not adequate should enforcement action be stopped. The case of *Sujon Miah* (Liverpool Crown Court, U940948, December 1994) confirmed that these considerations must also apply when it is a question of refusal of entry and removal. In order to ensure that full information about the situation to which the child would be returned is available, the local social services department could be asked to assess it, using similar criteria to those required under the Children Act 1989 in deciding whether to permit a child for whom it has responsibility to emigrate.

Children at school

The only way in which children are likely to be allowed to remain in the UK in their own right (that is, without being British citizens or without their parents living in the UK with them) is as students. This means that the child must be going to a private, fee-paying school, must have the money to pay the school fees and to live here and, if it is not a boarding-school, there must be adequate arrangements for looking after the child. The Home Office must also be satisfied that the intention is for the child to leave at the end of the studies. The immigration rules do not permit visa nationals to change their status to become students, so if the child is a visa national the application would be outside the rules and there would be no right of appeal if it were refused.

There is no provision in the rules for a child to stay in the UK in order to attend, or to continue to attend, a state school. This can create problems when the child has been in the UK with the family for a short-term purpose, for example if the parents are students, or diplomats or other workers posted to the UK for a term of duty, who then have to take up another post when the child is at a critical stage of education. An application to the Home Office may be made, exceptionally, for permission to continue in these studies and because of the delays in response and the possibility of appealing against any refusal the child may be able to complete the relevant academic year while the application is pending. ▶See chapter 11 for more information on making applications to the Home Office.

Children over 16 are not required by law to attend school but they may be able to remain as students by going to full-time studies (at least 15 hours' daytime classes per week) at a college of further or higher education, or a private college. See chapter 9 for information on grants and fees for further education.

Children born in the UK

Children born in the UK in or after 1983: immigration status

Since 1 January 1983, not all children born in the UK have been born British citizens (▶see chapter 17). Only a child with a British or a settled parent is automatically born British in the UK. When the parents are not married, only the mother's status counts. Other children born in the UK have no claim to British nationality by birth and are subject to British immigration control. There is a special section in the immigration rules to cover children born in the UK.

Technically, a child born in the UK and not born British does not have, or need, any leave to remain in the UK. These children are not illegal entrants or overstayers just because of their parents' status. They may therefore remain in the UK indefinitely, so long as they do not leave the country. A child who has never been granted such leave cannot be deported, unless his or her parents are deported, in which case the child can in law be deported as part of the family unit. If the parents leave voluntarily, there is nothing illegal in leaving the child in the care of other relatives or foster parents living in the UK. However, if the children leave the UK and their parents have also left, they will not be given permission to return unless they fit in to another category of the immigration rules. If children born in the UK live here until they are 10 years old, they gain the right to register as British citizens (▶see chapter 18).

If parents wish to obtain leave to remain for their non-British children born in the UK, the Home Office will grant this if the parent has leave to enter or remain. The child will be given the same length of time as the parents. If the parents have a different length of stay, the child will be given the longer. If the parents are living separately, the child will be given the length of time that the parent with day-to-day care for him or her has. If one parent is settled, the child can be granted settlement. This would be relevant, for example, for a child whose parents were not married, whose mother was an overseas student so the child would not be born British but whose father was a British citizen. If the parents applied to the Home Office for settlement for the child, this would be granted. The Home Office will only require evidence that the child is the child of the parent(s) and of the parents' length of stay; it does not have to be shown that the child can be supported and accommodated. If a child is in the care of the local authority, he or she should be given indefinite leave to remain, or admitted for settlement.

If children travel overseas at a time when they have not yet been granted leave to remain in the UK, they will need to convince immigration officers on their return that there is a reason for admitting them to the UK under the immigration rules. If they are returning with their parents, or while their parents are still in the UK, they will normally be given the same immigration leave as the parents are given, or as the parents have.

Children who have been out of the UK for more than two years will not qualify to enter under this part of the rules but will need to meet the more restrictive criteria of the general rules on children in order to return.

If children have already been granted leave to remain, they are free to travel and are likely to be readmitted for the same length of time. They do not have to prove that there is support and accommodation available to them in the UK. Children who are not visa nationals do not need entry clearance. Children who are visa nationals do not need visas if they are returning within a period of leave to remain of more than six months but do require visas in all other circumstances. Once leave to enter or remain has been granted, it is important to apply to extend it in time, as children can become overstayers if this is not done.

Children born in the UK before 1 January 1983

Except for the children of diplomats, any person born in the UK before 1983 is automatically a British citizen by birth. This gives the child full rights to remain in the UK and to return at any time as an adult, even if he or she was taken abroad as a baby. There have been instances of people, mainly in West Africa, who have had difficulty convincing the British high commissions that they are the babies who were born in the UK. Others travelling on British passports have had difficulty in satisfying immigration officers that they are in fact British citizens. People have also been arrested in the UK and alleged to be illegal entrants. Although they have claimed that they were born in Britain, the immigration authorities have not believed them. In general however, people born in the UK before 1983 are able to return to the UK to live on production of their full birth certificate (the one which has details of both parents so that it can be confirmed that the father was not a diplomat). If the birth certificate is a recent copy obtained from the Office of National Statistics at St Catherine's House further evidence may be requested to connect the applying adult with the child who was born in the UK and left at a very young age.

Such evidence may be difficult to produce. If there are close family friends or relatives living in the UK who have remained in contact with the person throughout, they may be able to make statements to confirm their continuous knowledge of the person applying. If the person had been registered with a general practitioner or there are records of childhood immunisations or other medical treatment, this might be helpful. If he or she had lived here long enough to go to a childminder/nursery school/school and records can be found, these may also be of use.

Children whose parents are forced to leave the UK

The fact that a child is British by birth in the UK does not affect the parents' immigration status in any way. Thus parents who were students, for example, do not have any claim to stay on after their studies because of the birth of a child; overstayers do not gain any right to remain because their children can do so. The British-born children of such families cannot, of course, be deported, even if their parents and siblings are. But in practice the deportation of the rest of the family usually means that the British child is forced to leave as well.

However, the European Commission of Human Rights, in the case of *Fadele*, recognised that British children do in some circumstances have rights and expectations that they will be able to live in the UK and this may mean that their families should be allowed to remain with them. In that case, three British children were able to show that their travel to Nigeria and living there with their father, who had not been permitted to stay with them in the UK after their mother's death in a car crash, had caused them great hardship. The European Commission held that the father's removal from the UK was wrong and the Home Office had to pay for the family to return.

A European Court of Human Rights case, *Berrehab* (1988 11 EHRR 322), in addition provides a precedent to seek the return of a deported parent of a British-born child. The decision confirmed the right of a child to continuing contact with both her parents following the breakdown of their marriage (▶see page 36 for further details and chapter 2 for information on parents visiting the UK to keep in contact with their children).

Thus when children have been left here without their parents, the Home Office has recognised that carrying out the letter of the immigration rules might bring it into conflict with the ECHR. Its instructions to officials therefore state that enforcement action against children under 16 should be rare and 'only be contemplated when the child's voluntary departure cannot be arranged'. The instructions stress the importance of ensuring that arrangements have been made for the child's care abroad and that 'if there is any evidence, not just a suspicion, that the care arrangements are seriously below the standard normally provided in the country concerned or that they are so inadequate that the child would face a serious risk of harm if returned, consideration should be given to abandoning enforcement action'. It is therefore worth reminding the Home Office of these instructions when applying for leave to remain outside the rules for children. The local social services department might give its views about the standard of care expected in the country to which the child would be sent, and whether this would meet the standards required if approval had to be given for the child's emigration, under the provisions of the Children Act 1989.

More recent ECHR cases, however, have narrowed the scope of these decisions. The case of *Poku* (26985/95) decided that where parents have had immigration problems, or married after deportation decisions have been made, the deportation of a parent is not a violation of the right to respect for family life, because the adults of the family made a decision to marry knowing there could be immigration problems.

SECTION 1: FAMILY

4 Relatives other than children and spouses

Apart from children and spouses there are many other relatives who may need or want to come to stay permanently with family members settled in the UK. The immigration rules about this are very restrictive and only make provision for a limited number of relationships. There are similar rules for parents and grandparents over 65, and then more restrictive ones for adult sons and daughters, aunts, uncles, sisters and brothers and younger parents and grandparents. More distant relatives are not mentioned at all and their entry is therefore always at the discretion of the Home Office.

REMEMBER:
- people abroad wanting to settle in the UK must get entry clearance before they travel
- people applying in the UK must use the correct Home Office application form to make a valid application
- BUT some family members may be British citizens
- AND some people may not have to fit into the immigration rules; see below

People who may not have to fit into the rules

People who want to come to the UK because they have relatives settled in the country may qualify under some other parts of the immigration rules. They might, for example, qualify as persons of independent means, or only intend to visit their relatives.

a) **EEA nationals:** Community legislation gives the right to 'relatives in the ascending line' to join EEA nationals who have travelled to another EEA country and are engaged in economic activity there, or are able to support themselves. Thus it does not apply to most British citizens, as they have not travelled between countries to work, but may apply to Irish citizens, if they have travelled between the Republic of Ireland and the UK. Relatives in the ascending line means parents, grandparents and great-grandparents, who may be the relatives of a non-EEA spouse of an EEA citizen. The relatives themselves do not have to be EEA citizens. Thus, for example, the Colombian parents of a Colombian woman married to a German man working in the UK would qualify under this provision.

Support and accommodation has to be available but the other requirements of the British immigration rules do not apply. EEA nationals may also qualify in their own right under any other part of Community law, irrespective of the presence of their relatives in the UK.

b) **Commonwealth citizens with the right of abode:** Commonwealth citizens with British-born parents (when the parent is the father, he must be married to the mother), and Commonwealth citizen women married before 1 January 1983 to a man with the right of abode, have the right of abode (▶see glossary) in the UK. Commonwealth citizens with a grandparent born in the UK may qualify to come because of that relationship. ▶See chapter 7 for more details.

c) **People who have a guaranteed annual income of at least £25,000**, without working, who are over 60 years old and with close relatives living in the UK, may qualify as persons of independent means. ▶See chapter 7 for more details.

d) **Visitors:** people may not want to stay permanently but may want to be able to visit relatives frequently. It may therefore be better to apply as visitors and not to give the immigration authorities any reason to think that more than a visit is intended.

Parents and grandparents

WHAT THE RULES SAY

Parents or grandparents who are coming to the UK in order to live with their adult children or grandchildren have to satisfy the entry clearance officer that:

- they are widows or widowers aged 65 or over, or
- they are travelling together as a couple and at least one of them is 65 or over, or
- if they have married again, they are 65 or over and they cannot look to the spouse or children of the second marriage for support
- if they are under 65, they must be living alone in the most exceptional compassionate circumstances
- the children or grandchildren in the UK are able to support and accommodate them, in accommodation exclusively occupied by them, without recourse to public funds
- they are wholly or mainly financially dependent on the children or grandchildren settled in the UK
- they have no other close relatives in their own country to whom they could turn for financial support
- they are not people to whom any of the general grounds for refusal apply ▶see pages 222–3.

WHAT THE RULES MEAN

Age requirement

This is interpreted strictly and it is important to show the age of the applicants, by a birth certificate if possible. There can be serious problems in countries where there was not a system of registration of births when the parents or grandparents were born. Elderly people may not know exactly when they were born and may date their age from local events, also unrecorded. When they obtained their passports, they may have given an approximate age for this purpose. The British authorities may take this as the only definite proof of age and it may be very difficult for the parents or grandparents to satisfy them at the time of any application for settlement that a different date of birth is more correct.

Since 1 October 1994, the rules no longer exempt widowed mothers and grandmothers from the age requirement. In the past, this exemption was applied only to widowed mothers, not mothers who were divorced or who had never been married. Like all fathers, they had to be 65 before their applications were considered under the rules relating to parents. Younger parents may still apply to join their children but will have to fit into the more restrictive rules about 'other dependent relatives'; see below for more details.

Previous financial support

This means that *before* coming to the UK the parents or grandparents must have been financially dependent on their children in the UK. If they are visiting the UK at the time of the application, and have been financially dependent during the visit but were not before, this requirement will not be satisfied. The Tribunal case of *Kartar Kaur* (11549) confirmed this; the Home Office must consider what would have been the situation had the person remained in her country of origin, and the fact of being dependent is necessary.

It is demeaning for elderly people to have to show that they cannot maintain themselves. It can also be difficult to prove, as many people do not keep records of all the money they have sent to their families abroad. If money has been sent through postal orders, people may have kept at least some of the counterfoils; if it has been sent through a bank account, the bank may have records. Registered letter slips, showing at least that something valuable was sent, can be useful. So are letters from the parents, mentioning money sent, from as far back as possible.

If money was taken in cash by visiting relatives or friends, it may be more difficult to do anything more than assert this fact. It may be helpful to have letters from the couriers, confirming when and how much money they took, or letters from the parents confirming they received the money. When parents or grandparents have other means of support, for example an occupational pension, it has to be shown that the money they receive from their children is more than the pension, so that they can show they are mainly, if not wholly, dependent on the children.

This requirement discriminates against people who have been thrifty, or people who live in a country where an adequate old-age pension is paid. Retired people in the United States, for example, are unlikely to be financially dependent on their children rather than on any pension or insurance. It also means that parents or grandparents who own property, for example their own home, may not be considered dependent, even though they intend to leave the home to their children and do not wish to keep it themselves. If they have already passed on property or capital to their children, before they die, and no longer own it, they may be considered to have become dependent by choice, not of necessity, and therefore not to qualify under the rules.

No other relatives to turn to

This requirement is also difficult to meet, if there is more than one adult child in the family and they do not all live in the UK. It does not take adequate account of cultural differences; in parts of the Indian sub-continent, for example, it is generally accepted that it is the sons' responsibility to care for their aged parents, not the daughters', who, when married, have a corresponding responsibility to their husband's parents. Thus when the sons are in the UK but the daughters are in India, it has to be argued that they cannot usually be expected to care for their parents and that the parents themselves, as well as the son-in-law's family, would not feel that it was right. If there is another son still in India immigration officials will expect that he should care for his parents, even if he lives a long way away and the care he would provide would not be acceptable to the parents. In all cases when there are other relatives living in the same country as the parents it is therefore important to show why they are not able to care for the parents and to explain the relevant cultural patterns.

It can also be argued that the children abroad do not have the resources to look after their parents adequately. This has sometimes been successful, for example in some Filipino cases. Although there may be several children in the Philippines, applications have succeeded by showing that their economic circumstances are such that they cannot manage to look after their parents, or even their own families, without the financial support they receive from the UK.

If other close relatives with whom the parents previously lived have died, their death certificates should be produced. If circumstances have changed, making other relatives no longer able to care for the parents, this should be explained.

Emotional dependence

Under previous rules, the concept of emotional closeness to a particular child has also been argued, with some degree of success. It is necessary to spell this out, to show why living with one particular child would be the best solution for the parents. The parents may have to show they attempted to live with other relatives, or other relatives may have to explain why they are unable or unwilling to look after them, before they will be allowed to come to the UK.

The cases of *Bastiampillai* (1983 Imm AR 1) and *Dadibhai* (October 1983, unreported) have confirmed that the other relatives must have both the ability and the willingness to provide all the support needed by the parent. This includes all the financial and emotional support necessary. It may be useful to quote these cases to entry clearance officers who may attempt to refuse merely because there are other relatives living in the same country. However, emotional dependence will not overcome the primary need for *financial* dependence to be shown, which is now specifically required by the rules.

Support and accommodation

The requirements for this are similar to those for spouses and children, and similar evidence should be provided; ▶see chapter 11 for more details. The main difference is that because there is no other legal liability in British law for an adult to maintain his or her parents or grandparents (unlike a spouse or children) it is more likely that entry clearance officers will request an undertaking to support them.

This means that as well as providing evidence of ability to support the parents, the sponsor may be required to sign a formal undertaking (▶see appendix) to do so, which also confirms his or her understanding that this undertaking may be made available to the DSS. The undertaking gives the DSS the power under the Social Security Contributions and Benefits Act 1992 to reclaim from the person who signed the undertaking any income support that the sponsored person may claim. Before 5 February 1996, it did not debar the sponsored person from claiming benefits, but meant that the sponsor could be treated as a liable relative and the DSS could attempt to reclaim income support from him or her. This was rarely done; JCWI knew of only one case of the DSS successfully taking a sponsor to court, in September 1990, although it had more frequently discouraged claims from sponsored parents.

From 5 February 1996, changes in the benefits regulations meant that people about whom undertakings have been signed are ineligible to receive income support, housing benefit and council tax benefit for five years, either from their arrival in the UK or from the date on which the undertaking was signed, whichever is the later. It is not clear how the Benefits Agency will check whether people are entitled to claim, or who they will check; this is an important area to monitor.

For more details on sponsorship and undertakings ▶see chapter 10.

How to apply

It is important to remember that if the parent or grandparent's application for settlement fails, this will have other consequences. It will be more difficult in the future for the person to make visits to the UK, because it will be more difficult to convince the immigration authorities that he or she intends to leave the UK at the end of the visit. Thus the long-term as well as the short-term plans of the person and the family should be considered before making an application which does not precisely fit into the rules.

Applying abroad

Parents or grandparents abroad need to apply for entry clearance at the British embassy or high commission nearest to where they live; they cannot get permission to enter to settle with their children at a port of entry. ▶See chapter 11 for details of the entry clearance application process and the documents and evidence required.

In the countries of the Indian subcontinent, people over 70 years old applying for settlement are considered in a priority queue, so they should not have to wait long for an interview. There are no special provisions made for the elderly in other countries. Parents or grandparents will need to provide evidence that they satisfy all the requirements of the rules and may also be asked detailed family questions.

Applying in the UK

If the parents or grandparents are already in the UK, for example as visitors, they may apply to the Home Office, on the official application form SET(F), for permission to stay with their children. Attached to these forms is a page headed 'Sponsorship declaration', but which is in fact an undertaking. It states also, 'completion of this declaration by the applicant's sponsor is not compulsory but an application will normally be refused if the sponsor refuses to do so. This form should only be completed if the sponsor is resident in the UK.' To make a valid application, people must send the Home Office the fully completed form, together with all the documents requested or explanations of why the documents are not available and when they will be.

When people have entered for a different purpose shortly before applying for settlement, there is the possible danger that they could be treated as illegal entrants, if it is thought that they came to the UK claiming to be visitors when in fact they intended to stay. It is rare for elderly people applying to stay with their children to be treated in this way. Parents and grandparents over 65 may be permitted to remain, provided there is support and accommodation available. However this possibility makes entry clearance officials overseas more reluctant to grant visit visas to elderly parents or grandparents who appear to be alone or in need of care overseas.

It is important to make the application to the Home Office before the person's leave to remain has expired; ▶see chapter 11 for information about making the application. As long as the application is validly made in time, the person is legally in the UK while it is under consideration and will have a formal right of appeal if the application is refused. Remember that the Home Office will look at the parent's situation in the country of origin, before coming for the visit. Although, for example, parents visiting children in the UK are likely to be financially supported in the UK during the visit, the relevant consideration for the Home Office is how they were supported in their country of origin before they travelled for the visit. It is therefore important to provide evidence of funds sent abroad as well as how the people are being supported at the time of the application.

The Home Office publishes statistics only for the Asian subcontinent on permissions granted. In 1995, 680 mothers and 320 fathers were allowed to remain and 110 mothers and 30 fathers granted entry clearance. The total for grandparents was 50. 650 'other dependent relatives', most of whom will have been parents, were refused.

Parents joining young children

There are no provisions in the immigration rules for adults to come to, or remain in, the UK because they have children born or living in the country who need their care. However it is possible for parents of British children who are still under 18 to apply to remain with them, outside the immigration rules but quoting the provisions of Article 8 of the European Convention on Human Rights on the right to respect for private and family life. It is important to explain the strong reasons why the children cannot go to live in the parent(s)' country.

Two cases considered by the European Commission and Court of Human Rights, *Berrehab* and *Fadele*, had confirmed that children's rights may be infringed if they are separated from their parents. More recently, the case of *Poku* (26985/95) found that there was no violation of Article 8 when a couple, both of whom had a child from a previous relationship as well as two children of their own, had married when the wife was already threatened with deportation. The Commission held that the couple 'must be taken to be aware of her precarious immigration status and the probable consequential effects' when they got married and the inevitable loss of contact between the children of the previous relationships and one of their parents was not a breach of the Convention.

From 1 October 1994 the immigration rules also make limited provision for a legally-separated or divorced parent to visit the UK to exercise rights of access to a young child here. This is discussed more fully on pages 35–36.

Relatives other than parents and grandparents

WHAT THE RULES SAY

The rules are even more strict about parents under 65 and 'other dependent relatives'. Adult sons, daughters, uncles, aunts, brothers and sisters may apply to join their relatives here. They have to show:
- that they are related as claimed to the person they wish to join
- that they are financially dependent on the person here
- that they have no other close relatives to turn to in the country in which they are living
- that they are living alone outside the UK in the most exceptional compassionate circumstances
- that they can be supported and accommodated in the UK in accommodation exclusively owned or occupied by the sponsor without recourse to public funds.
- that they are not people to whom any of the general grounds for refusal apply ►see pages 222–3.

WHAT THE RULES MEAN

The Home Office publishes statistics only for the countries of the Asian subcontinent on how many people are allowed to come or to stay in the UK as 'other dependent relatives', not parents and grandparents. In 1995, 90 were allowed to remain and 100 granted entry clearance. This rule also covers parents who are not yet 65, or parents who are separated or divorced or have never been married. Although there may well be compassionate circumstances involved there is no objective definition of 'exceptional compassionate circumstances' which will be decided by the immigration official dealing with the case.

The case of *Manshoora Begum* (1986 Imm AR 385) struck out a previous requirement of this rule, that the relative had to have a standard of living lower than the average in his or her own country. The Divisional Court agreed that this requirement was unreasonable, since the fact of receiving money from abroad at all, another requirement of the rule, could bring people above the average standard of living in several countries. Applications will still be decided on a case by case basis, because of the necessity of proving that there are exceptional compassionate circumstances. It is therefore important that the relatives applying give the fullest possible details of their circumstances to the immigration official dealing with the case, with any evidence they can produce, as discussed above.

The requirement of 'living alone' does not always need to be taken literally. A mother living with her young baby, for example, could be counted as 'living alone'. But when the 'exceptional compassionate circumstances' are caused by another family member with whom the person lives, the application must fail. This was decided in a Tribunal case, *Ibraheem* (11788), when a father applying to join his son in the UK lived with his other son, a violent drug addict. He therefore did not qualify as 'living alone' although his circumstances were compassionate.

More distant relatives

In exceptional circumstances it may be necessary for more distant relatives to apply to come to, or remain in, the UK with other family members. Applications for this can still be made, outside the immigration rules. There are no provisions in the rules for any other relatives to come to the UK: cousins, half-brothers, 'de facto' mothers of adopted children or stepmothers all apply outside the rules, at the discretion of the immigration authorities, and would be asking for special treatment because of their special circumstances. The Home Office has refused people applying to remain in the UK on the basis of a same-sex relationship, suggesting that they have applied under this rule, but to remain with a person who is not a close relative, and therefore they do not qualify. The Immigration Appeal Tribunal held in the past that this was wrong and that applications should be considered on grounds analogous to the marriage rules ▶see page 31 for further information.

The Home Office can grant applications outside the rules, so it may be worth trying if there are exceptional circumstances. It is important to show the immigration authorities what the strong exceptional compassionate reasons for the application are, for example when there was a close emotional relationship between the relative and the person settled in the UK. A person who had been brought up by a great-aunt or a cousin, and who had a quasi-parental relationship with that person, will need to explain this family background, why it had happened and why there were no other closer relatives who could support the person in the country of origin. If the person is elderly, it is more likely that exceptional compassionate reasons will be accepted. If the person has physical or mental disabilities, medical evidence to show this is required.

However, it is important to remember that if the application for settlement fails, this will have other consequences. It will be more difficult in the future for the person to make visits to the UK, because it will be more difficult to convince the immigration authorities that he or she intends to leave the UK at the end of the visit. Thus the long-term as well as the short-term plans of the person and the family should be considered before making an application outside the rules.

SECTION 2: REFUGEES

5 Refugees and asylum-seekers

The basis of the law on refugees is the 1951 UN Convention relating to the Status of Refugees, not any decisions or measures made under UK law. The definition of who is a refugee is made internationally; but the methods of deciding whether individuals fit in to this definition, and the standard of proof and evidence required, are matters for individual countries' laws. But as the process of harmonisation of laws within the European Union continues, these decisions too are being made in European committees and then implemented nationally.

Before 1993, the UK had no specific asylum law and asylum was mentioned almost as an afterthought in the immigration rules, after all other ways in which people might qualify to come to the UK had been listed. There are now two laws, the Asylum and Immigration Appeals Act 1993 and the Asylum and Immigration Act 1996, voluminous immigration rules explaining the separate procedure and listing the factors which the specialist Asylum Directorate at the Home Office must take into account in considering asylum applications, and a separate system of appeals against refusal of asylum. The 1993 Act states that 'nothing in the immigration rules shall lay down any practice which would be contrary to the Convention' but the Home Office can still make far-reaching administrative changes in how it deals with applications, often giving people no notice about them.

The Home Office considers each person's application for asylum in detail. If it is satisfied that people meet the criteria of the UN Convention, they will be granted **refugee status** and will normally be given leave to remain for four years. This may also be called **asylum**. If it does not believe that people meet these criteria but accepts that there are strong reasons why they should not have to return to their country of origin at that time, they will be granted **exceptional leave** to enter or remain, outside the immigration rules. This is normally given for one year initially and then for two periods of three years. If the Home Office does not accept either of these, and the person does not fit into any other part of the immigration rules, the application will be refused and the person will have certain rights of appeal.

Because the administrative and legal systems are new, and so rapidly-changing, it is particularly important to get good advice and representation in dealing with asylum applications.

The UN Convention relating to the Status of Refugees

The UN Convention defines a refugee as

- a person who has a well-founded fear of persecution for reasons of race, religion, nationality, membership of a particular social group or political opinion and who is outside the country of his nationality and is unable or, owing to such fear, is unwilling to avail himself of the protection of that country; or who, not having a nationality and being outside the country of his former habitual residence...is unable or, owing to such fear, is unwilling to return to it.

The Convention was signed in 1951 and was prepared and debated in the aftermath of the Second World War, mainly in the context of the thousands of displaced people in Europe. In 1967 a Protocol was added to it, extending the definition of refugees to non-Europeans and to people forced to seek refuge because of events that took place after 1945.

Interpretation of the Convention and Protocol

There are no internationally agreed procedures or standards in deciding who falls within the UN definition. Governments which have signed the Convention and Protocol choose the criteria they will use to decide whether people qualify and what standard of proof is necessary. This varies between countries of refuge and according to the countries from which people are fleeing.

The UN High Commission for Refugees has prepared a *Handbook on procedures and criteria for determining refugee status* on the interpretation of all the phrases in its definition. This is very helpful in preparing an asylum case, as its principles are generally accepted by the Home Office.

European definitions

The Justice and Home Affairs Council of the EU agreed a joint position on the interpretation of the definition of a refugee in November 1995, to inform the decisions made by individual countries. This stressed that 'persecution is generally the act of a state organ...in addition to cases in which persecution takes the form of the use of brute force, it may also take the form of administrative and/or judicial measures which either have the appearance of legality and are misused for the purposes of persecution, or are carried out in breach of the law'. These may be 'general measures to maintain public order' which are implemented in a discriminatory way or to camouflage measures against particular groups, measures directed against specific categories which have been 'condemned by the international community, or where they are manifestly disproportionate to the end sought', or measures taken against an individual for a Convention reason, in particular where the action is 'intentional, systematic and lasting'. Persecution not by the state will only be considered if it is 'encouraged or permitted by the authorities'. This clearly creates problems for those in danger from non-state authorities, for example the Liberation Tigers of Tamil Eelam, or in a situation where the state has broken down, such as Somalia or Zaire. At the time of writing, the UK had not yet accepted this definition in its asylum practice.

It is important to consider all the individual phrases in the UN Convention definition in deciding whether someone has a claim to asylum.

Well-founded fear

There is no internationally agreed definition but it has been accepted that 'well-founded' means 'serious possibility' or 'reasonable degree of likelihood'. But it is up to the Home Office to decide, using both subjective and objective criteria, whether this has been shown. The standard of proof is at the lower end of the scale of the balance of probabilities – the normal civil standard of proof – that it is more likely than not that the person would be in danger of persecution if sent back. In asylum cases, it must only be shown that there is a 'reasonable degree of likelihood' of such danger. This was decided by the House of Lords in the case of *Sivakumaran* (1988 Imm AR 147), which concerned six Sri Lankan Tamils who had been refused asylum and returned to Sri Lanka.

The standard of proof was again confirmed in the Tribunal case of *Koyazia Kaja* (11038), where the Tribunal stressed that a lower standard of proof is required in asylum cases than in normal civil cases, both for the Home Office and the appellate authorities: 'a lesser degree of likelihood... reasonable chance, substantial grounds for thinking, a serious possibility' are all ways of expressing the standard of proof needed to show the reasonable degree of likelihood that a person has been persecuted in the past or would face persecution if returned.

The Home Office considers applications in the light of the detailed information it has about the situation in different countries and how the person's history fits in with this. Refugees must satisfy the Home Office that they have a genuine fear for their safety. Often there is no proof or evidence to substantiate that fear and the decision will depend on the Home Office's assessment of the person's credibility – but as this is almost invariably negative, evidence becomes even more vital.

Persecution

There is no internationally accepted definition of persecution, but at the very least it includes constituting a threat to life or freedom, or other serious violations of human rights. The Convention has been interpreted to mean that there must be a danger to the person *individually*, though the reason for this may be membership of a particular group. It is not usually held to cover people who are living in a generally unstable or dangerous situation, for example because there is a civil war in the country of origin. It is also possible that discrimination against a person in many and persistent ways, combined with other factors such as an atmosphere of insecurity, can amount cumulatively to persecution. The European joint position states that 'acts suffered or feared must: be sufficiently serious, by their nature or repetition; they must either constitute a basic attack on human rights, for example life, freedom or physical integrity, or... manifestly preclude the person who has suffered them from continuing to live in his country of origin' as well as being based on a Convention ground.

Persecution is distinct from prosecution, though the two can be connected. People who fear to return to their country because they may face criminal charges, even when these are connected with political activity, cannot normally claim this in itself to be persecution. This was confirmed by the Court of Appeal in *O v IAT and Secretary of State for the Home Department* (1995 Imm AR 494). However, when the criminal penalties for a certain action in a particular country are disproportionate to those in most other countries, or when it is alleged that the real reason for the prosecution is because of the person's political or other opinions, this may show persecution.

Reason for fear of persecution

Refugees have to show that the persecution they face as individuals is for one of the reasons listed in the UN definition: race, religion, nationality, membership of a particular social group or political opinion. It is up to the people seeking asylum to satisfy the Home Office about their situation and the danger in which this would place them if they had to return. The part of this definition where there is most development in the law and which may be most difficult to establish is the membership of a social group. The UNHCR *Handbook* (see above) defines this as 'persons of similar background, habits or social status' and states that fear of persecution on these grounds may often overlap with others.

People who have argued that their fear of persecution stems from membership of a social group include westernised women from Iran and gay men and lesbians from several countries. Canada has granted asylum to a Saudi Arabian woman on the grounds of her activities challenging sex discrimination and to a woman from Trinidad who had suffered physical abuse from her husband, on the grounds that there was no network of support for women in her position in Trinidad. The United States has granted asylum to women facing genital mutilation, for themselves or their children, and to a gay man from Mexico. The Home Office has not yet accepted these arguments but has occasionally granted exceptional leave to remain to gay men from such countries as Iran and Argentina. However, a man from the Turkish Federated State of Cyprus lost his court case, *ex parte Binbasi*, reported in 1989 Imm AR 595 because it was not accepted that if returned he had to 'practise' his homosexuality. The Tribunal decided in the cases of *Golchin* (7623) and *Jacques* (11580) that homosexuals are not a 'social group' but in *Vraciu* (11559) that they are in Romania. At the time of writing, the High Court had held that *Syeda Shah*, who had suffered domestic violence from her husband in the UK and his family in Pakistan, had an arguable claim for asylum and had remitted her case for reconsideration by a special adjudicator. There is therefore room for further argument on particular cases.

People who have a well-founded fear of returning for other reasons not listed in the UN definition, for example family pressure, danger of criminal attacks, or the bombardment of their town or village by military units, may not fit into the terms of the Convention. However it is often still worthwhile making an application for leave to remain on these grounds, as the Home Office may decide to grant exceptional leave to remain, perhaps tacitly observing the UK's obligations under article 3 of the European Convention on Human Rights not to return people to torture or inhuman and degrading treatment. People do not have to have suffered persecution in the past, though any evidence to show that they had would be helpful. If it is likely that persecution would be suffered in the future, any evidence about the general situation in the country, or of what has happened to people of that racial, religious or other group and of the activities the asylum-seeker might feel compelled to carry out on return would be helpful.

Outside the country of nationality

Under the Convention, people cannot be refugees while still in the country in which they fear persecution. They must leave that country before claiming asylum in a safe country. It is therefore theoretically impossible for people to apply for visas to come to a country for asylum, but the Home Office has stated that such applications may, exceptionally, be considered at British embassies and high commissions. It is rare for them to succeed.

Criminal convictions

People may be excluded from the definition of a refugee if they have committed 'a crime against peace, a war crime, a crime against humanity or a serious non-political crime outside the country of refuge before recognition as a refugee or have been guilty of acts contrary to the purpose and principles of the United Nations' and can be refused asylum on these grounds. A 'serious non-political crime' is not closely defined because of the differences in countries' criminal laws, but would have to be a crime for which death, or a very serious penalty, could be imposed. This clause would not automatically exclude people whose prosecution had been initiated for political or other reasons and could therefore be considered to be part of the persecution from which they were attempting to flee.

There is a growing trend for governments to use this clause to exclude political activists who have any connection with armed groups. There are few legal cases on it but all the courts up to the House of Lords decided in the case of *T* (1996 Imm AR 443) that an Algerian who claimed to be a member of the Front Islamique du Salut (FIS) and to have been involved in two bomb attacks was excluded, even though the reason for his crimes was political. The Tribunal held that he was 'actively involved in a terrorist organisation' and that although the only definition of terrorism in law, 'the use of violence for political ends', might suggest that a terrorist crime was a political crime, it was not prepared to accept that he could qualify as a refugee. The Court of Appeal agreed that the crimes involved were 'grossly out of proportion to any genuine political objective', and the House of Lords that 'the link between the crime and the political object which Mr T was seeking to achieve was too remote', so he was excluded.

The case of *Chahal* in the European Court of Human Rights, November 1996, held that there is no similar exclusion from the provisions of Article 3 of the European Convention on Human Rights, prohibiting the return of a person who would face inhuman and degrading treatment. Mr Chahal had been detained in Bedford prison for over six years contesting his return to India. This may therefore be a useful alternative argument.

Once people have been recognised as refugees, they may lose their protection from expulsion if they are convicted of 'a particularly serious crime' in the country in which they have been given refuge. The nature of such crimes is not spelled out but could include large-scale drugs importation, for example.

Deciding if people qualify for asylum

It may be useful for an adviser to go through the following points, and to decide whether people qualify under them, to check whether they are likely to fit in to the narrow definition of a refugee.

1. Is the person afraid to return?
2. Is what she or he fears 'persecution'?
3. Is the reason for the fear a 'Convention reason', that is, because of the person's race, religion, nationality, membership of a particular social group or political opinion?
4. Is the fear well-founded?
5. Is the person excluded?

Policies to discourage asylum-seekers

Visas and carriers' liability

The policy of the British government, and indeed all European and Western governments for a long time, has been to attempt to discourage people from coming to seek asylum. Other countries also operate the policies discussed here in their UK context. The Home Office has initiated new processes and legislative changes in order to avoid taking responsibility for asylum-seekers and refugees. Citizens of certain countries were made into visa nationals – people who always need to obtain entry clearance in advance of travelling – in order to make it harder for them to reach the UK. Iranians were made visa nationals in 1980, Sri Lankans in 1985, Turks in 1989, Ugandans in 1991, most of the former Yugoslavia in 1992, Sierra Leone and the Ivory Coast in 1994, the Gambia in 1995 and Tanzania and Kenya in 1996, for this reason.

People without visas still manage to board planes in order to seek asylum. The Home Office next enlisted the airlines in immigration control, through the Immigration (Carriers' Liability) Act 1987. This provided for fines on airlines for each passenger they bring to the UK who does not have the correct documents; in July 1991 the fine was doubled to £2000 per passenger. The airline is still liable to be fined even if the incorrectly-documented person is granted asylum (although in practice the Home Office may then waive the fine). This means that airlines may be reluctant to allow passengers to board planes.

The 1993 Act provided for carriers' liability to be extended to transit passengers and for the Home Office to decide, by order, which transit passengers are required to have visas. Immigration (Transit Visa) Orders currently provide that nationals of Afghanistan, China, Eritrea, Ethiopia, Ghana, Iran, Iraq, Libya, Nigeria, Somalia, Sri Lanka, Turkey, Uganda and Zaire need transit visas, for however short a stay in transit in the UK. The intention is to deter people from those countries from being able to apply for asylum while in transit. Other visa nationals who have less than 24 hours between planes do not need transit visas.

Immigration officials may be stationed at airports abroad, to 'advise' airlines whether passports and visas are genuine. This is very dangerous for people not permitted to travel, as their national authorities may be alerted to their attempts to leave. There is evidence that people have been turned back from check-in desks and not allowed to fly to the UK. There have also been instances when airlines refused to let people off planes in the UK, on some occasions with the connivance of immigration officers, so that they could not apply to enter and therefore the airline would not be fined. Some of these people, who had been able to make contact with advisers in the UK, brought civil actions against the immigration authorities and were awarded damages for this.

Asylum-seekers by definition are often not able to approach the authorities of their own country to obtain passports, or the authorities of another country to obtain visas, without putting themselves in greater danger. They are also applying outside the immigration rules, because people cannot be considered as refugees until they have left their country of origin. Thus visa requirements and sanctions on airlines do not produce the result of fewer people needing and seeking asylum but of asylum-seekers having to resort to forged documents and visas in order to be able to escape. This means that many asylum-seekers can only come to the UK with the help of 'agents' who are able to obtain documents. The UN Convention makes it quite clear that this should not affect the person's application, stating that a country 'shall not impose penalties, on account of their illegal entry or presence, on refugees...'. The case of *Naillie* (1992 Imm AR 395) held that a person who travelled to the UK with forged documents, but who applied for asylum on arrival, is not an illegal entrant. However, the 1996 Act extends the criminal offence of illegal entry to those *seeking* entry by means which include deception ▶see page 266, so this may be superseded.

Detention of asylum-seekers

Large numbers of asylum-seekers are detained when they apply for asylum on arrival in the UK. It has been Home Office policy since at least 1989 to increase the numbers of asylum-seekers detained, hoping this may discourage others from coming. On 19 July 1993 317 asylum-seekers were detained, on 15 April 1994 there were 651 and on 28 October, 702. By 31 May 1996, there were 751, and by 1 October, 864.

Definition of a claim for asylum

Section 1 of the Asylum and Immigration Appeals Act 1993 defines a person's claim for asylum as being 'a claim made (whether before or after the coming into force of this section) that it would be contrary to the UK's obligations under the Convention for him to be removed from, or required to leave, the UK'.

This definition is very restrictive and could cause great danger to asylum-seekers. The UN Convention defines a refugee (▶see above) but does not define asylum. The Convention definition does not include many important situations, for example, a state of disturbance or civil war in the country of origin. The Act does not mention any other relevant international instruments the UK has signed, for example the European Convention on Human Rights, which in Article 3 forbids torture or inhuman or degrading treatment, or the UN Convention against Torture, Article 3 of which forbids the expulsion of people to a territory where they may be tortured.

Because the definition is '*the UK*'s obligations under the Convention' this means that anyone who has travelled through another country on the way to the UK may be returned to that country, if the immigration officers are satisfied that that country is 'safe'. If the person is not being removed direct to the country of danger, but to somewhere else where the asylum claim should be considered, there are no obligations on the UK under the Convention. The principle of people applying for asylum in the first safe country they reach has been applied by the British and other governments for a long time. It was codified between countries of the EU in the Dublin Convention (▶see page 93) and, even though the Convention has not yet been ratified by all signatories, the idea of a 'safe third country' has now been incorporated into British law.

How the Home Office deals with asylum applications
Decision-making criteria

The immigration rules, HC 395, now amended by Cm 3365 ▶see appendix, set out the criteria which govern both the Home Office decision and the grounds on which appeals can succeed. Paragraphs 340–4 list factors which may be taken into account in assessing applicants' 'credibility'. This is vital, as the success of the application basically depends on whether the Home Office Asylum Directorate believes the person's account. If it does not, the application will be refused. All asylum decisions are made by the Home Office Asylum Directorate. If people apply for asylum at a port of entry, immigration officers take the details but refer the case to the Home Office for decision. People already admitted to the UK for some other purpose may apply direct to the Home Office for asylum, whatever their status under immigration law.

The United Nations High Commission for Refugees has stated: 'It is not advisable to list... the factors which should be given special consideration in assessing an asylum-seeker's credibility. Evaluation of credibility is a process which involves the consideration of many complex factors, both objective and subjective, which are impossible to enumerate. Since all these may be equally important, singling out any of these factors will, by necessity, be incomplete and arbitrary.' The Home Office, however, does so. Its list begins:

- A failure, without reasonable explanation, to make a prompt and full disclosure of material factors, either orally or in writing, or otherwise to assist the Secretary of State in establishing the facts of the case may lead to the refusal of an asylum application.

This includes failure to report for fingerprinting, as well as failure to respond to questions relevant to the claim or to report for an interview. It can also create problems for people unable to give full details initially on arrival, as any further elaboration and explanations given later may be disbelieved.

The 'matters which may damage an asylum applicant's credibility' are listed:

- that the applicant has failed without reasonable explanation to apply forthwith upon arrival in the UK, unless the application is founded on events which have taken place since his arrival in the UK

This is aimed at people who enter the UK in some other capacity, for example as visitors or students, and only later apply for asylum.

Many applicants will be unable or unwilling to apply immediately on arrival in the UK. People who have been tortured or brutally treated by officials will not be able to tell their story to the first British official they meet; organisations dealing with torture victims know that it can take a long time to build sufficient trust to talk freely about such experiences. This requirement is contrary to the spirit of para 198 of the UNHCR *Handbook* which states that people may well be afraid to give full and accurate accounts of their cases because of their past experiences. Para 203 states that the benefit of any doubt should be in their favour.

In many cases, people may legitimately hesitate before making an asylum application once they have escaped from immediate danger. Applying for asylum is a drastic step: it means cutting off all possibility of return to one's home country and may put relatives and friends in danger. People are often reluctant to do this and need time to think through the consequences with advisers or with others from the same community. Asylum-seekers without access to legal advice will not know what the Home Office will consider to be a 'material factor' relevant to their case.

- **that the application is made after the applicant has been refused leave to enter or has been recommended for deportation or has been notified of the Home Office's decision to deport or remove him**

    These are administrative matters to do with British immigration law and may bear no relation whatsoever to the strength of the person's claim for asylum.

- **that the applicant has submitted manifestly false evidence in support of his application, or has otherwise made false representations, either orally or in writing**

    This may contravene Article 31 of the UN Convention, which accepts that asylum-seekers may need to disguise their intentions or their identity in order to flee to safety. It is not clear exactly what could be included in 'false representations'; whether this includes entering as a visitor, for example, or whether the Home Office means giving incorrect information in relation to the asylum claim.

- **that the applicant on arrival in the UK did not produce a passport, without reasonable explanation, or produced an invalid passport and did not tell the immigration officer**

    For all the reasons discussed above, asylum-seekers may not feel secure enough on arrival to reveal all the details of their case, and this may well include details of the documents on which they are travelling, as they may expect immediate refusal and return to the country of danger if they reveal they are using false documents.

- **that the applicant has otherwise, without reasonable explanation, destroyed, damaged or disposed of any passport, other document, or ticket relevant to his claim**

The Home Office states that almost two-thirds of people applying for asylum at the ports have no travel documents when they arrive. It believes that people have destroyed documents or returned them to agents who will use them again, or that they may have travelled through another country to which they would be returnable but that they are attempting to hide this so that their application will be considered in the UK. It may also be more difficult for the Home Office to establish people's identity if they have no travel document.

- that the applicant has undertaken any activities in the UK before or after lodging his application which are inconsistent with his previous beliefs and behaviour and calculated to create or substantially enhance his claim to refugee status

This may be difficult for asylum-seekers to interpret, as a person who has been in clandestine opposition in his or her home country may be able to act more openly once in the relative safety of the UK, and have difficulty in showing that this is a continuation of long-held beliefs. Equally, public involvement in the UK may make it more dangerous to return to the country from which asylum is sought. The case of *Senga* (9.3.94, in the Divisional Court) held that in certain circumstances the fact that an application for asylum had been made could put a person in more danger from the authorities of his or her country.

- that the applicant has lodged concurrent applications for asylum in the UK or in another country

If applications are made in more than one country, the question may then arise which country was the most appropriate one to consider the asylum application and, if it was not the UK, whether the person could be returned there. It would also be possible for the Home Office to request details of the application from the other country and then compare them with those given in the application made in the UK, to see if there were any discrepancies in the information, which would also go against the person's credibility.

- that if there is a part of the country from which the applicant claims to be a refugee in which he would not have a well-founded fear of persecution and to which it would be reasonable to expect him to go the application may be refused

This means that the Home Office, and the appellate authorities, may assess the safety of a part of a country (Colombo for Tamils from Jaffna, Islamabad for an Ahmadi from Karachi, for example) or make arrangements to send a person to a particular area, if the main airports are in a place which is not considered safe. It is unclear when it would be considered reasonable to send a person to part of a country where he or she had never lived before or had no connections. This is also a derogation from responsibilities under the UN Convention. The UNHCR *Handbook* states in para 91 that 'the fear of being persecuted need not always extend to the whole territory of the refugee's country of nationality' and Article 1A refers to a country, not to parts of a country. The case of *Jonah* (1985 Imm AR 70) held that it was unreasonable to expect a Ghanaian trade union activist to have to give up all this work and to live separately from his wife and family in a remote area in order to avoid coming to the notice of the authorities.

- **the actions of anyone acting as an agent of the asylum applicant may also be taken into account**

  No definition of an 'agent' is given. An asylum application can therefore be prejudiced by corrupt 'agents' in the country of origin, incompetent advisers in the UK or any friends or relatives who mistakenly try to help. It is therefore even more essential that any adviser is sure that the information put forward on a client's behalf is full and correct and that it has been agreed with the client.

- **If an applicant is part of a group whose claims are clearly not related to the criteria for refugee status in the Convention and Protocol he may be refused without examination of his individual claim**

  This is a further provision which allows for accelerated and unsafe decision-making. It is in direct contravention of the UN Convention, which insists that each case be assessed individually. It begs the question of what is a group, and what or who is 'clearly' outside the Convention. It allows for the kind of stereotyped, cursory decision-making which in the past has allowed Tamils and Kurds, later granted full refugee status, to be labelled initially as 'bogus' by Ministers and officials.

  These criteria show clear influence of European debates. Many of them were discussed in the meetings of European Interior Ministers, in 1992 and 1993, which passed a Resolution on 'manifestly unfounded' asylum cases mentioning similar criteria. Ministers have also discussed and agreed joint positions on minimum conditions for reception of asylum-seekers and provision of the basic means of survival but the UK has not yet implemented these proposals.

Connections with another country

If an asylum-seeker has close connections with another country as well as the one from which she or he is claiming asylum, the Home Office may suggest that asylum is not necessary because there is another country to which he or she could go. People who are dual nationals are always expected to go to the safe country of nationality. This has been used, for example, for people of Jewish origin, who have been told that they could go to Israel. The Court of Appeal agreed with this view, in the case of *Miller v IAT* (1988 Imm AR 358).

How to apply for asylum

Applying overseas

In very rare cases, refugees may apply for entry clearance to come to the UK. There have been limited government programmes for refugees from particular countries, for Chileans in the 1970s and for some Vietnamese during the 1980s, for example. This is a government decision to accept a quota of people who are already recognised as refugees. They will normally be given permission to enter for four years and granted settlement at the end of that time. People who have come in this way may be referred to as 'programme refugees'.

In 1992 the government announced that up to 1000 Bosnian ex-detainees, and their families, would be allowed to come to the UK. They were allowed in very slowly and were not formally recognised as refugees. On arrival, they were given a strange status, 'temporary refuge', in the UK, usually for six-month periods, and were told not to expect to be allowed to stay longer. In fact, they have been granted extensions of exceptional leave to remain.

If asylum-seekers are applying in their own country, they do not fall within the terms of the UN Convention if they are applying for entry clearance. Applications cannot succeed under the immigration rules, as there are no such provisions. The British authorities have to decide whether to make an exception to the rules to consider the applications of such people.

If asylum-seekers are applying in another country, where they have managed to escape temporarily, the immediate presumption is that the application for asylum should be made to the authorities of the country in question, unless it can be shown that that country also is not safe. It is unlikely that an application will succeed unless the person already has very close ties with the UK, for example a spouse or young children already settled or granted refugee status.

Applying on entry to the UK

People seeking asylum at an air- or sea port should apply to the immigration officer for asylum, explaining the danger they would be in if they had to return. People may feel able to do this but equally may not want or dare to give full details to an official, having been persecuted by officials until then. People also may not know the correct procedure for applying for asylum, and may believe it would be safer or better to gain entry to the UK in some other category, for example as a visitor, and later apply for asylum once in the UK. But the immigration rules suggest that people should apply 'forthwith on arrival' and, with effect from 24 July 1996, those who apply after entry are not entitled to any welfare benefits to survive.

When people apply for asylum at a port of entry, a decision on the application is not made immediately. Most people's cases will be considered under the 'short procedure' and they will be interviewed in detail about their claim shortly after arrival. Sometimes immigration officers may carry out a shorter 'pro-forma interview' to establish basic details about the person and his or her claim. If they are satisfied the application should be considered here, and that the person should be given temporary admission, they will issue an on-entry Standard Acknowledgement Letter (SAL1), which the asylum-seeker may use as proof of identity. All applicants will be fingerprinted. While the application is under consideration the applicant may either be detained in a prison or immigration detention centre or be given temporary admission to live at a named address. All decisions are made by the Home Office Asylum Directorate though they are passed on to the person concerned by immigration officers.

The short procedure

In May 1995 the Home Office began a two-month pilot of a scheme to deal with and decide asylum applications very much more quickly. In this pilot scheme, people from Nigeria, Ghana, India, Pakistan, Poland and Romania applying in-country were interviewed almost immediately on submitting their asylum application, and then given five days in which to produce further supporting evidence. During this period, most of the applications were decided within three weeks. In November the Home Office extended the procedure to nearly all people who applied for asylum on arrival at Gatwick airport (possibly related to the expansion of the detention centre there) and then to another 30 nationalities applying in-country as well as at Gatwick.

On 20 March 1996, the Home Office announced that the short procedure would eventually apply to *all* asylum-seekers except nationals of Afghanistan, Bosnia, Croatia, the Gulf states (except Kuwait), Iran, Iraq, Libya, Liberia, Palestine, Rwanda, Somalia and the former Yugoslavia. The period for submitting written representations was extended from ten days to a month in cases where people are not detained, and remained at five days for detainees. This is how the majority of new applications were considered by autumn 1996. The Home Office has stated that further information submitted after the deadline will be considered if it arrives before a decision has made. It explains its views on the short procedure as follows:

'we now see the procedure as likely in due course to be suitable for the great majority of asylum claims. There are practical constraints on moving very quickly to that situation, and in particular we must clearly continue to devote a very significant part of our overall resource to clearing the current backlog of undecided applications. But we are already working on the presumption that most nationalities of applicant may be suitable for the short procedure. In *individual* cases, it will become apparent from time to time that the application cannot be resolved quickly and in those cases the short procedure will cease to apply as soon as that judgment is made... There will continue to be some nationalities on which we do not use the short procedure at all, either because we do not have the resources available; or because experience suggests that a significant proportion of cases may take longer to decide than the procedure expects; or because an interview may not normally be necessary (for example, where we can move quickly to grant exceptional leave). We are also, of course, *not* including unaccompanied minors... We are now moving incrementally to the situation where the normal expectation for *included* nationalities will be a short procedure interview.'

From May 1995 to June 1996, 6734 asylum-seekers' cases were considered under the short procedure. Where decisions had been made, 5735 were refused and 3 were granted asylum. The use of the short procedure has serious consequences for Home Office decision-making on asylum.

'Third country cases'

If people have not come directly from their country of origin, but have spent some time in any other country on the way to the UK, immigration officers question them in detail to see whether that country would be a more appropriate one in which to seek asylum. Under the UN Convention, people seeking asylum are assumed to have come direct from the country of danger, and, governments consider, should apply for asylum in the first safe country they reach. It is therefore probable that asylum-seekers who have travelled through countries believed to be safe, for example other EU countries, will be refused in the UK and may be told that their claims are 'without foundation' because they do not 'raise any issue as to the UK's obligations under the Convention' (because the people are able to go to another safe country). Immigration officers can make removal arrangements to the country from which the asylum-seekers travelled, provided they are satisfied that that country will not return them to the country of danger. There is a right of appeal against such a refusal, but normally only under the 'fast track procedure' or after removal ▶see chapter 16 for more details.

EC governments signed a Convention on asylum-seekers in Dublin in June 1990. The text of the Convention is printed at the end of the 1990 Immigration Appeals reports. This confirmed that asylum-seekers in any country in the EC should have their applications considered in the first EC country they reached and that it would not be considered in any other country. This Convention had been signed but not yet ratified by all EC governments at the time of writing (the UK ratified it in July 1992), so is not yet in force. It is not followed in practice, as refused asylum-seekers are usually sent to the last safe EU country through which they travelled before coming to the UK, rather than the first safe country they arrived at in the EU. However, this last country may remove them again to the country they went through before, so it can be very hard to check what happens.

The Home Office states that if asylum-seekers have close relatives in the UK, their applications may be considered in this country even if they have come through another. 'Close relative' normally means only a spouse, a child under 18, or a parent if the applicant is a child under 18. Others who have travelled through another country which is considered 'safe' are likely to be returned there and it is unlikely that this can be delayed or contested unless there is evidence that the other country will return asylum-seekers to a non-EU country, or that it is not 'safe'.

Fingerprinting

The 1993 Act provides for fingerprinting of all people who have made asylum claims and their dependants. It also gives immigration and police officers the power to arrest without warrant anyone who does not comply with the fingerprinting requirement and states that fingerprints are to be destroyed either within a month of the person being granted settlement or after ten years. Fingerprinting normally takes place early in the asylum application process. The Asylum Screening Unit at Croydon (▶see pages 95–96) which records asylum claims and issues Standard Acknowledgement Letters (SAL2s for those who applied after entry) to confirm that a claim is made is the main office where fingerprinting takes place but it is also done at ports and other Home Office Public Enquiry Offices.

When a child is fingerprinted, another adult, either the parent or guardian or another responsible person, must be present. The Home Office has not stated any lower age limit for fingerprinting children, though in practice children under 16 are not normally fingerprinted.

In respect to fingerprinting, the 'dependants' of an asylum-seeker are defined as

- a spouse and
- children under 18 of an asylum-seeker who are
- not British citizens and
- do not have indefinite leave to remain in the UK.

This is intended to ensure that only people whose stay in the UK depends on an asylum claim are covered by these provisions. It is usual for these family members also to be listed on the asylum-seeker's SAL.

Other applications

When people's cases are not considered under the short procedure they may be called back to the airport for an interview to complete a questionnaire giving details of their claim. These are known as the 'asylum interview record'. If people are detained, they will be interviewed more quickly by the immigration service. The immigration officer will fill in the questionnaire at the interview and send the completed form to the Home Office for consideration. Representatives may request copies of any questionnaires filled in by immigration officers, and other notes of their interviews, in order to ensure that the further details are in conformity with the bare facts recorded earlier, or to explain what may have gone wrong at an initial interview.

People given temporary admission may be given a different political asylum questionnaire (PAQ) to complete themselves within a given period, normally four weeks. It asks for personal details about themselves and their families, about their travel to the UK, about their past education and employment history and about the reasons for their claim to asylum. It is important that people should have help and advice in filling these in, to ensure that all relevant information and any supporting evidence is sent to the Home Office in order that a decision on whether a person has a well-founded fear of persecution for any of the reasons listed in the UN Convention and the immigration rules may be made.

If the Home Office is not satisfied from the information in the questionnaire that the person qualifies for refugee status or exceptional leave to remain, or does not send one out, it is usual for an interview to be arranged with the asylum-seeker. People may be asked to return to the airport for a further interview before a decision is made.

At Heathrow airport, an advice service, the Refugee Arrivals Project, ▶see chapter 19 for address, advises and helps asylum-seekers to find accommodation and financial support, and seeks the release of those initially detained. It also refers asylum-seekers to sources of legal advice on their cases, such as the Refugee Legal Centre or solicitors.

Applying after entry to the UK

People may apply for asylum after being allowed into the country for any other purpose, for example as visitors or students. They should then apply to the Home Office for a change of status. The majority of applicants' cases are dealt with under the short procedure ▶see above, so they may be interviewed about the detail of their asylum claim straightaway. It is important that they should be accompanied to this interview, so records can be kept and any problems noted at the time.

If the case is not considered under the short procedure, before issuing a Standard Acknowledgement Letter (SAL2) to confirm the application has been made, the Home Office must be satisfied as to the identity of the asylum applicant. Particularly in relation to after-entry applicants, who may not have passports, other evidence such as birth certificates is requested, or people are interviewed in some depth about their method of entry to the UK, to see if this appears credible. These interviews are normally carried out by the Asylum Screening Unit at Lunar House, and only when its officials are satisfied about identity will a SAL2 be issued. The asylum-seeker will also be fingerprinted. It is helpful for an asylum-seeker to be accompanied to a Screening Unit interview, to ensure that questions are only asked about identity and not about the substance of the asylum claim, as this should be dealt with by specialist asylum workers, and to be there should the Home Office decide to interview the person immediately under the short procedure.

From July 1994, a frequent Screening Unit practice was not to issue a SAL on first application, but to give asylum-seekers a form, GEN 32, asking them to come for a further screening interview in a month's time, and a PAQ to complete and bring back at that interview. The implication is that if the PAQ cannot be completed in time, the SAL will not be issued, but people can ask for more time to complete the application.

While a decision is pending an asylum-seeker is not liable to detention, provided that the application was made while he or she was legally in the UK. The Home Office may then grant asylum or exceptional leave to remain on the basis of the response to the questionnaire. It has stated that it will not normally refuse an application without interviewing the asylum-seeker to give him or her a chance to put forward any other information and evidence.

In practice, applications have been refused on the basis of questionnaires alone. In July 1994 the Home Office stated that it would no longer normally interview asylum-seekers from Pakistan applying on the basis of membership of the Pakistan People's Party as it had since been returned to power, or nationals of the Czech Republic, Slovakia and Poland claiming to fear persecution from the previous Communist regimes. It would rely solely on the information given in questionnaires, unless there was any particular individual reason put forward to suggest that the person had a claim under the Convention.

People who have overstayed, or who the Home Office has treated as illegal entrants, may apply for asylum and the application will be considered. The Home Office will however be suspicious if the application was made long after the person came to the UK, and may suspect that it was made mainly in order to delay removal. The immigration rules on asylum (▶see above) say that if an application is not made 'forthwith' on arrival in the UK, this is a factor the Home Office may take into consideration.

Asylum interviews

The basis of the asylum claim is the information which the Home Office receives from the asylum-seeker and the assessment it makes of whether the claim is 'credible'. In view of the seriousness of the issues involved and the possibility of misunderstandings, it is very important that someone should accompany an asylum-seeker at any interview at the port or at the

Home Office and make a full written record of the interview. This may be the solicitor or adviser who is helping with the asylum application, or they may send a clerk, a junior or freelance worker, who keeps a full record of the interview. Clerks may become very experienced in asylum and immigration procedures but will not normally give legal advice.

The immigration authorities have made it more difficult for people to be accompanied or represented by use of the short procedure and by refusing to delay interviews so that a representative or clerk may reach the airport to attend. In November 1996 the Home Office issued draft guidance for representatives at asylum interviews, making clear its view that 'representatives and their interpreters may attend interviews as observers at the discretion of the interviewing officer...observers must refrain from interrupting during the interview, they will be permitted to add their comments at the end of the interview.' Representatives have contested the restrictive nature of this guidance.

Many asylum-seekers do not speak English and their interviews will therefore be carried out through an interpreter, normally employed by the Home Office or immigration service on a sessional basis. If the representative or clerk at the interview is not fluent in both languages, an independent interpreter should also be present at the interview, to note any difficulties in interpretation. The Home Office has agreed that this is permissible. It states, 'minor discrepancies in translation should be noted throughout the interview and brought to the attention of the interviewing officer at the end of the interview. The interviewing officer should be made aware immediately of any major difficulties over interpretation.' If the asylum-seeker does not understand the official interpreter, it is important that he or she makes this clear to the interviewing officer, and a new interview with an interpreter in the correct language or dialect should be arranged. In practice, this is likely to be very hard to do, when there is no independent corroboration of interpretation problems.

The Home Office relies on the detailed information given by the asylum-seeker as the basis for the claim for asylum. Thus filling in the questionnaire and responding at interview are of paramount importance. It is necessary to explain in detail exactly what has happened to the person, what activities he or she has engaged in which could result in persecution, what has happened to members of the family or the particular group to which the asylum-seeker belongs. It may be simplest for an adviser to go through this with the asylum-seeker in date order, before any interview if possible, in order to prepare a clear statement either on the questionnaire or as a separate letter, explaining what has happened and why the person qualifies for asylum.

It is vital that all information given to the Home Office in connection with an asylum application is totally accurate and complete. Mistakes made at this point are extremely hard to correct later, as the Home Office will not believe the corrections. The Home Office will check any inconsistencies in successive representations and may use these to cast doubts on the applicant's 'credibility'. Also if further elaboration of an initially-sparse and concise or terse statement is sent later, the Home Office may allege that the further details are an exaggeration of the person's claim or his or her personal involvement in the claimed activities and may therefore disregard them, or suggest that the elaborations cast doubt on the credibility of the initial application. Thus any statement in support of an application should be thoroughly checked with the asylum-seeker, and translated into the language used if the statement was taken through an interpreter, before it is sent to the Home Office.

The Home Office has made it clear that it gives priority to applications made after the 1993 Act came into force, in order to continue to try to meet its target timetable of three months for deciding asylum applications. In June 1996 the average length of time for a decision was 45 months for an application made before July 1993 and 11 months for one made afterwards. At the end of December 1996, 55,695 people were waiting for a decision on their asylum applications.

Sources of information

It is helpful, when possible, to have corroborative evidence to support information given by an asylum-seeker.

Amnesty International has detailed information about most countries of the world and its researchers may be able to provide references or information to support what the asylum-seeker has said. It publishes a yearly review, with brief details about each country and many detailed briefings and bulletins, which are invaluable.

The Minority Rights Group publishes in-depth studies of particular groups which are very helpful.

The Refugee Legal Centre may have up-to-date information about the Home Office's current practice with regard to particular countries and information about those countries, but does not yet have facilities for other organisations to use.

The Medical Foundation for the Care of Victims of Torture is able to provide medical reports from doctors and psychiatrists, on their assessment of physical and mental scars, to confirm information given by asylum-seekers.

Human Rights Watch produces reports on the human rights situation in particular countries, mainly in Africa, Asia and the Middle East.

The Immigration Law Practitioners' Association has published useful booklets, both on making applications for asylum and lists of academic and other experts on different countries, who may be able to provide background and corroborative evidence.

The United Nations High Commission for Refugees may offer support in particular cases or its views on the situation in particular countries. It produces a CD-ROM of collated material relevant to asylum claims, called Refworld.

The Electronic Immigration Network is setting up a series of bulletin boards and a database of immigration and asylum decisions and other relevant information.

▶See chapter 19 for the addresses of all these organisations.

While an application is pending

Welfare benefits

Section 11 and Schedule 1 of the 1996 Act were added at a very late stage, after JCWI's challenge to the DSS' regulations excluding asylum-seekers from benefit ▶see chapter 10. They provide the legislative framework to exclude 'any person who has made a claim for asylum' from entitlement to income support, housing benefit and council tax benefit. The only asylum-seekers who are still eligible to claim these benefits are people who apply for asylum on arrival in the UK, or within three months of the Home Office declaring their country has undergone a 'serious upheaval'. No such declarations had been made at the time of writing.

While an application for asylum which was made on arrival in the UK is being considered, therefore, the person is eligible to claim income support but this will be paid at the urgent cases rate. This means that an asylum-seeker is expected to survive on 90% of income support, although full income support premiums and normal housing costs are paid, as well as full premiums for any children.

Since the introduction of Standard Acknowledgement Letters in November 1991, the Benefits Agency has preferred these to all other forms of identification. When people do not have SALs, for example because they applied before November 1991, or they have separated from a person whose dependant they had been, the Benefits Agency often requests up-to-date letters from the Home Office confirming their status and threatens to stop benefit if these are not produced. Since February 1996, SALs are different for people who applied for asylum on arrival (now called SAL1) who may be eligible for benefits and those who applied after entry (SAL2), who are not.

People who applied for asylum from 5 February 1996 onwards and who applied after they had been admitted to the country for any other purpose do not qualify for income support at all. Neither do people who have been refused asylum and are appealing against that refusal. However, if their applications or appeals are successful and they are recognised as refugees they may then claim backdated benefit for the period of their application or appeal.

People who applied for asylum on or after 25 July 1993 do not have full rights to housing as homeless persons (▶see page 200). People who applied after 18 August 1996 have no rights to consideration for housing at all, unless they claimed asylum 'on arrival', when they may qualify for temporary housing as homeless people.

The government's intention is to ensure that people who apply for asylum when already in the UK are not entitled to any financial help. At the time of writing, the Divisional Court had decided in the case of *R v London Borough of Hammersmith ex parte M and others* on 8 October 1996 that asylum-seekers who are 'in need of care and attention which is not otherwise available to them' are covered under s. 21(1)(a) of the 1948 National Assistance Act. This means that local authorities are required to provide accommodation and food for them, normally through Social Services departments. The Court of Appeal upheld this decision on 17 February 1997. When asylum-seekers are able to receive such help, doing so has no effect on the Home Office's consideration of their cases.

The Home Office is often very slow in considering asylum applications, and some are still pending from before the Asylum and Immigration Appeals Act 1993 came into force. However there is political pressure for it to deal with new applications more quickly, hence the invention of the short procedure.

Working

The Home Office has stated that if an asylum application has not been decided after six months, it will give the asylum-seeker permission to work while waiting for the decision. This permission is not automatic. People who applied after entry to the UK should go to the Home Office special office in the Whitgift Shopping Centre, opposite Lunar House, with a letter from their representative if they do not speak English, stating the date on which the asylum application was made and that no decision has yet been reached, and requesting permission for themselves and their spouse, if any, to work. This permission will normally be granted on request to asylum-seekers, but more rarely to spouses and, if granted, will be endorsed on the SAL2. The Home Office has also said that if an asylum-seeker is offered a specific job, permission to work may be given before six months have elapsed. For port applicants, an application should be made in writing to the immigration service at the port, and permission will be endorsed on the SAL1 or IS96.

When asylum-seekers have been permitted to work, this permission will not normally be removed if they are refused asylum and appeal against the refusal. However, their SALs will be withdrawn, so it may be difficult for them to show proof that they may work. When asylum is refused within six months, and people appeal, they will not normally be allowed to work during the appeal period, however long this takes.

Special groups of asylum-seekers

Unaccompanied child asylum-seekers

The immigration rules on asylum make specific provision for unaccompanied child asylum-seekers, recognising their particular vulnerability. The rules suggest that more consideration should be given to the objective risks in a country rather than the child's understanding of them. Children will not normally be interviewed, but if an interview is considered necessary, a 'parent, guardian, representative or another adult who for the time being takes responsibility for the child' must be present. The Home Office also intends to deal with these applications more quickly than average. It has an Unaccompanied Children's Module in the Asylum Directorate which deals with all questions about unaccompanied children and makes inquiries to substantiate their cases. If an interview is considered necessary, caseworkers have received training in dealing with children. If the application is refused, the appeal also should be expedited. The Home Office has stated that it 'will not seek to remove an unaccompanied child under the age of 18 from the UK unless it is possible to put in place acceptable reception and care arrangements in their country of origin. If this does not prove possible the child will be granted exceptional leave to enter or remain.'

In debate on the Asylum and Immigration Appeals Bill in 1993, the House of Lords agreed to set up an advisory panel to help unaccompanied child asylum-seekers, but this amendment was defeated in the House of Commons. The government however has set up a panel, on a non-statutory basis, in connection with the Refugee Council. It provides unaccompanied children with an individual adviser, who can help them in dealing with British authorities such as social services departments, schools and immigration, find interpreters and offer support and help; ▶see chapter 19 for address. When a child applies for asylum after entry to the country, it is essential that the Refugee Council adviser goes to the Screening Unit with the child, otherwise staff may refuse to process the claim.

Detained asylum-seekers

The 1993 and 1996 Acts contain no additional powers to detain people. However, the Immigration Act 1971 already gives a power to detain indefinitely, and without bringing before a court, anyone whose application for entry to the UK is being considered or has been refused by the Home Office, and anyone whom the Home Office has made a decision to deport, or who is alleged to be an illegal entrant, pending removal. This includes people who are seeking, or who have been refused, asylum. Since 1991 the Home Office has been increasing the provision of detention places, mainly for asylum-seekers.

In a letter to Amnesty International British Section of 13 July 1993, the

Home Office stated: 'It remains our policy that we should not routinely detain asylum seekers...the decision to detain in a particular case rests with the Immigration Service who consider cases on an individual basis and will take into account all the known facts. Cases in which the applicant is detained receive a very high priority and the need for continued detention is regularly reviewed...' It also stated that most detainees are in immigration service establishments, or Haslar, a prison which holds mainly Immigration Act detainees, but ordinary prisons may be used 'when an individual is either unstable, violent or has special medical needs. A further consideration in the allocation of detainees is the need, so far as possible, to detain people in locations convenient to friends, relatives and legal representatives.' Advisers may wish to remind the Home Office of this in relation to particular individuals.

The Home Office's actions belie its words. Campsfield House, near Kidlington, Oxfordshire, was opened as an immigration detention centre, primarily for asylum-seekers, in November 1993, and holds 200 people. In June 1994, it was announced that Immigration Act detainees would be kept mainly in five prisons, Doncaster, Rochester, Holloway, Winson Green and Haslar, as well as immigration detention centres, thereby 'improving services to detainees' because of the concentration of people. Doncaster has not in fact been used, but Tinsley House near Gatwick was opened in spring 1996, holding another 150 people.

It is important to continue to request temporary admission for detained asylum-seekers. The Home Office states that detention is reviewed monthly, so it is well worth continuing to fax and to telephone to request temporary admission, when there is an address to which the person could be released and no reason to suggest that he or she would abscond. The passage of time since the person has been detained may also be a reason to urge release, particularly if it is clear that there is a lot of information for the Home Office to consider and the case will take some time. The 1996 Asylum and Immigration Act makes bail applications for alleged illegal entrants a possibility as well as for those with appeals pending; ►see chapter 15 for more information.

Refusal of applications

The Asylum and Immigration Appeals Act 1993 was accompanied by a change in Home Office policy. The proportion of refusals of asylum has risen steeply since the Act, from 15% in the 18 months before July 1993 to 75% in the 15 months afterwards and up to 80% by late 1996.

Curtailment of leave

People who make asylum applications while they have permission to be in the UK (eg as visitors, students, workers or spouses within a year of arrival) have a right of appeal if refused asylum, within seven working days of the refusal. But in addition, the 1993 Act gives the Home Secretary the power to curtail any leave to enter or remain they and their dependent family members already had at the same time as refusing their asylum application. There is no appeal against a decision to curtail leave under this Act, so people who apply for asylum while legally in the UK (for example as visitors or students) risk being deported without being able to complete their visit or studies here if they apply for asylum and this is rejected.

Leave may be curtailed if the applicant 'does not meet the requirements of the rules under which leave was granted'. The Home Office Minister stated in Committee on the 1993 Bill in the House of Commons that it was not the intention to apply this section to 'genuine students' but did not clarify this further and rejected amendments that would have done so. Deportation decisions may be made at the same time as curtailment, even though people do not yet know they have become overstayers or have broken conditions of stay. If no deportation decision is then made, the person may be forced into a position of illegality by remaining in the UK, without leave, in order to be in a position to appeal against deportation and argue that the curtailment decision was wrong. At the time of writing, these powers had not been frequently used. An Order amending the 1988 Immigration Act, to provide that there is a full appeal against deportation after curtailment in these circumstances, also came into force on 26 July 1993.

Moreover, if a person applied in time to remain on some other ground as well, for example because she has married a British citizen, and has lodged an appeal against refusal of asylum, any argument about the merits of the marriage case will be heard in the same appeal. All outstanding appeals against refusal, on whatever grounds, will be dealt with together.

Rights of appeal

There are two parallel asylum appeals systems currently in operation – for those refused asylum before 26 July 1993 and those refused on or after that date.

People refused asylum before 26 July 1993

Appeals lodged against these refusals are heard and decided under the immigration appeals system and the Immigration Appeals (Procedure) Rules 1984, not under the Asylum and Immigration Appeals Act. Because of the delays in hearing appeals the systems will continue in parallel for some years. The main differences between the systems are that in the old one there are no time limits within which immigration appeals must be heard, there is always a right to apply for leave to appeal to the Tribunal after an adjudicator dismisses the appeal and then for judicial review of the Tribunal's decision.

Before 26 July 1993 people who applied for asylum on arrival and did not have prior entry clearance had no right of appeal against refusal. The

Home Office operated a two-tier refusal system; after considering the application, it wrote a letter stating it was 'minded to refuse' the application, giving detailed reasons and inviting the person to put forward further evidence or information to contest this decision. It was possible for people to be granted asylum or exceptional leave after such reconsideration, or for the application to be refused formally and removal arrangements made.

People refused asylum on or after 26 July 1993

The system of appeals under the Asylum and Immigration Appeals Act 1993, as altered by the Asylum and Immigration Act 1996, applies to them. The details of the appeals system are in the Asylum Appeals (Procedure) Rules, also amended after the 1996 Act, and Schedule 2 to the 1993 Act. The 1993 Act provided for 'special adjudicators' who deal only with appeals involving asylum, and that all people refused asylum in the UK and required to leave the country have some chance of appeal.

There are three separate types of appeal for refused asylum-seekers:

- **people who have come through another country** ('safe third country cases'). People who have come through any European Union country or any other country the Home Office lists in an Order (currently the United States, Canada, Switzerland and Norway) have no right of appeal while they are still in the UK. They can be sent back to the country they came through and can only appeal from there. People who have come through other countries not listed in the Order are able to appeal while still in the UK, under the 'fast-track' system.

- **when the Home Secretary 'certifies' a claim for asylum** falls within specific categories, there is only a 'fast-track' appeal against refusal, with no right to apply for leave to appeal to the Tribunal. This includes people who are to be sent back to a country in which it 'appears' to the Home Secretary that 'there is in general no serious risk of persecution' (the 'white list' countries). These countries are at present Bulgaria, Cyprus, India, Ghana, Pakistan, Poland and Romania, but others could be added at any time. It also includes people who arrived in the UK without passports or with invalid passports and people whose fear of persecution is not for one of the five reasons listed in the UN Convention on Refugees. The only exception is where there is a 'reasonable likelihood' that people have been tortured in the country to which they are being sent. Advisers should therefore obtain medical evidence as a priority wherever possible. Decisions may be delayed if there is a date fixed for a medical examination or report.

- **other asylum refusals**, whether the application was made on entry to the UK, or after arrival in the country when the person still had leave to remain. People have to lodge appeals within seven days and if they lose before a special adjudicator they may apply for leave to appeal to the Tribunal. People who applied for asylum when they did not have leave to remain will not have an appeal then but will have an appeal against deportation or removal and can argue their asylum claim there.

▶Full details of the appeal systems are discussed in chapter 16.

When applications are successful
If refugee status is granted

If the Home Office gives refugee status, it will state this on a standard letter and refugees will be given permission to remain in the UK for four years. The letter explains that they have been given refugee status under the UN Convention, that they have full rights to live and work and to claim benefits in the UK, that they are entitled to grants and to home fees as students, and gives details of the Refugee Council and World University Service as organisations giving advice on benefits and education respectively. Near the end of that four-year period they may apply for settlement, and this is normally granted, although there is no provision in the immigration rules for this. If they have been out of the UK for long periods, usually of more than three months, the Home Office may grant an extension rather than settlement. For example, JCWI knows of an instance of a refugee being refused settlement and being granted a further year's extension of stay, because he had been out of the UK for over a year. He had been visiting his sister, who had recently been able to leave Somalia for Italy and was applying for asylum there. Any such refusals should be contested.

There was an argument that all people recognised as refugees who had been receiving urgent cases rate income support while their asylum application was pending could make backdated claims for the full amount of income support for that period. JCWI knew of one successful claim, but in November 1996 Social Security Commissioner Howell, in decisions CIS 564/94 and CIS 7250/95, rejected this argument. People who applied for asylum after 5 February 1996, who did not then qualify for benefits but who are later recognised as refugees, may make backdated claims for urgent cases income support for the period of their application or appeal, within 28 days of their refugee status being granted.

A person recognised as a refugee is also entitled to a travel document from the authorities of the country which has granted asylum; this is known as a 'Convention travel document' or CTD. Since 19 August 1996, the Home Office issues machine-readable dark blue documents; previously, they were pale blue cardboard-covered ones. Refugees are entitled to these documents but there have often been long delays before a document is issued. At the time of writing, delays were about six to eight weeks. The documents are valid for all countries except the one from which the person needed asylum and entitle the refugee to travel and to return to the UK within the period of leave given, without needing a visa.

Refugees may also be required to register with the police. The Refugee Council will pay the police registration fee for refugees who are on benefits.

Few people are recognised as refugees – only 1,960 in the first eleven months of 1996, 6% of decisions made.

Exceptional leave to remain

If refugee status is not granted but the Home Office believes it would be wrong to force the person to return at the time, a lesser status called 'exceptional leave to remain' may be granted. It is given either because of the general situation in a country, or on an individual basis, normally for a year at first and then for two periods of three years. People should use official Home Office application forms, and may apply for settlement after seven years' exceptional leave and this is normally granted.

The Home Office sometimes makes statements that a whole group of people will be covered by a policy of granting exceptional leave to remain. This was granted, for example, to Poles who were in the UK before March 1983, Tamils from Sri Lanka who arrived before May 1985, until December 1992 to Lebanese people who had a fear of returning during the civil war, Kuwaiti citizens after the Iraqi invasion (but not automatically to people of other nationalities who had been resident in Kuwait), Chinese citizens who were in the UK before 4 June 1989 and Liberians during the 1990 civil war. A new status, called 'temporary refuge', was invented for the Bosnian ex-detainees allowed to come in 1992–94. It was given for six months initially.

When such an exceptional leave policy has been announced, it is not normally necessary for a person who falls within its remit to make a detailed application for asylum to the Home Office. A statement that he or she qualifies under the policy, with a brief outline of the reasons, should suffice. However, if the person might in fact qualify for refugee status and wants to attempt to obtain this, full details should be sent.

Exceptional leave may also be given for personal or compassionate or humanitarian reasons. This status is granted entirely at the discretion of the Home Office and there is no provision for it in the immigration law or rules, or in international conventions. The Home Office has stated that in the past exceptional leave was sometimes granted because delays in dealing with asylum applications made it impracticable to remove people. It made a policy decision at the passage of the Asylum and Immigration Appeals Act to grant it much more rarely. In the first half of 1993, 76% of decisions on asylum applications were to grant exceptional leave; in the second half, it was 22%, while outright refusals rose. By 1996, only 14% of decisions were to grant exceptional leave.

The Home Office may expect people granted exceptional leave to continue to use their national passports. If the country of origin of a person granted exceptional leave will not issue or renew a passport, the Home Office will normally issue a travel document. It usually requires written confirmation from the authorities of the country concerned, usually its embassy in the UK, that a passport will not be issued and may ask for details of the reason and urgency of the travel, before issuing a document. From 1 January 1994 the Home Office has stated that this policy will be rigidly enforced for those granted exceptional leave to remain before the Asylum and Immigration Appeals Act, but those granted exceptional leave after 26 July 1993 should be given travel documents with less trouble. It also raised the fees for these non-Convention travel documents and made them non-refundable if the document is refused. These travel documents are brown-covered, again machine-readable from 19 August 1996, and are valid for all countries except the person's country of origin and for the same length of time as the exceptional leave to remain. People may travel and re-enter the UK without visas within the time granted to stay.

Stateless people allowed to remain in the UK under the provisions of the 1954 UN Convention on Statelessness may be issued with a red-covered travel document. These are rare, as there is no provision within the rules or policy guidelines for making applications under this Convention.

Family reunion

People with refugee status The spouse and the children under 18 of a person granted refugee status may have travelled to the UK together with the refugee, in which case they will be granted permission to stay for the same period as the refugee. If they apply to join the refugee later, they have the right to do so. If they require visas, these should be granted simply on establishing the relationship; there is no visa fee. It is not necessary for a refugee to prove that she or he can support and accommodate the spouse and children. However it is Home Office practice not to make this exception when a refugee marries after being granted asylum. The spouse would need to apply for entry clearance and meet all the other requirements of the immigration rules.

There is no right for any other members of the family to come and they normally have to wait until they fit into the immigration rules. Elderly parents, for example, can only come to join their adult children once the son or daughter has gained settlement, normally after four years as a refugee.

People granted exceptional leave to enter or remain have no right to be joined by any family members. If the whole family has travelled to the UK together and one member has been granted exceptional leave, it is usual for the spouse and children to be granted this too. However, if the other family members have remained outside the UK they are unlikely to be granted entry clearance. The Home Office has stated that family reunion will not normally be allowed until the person with exceptional leave has been in the UK for four years, and the other criteria of the immigration rules on families, most importantly that there is adequate support and accommodation for the family, are met.

The Home Office first stated that such applications would be considered when Sri Lanka was made into a visa country in 1985. People who could prove 'severe hardship' through being separated from family members could apply in Colombo but very few visas have been granted on this basis.

Families may make applications for entry clearance to join someone with exceptional leave earlier than this, but the Home Office will only grant the application if it can be shown that there are 'compelling compassionate circumstances'. The Home Office did not, for example, consider the case of a Kurdish child who had cerebral palsy compelling enough; neither was his death considered compelling enough to allow his brothers and sisters to join their parents afterwards until the family's solicitors had begun a judicial review application. This rigid operation of the policy creates a very difficult situation both for families abroad and for the person here. Refugee community groups and others have been campaigning against this and it has now become somewhat easier for children to join parents when both are in the UK with exceptional leave.

From 1988 until 28 January 1994 the Home Office operated a concession for Somali family members, in Somalia, or in refugee camps in Ethiopia or Djibouti, who were unable to travel to a British embassy to apply for entry clearance. Their sponsors in the UK were able to apply to the Home Office for entry clearance on their behalf and provide the documents here, so that the Home Office could then inform the British post that entry clearance should be granted. This made the process easier for displaced families for a while, but the concession was withdrawn when the Home Office believed it had become safe for people to travel again. The Home Office also argued that, when it refused applications, there was no right of appeal unless the family members made a further visa application abroad, knowing it would be unsuccessful, and then appealed after the inevitable refusal. The courts have agreed with this interpretation, thus making family reunion almost impossible.

The families of asylum-seekers, that is, people whose asylum applications have not yet been decided, have no right to come to the UK to join them. If families manage to arrive, and explain at the port that they are coming to join an asylum-seeker, it is probable that they will be given temporary admission to remain until the main applicant's case has been decided. They will then be granted leave in line with him or her if the application is granted. However, there is no automatic right for them to be allowed in and they can be refused entry at a port or airport. In that case, they may wish to apply for asylum in their own right, even if the danger they would face is mainly because of their connection with the relative they are coming to join, so that this application can be considered too.

Other rights connected with asylum

People granted either refugee status or exceptional leave to remain are entitled to claim any welfare benefits in the UK, on the same basis as other residents. This does not affect their immigration status. They will be treated as home students for the purposes of assessment for fees for studies. Asylum-seekers however will be treated as overseas students until they have been given leave to enter or remain. People with refugee status become eligible for consideration for student grants straight away; people with exceptional leave have to wait for three years. Refugees and people granted exceptional leave to remain are both free to work without needing work permits.

Transfer of asylum

People who have been granted asylum in one country may wish to transfer their asylum to another country. If they have obtained asylum in the first country to which they went but have many relatives in another country, or if there is a much larger community of their nationality or religion in another country, they may wish to change their country of asylum. Transfer of asylum is always difficult, as most countries do not wish to add to their refugee population. People have to make a very convincing case to show that they are having difficulties in their country of first asylum or have very strong connections, usually immediate family, in the second country.

Loss of asylum

Once a government has granted a person refugee status, it will not normally revoke this because of any change in the country of origin which may later make it safe for the person to return. Under the UN Convention, a person may lose refugee status after it has been granted if he or she is convicted of any crime which would have excluded him or her from being granted refugee status, but this has so far been rare. The Home Office standard letter to people granted refugee status makes mention of this possibility, particularly in relation to political activities, but this seems mainly designed to discourage refugees from political activities, and to stress fears about terrorism, rather than because any action will be taken.

Refugees can themselves renounce their asylum if they wish to return to their country of origin or again use their national passports. When refugee status is granted, the Home Office will normally keep the person's passport, if it was available at the time of decision, and will issue on request a refugee travel document, which is valid for every country except the one from which asylum was granted. By requesting the return of a passport, or going back to the country, the person shows that he or she is again seeking the protection of that country and has therefore lost refugee status. However, the permission to remain under British immigration law remains the same. A refugee who was settled in the UK but who returned to his or her own country remains settled and is subject to the normal returning resident rules. These state that a person must return to the UK within two years of leaving and must intend to return for the purpose of settlement; ▶see page 229 for further information. People who were refugees who go back to their country of origin will not have any special consideration on returning to the UK.

People with exceptional leave to remain normally still use the passport of their original country. If they travel to any other country, they should be readmitted to the UK if they return within the time limit of their previous permission to enter or remain. However, if they return to their country of origin this could be dangerous, as they may be refused re-entry, on the grounds that they no longer need an exception to be made as they have shown it was safe to return, or they may need to make a new application to re-enter on asylum grounds. This will be considered by the Home Office on the basis of their current circumstances. If they are readmitted without serious problems, it may be more difficult for them to gain an extension of their stay in the future. It will be clear from their passport that they have travelled back to the country to which they said they could not return, and the Home Office may ask more questions to determine whether it is now safe for them to return permanently. If the country is one for which there is a blanket policy, and if there was an emergency reason for travel there, such as the serious illness or death of a close relative, further leave will probably be granted but this cannot be assumed.

SECTION 3: THE EUROPEAN ECONOMIC AREA

6 The European Economic Area

European Community (EC) legislation and British immigration law are not always compatible. This is not surprising, because they are based on completely different premises. One of the aims of the European Union (EU – the term more commonly used for the European Community since the Maastricht treaty) is to minimise barriers for EU citizens travelling between EU countries for what are defined as economic purposes. On the other hand, the aim of British immigration law is principally to deter economic migration from people who are not EU nationals. Where the two systems of law clash, Community legislation in theory overrides individual national laws.

The countries of the EU in January 1997 are Austria, Belgium, Denmark, Finland, France, Germany, Greece, Ireland, Italy, Luxembourg, the Netherlands, Portugal, Spain, Sweden and the UK. There are applications for membership from several other countries, including Cyprus, Hungary, Malta, Turkey and several in eastern Europe, but joining is usually a long-drawn-out process which has to be agreed by all existing members. Citizens of EU countries are, by and large, able to move freely between all other EU countries and the individual national immigration laws do not apply to them.

From 1 January 1994, five of the European Free Trade Association (EFTA) countries – Austria, Finland, Iceland, Norway and Sweden – joined with the EU to form the European Economic Area (EEA). Nationals of these countries have the same freedom of movement rights as EU citizens. Liechtenstein joined in May 1995; Switzerland in a referendum decided not to. Although Austria, Finland and Sweden joined the EU from 1 January 1995, Iceland, Liechtenstein and Norway did not, so the EEA remains a separate entity.

There are also Co-operation Agreements or Association Agreements between the EU and a number of other countries. The Association Agreements with Turkey, Bulgaria, the Czech Republic, Hungary, Poland, Romania and Slovakia and the Cooperation Agreements with Algeria, Morocco and Tunisia give workers or business people from these countries some varying extra rights in the EU ▶see page 123. New agreements are under negotiation with Slovenia, and some Middle Eastern countries.

European institutions

The EC was set up in 1957 by the Treaty of Rome, which provided for the gradual reduction of barriers to free movement of workers, capital, goods and services between EC countries. An amendment to the Treaty, the Single European Act (SEA), came into force from 1986. The intention of this Act was to create a single internal market in goods and services and the free movement of people within the whole EC area, by harmonising the laws of the individual countries in specific areas.

The next European agreement, the Maastricht Treaty on European Union (TEU) was ratified and came into force on 1 November 1993. Under this treaty, the EC was subsumed into the European Union. It covers economic policies, including freedom of movement of workers and visa policies. The general body of law which has been agreed before then, however, is still known as Community legislation. Under the terms of the justice and

---

HISTORICAL BACKGROUND TO THE EUROPEAN ECONOMIC AREA

1957 Treaty of Rome set up the **European Economic Community** (EEC), also called the Common Market, of France, West Germany, Italy, Belgium, the Netherlands and Luxembourg

1973 UK, Ireland and Denmark joined EEC

1986 Single European Act which joined the EEC (now including Greece, Portugal and Spain) and other European treaty groups, to be called the **European Communities** (EC)

1993 Maastricht Treaty on European Union ratified by UK; EC now subsumed into the **European Union** (EU). The Treaty came into effect throughout the member states on 1 November 1993.

1994 EU joined by Austria, Finland, Iceland, Norway and Sweden to form **European Economic Area** (EEA). Nationals of all these countries had full EU migration rights.

1995 Austria, Finland and Sweden became full members of the EU. Liechtenstein joined EEA.

1996/ ongoing Intergovernmental Conference discussing amendments to the
1997 Maastricht treaty.

BUT because the law relating to the free movement of EU nationals was developed during the period of the European Economic Community, it is still called Community or EC legislation. The EC is now the first of the 'three pillars' of the European Union and is the term used when discussing economic policy, which includes the free movement of EEA national workers and visa policies for other nationalities. The 'second pillar' is the Common Foreign and Security Policy (CFSP) and the 'third pillar' Justice and Home Affairs matters, which include refugee and immigration policies. Some campaigning groups urge that all migration policies should come under the 'first pillar' as this means that they would be subject to the jurisdiction of the European Court of Justice. The term EU is used when discussing the three pillars together.

home affairs pillar of the TEU, common policies on immigration and refugee issues are negotiated by the member states under a procedure known as 'intergovernmental cooperation.' The Maastricht treaty is subject to periodic revisions and developments, and is currently being discussed in the ongoing Intergovernmental Conference of 1996–97.

There are several Europe-wide institutions that debate proposed change within the Union and provide for its implementation.

The European Parliament, which sits in Strasbourg but also has offices in Brussels, has directly-elected members (MEPs) from each EU country and debates proposals for change in Community legislation and resolutions on particular areas. It can investigate particular areas and produce reports. The Parliament has limited powers to initiate new legislation, or propose amendments to policies recommended by the European Commission. It can however receive complaints from individuals about EU policies and laws and, if necessary, make references to the European Court of Justice.

The European Commission, based in Brussels, is the executive cum civil service of the EC. It has 20 appointed members, representing all the EU countries, and drafts legislation for the EC. The UK's commissioners at the time of writing are Leon Brittan and Neil Kinnock, and the Commissioner mainly dealing with migration is Padraig Flynn. It has its own supporting bureaucracy, also recruited from all the different EU countries.

The European Council, also called the **Council of Ministers**, is the legislative body. It consists of Ministers from the 15 EU countries and takes the final decisions, having taken account of the views of the European Parliament.

EC policies are given effect in the administrative and legal systems of the member states through **regulations and directives**, which are proposed by the European Commission and agreed by the European Council. Regulations are 'binding in their entirety and take direct effect in each member state'. This means that each country has to take immediate measures to bring them into force. There are regulations on the freedom of movement of workers, and the rights of workers to remain in a member state after finishing employment there. Directives are 'binding as to the result to be achieved', meaning that countries may use different means to bring them into force. There are directives on the right of establishment for the self-employed and service providers, and on limitations on the right of free movement for reasons of public policy, public security and public health. In immigration matters, Britain incorporated provisions of directives by section 7(1) of the Immigration Act 1988, which came into force on 20 July 1994. The delay appeared to be because the Home Office had difficulties in working out a way to do this compatible with the rest of the immigration control system.

The European Court of Justice (ECJ), in Luxembourg, decides on legal cases brought under Community law. Its interpretation of Community legislation has to be followed by individual countries. Under Article 177 of the Treaty of Rome, national courts and tribunals at any level can refer cases to the ECJ for a ruling on the Community law implications of a judgement; governments may also seek rulings from the Court.

All these institutions decide matters of Community law. However member countries still keep their own individual laws for areas which are not covered by the Community. This includes laws which relate to non-EU citizens, including therefore migration and asylum laws and procedures. The governments consult with one another regularly through a number of official and semi-official coordination groups. From 1 November 1993 such groups were formalised in the K4 Committee, set up under Title VI of the Maastricht treaty. This covers migration and justice matters, under the Council of Interior and Justice Ministers, and has set up a series of Steering Groups. Steering Group I, formerly the Ad Hoc Immigration Group, is responsible for asylum and immigration matters, with subordinate working groups on such subjects as asylum, immigration policy, control of external frontiers, visas and information clearing houses. These working groups can produce policies to be agreed at European six-monthly summits by the representatives of the governments concerned, who then take the decisions back to their own national governments for implementation.

The working groups are therefore a way around the normal EC institutional procedures. They remove the exclusive right of the European Commission to propose and introduce legislation, and also avoid debate in the European Parliament and the judicial control of the European Court of Justice. They contribute to the process of making immigration laws more uniform throughout the EU and the process of harmonisation of laws between the countries is a continuous one.

Freedom of movement

The Treaty of Rome provided for the freedom of movement of goods, services, capital and workers between EC countries. The definition of workers included only EC citizens and not other people living in any EC country, who are known in EU terminology as 'third country nationals'. The definition now applies to nationals of all EU and EEA countries. People holding valid passports as citizens of any individual EU country are Union citizens; each EU and EEA country has its own citizenship law establishing who are its citizens. In other respects it is a broad definition, as 'workers' includes:

- people who have a job to come to, or who are working
- people who are involuntarily unemployed and are looking for work in another EEA country
- people who have worked in the UK but are unemployed by reason of permanent disability through illness or injury, or who have reached retirement age

- people who wish to set up a business in another EEA country
- people who wish to be self-employed
- people who are coming to provide services.

Three more EC directives, on the freedom of movement of students (93/96/EEC), retired people (90/365/EEC) and other self-sufficient people (90/364/EEC), have been in force since 30 June 1992 and extend free movement rights to:

- students enrolled at recognised educational establishments for the principal purpose of following vocational training courses, who have sufficient resources to avoid becoming a charge on public funds and who are covered by sickness insurance
- people who are receiving invalidity or retirement pensions which are sufficient to support them without becoming a charge on public funds and who are covered by sickness insurance
- any other people who have the resources to support themselves and their families without becoming a charge on public funds, and who are covered by sickness insurance.

Under the terms of the SEA and the TEU, the EU institutions sought a more general 'right to travel' across frontiers between the member states which would extend to third country nationals as well as EU citizens. Article 7A of the TEU asserts that 'The Community shall adopt measures with the aim of progressively establishing the internal market over a period expiring on 31 December 1992...the internal market shall comprise an area without internal frontiers in which the free movement of goods, persons, services and capital is ensured'. However, the member states have not yet agreed the common terms for immigration controls at their external borders and as a result immigration controls at internal frontiers remain in place throughout much of the EU.

There is no political and administrative agreement on the meaning of the right to free movement within an EU which has no internal frontiers. In the English courts, in the case of *Vitale* (1996 Imm AR 275) it was held that the creation of a 'European Union citizenship' under the terms of Art 8A of the TEU had not led to a general right of free movement and establishment in addition to the right of freedom of movement for workers. In the joined cases of *Castelli* and *Tristan-Garcia* however, the Court of Appeal ruled that the mere fact that an individual was unemployed and not actively seeking work, and had been required to leave the UK by the Secretary of State, did not render that person unlawfully resident and outside the provisions of EU law. A subsequent Court of Appeal decision in the cases of *Remelien* and *Wolke* allowed the possibility that an EU national who was not working and who had been required to leave the UK could be deprived of social security benefits. This is despite the fact that, following the decision in *Castelli* and *Tristan-Garcia*, such a person had to be regarded as lawfully resident in the country. The situation is therefore still unclear.

The European Commission has attempted to break the deadlock on this issue by proposing a series of three 'Right to Travel' directives which, if enacted, would lead to the dismantling of immigration checks at EU border crossings. The Dublin European Council meeting of December 1996 considered a proposal that the right of movement across internal frontiers should be added to a separate chapter of a revised Treaty, with states being given the opportunity to opt out. The question will remain controversial.

Entry procedures

EEA citizens do not require permission to enter the UK and no formal time limit can be put on their stay. When they enter the UK, their passports are not stamped though they may be given a form explaining their status and the process for applying for a residence permit should they wish to do so. They are free to remain in the UK, to work or to study and do not need to apply for any further permission to stay, as this is an automatic right under Community legislation. They are eligible to claim most benefits on a similar basis to people settled in the UK. The European Court of Justice agreed in the case of *Antonissen* (191/89, [1991] 2 CMLR 373) that UK legislation giving the power to require an EC national to leave if he or she has not been able to find work or live on anything other than income support within six months and is believed to be without reasonable prospects of employment is not contrary to the Treaty of Rome; see pages 121–2 and 189–90 for more details.

Individual countries do have the right to restrict some jobs to their own nationals, but these areas are defined in Community legislation. Some public service jobs, for example, may be restricted, but only those which involve the official in some exercise of discretion. Because of this provision, from 1 June 1996 the UK has restricted recruitment to higher-level civil service jobs to British nationals; previously, Irish and Commonwealth-country citizens had also been eligible. From 1 January 1994, citizens of all EEA countries have had freedom of movement throughout the EU and EEA areas. Only EU citizens have the right to vote in European and local elections if they are living in a different EEA country from that of their nationality.

Residence permits

EEA citizens may find it useful to have a document to show to anyone who has the right to request proof of identity or of status in the UK, for example a Benefits Agency official when the person is claiming benefit. In the UK, this is known as a residence permit and is a small dark blue folded card, including a photo of its holder. It is not compulsory and does not in itself give permission to the EEA national to remain. It is merely a document confirming the right that the person already has through the operation of Community legislation. Its main uses are as an identity document, as an aid to gaining settlement (see below) and as evidence of status should the EEA national wish to be joined by family members who are not themselves EEA nationals.

EEA citizens carrying out any kind of economic activity may obtain residence permits from the Home Office. In practice, the European Directorate at the Home Office is unwilling in many instances to issue residence permits to people who are not actually working at the time they apply, even if they have a lengthy record of employment in the UK. The permits of people who are self-employed or carrying out business are confusingly known as right of abode certificates. Application forms EEC1 can be obtained from the Home Office. If the person is working, the employer needs to confirm this fact, or if studying, the college. If the person is self-employed, evidence of the financial state of the business will be required. The Home Office also requires two passport-size photos and evidence that the person is an EEA national (normally a valid passport) and then issues a residence permit. These are normally valid for five years. EU directives allow a permit to be issued for a lesser period, of one year, if the person concerned is on a fixed term contract of employment which is for a period of one year or less. If the person is a seasonal worker who will remain in the country for less than three months, there is no requirement for the issue of a residence permit.

After four years holding a residence permit, EEA nationals may apply for settlement. This will be granted if they have been working or doing business for most of the four-year period. Absences for up to six months do not constitute a break in this period and part-time employment also counts. Though the immigration rules state that the person concerned should have been issued with a residence permit to qualify for settlement after four years, it is unclear whether this is a correct interpretation of relevant EU law. As a residence permit merely confirms the right of residence, derived directly from the terms of the Treaty, it would seem unreasonable to make the possession of such a document the route for obtaining permanent settlement rights. Evidence of employment throughout the relevant four year period should serve as well as a residence permit in support of an application for indefinite leave to remain.

Appeals for EEA citizens

Community legislation provides that EEA citizens have the right of appeal against any decisions made against them in the exercise of their free movement rights. This gives them more rights than others under British immigration law. EEA nationals do not require leave to enter, because they have rights to do so under Community legislation, incorporated into British law since 20 July 1994 when section 7(1) of the Immigration Act 1988 came into force. They can only be refused entry on grounds of public policy, public security and public health and these have been restrictively defined in European case law. There should also be no checking of EEA nationals at the internal borders of the EEA, other than seeing the outside of their passports to show their nationality, so it is unusual for them to be refused entry. In cases where EU nationals, or third country family members, are refused entry, they have a right of appeal to the Tribunal and may remain in the UK while the appeal is pending.

EEA citizens also have a right of appeal against being refused a residence permit or the curtailment of a residence permit. Under the Immigration Act 1971 people only have a right of appeal against refusal if they had leave to remain at the time they made the application that was refused. As EEA citizens do not have or need leave to remain, the Home Office has instituted a special review procedure for EEA nationals, who can apply direct to the Immigration Appeal Tribunal if they are refused a residence permit or if their permit is curtailed.

Deportation of EEA citizens

EEA citizens who are exercising free movement rights can only be deported for reasons of public policy, public security and public health. They cannot be deported for remaining in the UK without leave, because they do not require leave, or for claiming benefit. They will always have a right of appeal against deportation. Section 5(1) of the Immigration Act 1988, which restricts rights of appeal for people who have been in the UK less than seven years, does not apply because the deportation is not on the grounds of overstaying or breaking conditions of stay. 'Public policy' has been defined very tightly by the European Court of Justice, in the case of *Bouchereau* (C–30/77, 1981 2 All ER 924). This decided that an EC citizen cannot be recommended for deportation solely because of a criminal conviction, for example, but only if the person's continued presence in the UK can be shown to be detrimental to the UK.

Family members

Under Community legislation, the families of EEA nationals who have travelled to another EEA country for any purpose provided for in Community law are entitled to go to that country and to remain on the same basis as the EEA national. This applies to family members whether or not they themselves are EEA nationals. Family members who are visa nationals can be required to have visas before entry, but they must not be charged a fee for them and the issuing of the visa must be expedited.

Since 20 July 1994 family members entering the UK have been required to have an 'EEA family permit', a document created under the Immigration (EEA) Order 1994. This is an entry clearance sticker, endorsed to show that it is an EEA family permit for non-EEA national family members, and must be issued free. If the EEA national in the UK has a residence permit, the Home Office will grant family members residence permits for the same length of time.

UK citizens living in the UK do not count as EEA citizens for this purpose because they have not moved to the UK to work and therefore are not exercising free movement rights. However, a UK citizen who also holds the citizenship of another EU member state can benefit from EU citizenship status when, for example in issues of family reunification, this is more advantageous than UK law. In this way, for example, dual Irish/British citizens, even if they have lived in the UK all their lives, can have their family reunion applications considered under EU law. Home Office procedures for dealing with these dual national cases are considered below.

The family of an EEA national worker is defined in Regulation (EEC) 1612/68 as:

- a spouse
- children and grandchildren up to the age of 21 automatically; children over 21 if still dependent
- dependent parents, grandparents and great-grandparents
- other relatives who had been living 'under the same roof' or if they are dependent (this has not been more closely defined).

The definition of 'family' is slightly different for EEA nationals in the UK under the provisions of the later directives on students, retired people and others ▶see page 115. For students, only the spouse and their dependent children are covered. For retired people and others, family is defined as the person's spouse, their descendants who are dependants and dependent relatives in the ascending line of the EEA national or the spouse. They must all be covered by sickness insurance.

These people have the right under Community legislation to travel with, or to come to join, an EEA national who is engaged in any economic activity in any other EEA state. They do not have to fit into any requirements of British immigration law to do so; the primary purpose rule, for example, does not apply to spouses of EEA nationals. They will be allowed to enter or to remain for the same length of time as the EEA citizen. The only evidence the Home Office will need is evidence of identity, of the relationship and of the economic activity of the EEA national. Thus, for example, if a Ukrainian overstayer marries an EEA national who is working in the UK and applies to remain with her, the Home Office should not ask further detailed questions about the relationship but will grant leave to remain for the same length of time as the EEA national. However, the Tribunal held in the case of *Wong* (R12602) that the Home Office could interview couples to decide whether their marriage was one of convenience, as this would not give the non-EEA national rights of appeal under Community law.

Dual British/EEA nationals

In May 1994 the Home Office started to give family members of dual British and EEA nationals the choice of being treated under Community or British immigration law; this is most frequently relevant to Irish nationals.

Spouses may therefore opt to have their cases considered under the immigration rules ▶see page 18, when they may be given a year's stay if they meet all the requirements, and apply for settlement at the end of the year. Alternatively, they may, along with their spouses, be given five-year residence permits if the spouse is economically active. Although Irish nationals and other settled EEA nationals do not need residence permits, those who wish to be joined by non-EEA family members can apply for them, and their family members would also be granted residence permits for the same length of time. If they did not do this, family members would have to qualify under the British immigration rules for families.

Irish citizens are also in a special situation because there is no immigration control between the UK and the Republic of Ireland, and citizens of both countries are entitled to move and live and work in the other. No time limit is placed on their stay and they are automatically settled from arrival. People born in Northern Ireland are usually British citizens as well ▶see chapter 17. If they travel to Britain without any connection with another EEA country they have not therefore moved between EEA countries and do not gain EEA rights.

The Immigration Appeal Tribunal, in *Sahota* (13299) and *Zeghraba* (13448), disapproved of the Home Office practice of offering a choice of laws, ruling that the exercise of EU rights is not a matter of choice on the part of the people concerned, but of the proper interpretation of their position under the relevant provisions of Community law. Therefore, if Irish nationals fall within the provisions of EU law, as they always must, this standard should be applied.

British immigration rules regarding family members are more restrictive than the Community rules; for example, a British citizen living in France and engaged in any economic activity there has the right to be joined there by her husband, even if he was refused permission to join her in the UK under the primary purpose rule. The case of *Surinder Singh* in the ECJ, discussed in the Annex to chapter 2, decided that Community law also applies to British citizens who, after the exercise of their European free movement rights, return to the UK. After such a couple have lived and worked in another EEA country for some time, generally considered to be at least six months, they can return together to the UK under Community law, because the wife has exercised her rights of free movement.

In *Surinder Singh*-type situations, the issue arises as to the type of residence permit which should be granted to the third country spouse of a British citizen on return to the UK from another member state. Home Office practice is inconsistent here; in some cases granting leave for one year, followed by indefinite leave if the provisions of the immigration rules on spouses are met; in other cases granting a residence permit for five years in line with EU directives on residence permits. Arguably neither approach is correct. When the family's status depends on the residence status of the EU national family member, then the third country spouses of returning British citizens should be given an indefinite right of residence on arrival. This position follows on from argument relating to the family members of Irish nationals and dual nationals, considered above.

Public funds

EEA nationals are not required to satisfy immigration officers that they can support themselves without recourse to public funds. They are therefore eligible to claim any benefit, at any time, if they meet the qualifying conditions for the benefit. EEA citizens who are signing on and genuinely looking for work are entitled to income support/income-based jobseeker's allowance whether or not they have a residence permit. However, like all claimants, from 1 August 1994 EEA work-seekers have had to show that they are 'habitually resident' in the Common Travel Area of the UK, Ireland, the Channel Islands and the Isle of Man. The government's stated intention behind this change, which is discussed in more detail in chapter 10, was to disqualify some people, in particular EEA nationals, from claiming if they had not lived in Britain for long, or worked here.

The Department of Social Security guidance to Benefits Agency staff suggests that six elements of people's situation should be considered – their 'centre of interests', whether they have a permanent job, the type of job done, their intentions, their reason for coming to the UK and the length and continuity of their residence in the UK and elsewhere. The validity of the habitual residence test under Community legislation was challenged in the case of *Getachew* (QBCOF/95/1106/D), as it curbs freedom of movement rights and indirectly discriminates against other EEA nationals who are less likely than British or Irish nationals to meet the requirement. The case was lost in the Court of Appeal on 24 October 1996, the court holding that EEA work-seekers, as opposed to EEA workers, had no right to equal treatment in benefits entitlements. However, the Social Security Commissioners referred the case of *Swaddling* (CIS/7201/1995) to the ECJ in December 1996, on these grounds that the habitual residence test is a deterrent to the exercise of free movement rights. This case concerns a British citizen who had been living and working in France but was made redundant there, returned to Britain and was refused income support on the grounds that he was not habitually resident.

The Social Security Commissioners have accepted that EEA nationals do not require leave to remain. Thus as long as they are workers or pass the habitual residence test they are not initially considered 'persons from abroad' for benefits purposes ▶see chapter 10. However, the Employment Service offices have instructions to inform the Home Office when EEA nationals claim income support/JSA(IB) for more than six months and when they believe that the individual concerned has no 'genuine chance' of employment or is not 'actively, persistently and seriously' seeking work. Lone parents, who are considered unlikely to find employment because of child care responsibilities, are an example of the first category and people who are chronically ill an example of the second. If people do not have residence permits and have not worked in the UK, the Home Office may send them letters 'requiring them to leave the UK' and further income support/JSA(IB) may then be refused.

There is evidence that the Home Office has required EU nationals to leave the UK even when they have worked, if they have subsequently been unemployed and in receipt of benefit and, in the opinion of the Secretary of State, have no prospect of further employment. This controversial practice has not only led to the curtailment of benefit rights (subject to a right of appeal to the Social Security Appeal Tribunal) but also to refusal of family reunification for third country national family members when the EEA national is not currently in employment. There are challenges before the Immigration Appeal Tribunal in a number of such cases.

The point of the Home Office letters is to scare the claimants and to enable income support payments to be stopped; there are no effective practical sanctions the Home Office can take to enforce their departure, though if income support is refused they may have difficulties in remaining. The legality of this process is being contested in the cases of *Wolke* and *Remelien* who are applying to the House of Lords at the time of writing. If people remain in the UK after being 'required to leave' and then engage in any economic activity, they become entitled to residence permits and no further immigration action can be taken against them.

Once a residence permit has been granted, this is convenient evidence for the Benefits Agency of people's status and their eligibility to claim. EEA nationals cannot be deported solely for claiming, although they must be exercising their Treaty rights of free movement. Thus it is safe for EEA nationals to claim income support/JSA(IB) between jobs when necessary, as long as they are not voluntarily unemployed, or to claim benefits, such as family credit, as well as working.

EU nationals: the UK's definition

Each EU country has the right to determine who are its nationals for EU purposes, within common parameters. The Maastricht Treaty on European Union defined the rights connected to Union citizenship: to travel to, and live in, other EU member states, to vote and to stand for election in local and European Parliament elections in the country where they are living, to have diplomatic protection in other non-EU countries where their own country is not represented, to petition the European Parliament and to complain to the European Ombudsman. In practice, these rights add little to the rights of European nationals already defined in the Treaty of Rome and Directives.

The UK's definition of British nationals for EU purposes is:

- British citizens (excluding those from the Channel Islands and the Isle of Man)
- British subjects with the right of abode (see glossary)
- British Dependent Territories citizens connected with Gibraltar; it was decided that as Gibraltar is a territory in Europe its people should have free movement rights.

All other British nationals (►see chapter 17) are *not* EU nationals.

Many people living in the UK are *not* EU nationals. They include:

- people living in the Isle of Man and the Channel Islands, because these islands have their own immigration and citizenship laws; other EEA nationals are not able to go to live there either
- other kinds of British nationals
- Commonwealth citizens with the right of abode in the UK who are not British
- other people settled in the UK who are not British.

All these people are not EU nationals and do not have freedom of movement rights. They have no rights in the other countries of the EEA. They need to fit in to the individual countries' immigration laws in order to travel there.

Other EU countries with overseas responsibilities have also defined their nationals for EU purposes. France, for example, has defined people from Guadeloupe and Martinique as Union citizens but not people from other overseas areas. Portuguese citizens from Macau are Union citizens.

Association and Co-operation Agreements

The EC negotiated agreements with several countries which give their nationals some advantages in migration or work matters. The British immigration rules refer to the Association Agreements with the Czech Republic, Poland, Romania, Slovakia and Hungary, implemented in 1994–6, and a similar agreement with Bulgaria has since been signed. These Association Agreements provide for nationals of these countries to come to the UK as business persons without having to have the £200,000 capital demanded of others, and, for all except Hungarians, to come as self-employed persons. They may be given leave to enter for a year initially, and an extension of stay for three years, then settlement after a total of four years and on showing the Home Office audited accounts. The EC-Turkey Association Agreement, in force since 1980, does not give Turkish citizens rights to come to the EC. However if they have been working with permission in an EU country for a year they have the right to continue in that job for a further three years. This was confirmed by the case of *Kus* (C–237/91) in the ECJ, when a Turkish man who had been allowed to work in Germany because of his marriage to his German wife was allowed to continue to work and live in Germany after his divorce. A further case, *Sevince* (C–192/89), confirmed that Turkish citizens who have worked legally in a job for three years are entitled to change employment in the same field and after four years may remain and work in any job. The Association Agreement could therefore be relevant to a Turkish national admitted, for example, as a spouse for a 12 month period, who worked for this period, but whose marriage has broken down. In such cases the person would lose the possibility of remaining on the grounds of the marriage, but might acquire further leave to remain if the employers confirm that they wish to continue the employment. Similarly, a Turkish national who has completed at least one year of a work permit should not lose the right to remain in residence if the Overseas Labour Service of the Department for Education and Employment refuses to extend the work permit. Provided the employer wishes to continue the employment, the Home Office may be required to grant further leave to remain under the provisions of the Association Agreement.

The Co-operation Agreements with Algeria, Morocco and Tunisia, made in 1987, do not confer any rights to enter or to continue to work. They prohibit discrimination against nationals of those countries and their families 'as regards working conditions or remuneration' and in the field of social security, in relation to other EU nationals, provided they have been working with permission. The Co-operation Agreement with Yugoslavia was suspended in 1991, but new agreements may be made with the independent states. The Euro-Mediterranean Partnership was developed at a conference in Barcelona in November 1995. This aims to bring all the countries adjacent to the Mediterranean into a network of co-operation agreements with the EU. The existing Co-operation Agreements appear to be providing the model for this process, with the possibility that service providers, if not workers, will have some degree of free movement.

Negotiations for a new agreement between the EU and the group of countries collectively known as the African, Caribbean and Pacific (ACP) countries began in 1997. With the object of drafting a fifth Lomé Convention, ACP countries have served notice that they intend to negotiate for higher levels of protection in EU law for their nationals living and working in the member states. This could lead to developments similar to the Co-operation Agreements.

The removal of internal frontiers

The Single European Act of 1985 was intended to provide for an area without internal frontiers, with the free movement of goods, capital, workers and services between the twelve EC countries. 1 January 1993 was the target date for this but it was not met. Maastricht measures working towards European union have also not been implemented. The British government's view is that the agreements do not mean the end of immigration checks at the UK's borders. It has continued to carry them out for people travelling within the EEA. EEA nationals are normally only asked for proof that they are EEA nationals – to show the cover of their passport from one of the 18 countries – but others are still subject to full immigration examination. The European Commission has stated that it does not endorse the continuation of such checks. A judicial review application claiming that these checks are unlawful, *ex parte Flynn* (1995 Imm AR 594), was unsuccessful.

The Schengen group

All the EU countries except the UK and Ireland are members of a core group known as the 'Schengen group' because the original agreement to set it up was signed in the Luxembourg town of Schengen. This agreement dates from 1988, when five EC countries completed negotiations for an internal market and barrier-free zone between them. By 1993, all the EC countries except Denmark, Ireland and the UK had joined the Schengen group; Denmark and the other Nordic countries joined in April 1996.

The agreement came into force on 26 March 1995 for seven countries (Belgium, France, Germany, Luxembourg, the Netherlands, Portugal and Spain), theoretically making a border-free zone between them and common criteria for nationals of other countries coming in to them. At the time of writing, France had not opened its borders with the Benelux countries, because of fears of drug dealers, and there is no uniformity of treatment of other third-country nationals wanting to visit any Schengen country.

Third country nationals as service providers

Service providers are defined in Community legislation as a special category of workers who reside in another member state for a temporary period whilst they are providing a specific service. Typical service providers are employees of companies based in a member state who have been sent to a second state to provide a service for a finite short or long period.

The ECJ has accepted that such service providers need not necessarily be EU nationals. This principle was first considered in the case of *Rush Portuguesa* (C–113/89), which concerned the residence status of Portuguese national employees of a Portuguese firm with a contract for civil engineering works in France. At the time, the transitional conditions which governed Portugal's admission to the EC allowed freedom of movement for self-employed workers and service providers, but not for Portuguese workers seeking employment with employers based in France. The ECJ ruled that the status of the company as an undertaking lawfully entitled to provide services on a commercial basis in another member state was sufficient to secure a residence status for its employees who were providing those services.

In a further case, *Vander Elst* (C–43/93), a Belgian employer won recognition from the ECJ that the firm's Moroccan employees who had been directed to provide services on its behalf in France were entitled to consideration for their position in that second country under the provisions of Community legislation, rather than French domestic employment law. By these decisions, it is arguable that there is a right for third country national employees of an undertaking in a member state to travel to, and trade on behalf of their company in, a second member state. However, Article 59 of the EC Treaty, which deals with service provision, sets out the possibility that rights might be extended to third country national service providers, but only with assent to an amendment to the Treaty. To date, no agreement on such an amendment has been forthcoming.

Future developments

Refugees and asylum-seekers are likely to face even greater problems in gaining refuge in the EEA. The Dublin Convention, agreed in June 1990, signed by all EU countries but not yet ratified by all, provides that if one EU country refuses an asylum application no other EU country should then consider the person's case. People would therefore have only one chance of gaining asylum in all EU countries. Although the Convention is not yet in force, most countries, including the UK, have incorporated similar provisions into their national laws, so that their practice already excludes asylum-seekers (▶see chapter 5). Thus countries which had more liberal practices are becoming more restrictive, to reduce numbers of asylum-seekers because of pressure from countries with harder-line policies.

Immigration laws of individual countries are being harmonised so that there will be similar requirements for entry to all countries. For example, there is now an 'EU common visa list' of countries whose nationals require visas to come into any EU country. It includes most black and Third World countries. The UK implemented it from April 1996, when 14 new countries were added to its visa list. There are also proposals for a 'Eurovisa' to allow people to visit all countries of the EU with a single visa, and to give a permitted stay of up to three months in total, rather than the present British maximum of six months. These are not yet in force.

Because the procedure of intergovernmental groups drafting Conventions to be agreed by all countries has been so slow and ineffectual, the European Commission has begun to try to carry out Community policy by preparing new Directives itself, rather than leaving it to intergovernmental processes. It produced three proposals for directives in July 1995:

- a directive on the elimination of controls on persons crossing the internal frontiers of the Union. The UK government opposes this, and to be enforced it must be agreed unanimously.

- amendments to the directives on movement and residence of workers and the self-employed, to bring them into line with the abolition of internal frontiers

- a directive on the right of third country nationals to travel in the EU. In general, this would entitle people to travel for three months in the territory of the EU, without being subject to border checks.

The Commission set the target date for implementation of these directives as 31 December 1996. This target was not met, but discussions on these and other proposals continue. The European Council meeting in June 1996 passed a resolution listing 12 priorities for co-operation in immigration and asylum matters, to be implemented in the next two years. These included harmonisation of procedures for granting asylum and alternative protection and of conditions for the reception of asylum-seekers. In December 1996 it discussed proposals for change in the European treaties to develop 'an area of freedom, security and justice, in which the free movement of persons would be ensured', which would include the abolition of controls at internal borders, and to prohibit discrimination based on grounds including race, ethnic or social origin or sex.

In summary, the laws and procedures in relation to EEA nationals, and increasingly all immigration laws, are subject to change from different sources in Europe, rather than primarily from the Home Office and the British Parliament. The processes of change may be very slow, but it can be even harder to keep abreast of discussions and developments.

SECTION 4: NON-EEA WORKERS

7 Workers and business people

The following groups of people do not need specific permission to work in the UK:

- people who are settled (allowed to stay permanently)
- people who have been allowed to enter or remain to join close relatives settled in the UK, for example husbands and wives, and have been allowed in for a year initially
- people granted refugee status or exceptional leave to remain
- Commonwealth citizens who have been allowed in as working holiday-makers or because they had a grandparent born in the UK
- other people who have no restriction or prohibition on working stamped on their passports

These are all people who have been able to come to the UK for some other reason but are able to work.

It is very hard for non-EEA nationals to be allowed to come to the UK *in order to* take up work. British immigration law and rules on coming to the UK to work are designed mainly to protect jobs in the UK for people already allowed to live and work in this country, and to encourage investment in businesses only from people with a very substantial amount of money to invest. The work permit scheme is not designed to help people to come to work in the UK. It ensures that employers will only go through all the paperwork and delays involved if the worker is essential. People may only come to set up a business or to live off their capital if their means are substantial; the only provisions for people from abroad to set up small businesses are for Poles, Bulgarians, Czechs, Romanians, Slovakians and Hungarians, under Association Agreements with the European Community.

Workers

The work permit scheme

Work permits are granted to employers by the Department for Education and Employment (DfEE), not the Home Office. In May 1989 that

Department published a discussion paper on changes in the scheme, in order to streamline it and to make it easier for transnational companies and large employers to transfer workers. The results were announced in February 1991 and most of the scheme came into effect on 1 October 1991. The main proposed change that has still not come into force was charging employers fees for work permits; in March 1991 the Department suggested that this should not be more than £100.

How the work permit scheme operates

Work permits are issued to employers, not to workers, to enable them to employ a named worker in a particular job at a particular rate of pay. They thus give extremely specific permission and if the worker changes jobs, even within the same company, a new permit is necessary. Permits are issued by the DfEE Overseas Labour Service, not by the Home Office. The possession of a work permit means that the immigration authorities should allow the person to enter the UK, or to remain, in order to do the job.

Employers have to apply to the DfEE for a work permit. They obtain application forms from the Department's central distribution service in Bristol but return them to the headquarters in Sheffield ▶see chapter 19 for addresses. The application form for most work permits is form WP1, which comes with an explanatory leaflet WP1/5; the form for training and work experience permits is WP2. There is a specific form for entertainers, sportspersons and models (WP3) and an extra one for footballers (WP4). The forms come with explanatory leaflets about the scheme and it is important that employers do their best to comply with the requirements or the application may be rejected out of hand.

From 1 October 1991, there has been a two-tier system, making it easier for employers to obtain permits to employ workers in high-level posts. Part 1 includes transfers within transnational companies, board level posts, posts involving substantial financial investment in the UK and 'occupations which are acknowledged by the industry or profession as being in acute short supply nationally and likely to be so within the EEA'. The DfEE has a special register, which is frequently updated, of occupations which it considers to fall into this category. A recorded telephone message at the Department on 0114 259 4203 gives current information. These 'shortage occupations' are very restricted; in January 1997 they included only some specialities in NHS medicine and nursing and professions ancillary to medicine, and veterinary surgeons. They may alter at short notice.

When a job is listed as falling in this category, the employers only have to fill in part of the WP1 form, to show the level of the job and the experience and qualifications of the person concerned, and to show how it falls into one of these categories. The employers do not have to show in so much detail that they have advertised the job or attempted to train other workers to do it. It is still necessary to provide some evidence to show that the job could not be done equally well by someone resident in the EEA, so it is not a foregone conclusion that the 'resident labour test' will be waived. However the Department says these permits will be issued 'with the minimum of checks'.

Part 2 covers all other jobs. The DfEE publicity makes it clear that permits will not be issued for manual, craft, secretarial or similar-level jobs, nor for resident domestic workers such as nannies and housekeepers. Permits may be issued for 'keyworkers', who are defined as 'overseas nationals having technical or specialised skills and expertise essential to the day-to-day operation of the company'. They have to possess particular skills, knowledge or experience, and the employer has to show that the jobs of other people depend on them. These permits may also be issued to people with extensive knowledge of languages and cultures outside the EEA who will spend at least 60% of their time using this knowledge, and to some senior workers in the hotel and catering industry, such as hotel managers, head chefs and senior waiters and reception staff, with at least five years' experience abroad. There are stringent advertising requirements to show that no resident or EEA worker could be found. Keyworker permits are issued for a maximum of three years and the workers are expected to train a person as their replacement during that time.

The main requirements of the scheme in general are:
- the worker from abroad will not be taking a job which could be done by anyone already permitted to work in the UK or by an EEA national. Employers are required to sign a declaration confirming that no other worker has been displaced by the worker from abroad.
- the job must be one requiring a degree or equivalent professional qualification; or senior executive or administrative skills; or for highly qualified technicians with specialised or rare skills
- the person must usually have had at least two years work experience, normally abroad, in a similar job to that for which a permit is now being requested. The DfEE requires original written proof of these jobs from previous employers and of academic qualifications. The employer's word is usually accepted when the application is for an inter-company transfer or a Part 1 job. People in the UK as students or visitors will not normally be permitted to change to employment. Experience gained in the UK illegally, or while here temporarily free to work, for example as a working holidaymaker, will not normally be considered.
- the person must have all the skills and qualifications necessary for the job. Permits are normally only given for highly skilled professional jobs, so evidence of studies and qualifications may be very important.
- there must be a genuine vacancy
- for jobs in Part 1, the employer has to show either that the employee has been employed in a sister company abroad and is required in the UK, or that the job is one at board level and there is no other suitable candidate,

or it is essential to new foreign investment and creation of jobs in the UK, or the job is on the acute skills shortage list
- for jobs in Part 2, the job must normally have been advertised in appropriate newspapers or professional or trade journals which are also available in the EEA (*both* of these for keyworker jobs), with at least four weeks allowed for responses.

This may be a problem when a person is in the UK already and doing the job, or has been offered the job before the fact of needing a work permit was known. The form requires evidence of all the attempts made to find someone already allowed to work, including copies of the advertisements, details of the response to them, including how many respondents were EEA nationals, and explanations of why the other applicants were not suitable.

The DfEE states that applications will normally be decided within six to eight weeks, but if another government department is involved it may take longer. Hotel and catering applications may take three months.

Applying when the worker is abroad

People coming to work need entry clearance. A work permit counts as prior entry clearance for non-visa nationals; visa nationals need visas as well. Normally people have to be outside the UK while the employer is applying for the work permit. If the Overseas Labour Service grants the permit, it sends it to the employer, who sends it to the worker abroad.

Applying in the UK

Since 1 October 1991, any application for a work permit or for an extension of a work permit holder's permitted stay is made direct to the DfEE, not to the Home Office. It is therefore very important that the application is made while the person's leave to remain is still valid, so that he or she remains legally in the country while the application is pending and does not become an overstayer. The person's passport does not need to be sent with the application, but after the application has been decided, the employer will be told to send the passport to the Home Office.

It is very rare for a person in the UK for some other purpose to be granted leave to remain as a work permit holder. The immigration rules do not permit people who entered without the appropriate work permit or entry clearance to remain as workers and it is very difficult for people who entered for any other purpose to be allowed to stay for work. If an employer applies for a permit for a person who is in the UK at the time, without a work permit, the DfEE may recommend a permit but the case then must be referred to the Home Office to decide whether to grant the person leave to remain. The Home Office can refuse to grant leave to remain to take up the job even if the DfEE has recommended that a permit be granted. Applications may be started when the person is in the UK, then the DfEE be informed, with proof, that the person is leaving or has left the UK at the time the application is likely to be decided. If the permit is granted, the person may then return.

When a permit is granted

If the worker is not a visa national he or she needs no further documents except a passport in order to come to the UK. A visa national needs a visa as well, but will be given it on application to the British embassy or high commission, provided the job is still available. Work permit holders arriving in the country can be refused entry by immigration officers if it is believed that false representations were employed in order to get the permit (even if they did not know that this had been done) or that the job is no longer available, or if any of the general grounds for refusal (▶see pages 222–3) apply. If the permit is for less than 12 months, they also have to satisfy the officers that they intend to leave at the end of the period of employment.

The worker will be admitted for a period of four years, unless the permit is for a shorter period, when the worker will be admitted for this period. During this time, it is possible for the person to stop working and to remain in the UK legally, but only to change jobs if the new employer first obtains a new permit. The same criteria apply to the new application, except that the worker does not need to be outside the country while the application is pending, having already obtained entry clearance for the purpose of work. Because of the requirement of previous experience abroad, changes of employment will usually only be allowed within the same type of occupation.

Extending a permit

Work permit application forms require the employers to specify the period of employment. They are not able to state 'indefinitely' but have to justify the period requested. The DfEE expects that most permits will be required for a short, finite period and employers will have to make out a special case for a permit for permanent employment. The 1991 regulations state that only 'in exceptional circumstances will permits be granted or extended for the four year period which can qualify the overseas national to apply for indefinite leave to remain in the UK'. Keyworkers are normally given permits up to a maximum of three years and are expected to train their replacements in this time. If a permit is granted for a limited period and the employers want to continue to employ the worker there is a specific form, WP5, to apply for an extension. The employers must again show why this is necessary, for how long and why it has been impossible to train, transfer or recruit a local replacement for the job. When there is a strong case for an extension, it may still be granted.

Work permit holders pay national insurance contributions and tax. They are therefore entitled to any benefits for which they qualify as a result of their contributions. They also have the same rights under employment law as any other workers; the work permit does not alter any contract of employment or remove any trade union, employment or negotiating rights. However, workers who wish to continue to live in the UK may be deterred from making complaints by the fact that the permit depends on the employer and their chance of remaining in the UK depends on keeping a work permit.

Families of work permit holders

The wife or husband of a work permit holder qualifies under the immigration rules to come to live with the permit holder in the UK. So do the unmarried children under 18 of work permit holders, provided both parents are living, or coming to live, in the UK. Family members must also obtain entry clearance from the British embassy or high commission before travelling. They will have to prove their relationship to the work permit holder, that they intend to live together with the work permit holder in the UK and do not intend to remain longer than him or her and that there is adequate support and accommodation for them in the UK without recourse to public funds (see box on page 180 for definition). There are more details about the procedures in the chapters on spouses and on children. No other relatives have any claim under the rules to join a work permit holder before he or she is granted settlement.

Work permit holders' passport stamps will usually state that they cannot take employment paid or unpaid without the consent of the Secretary of State for Employment and that they cannot do business without the consent of the Home Office. Their families' passports will usually just be stamped with a time limit, in line with the work permit holder's. Before 1 October 1994, the immigration rules specifically stated that the spouse and children of work permit holders should not be restricted from taking employment. From 1 October 1994 the rules state nothing about permission to work for family members but the Home Office states that its practice will be not to impose restrictions where these are not specifically mentioned. The spouse of a work permit holder is therefore free to work without needing a permit in his or her own right. From 8 November 1996 permit-holders and families may also have a condition requiring them to maintain and accommodate themselves without recourse to public funds; this means only public funds as defined in the immigration rules ▶see chapter 10. The children are entitled to state education from the ages of 5 to 16. The permit holder and any family members are entitled to National Health Service medical treatment immediately on arrival.

Settlement

After four continuous years working in a job or jobs for which permits have been granted, the worker will qualify to settle. Near the end of the four years the worker must make an application to the Home Office for permission to settle, on the official Home Office application form SET(O), enclosing his or her passport, confirmation from the employer that the job is still continuing and all the other documents requested on the form. If there have been periods of unemployment, or periods when the person was working without a permit, these may not count towards the four years; the person may have to work again for a four year period, with a work permit, in order to qualify for settlement. In practice, a short period of under three months without a job should not be counted as a break in employment but the person should explain the reasons for any longer absence on the form. Any other family members who have been admitted to be with the work permit holder should apply for settlement in line with him or her, on the same form. If the children of work permit holders have become 18 during the four years of the permit, they will be allowed to settle with the rest of the family, provided they are still unmarried and financially dependent.

Permit-free employment

The immigration rules list a number of occupations for which work permits are not necessary, and the immigration authorities deal with applications for people to come to do them. These jobs are known as 'permit-free employment' and are normally jobs for which it is unlikely that someone already resident in the UK will qualify. People coming for any of these jobs need to obtain entry clearance from the British high commission or embassy in their country of origin, but the employers do not need to apply to the DfEE. The person will need confirmation of the job offer and should then fill in the application forms IM2A and IM2C at the British embassy or high commission and pay the fee (see appendix). The entry clearance officer may refer the application back to the Home Office to confirm details of the job or the employers before making a decision about granting entry clearance.

The occupations which can be considered for permit-free employment are:

- **ministers of religion**. The rules now give a definition of the Home Office's understanding of these jobs. A minister is 'a religious functionary whose main regular duties comprise the leading of a congregation in performing the rites and rituals of the faith and in preaching the essentials of the creed'. They have to show that they will be working full-time as ministers and that they are capable of filling the position required by the religious group requesting them to come. They will be asked for evidence of any formal qualifications and of past experience of religious work for at least one year, or that they are ordained, after at least one year's full-time or two years' part-time training, as well as for details about the job and pay offered. Pay or fringe benefits such as accommodation must be sufficient to show that they and their dependants can be supported and accommodated by the religious community or denomination which will employ them. The community needs to show that there is a genuine need for the person to come to work there. The entry clearance officer will require a letter from the religious group giving full details of the position offered.

Although the immigration rules specify that entry clearance is necessary, in the past the Home Office might, exceptionally, consider applications made on behalf of ministers of religion who are already in the UK as visitors. Congregations may have invited priests from abroad to visit, to see if they are mutually compatible, and then decided to offer them a post. It was possible for this application to be considered in the UK without the visitor having to leave and for permission to remain as a minister of religion to be granted, provided the other criteria of the rules were satisfied.

The Home Office changed this policy from 20 June 1995. From that date, it stated it would only consider applications within the UK when 'a bona fide minister of religion had been granted a visa or leave to enter as a visitor specifically to attend an interview for a job in the UK as a minister and was offered the job; or... specifically for a preaching tour of the UK, was asked to fill a vacant post as a minister in this country, the job offer appeared to be genuinely unexpected at the time the applicant entered the UK and there were good community relations reasons for allowing him to stay.' Thus most ministers need to have entry clearance for this purpose in advance of travelling.

When the Home Office considers such applications, it has a standard letter and list of questions which it sends out to religious organisations applying for a minister to remain to work with them. It appears to assume that applications where detailed questions will be necessary are from smaller and non-mainstream religious groups. It asks organisations, among other things, to 'state the number of people employed by the place of worship/organisation, and say what their duties are' and 'give the date when the organisation/place of worship became established in the UK and details of all properties it owns, and the use to which these are put', as well as questions about the specific duties of the post and whether it is a newly-created one or, if an existing one, why the previous post-holder has left.

In practice, it may be more difficult for people from non-Christian religious organisations and non-mainstream Christian churches to convince entry clearance officers or the Home Office of their status.

- **missionaries**. A missionary is defined as 'a person who is directly engaged in spreading a religious doctrine and whose work is not in essence administrative or clerical'. They have to show evidence of previous experience or training in missionary work, and must be sent to the UK by an overseas organisation.
- **members of religious orders**. They may come to live in a monastery or nunnery and be part of its life, or to teach in a school run by the order and part of it. If they are teaching in an outside school, the school must obtain a work permit to employ them. It is assumed that the religious order will be providing board and lodging for its members.

- **representatives of overseas newspapers, news agencies and broadcasting organisations** on long-term assignments to the UK. Their permanent employment will be with the organisation abroad and they must have been engaged outside the UK but their place of work will be the UK for prolonged periods.
- **representatives of overseas firms which have no branch or subsidiary in the UK**. The firm must be based overseas and the representative must be an existing senior employee with the power to make decisions and negotiate on behalf of the company. The Home Office sends out a standard letter to inquirers, explaining the documents needed for entry clearance, about the person and about the company. The representative must be a full-time employee and may not be a majority shareholder in the firm. During the first year, the representative is expected to set up a registered branch or wholly-owned subsidiary of the company in the UK, and to continue to run it.
- **private servants of diplomats**. They must be at least 18 years old, and be employed full-time as a servant of a diplomat or of a family member forming part of the household of a diplomat, for example as a housemaid or a chauffeur. They are not exempt from immigration control (see below) because they are employed by an individual diplomat, not by the embassy or high commission. It is therefore not possible for someone who is exempt from control through a job at an embassy or high commission to change status within the UK to work for an individual diplomat, as entry clearance was not granted for this purpose.
- **operational ground staff of overseas-owned airlines**. They must have been transferred to the UK from work abroad for an airline which operates services to and from the UK, at a level of station manager, security manager or technical manager at an international airport and will be working full-time in that job.
- **people employed by an overseas government or a United Nations organisation or other international body**. These are people who are not formally diplomats, but are based overseas and have formal contracts of employment with the international body or overseas government, not with the embassy or high commission in the UK.

All these people will be admitted for a year at first. They may apply for an extension for a further three years, on Home Office application forms FLR(O), and at that stage have to show the Home Office that they are still working in the relevant job and that all the same requirements, apart from entry clearance, have been met. The spouse and unmarried children under 18 of all these people may also be allowed in to join them, provided that they obtain entry clearance and can be supported and accommodated, in accommodation owned or occupied exclusively by the family ▶see chapter 11, and do not intend to remain in the UK longer than the worker's period of permission to remain. If only one parent is in the UK, children have to meet either the 'sole responsibility' or 'exclusion undesirable' criteria ▶see chapter 3. The rules from 1 October 1994 state nothing about whether family members are allowed to work; in the past, they were free to work and the Home Office has continued this practice. After four years' continuous work in the category, and provided the person is still working and the employers confirm that the person's work is still required, the worker and family can be granted indefinite leave to remain.

Short-term workers

Some people may be admitted to work for short and clearly-limited periods. The following categories of short-term worker do not need work permits.

- **teachers and language assistants** coming to schools in the UK under official exchange schemes approved by the DfEE or the Central Bureau for Educational Visits and Exchanges or the League for the Exchange of Commonwealth Teachers. Two years is the maximum period they will be permitted to stay.
- **seasonal workers at agricultural camps** under Home Office-approved schemes. These are mainly people coming to help with harvests. They must be students in full-time education abroad, aged between 18–25 (unless returning at the specific invitation of a farmer for whom they have worked before) and hold valid 'Home Office work cards' issued by the operator of an approved agricultural work camp scheme. They cannot be allowed to remain for more than six months or beyond 30 November of any year. Time as a seasonal agricultural worker will count as time as a visitor, so they cannot add to the six-month period.

People allowed to work outside the immigration rules

Voluntary work

The Home Office may allow people to come to the UK for voluntary work. They are advised to apply for entry clearance, with proof of the work they are coming to do, and each case is considered individually. Volunteers must be working for a charitable organisation, receiving no remuneration other than pocket money, board and accommodation. The work they do must be closely related to the aims of the charity and they must not be doing clerical, administrative or maintenance work. The maximum period allowed is 12 months and volunteers are expected to leave the UK at the end of this time, and are not able to take or seek full-time employment.

Academic work

After students have completed higher degrees, universities may want to continue to benefit from their research and knowledge. It may be possible for the university to obtain work permits for students to stay on outside the rules as lecturers/demonstrators and to be paid for this work, because of the very specialised knowledge and experience required. They do not need to be outside the UK while the application is made, and it is possible but rare for an international student's status to be changed in this way.

Visiting academics may also be allowed to work in the UK but without needing work permits. These would normally be people employed and paid by a foreign university, coming with entry clearance to do academic work or research for an academic year and allowed to do this exceptionally, outside the immigration rules, for this period.

Domestic workers

There is no provision in the immigration rules for domestic workers to come to the UK, other than those working for diplomatic families. Work permits for this type of work have not been issued since 1980. However it is well known that servants come into the UK with their employers. This is completely outside the immigration rules, and is a concession to rich or expatriate families who want to continue to employ servants who have worked for them overseas. The Home Office formalised this concession from May 1991 and produced an information leaflet for domestic workers, copies of which should be given to the worker and the employer when the worker is granted entry clearance.

Under the terms of the concession:
- the worker must be at least 18 years old
- if the employer is visiting the UK, the worker must have been employed by that employer for at least 12 months
- if the employer is coming to the UK for any other purpose, the worker must have been employed by that employer for at least 24 months
- the worker must have entry clearance before travelling to the UK. The employer must give a written undertaking to provide adequate maintenance and accommodation, including a separate bedroom, for the worker, and set out the main terms and conditions of employment in writing. The worker must have a copy of this statement, and confirm that he or she agrees to it. The British embassy or high commission should check the type and hours of work involved, and that the worker wants to come to the UK. The British post must interview the worker, at least on the first application for entry clearance, to ensure that she or he understands the position.
- both worker and employer must be given, and confirm they understand, a brief leaflet explaining the position. The leaflet was revised in February 1996 and explains that workers will not be permitted to change employment in the UK but if they lose their job they can remain for the period of permission granted provided they can support themselves without working. It also tells the worker that 'everybody in the UK has the full protection of the criminal law' and that it is against the law to 'keep you locked in the house against your will; or have sex with you without your consent; or behave violently towards you'. It is not clear how many

workers actually see, or are able to keep or understand, this leaflet.

When a domestic worker arrives in the UK, the immigration officers usually give him or her leave to enter for the same length of time as the employer. If the employer is a visitor, the domestic worker's passport will also be stamped for six months, with a prohibition on working, paid or unpaid, except for the named employer. If the employer is a British citizen or settled in the UK, the worker will normally be given leave to enter for a year, with the same employment conditions. The worker may apply to the Home Office to extend this leave, on form FLR(O), and the application is likely to be granted provided the employer still lives in the UK and continues to employ the worker. The Home Office information leaflet states that if domestic workers apply for settlement after four years' work for the named employer, and the employer still wishes to continue to employ them, the application may be granted. Form SET(O) should be used.

Because this concession is completely outside the immigration rules, these workers have no rights. They have no right to change their employment and applications to do so will be refused, so the workers are completely dependent on their employers' goodwill. If they lose their jobs, or have to leave because of unbearable treatment and exploitation, they do not qualify for leave to remain in the UK or to claim welfare benefits such as income support and are in a very vulnerable position. Any application they make for further leave to remain in the UK on compassionate grounds, or to pursue any criminal case against their employers, is made exceptionally, outside the rules.

Some campaigns for exploited workers have been successful. There is a support group, Kalayaan (meaning freedom in Tagalog, one of the main languages of the Philippines), for exploited workers, and those who have been forced through ill-treatment to leave their employers ▶see chapter 19 for address. The group provides moral and physical support and refers people for legal help and advice. It has members from many different nationalities.

Exemption from control

Diplomatic work

Diplomats and others working at embassies or high commissions in the UK do not need work permits, because under international law they are considered to be employed in the country of the embassy. Their admission to the UK is therefore mainly the responsibility of the Foreign and Commonwealth Office, which is given lists by the countries concerned of their diplomatic staff. They require entry clearance explaining their status, but this will be granted on proof of their employment. The entry clearance states that they are 'exempt' from immigration control and therefore their passports are not stamped, or may be stamped only with the date, when they travel into the UK. They may remain as long as they are employed by the embassy or high commission. Time spent working while exempt from immigration control does not qualify a person for settlement under the rules but can count under the 10-year concession see pages 238–9.

When a person who is exempt from control leaves the job at the high commission or embassy, for whatever reason, the exemption continues until the Home Office specifically cancels it. When the Home Office is informed that the job has ended, it will remove the exemption, and write to the person concerned to state this and to grant leave to remain for a period of 28 days, in order that the person may either make arrangements to leave the UK or make a new application for permission to remain longer. There is a right of appeal against removal of exemption, but the appeal cannot succeed unless the person is still employed in an exempt category. If the person wishes to remain longer in the UK, it is important to make a fresh application to the Home Office within the 28 days' leave granted, so that there may be a right of appeal against any refusal.

It is not possible for people who are in the UK in another capacity to change status in order to work at an embassy or high commission. They need to leave the UK to apply for entry clearance. Occasionally, if the person has been in the UK in breach of immigration control, he or she will be refused permission to return for this type of employment as the immigration authorities cannot then control how long the person remains.

Training and work experience

The DfEE operates a Training and Work Experience Scheme (TWES) to 'assist businesses and organisations in their international development and to help other countries by increasing the skills and experience of their citizens'. Under this scheme the DfEE issues permits to employers to give people the chance to have a period of training or work experience in the UK. TWES is currently under review, but no changes are expected to be announced before late 1997.

For training permits, the employers have to show that the training will lead to a recognised professional or specialist qualification at postgraduate level, that the person already has a degree or equivalent qualification, the training is for a minimum of 30 hours a week and essential for the gaining of the qualification and the salary and conditions 'reflect the normal rates applicable to the profession'. The DfEE needs to be satisfied that the firm is providing adequate training and that the person is progressing. Permits for training necessary to obtain a professional qualification, for example in law or accountancy, will be granted to cover the length of the training. People are expected to complete it in the shortest possible time and to leave the UK at the end of the period.

The length of the training does not have to be agreed at the outset because approval is given in stages depending on progress. If the qualification will take more than three years, such as accountancy or law, the person may be admitted for three years, or until shortly after the date of the first examination, and further extensions may be given to cover the next examinations, up to a maximum of six years. Extensions may be granted in order to re-sit examinations, though not more than three chances will be given.

For work experience permits, people should be between 18 and 35 and 'at or near the start of their career'. They must be in a supernumerary post, or on a one-for-one exchange, and can be paid only a 'modest spending allowance'. The length of the programme must be agreed at the outset with the DfEE and extensions will not be granted. It may be possible for students who have qualified in the UK to be granted work experience permits to obtain six months' or a year's work experience in the subject they have been studying academically, before leaving the UK. People will normally be admitted for 12 months at a time and two years is the maximum time that can be granted for work experience.

In both cases, employers need to obtain permits from the DfEE, showing that they are offering a genuine training or work experience programme to the person, why experience in the UK is needed and how it will be used abroad. It is important that both the employer and the trainee understand and sign a declaration on the application form that the employment is temporary and that the person will be leaving the UK at the end of the training period. People already in the UK as students may be allowed to switch category, but all others must ensure that their prospective employer has obtained a permit before they travel.

It is the workers' responsibility to ensure that their employers apply to the DfEE for extensions of their permit and leave to remain within the time given, so that they do not become overstayers. Home Office decisions about granting further leave to remain depend on DfEE decisions about permits. The Home Office refuses the person permission to stay if an extension of the permit has been refused. A person who 'does not hold a relevant document which is required by the immigration rules' has no right of appeal against refusal. These documents are defined as entry clearances, passports or identity documents and work permits or permissions to work after entry. Thus people whose employers are refused training permits for them will be told that they have no right of appeal against refusals of entry clearance or of leave to remain.

The spouse and children under 18 of people with training or work experience permits may be granted entry clearance or leave to enter or remain in line with the permit-holder. If they need to apply to stay longer, they must make the application to the DfEE, along with the permit-holder, *not* to the Home Office.

Student nurses

Student nurses are treated as students, not trainees, throughout their nurse training period. They deal only with the Home Office to extend their permitted stay, even though it is clear that they are working while they are training and are receiving training bursaries. The hospitals do not have to apply for permits for their student nurses. In the past, student nurses were the only people for whom the rules made provision to stay to work in the UK after the completion of their studies. Before 1 October 1994, the immigration rules allowed hospitals to apply for work permits for nurses after they had qualified, and the nurse did not need to leave the UK while the application was pending. This exception no longer exists. General nursing is no longer on the register of occupations in short supply, though some NHS specialisms, such as paediatric intensive care or mental health, are still on the list.

Other ways of being able to work in the UK

British-born grandparents

Commonwealth citizens with a British-born grandparent can come to the UK to work or to seek work. They need to prove their descent from the person born in the UK, by having the grandparent's birth certificate, the grandparents' marriage certificate, the birth certificate of the father or mother descended from them, the parents' marriage certificate and the applicant's birth certificate. If the parents or grandparents were not married, any other evidence to show the relationship will be helpful, such as affidavits from people who knew them to confirm that they are the parents, or any evidence from school or medical records showing the family connections. The person applying needs to be at least 17 years old. People coming to the UK for this purpose need entry clearance; people already in the country, for example as visitors, may be permitted to change their status and should apply on form FLR(O).

People will be allowed to enter or remain for four years, without any restrictions on employment. At the end of the four years they may apply for settlement, which will be granted provided they have been working and are able to support and accommodate themselves without recourse to public funds ▶see chapter 10.

Working holidaymakers

Commonwealth citizens, aged between 17 and 27, may be allowed to come to the UK for up to two years on a working holiday. Since 1 October 1994, they need entry clearance; they also have to show that any work they will take will be incidental to their holiday, and that they have the money to support themselves without recourse to public funds and to pay their return fare. From 1 October 1994, the rules state that they should not intend to 'engage in business, provide services as a professional sportsman or entertainer or pursue a career in the UK'. The Home Office's intention is to stop people from working throughout the two years, or taking professional jobs.

Working holidaymakers' passports are endorsed with leave to enter on condition that 'the holder does not enter employment paid or unpaid other than as a working holidaymaker and does not engage in any business or profession without the consent of the Secretary of State for the Home Department'. The Home Office states that they should not work for more than 25 hours a week or for more than half of their time in the UK. They may also have a formal condition requiring them to maintain and accommodate themselves and any dependants without recourse to public funds.

The rules about the families of working holidaymakers state that married people are only able to be working holidaymakers if their spouses also qualify and intend to be working holidaymakers too. People with children who will become five years old during their potential time as working holidaymakers are not eligible, and children will only be allowed in if they will still be under five at the end of their time in the UK. It is no longer possible to aggregate several periods of time as a working holidaymaker to make up the two years total; the time is to be counted from the first entry as a working holidaymaker.

In practice, many more white than black Commonwealth citizens have made use of this provision and the majority of the people coming have been Australians, New Zealanders and Canadians. During the 1980s and early 1990s it became more widely known, and numbers of young people from West Africa and the Asian subcontinent applying as working holidaymakers rose. The Home Office stated at that time that no centralised figures were kept for entry clearance or leave to *enter* as working holidaymakers but in 1994, 11,240 people were given leave to *remain* as working holidaymakers, including 740 from the Indian subcontinent, 660 from Ghana and 640 from Nigeria, compared with 1520 from South Africa, 1950 from Australia and 1310 from New Zealand. It is widely believed that this increase in numbers from black Commonwealth countries is the reason for the Home Office changing the rules and now requiring entry clearance. In 1995, 15,556 working holidaymaker applications in Canberra were granted and 14 refused; Kingston granted 107 and refused 7; Accra granted five applications and refused eight.

Au pairs

Young people between the ages of 17 and 27 who are unmarried, who have no dependants and who are citizens of Andorra, Bosnia-Herzegovina, Croatia, Cyprus, Czech Republic, the Faroes, Greenland, Hungary, Macedonia, Malta, Monaco, San Marino, Slovak Republic, Slovenia, Switzerland or Turkey may come as au pairs for up to two years.

Many people from EEA countries also come to the UK as au pairs but do not have to qualify formally under the rules. An au pair is supposed to be living as part of an English-speaking family and to help in the home for not more than five hours per day, with two free days per week, in return for pocket money (the Home Office suggests up to £35 per week) and board and lodging. The main purpose of his or her stay is to learn English. The two years period cannot be aggregated but is counted from the first date that leave to enter as an au pair was given. Entry clearance is not compulsory for non-visa nationals, but it is not possible to change status within the UK to become an au pair; people in the country for another purpose have to leave and then return and ask for leave to enter as au pairs.

Unauthorised workers

People who are restricted or prohibited from working under the immigration conditions of their stay do sometimes work. If they do so while their leave to remain is still current, they are committing an offence under section 24(1)(b)(ii) of the Immigration Act 1971. They can be charged to appear in a magistrates' court or the Home Office can make a decision to deport them, on the grounds of a breach of their conditions of stay (▶see chapter 14 for more details of these processes). They are therefore in a dangerous position and are liable to pressure and blackmail from employers. Unauthorised workers may be working in very bad conditions or for very low pay, but dare not take action to force improvements because they are vulnerable to the employers informing the Home Office of their work or sacking them summarily. Although unauthorised workers have the same legal rights to contest unfair dismissal etc. they are unlikely to do so as this will draw attention to their presence in the UK.

People may also be working illegally without being aware of this. Students often believe, erroneously, that they are free to work during their holidays, or that the fact that they have been able to obtain national insurance numbers gives them permission to work. This is not the case. Some students are completely prohibited from working and need to apply to the Home Office for this prohibition to be removed before they can work. Other students' passports state that they can only work with the consent of the DfEE. This means that the employer needs to obtain permission from the local Jobcentre to employ the student before the student is legally free to work (▶see chapter 9 for full details).

Overstayers who are working are not working illegally because any restrictions on working placed on their stay came to an end when the leave to remain finished. If they are caught, they can be prosecuted or deported for overstaying, but not for working in breach of conditions.

From 27 January 1997, the Asylum and Immigration Act 1996 created a new offence for an employer knowingly to employ a person who is *not* in a group listed in a Home Office Order. These groups are people 'permitted to work under the immigration rules', asylum-seekers who have written permission from the Home Office to work, and people appealing against a Home Office refusal who had permission to work before the refusal. The Home Office does not normally restrict people on appeal from working, so this creates situations when people are able to work legally but employers would be committing an offence by employing them. The Order also lists the documents which employers may check to establish whether any new employees are permitted to work. Employers must keep a copy of a document, such as a P45 or P60, or a passport or a SAL, to show that they carried out this check, as a defence against possible prosecution. If the employers carried out this check, they are not liable to prosecution even if it is later established that the person was not allowed to work.

The Home Office has stated that this provision was intended for use against particular rogue employers, such as some organisers of agricultural work gangs, and proprietors of bogus colleges. However its ambit is much wider and there are fears that it will result in more discrimination against black and 'foreign-sounding' people in recruitment. It must be monitored closely.

Business people, the self-employed and persons of independent means

Business people

The immigration rules are designed to ensure that only wealthy business people will be permitted to come to set up or to join businesses. Entry clearance is necessary. People have to show:

- they have at least £200,000 capital of their own to put into the business. This capital has to be readily available, either in the UK already or easily transferable to the UK, which can be put into the business. The immigration authorities are entitled to ask about its provenance, so borrowing money from a rich friend or having money in trust will not be adequate. The business should need this amount of new financial investment.
- they will be involved full-time in running the business, will be able to meet their share of any liabilities and there is a genuine need for their time and investment. This means that they should not have other time-consuming activities outside the UK. They will not be allowed to do other work. This is intended to ensure that people coming to do business are actually needed for the business and that this part of the rules is not being used as a way for rich people who do not otherwise qualify to come to join their relatives.
- they have a controlling or equal interest in the business with a proportionate financial investment in it, showing that they are owners of the business rather than its employees
- they have to show that new, full-time employment will be created for at least two people already living in the UK as a result of the admission of the business person from abroad

- if they are planning to set up a new business, they have to show that they have enough money left over after the investment of the £200,000 to support themselves and their family, without doing any other work, until the business can reasonably expect to make a profit
- if they are joining an existing business, they need to show its audited accounts for previous years and a written explanation of the terms on which the new partner will be joining. They need to show that the share of the profits they will receive is likely to be adequate to support them and any dependants.

Business people are normally granted leave to enter for a year initially and can apply to the Home Office, on form FLR(O), to extend this near the end of the year. If there is evidence that the business is continuing, the money has been invested and is being used in the business and the new employment has been created, an extension of three years should be granted. The spouse and children under 18 of the business person may be granted entry clearance to come to join him or her and will be granted an extension of stay in line with the business person. After four years, they can all apply to settle, and this will be granted provided the business is still continuing and is making enough profit to support them, and full yearly accounts are provided. There are separate provisions for Polish, Bulgarian, Czech, Romanian, Slovakian and Hungarian citizens, who benefit from an EC Association Agreement ▶see chapter 6.

Self-employed people

The immigration rules before 1 October 1994 provided for a separate category of self-employed people, who had to meet most of the same criteria as business people, including the £200,000 capital. It was intended to provide for people wanting to set up as professionals, for example, architects, accountants or doctors in private practice. They have now been subsumed into the business category. There is however a special concession for overseas lawyers setting up as consultants in the law of another country, who do not need to have £200,000 capital nor to create employment for anyone else.

Writers, composers and artists

There is a specific provision in the rules for self-employed writers, composers and artists to be given entry clearance. They do not need to have £200,000 but have to show that they have established themselves abroad and will be able to make enough money to support themselves and any dependants without recourse to public funds, from the proceeds of their artistic work. They are not able to take any other employment in the UK but if they also have savings or private means they may use them to support themselves as well as their art, composing or writing. Writers will not normally include freelance journalists; artists may include art photographers and sculptors but not performing artists, such as actors, musicians, dancers and singers, who need to obtain work permits. Writers, composers and artists will be allowed in for four years; the spouse and children under 18 will be granted extensions of stay in line, and they can all apply to settle near the end of the four year period.

Investors

The 1994 rules created a new category of 'investors', people who have at least £1 million of their own and disposable in the UK and who intend to bring this money to the UK and invest at least £750,000 of it in UK businesses which are not mainly engaged in property investment or in government bonds in the UK, and who intend to make the UK their main home. They are not allowed to work, but may be self-employed. They need entry clearance and, like business people, may be admitted for 12 months initially and then be given an extension for three years and settlement at the end of that time if they still meet all the requirements of this rule. The spouse and children under 18 will be granted entry clearance to join an investor and be given extensions and settlement in line with him or her.

Retired people of independent means

From 1 October 1994, people 60 years old or older who have a guaranteed income of at least £25,000 per year without working, doing business or getting help from anyone else, or claiming public funds, may be allowed to come to live in the UK. They must apply for entry clearance and show that they have the requisite amount of money and that they plan to live on it, without doing any work or business, and that this will produce enough money to support themselves and their dependants. They also have to intend to make their main home in the UK and show that they have a 'close connection' with the UK.

In the past, there was no age limit for persons of independent means. Under the previous rules, the Immigration Appeal Tribunal interpreted 'close connection' as having close relatives either settled or living in the UK for some time, for example as students, or the applicant having spent a substantial period of time in the UK in the past. An adjudicator's decision (*Sum Yee Thong*, TH/30896/87) held that having a gay partner in the UK is a 'close connection'; the Home Office was refused leave to appeal to the Tribunal against this.

The spouses and children under 18 of persons of independent means can be given entry clearance to come to join them. They will all normally be given permission to stay for four years on arrival with a prohibition on working and can apply to settle near the end of that time. This will be granted as long as the money has remained available throughout the period, they have made the UK their main home and they have not needed to have recourse to public funds.

SECTION 5: TEMPORARY PURPOSES

8 Visitors

Visitors who are visa nationals (see glossary) have to obtain entry clearance from a British high commission or embassy before travelling. Visitors who are not visa nationals do not need to obtain entry clearance but may do so if they wish or alternatively may apply for permission at a British port or airport. They have to satisfy the same requirements of the immigration rules whether they are applying in the UK or abroad. Since the 1994 immigration rules, HC 395, there have been specific rules for visitors in transit and for medical visitors, discussed below, who have to meet different or additional criteria from those visiting family or friends, or tourists.

▶See chapter 11 on the advantages and disadvantages of applying for optional entry clearance and for the procedure for applying for entry clearance and any action to contest refusals. Statistics show that there is a higher refusal rate for people applying at British posts abroad than for people applying at a port of entry, although the formal requirements of the immigration rules are the same. In Jamaica in 1994, for example, the refusal rate of entry clearance applications for temporary purposes was 1 in 7, while the refusal rate for Jamaicans arriving at UK airports was 1 in 66.

WHAT THE RULES SAY

The immigration rules on visitors state that people must:
- be genuinely seeking entry for not more than six months as a visitor
- intend to leave at the end of their visit
- not intend to take employment paid or unpaid, or to produce goods or provide services, including selling goods or services direct to the public, during the visit
- not intend to study at a state school
- maintain and accommodate themselves and any dependants from resources available to them, without working or recourse to public funds, or be maintained and accommodated by relatives or friends
- be able to meet the costs of their onward or return journey
- not be people to whom any of the general grounds for refusal apply
  ▶see pages 222–3.

If the immigration officers are satisfied that the people qualify, they may be given leave to enter for six months. A shorter period may be given if the immigration officers believe this is appropriate.

Business visitors are able to 'transact business', defined as including attending meetings and briefings, fact-finding, negotiating or making contracts with UK businesses to buy or sell goods or services. They must have their main place of business and home outside the UK and not engage directly in business here.

Transit passengers also have to show

- they are in transit to a country outside the Common Travel Area ▶see page 224 and are assured of entry there
- they have the means to pay for the ticket
- they intend and are able to leave the UK within 48 hours

Any application for an extension beyond 48 hours is to be refused.

WHAT THE RULES MEAN

People may wish to come to visit the UK for many different reasons – to see relatives or friends, purely on holiday, to make or renew business contacts, to help in a family crisis or emergency. The immigration rules are the same for visitors, whatever the purpose of the visit, but the way they are interpreted for people from different countries and economic backgrounds is very different.

The intention test

- that they are 'genuinely' seeking entry for the length of time they ask for, not exceeding six months

This is the most difficult part of the rule to satisfy, because it is a subjective test of a person's intention which cannot be proved either way. Immigration officials will go into details about the person's life and background to see if they believe the person's story. They may ask a lot of questions: why will you need to go back after only two weeks? who will look after your children/farm/business while you are away? surely you can't afford to spend this amount of money on so short a time; aren't you planning to stay longer? if you found a place to study in the UK, would you do so? They will often search luggage and read any correspondence, including letters carried by the passenger to give to other people in the UK, making inferences from what is said, or not said.

If there are definite reasons why visitors have to return, they should try to have evidence of this. For example, a person in employment could have a letter from his or her employer, confirming the length of holiday and when the person is expected back at work. A student could have a letter from the college, confirming when the next term will begin. For someone without such a structured life, it can be more difficult and immigration officers openly admit to using something they call 'nose' – their alleged sixth sense telling them when someone is not genuine. They are also encouraged to think 'would I do that?' in connection with information they are told, but they may not appreciate the differences in cultures which place greater importance on particular events. Because it is up to the visitor to prove intentions, not up to the immigration officer to disprove them, it is very easy for officers to refuse without any objective proof.

Certain groups of people are more likely to be refused because officials are not satisfied about their intentions. They are: people from poorer countries; people who are relatively poor by the standards of the country from which they come; people with many relatives in the UK, particularly if the visitors are young and single, or elderly; people with a family history of immigration to the UK; people who are unemployed or who have just finished their studies. A list is circulated to immigration officials every month of the 'top five nationalities' refused entry in that month; once a country appears on that list, its nationals, especially those in the above categories, will be subject to close examination. Immigration officers are also expected to refuse people in roughly the same proportion and may have unofficial quotas of refusals to meet.

The support and accommodation test

- that during the visit they will be able to maintain and accommodate themselves, or be maintained and accommodated by relatives or friends, without working and without claiming public funds.

This means that officers are able to inquire into the money that visitors are bringing with them and the money that their friends and relatives may have to support them. When people apply for entry clearance abroad, entry clearance officers usually require evidence of financial support. If visitors are bringing their own money, evidence such as their bank statements or a letter from their employers confirming their salary will be required. If they are being supported by friends or relatives in the UK, a letter of invitation from the person confirming willingness to support the visitor is necessary, together with the sponsor's bank statement or other evidence of resources.

Immigration officers may decide that a person has either too little money, and therefore may want to work or to try to claim benefits here, or too much money and may therefore be planning to stay for a longer period than that stated. This is a very subjective calculation; what might be considered too much money for a Guyanese citizen, for example, could be thought perfectly adequate for a North American. Immigration officers may also make suggestions, for example – would you work if you could find a job? – and use the answer, if affirmative, as a reason for refusal.

When visitors come without entry clearance, it may be useful for the sponsor to come to the airport to meet them, with evidence of the financial support available. If the sponsor does not go to the airport it is useful if the visitor has a telephone number for the sponsor, so that the immigration officers can make contact without delay, should they wish to do so.

Meeting the cost of the return journey

This usually means that the visitor should have a return or onward ticket, or the means to purchase one. However, officials will not automatically assume that the possession of a return ticket means that a person is a genuine visitor who plans to return: they may say that the return half of the ticket can be traded in if a person decides not to leave.

Length of time for visits

From February 1988, the immigration rules stated that in most cases visitors should be admitted for six months automatically, even when they intend to stay only for a few days. From 1 October 1994, the rules have been less clear, stating only that people 'may be admitted for a period not exceeding six months, subject to a condition prohibiting employment' so there is more scope for immigration officers to admit people for less than six months. However, if a visitor asks for six months, this may well be interpreted as indicating a wish to stay longer than a 'normal' visit; the support and accommodation requirements will also be much more difficult to fulfil.

Medical visitors

Medical visitors have to show, in addition to the normal rules about visitors, that:

- the course of medical treatment is of finite duration and they intend to leave at the end of it
- they can provide evidence of the medical condition requiring consultation or treatment in the UK, arrangements for private medical treatment, the estimated cost and duration of treatment and of funds available to pay for it. An undertaking of intention to pay can also be demanded.

If the person is suffering from a communicable disease, the Medical Inspector (at the port of arrival) must be satisfied that there is no danger to public health. There is nothing in the rules to state that immigration officials should take into account the availability of treatment in the person's home country. However, this is normally something that is considered if it is proposed to spend a lot of money on treatment. Medical visitors can be admitted for up to six months initially.

Working holidaymakers

The immigration rules provide for 'young Commonwealth citizens between the ages of 17 and 27' to come to the UK for 'working holidays' of up to two years. Since 1 October 1994 they must have entry clearance before travelling to the UK. They have to satisfy immigration officials that they are intending to be in the UK on holiday, that they are able to support themselves if they do not find work and that they can pay for their trip home. They have to show that any work they take is 'incidental to their holiday' and is not the main purpose of coming to the UK and that they do not intend to settle into long-term work.

Applying for entry clearance

Since the summer of 1992, visa officers in some British high commissions and embassies have operated an unofficial 'pre-sift' process of people applying for visit visas. They make an initial examination of visa applications, to decide which are unlikely to succeed. The visa officers then tell some people that they may proceed with their applications but they are likely to be refused and they might therefore wish to withdraw the applications and therefore not pay the non-refundable fee. Foreign Office instructions state that 'previous refusals, those with inadequate documentation, those producing obviously fraudulent documents and... applicants from poor backgrounds with no friends or relatives in the UK' may be treated in this way. In an experiment in New Delhi from June to December 1991, 8000 people withdrew their applications; as a result, the refusal rate fell from 15% to 9% and the High Commission believed that this was a useful economy.

The only redress people may have when their applications have been 'sifted' is to pursue a formal application, which is likely to be prejudiced by the initial officer's views. Because this takes place abroad and people often do not understand the bureaucratic procedures at the High Commissions, there has been little knowledge of or protest against this practice. It has no justification in law.

The Asylum and Immigration Appeals Act 1993 removed rights of appeal against refusal of entry clearance for visitors, prospective students and students coming for courses of six months or less. There is therefore no formal means of contesting decisions in these cases. The government set up an 'independent monitor' of refusal decisions, Dame Elizabeth Anson, previously an immigration appeal adjudicator. She reviews the papers concerning a random sample of visitor refusals, to assess whether they are in accordance with the law. In her first report, she criticised the 'pre-sift' practice and urged that applicants should be clearly informed of their right to pursue the application. She repeated this in her 1995 report, and also stated that 1% of the refusals she reviewed were incorrect in law, and in another 3–4%, the facts of the case did not warrant refusal. In 1996, she was particularly critical of refusals of elderly parents.

Arrival in the UK

Leave to enter

People who are admitted as visitors will normally have their passports stamped with the immigration officer's square date stamp, showing the date and the port at which they entered, and 'leave to enter for six months, employment prohibited'. After 8 November 1996, the stamp may be 'leave to enter for six months: employment and recourse to public funds prohibited'. ▶See chapter 13 for examples of passport stamps. *It is the passport stamp given at the airport that shows how long people can stay in the UK*, not the entry clearance from a British post overseas. The time begins to run from the date on which this stamp was given. Visitors should keep a note of this date separate from the passport so that even if the passport is lost they will know how long they can stay and when they need to apply for an extension of stay if that is necessary.

It is unusual for people to be admitted for less than six months and when this is done it shows that immigration officers were suspicious. For example, many passengers on the well-publicised charter flight from Jamaica which arrived at Gatwick airport on 21 December 1993 were given leave to enter only until 17 January 1994, the return charter date.

Transit passengers

Transit passengers will be admitted as visitors for up to 48 hours. This time will not be extended. There are special arrangements for most visa nationals not to need visas when they are in transit and booked on onward flights, normally within 24 hours of arrival. However, Immigration (Transit Visa) Orders made transit visas necessary from 22 July 1993 for nationals of Afghanistan, Iran, Iraq, Lebanon, Libya, Somalia, Sri Lanka, Turkey, Uganda and Zaire, from 24 October 1995 also for Chinese, Ghanaian and Nigerian nationals and from 1 September 1996 for Eritreans and Ethiopians. If they arrive without transit visas, the airlines carrying them are liable to the £2000 fine per passenger under the Immigration (Carriers' Liability) Act 1987. Lebanese nationals no longer require transit visas.

Work and business

Visitors are not permitted to work in the UK. This includes voluntary and unpaid work and other activities which would not normally be considered work. The Immigration Appeal Tribunal has decided that people coming intending to spend their visit looking after a relative's children cannot be treated as visitors but would be working as childminders (a job for which work permits are not available).

Visitors may transact business (such as attending meetings and briefings, fact-finding, negotiating or making contracts with UK businesses to buy or sell goods or services) provided they are based abroad. Business visitors may make or consolidate contacts in the UK, investigate new markets or learn new business techniques, but not set up in business in the UK, or set up a branch office for a business based abroad, as they would then need entry clearance as business people (▶see chapter 7).

Refusal of entry

Visitors who already have entry clearance will probably not be asked many questions by immigration officers as they have already been questioned in detail abroad. They can be refused at the airport if the immigration officer has reason to believe either that they lied, or deliberately concealed relevant information, in order to get entry clearance or that there has been a change in circumstances since entry clearance was granted, which means that the person no longer qualifies for it. If they are refused, they have the right to appeal against the refusal and to remain in the UK while the appeal is pending.

A change in the immigration rules, with effect from 1 November 1996, provides that entry clearance may be revoked if the entry clearance officer was deceived, or if there has been a change of circumstances, or if exclusion is conducive to the public good. It is not clear how an entry clearance officer would find out, nor what the effect on appeal rights would be.

Visitors who do not have entry clearance may be refused entry if they do not satisfy immigration officers that they qualify under the immigration rules for entry. If they are refused entry, they can be sent straight back without any right of appeal. Representations can be made to the immigration officers as to why they have made the wrong decision (▶see chapter 12 for further information).

The Asylum and Immigration Appeals Act 1993 removed rights of appeal for visitors refused entry when they do not have entry clearance. Thus there are no longer any formal channels for contesting such refusals, though in some circumstances judicial review may be possible ▶see chapter 16. There are many very worrying implications of this loss of appeal rights. Whenever officials are given a power with no procedures for review, they are more likely to make arbitrary decisions and refuse applications, knowing there will be no comeback on them. People from black and Third World countries are refused more often as visitors; for example, 1 in 376 Malaysians, 1 in 3202 United States and 1 in 2316 Canadian citizens were refused entry in 1995 and more than 1 in 4 Bangladeshis and Ghanaians were refused visas for temporary purposes in 1995. Even after going through the visa process, 1 in 117 Ghanaians and 1 in 236 Bangladeshis were refused entry on arrival in the UK.

Applying for extensions

WHAT THE RULES SAY

There is now *no* provision in the immigration rules for extending a visit beyond six months, except for medical visitors.

Visitors who have been admitted for less than six months initially may apply for extensions, on Home Office form FLR(O), to take them up to the six month limit. If they do this, they must show a good reason for their change of plans. The application can be granted if the total time for the visit will not be more than six months and the other requirements of the rules – about maintenance and accommodation, and about the visitor's intention to leave at the end of the visit – are still satisfied. Time spent in the UK as a seasonal agricultural worker ►see chapter 7 counts towards this six months, should an agricultural worker apply to remain as a visitor. Any applications to remain as a visitor beyond the six-month limit are outside the immigration rules, and therefore are dealt with at the discretion of the Minister. The 1994 rules state that an extension of stay 'is to be refused' if the visitor does not meet all the requirements of the rules, so extensions for more than six months may become even more difficult. The Home Office has stated that such applications will only be granted in exceptional circumstances.

This does not prevent people from applying. Provided that a valid application is made before the existing leave runs out, the visitor will be legally in the UK until a decision is made and for 28 days after any refusal decision. The Asylum and Immigration Appeals Act 1993 removed the right of appeal for those applying for a time longer than that permitted in the immigration rules, so there will be no right of appeal against the refusal. Home Office practice is to state that people should leave the country within 28 days of refusal, and they are given leave to remain for that purpose only. That means that the visitors will be able to remain legally in the UK for some time, whatever decision the Home Office makes. But if they do not leave the country, after the 28 days are over they are here without permission and the Home Office could make a decision to deport them.

People's passports will be marked to show that they have been refused an extension ►see chapter 13 for example. This may make it difficult to return to the UK, or to travel to other countries, in the future. Even if the visitors leave the UK before the Home Office replies, they will be on record as having asked for something outside the rules. The Home Office assumes that everyone knows what the rules are and that applicants for extensions deliberately asked for something which is not allowed. Officials may not be satisfied that the visitors intend to leave the UK at the end of the next visit because they did not do so the previous time.

Visitors should therefore be told about the possible long-term consequences of applying for extensions. It is important only to apply to extend a visit if it is really necessary, to set out the reasons for staying and the length of time required, and as far as possible to show that the visitors have done what they said they would do and left when they said they would.

How to apply for an extension

▶See chapter 11 about applying for extensions. It is important to be as clear as possible about the reasons for staying longer and the length of time required. People must use the official Home Office application form FLR(O) and send it to the Home Office, together with all the documents requested or explanations of why the documents are not available, before their leave to remain runs out. If they are applying for leave to remain for more than six months, they should also complete part 5.11, explaining what the special circumstances are. This may be a simple statement something like: 'I want to remain in the UK for another two months as a visitor before I have to return to college in my country' or 'I want to remain as a visitor for another three months in order to look after my sister whose baby is expected next week'. If there is any evidence to support either the reasons for the application or the necessity to leave the UK at the end of the further time, this should be sent to the Home Office. This might be confirmation of the reason why the person has to leave or a doctor's letter about any medical reasons for the visitor to remain longer. The passport must be sent to the Home Office with the application. People may request the return of their passports at any time; but ▶see pages 239–41 about the possible dangers of doing so.

There is no maximum time limit for medical visits, but in order to get an extension people have to show evidence of satisfactory arrangements for private medical consultation or treatment and its likely duration, and the progress of any treatment, from a registered medical practitioner who holds an NHS consultant post. This seems a strange stipulation, as the medical treatment must be private. They need to show evidence that they have paid past costs and are able to pay future costs of treatment and of their maintenance in the UK.

If the application is refused, as long as it was made in time, before the previous permission to stay ran out, the person will have the right to appeal against the refusal (because no time limit is laid down for medical visits) and to remain in the UK while the appeal is pending. ▶See chapter 16 for more information about appealing against refusals.

Visitors as carers

In a policy statement on carers, the Home Office confirms that allowing a person to remain must always be exceptional. The internal instructions on carers state that 'applications for leave to remain in order to care for a sick or disabled *relative* should normally be granted for a period of 3 months and on code 3 [employment prohibited]. The applicant should be informed that leave has been granted on the strict understanding that during this period arrangements will be made for the future care of the patient by a person who does not require leave to remain outside the immigration rules. Applications for leave to remain in order to care for a sick or disabled *friend* should normally be refused. However in emergency cases (eg where the patient has suddenly fallen ill and there is insufficient time to arrange permanent care whilst dealing with the immediate problems of the illness, or where there is nobody else in the UK to provide care) leave to remain may be granted for a period of 3 months as above.'

When a person is applying for leave to remain, the Home Office requires a letter from the patient's doctor, giving full details of the patient's illness and treatment, any other care being provided and the long-term prognosis. If people apply for any further extensions, the Home Office will request many more details both about the patient and the carer. Even if successive extensions are granted to a carer, the person will not qualify for settlement and will be expected to leave when the patient dies or recovers.

Visitors changing their status

The immigration rules provide for some changes of status for people who have come to visit the UK and prohibit others. The rules allow visitors:

- to apply to stay and settle with some close relatives; for example, parents coming to visit their children settled in the UK may apply to stay and settle with them (▶see chapter 4)
- to marry and to apply to stay with their spouses (▶see chapter 2)
- to apply for asylum (▶see chapter 5)
- **if they are not visa nationals**, to apply to stay as students (▶see chapter 9)

They should make applications to the Home Office, on the appropriate official Home Office form, before the time limit in their passport runs out, asking for a change of status and showing how they fit into the relevant parts of the immigration rules concerning their new status. It is important to explain why their plans have changed since they came in for the visit and what has made them decide to remain for a different purpose.

The rules do not allow visitors:

- to stay as working holidaymakers
- to stay in order to work or to be self-employed
- to stay in order to set up a business
- **if they are visa nationals**, to stay as students

This does not mean that they cannot apply for such changes, but that any application is likely to be refused, with no right of appeal. The Home Office would need to be satisfied that there were very exceptional reasons to consider granting them. People should be referred for specialist advice about the consequences of such applications.

Travel outside the UK

Frequent visits

There are no restrictions in the immigration rules on how frequently people can visit the UK. However, each time people return, they have to convince the immigration officers again that they fit into the immigration rules. Even if people just go on a day-trip to France, they need to prove all over again that they qualify to re-enter and they can be refused entry if the officer at Dover is not satisfied. It can be sensible to take proof similar to that which was used on the original entry.

Immigration officers can also consider information about past visits. This is particularly likely when people stay almost for the six-month visit limit and then return after a very short absence. For example, a person who has just spent five and a half months in the UK and has been away for three days may have difficulty in showing that he or she is a genuine visitor on return. The immigration officer may suspect that the person is attempting to get round the six-month visit period and may have other reasons for seeking to remain in the UK. This may be particularly difficult for people with close family members living in the UK.

Visa nationals

Most visa nationals need visas for every entry to the UK (►see glossary for list of visa nationals). Visa national visitors may have obtained either single-entry or multiple-entry visas from the British post which gave permission initially. A single-entry visa can only be used once. A multiple-entry visa is valid for any number of visit entries within the time for which it is given, usually six months, two years or five years. People who are considering travelling and returning to the UK should apply for multiple-entry visas initially: for example, if they are planning to go to other European countries as well as the UK, or want to go on haj with relatives living in this country and visit them before and afterwards.

Some British high commissions and embassies appear to have an informal practice of not granting multiple-entry visas until people have travelled to the UK and returned to their country of origin at least three times and have therefore established a history of keeping to the time granted them. Visitors who are visa nationals and who do not obtain multiple-entry visas have to apply to the British post in the country they visit for a new visa if they want to return to the UK. Since May 1991, it has not been possible for people to obtain re-entry visas in the UK.

SECTION 5: TEMPORARY PURPOSES

9 Students

Students and prospective students who are visa nationals (see glossary) have to obtain entry clearance from a British high commission or embassy before travelling. Those who are not visa nationals do not need to obtain entry clearance but may do so if they wish or may apply for permission at a British port or airport. They have to satisfy the same requirements of the immigration rules whether they are applying in the UK or abroad.

▶See chapter 11 on the advantages and disadvantages of applying for optional entry clearance, the procedure for applying for entry clearance and some ways of contesting refusals.

WHAT THE RULES SAY

People coming to the UK as **students** must show:

- that they have been accepted for a course of study at a publicly funded institution of further or higher education, or at a bona fide private education institution or an independent fee-paying school
- that they are able and intend to follow a full-time degree course at a publicly-funded institution, or a weekday daytime course involving attendance at a single institution of at least 15 hours organised daytime study of one subject or directly related subjects or a full-time course at an independent fee-paying school
- they intend to leave the UK at the end of their studies and do not intend to take employment or engage in business, apart from part-time or vacation work undertaken with the consent of the Secretary of State for Education and Employment
- they are able to meet the costs of the course and their accommodation and maintenance without working and without recourse to public funds
- none of the general grounds of refusal apply ▶see pages 222–3.

People who have genuine and realistic intentions of studying in the UK but who have not yet been accepted for a full-time course may be admitted as **prospective students**, for up to six months. They have to show that:

- they have a genuine and realistic intention of undertaking, within six

months of entry, a course of study which would meet the requirements of the rules
- they intend to leave the UK on completion of their studies, or on completion of their time as prospective students if they are not accepted as students
- they can support and accommodate themselves and any dependants without working and without recourse to public funds.

Students applying for courses which will last for six months or less, and prospective students, do not have any right of appeal against refusal of entry clearance, or refusal of entry if they had not obtained prior entry clearance. People who have already been in the UK for six months for any purpose will not be granted extensions of stay as prospective students.

Visa nationals who did not enter the UK with a visa as a student or a prospective student will be refused permission to change their status in the UK to become students.

WHAT THE RULES MEAN

Education institutions

All publicly-funded institutions are assumed to be bona fide, as are private fee-paying schools for children. The more detailed wording in the rules from 1 October 1994 about the type of institution students may attend appears to be aimed against adult education and community or village colleges which charge no, or lower, fees for their adult students, and which do not now meet the requirements of the rules. The Home Office does not have a formal procedure for the recognition of other private education institutions, but is believed to have its own list of institutions which it suspects are not providing education or are carrying on fraudulent practices. In 1988 there were raids at the London School of International Business and various institutions at Wickham House, London E2. Some students were arrested and others were refused extensions of stay. Some students at the Academic College of Education were refused on the grounds that the college they were attending was not adequate. However refusals of entry on the grounds that colleges are allegedly bogus are rare.

Full-time studies

Students will normally need a letter from the college at which they intend to study, confirming that they have been accepted on a particular full-time course. Depending on the college and the level of studies, the immigration authorities may also ask for details of the precise number of hours per week the student will be studying. They also need to know the level of fees and whether the whole fee, or a deposit towards this, has been paid. Universities and other institutions of higher education do not normally require students to pay a deposit.

'Full-time' for immigration purposes is defined as at least 15 hours organised daytime classes per week. Before 1 October 1994, this could occasionally be two or more part-time daytime courses at more than one institution which together made up 15 hours, if the student could show that this was the only or most convenient way to do a course. Since 1 October 1994, study must be at a single institution but can include two or more related subjects. If the full-time course is of first degree level or higher, it is assumed that the 15-hours requirement is met, even though there may not be formal classes for this number of hours.

Financial support

Students must show that they have the money to pay their fees and to live in the UK without needing to work and without recourse to public funds (▶see box on page 180 for definition). Student grants are not 'public funds' for this purpose, so students who qualify for a grant or for fees reimbursement can use this as evidence to show that they can support themselves. Overseas students now have to pay full-cost fees for their courses, which are usually several thousand pounds. Although they may be allowed to work part-time (▶see page 169 for details), any earnings from employment they may obtain will not be taken into consideration by the Home Office in assessing their financial viability. If a student's spouse has been permitted to stay in the UK with him or her and has permission to work, his or her earnings may be taken into consideration.

Students may provide evidence of their financial support in several different ways. If they are supported by a government or other scholarship, a letter from the scholarship-giving agency will probably be sufficient, confirming the amount of the money and the arrangements made about fees. If students are being privately supported, a letter from the sponsor confirming willingness and ability to support them and evidence to prove this, such as recent original bank statements or pay slips to show that money is available, will be necessary. When it is a friend supporting the student, or anyone else who has no immediately obvious interest in doing so, the immigration authorities may ask more questions about their and the student's motives. The additional requirement in the 1994 rules for students to show that they do not intend to take employment without consent from the Secretary of State is clearly connected to this but, like the intention to leave the UK at the end of the studies (see below), can create problems and the immigration authorities may interpret it in a discriminatory manner.

Ability to follow the course

Immigration officials also have to be satisfied that the student is academically able to follow the course – though they have no qualifications with which to make this assessment and may go just on their views of the student's proficiency in English when answering their own questions. The Immigration Appeal Tribunal decided in the case of *Pattuwearachchi*

(1991 Imm AR 341) that it is valid for a student coming to do a vocational course to decide at entry to follow an English language course first, and this change of plan did not invalidate the entry clearance granted. Entry clearance officers are encouraged to check with the local British Council office if they have doubts about any qualifications or certificates shown to them. Many institutions include an English language test as part of their application process.

Intention to leave the UK

Students have to show that they intend to leave the UK at the end of their course of studies.

In many cases, it is impossible to prove at the outset of a course what a person will do at the end of it and immigration officers therefore may make subjective decisions. Because official scholarship or sponsoring agencies often stipulate that a student must return, this part of the rules is rarely a problem for officially-sponsored students. However, privately-sponsored students may encounter difficulties. The immigration authorities may ask what benefit the course will be to a person after returning home and about the student's future career plans and whether the course is available in his or her home country. It may be helpful to have evidence of job advertisements from the country of origin which specify the qualification the student hopes to obtain, or even a job offer for return. It is certainly important to relate the qualifications to be obtained to employment prospects in the home country. Other evidence of commitments in the country of origin, for example having a spouse and children there, could also be helpful.

If students wish to continue to follow higher-level courses after the one for which they are seeking entry, they should explain this. The immigration authorities can decide whether these plans appear to them to be realistic either academically or financially. If a student has many other relatives who have become settled in the UK, particularly if they entered as students in the past, immigration officers may be particularly suspicious about their longer-term intentions.

Students not yet accepted on a course: prospective students

People hoping to study in the UK may not have made definite arrangements to do so before travelling. They may be travelling or intending to travel to the UK to look for a suitable course, or to come for interview at a particular institution. In these circumstances it is important that they explain their intentions to study to the immigration official and seek entry clearance or entry to the UK as a 'prospective student'. They then have to satisfy the immigration officials that they have the money to support themselves for the period while they are arranging their studies and that if they are not successful in obtaining a place they will leave the UK by the end of the period of stay granted.

Students or those seeking advice on their behalf may feel that, as they have no specific study plans, they should seek entry as visitors. This is not advisable. It is important that students make their intentions clear on arrival. The dangers of entering as visitors and seeking to change status once studies have been sorted out are twofold:

- people could be treated as illegal entrants (▶see chapter 14) because they did not reveal their true intentions, or the period for which they wished to remain, on arrival
- visa nationals (▶see glossary for list) cannot change their status while in the UK to become students

Since June 1989, the immigration rules have made it impossible for a visa national who enters the UK in some other capacity, for example as a visitor, to change to become a student while in the UK. It is necessary for such people who want to study in the UK to leave the country and then return after obtaining another visa abroad for the purpose of studies. People who hope to study but who have not yet obtained a place at a college to do so therefore should obtain visas as 'prospective students' for this purpose and then apply to extend their stay in the UK if accepted. The provisions for gaining a prospective student entry clearance are similar to those for students except that they have to show they have 'genuine and realistic intentions' of studying, within six months of entry, rather than a definite place at a college. Students from countries which have strict foreign exchange control regulations, for example Nigeria, may have problems in showing their financial support to undertake a course before they have been accepted on it.

Arrival in the UK

Leave to enter

Students will normally be allowed in for a year at a time, or for the duration of their course, whichever is shorter. Higher-level degree students may be admitted for the full length of their course, particularly if they have evidence of financial sponsorship for the whole time. The length of time and conditions will be stamped on their passports (▶see chapter 13 for examples of passport stamps).

Students will either be given a *prohibition* on working or a *restriction* on working. A student admitted for six months or less or who has a scholarship may be prohibited from working. Most students will be given a restriction on working, meaning that they can only work if they obtain permission from the Department for Education and Employment first (▶see page 169 for details). After 8 November 1996, they may also have a formal condition requiring them to support and accommodate themselves and any dependants without recourse to public funds.

Students who are not Commonwealth or EEA citizens and who are admitted for more than six months may also be required to register with the police. This means going to the local police station, or, in the London Metropolitan Police area, to the Aliens Registration Office, 10 Lamb's Conduit Street, London WC1X 3MX, within seven days, to give the police details of name, address, marital status and occupation, and to pay a fee (see appendix) for obtaining a small green police registration certificate. Students do not need to continue to report on a regular basis but any changes in the information recorded on the certificate, such as a change of address, should be reported to the police.

Refusal of entry

Students and prospective students who obtained entry clearance in advance of travelling have the right to appeal against any refusal of leave to enter and are able to remain in the UK while the appeal is pending. Students who are not visa nationals do not need to obtain entry clearance before travelling. However, if they are unable to satisfy an immigration officer at a port of entry that they qualify to enter, they may be refused entry and can be sent straight back. Representations may be made to the immigration officers as to why they have made the wrong decision (▶see chapter 12 for more details).

Unless there is some very important new evidence or exceptional and compelling compassionate reasons, it is very unusual for immigration officers to change their minds once a decision to refuse has been made. If they are not satisfied that a student is able to follow the course that he or she intends to do, further evidence from the academic institution may be helpful to show that the student does meet its admission criteria. If the reason for the refusal is related to the intention to leave at the end of studies, it is very difficult to alter the decision.

Prospective students and students intending to study on a course for six months or less have no right of appeal against refusal of entry clearance or of entry if they did not have prior entry clearance. Students on longer courses can appeal only after they have been removed from the UK.

Families of students and prospective students

Since 1 October 1994, when HC 395 came into force, the immigration rules have been the same for husbands of female students and wives of male students. Before that date the husbands of female students had no claim under the rules to come to join them. If an exception to the rules was made for a husband, he was allowed to remain for the same length of time as his wife, but was normally prohibited from working.

The rules state spouses of students and prospective students must show that:

- they are married to a person admitted to, or allowed to remain in, the UK as a student

- the couple intend to live together as husband and wife while the student is studying, and the marriage is still subsisting
- there will be adequate maintenance and accommodation for them, and any dependants, without recourse to public funds (▶see chapter 10 for definition)
- they do not intend to work unless permitted to do so
- they intend to leave the UK at the end of any leave granted
- none of the general grounds for refusal apply ▶see pages 222–3.

The status of the family is dependent on that of the student; family members will be given the same time limit on their stay as the student him- or herself and cannot be given a longer period. Spouses will be prohibited from working if they are given leave to enter or remain for less than 12 months.

This provision suggests that spouses may frequently be prohibited from working. If a student is admitted for a year, and the spouse follows later, the period of leave granted cannot be longer than the student's, and therefore is less than 12 months. Thus the spouse is prohibited from working. If they travel together, the spouse may be given a year and not be prohibited from working. Although the rules stipulate that family members may come to join a student 'admitted to or allowed to remain in the UK', the Home Office has confirmed in a letter to UKCOSA, the Council for International Education, of 12 October 1994, 'Where a student wishes to bring his family to the UK with him he can apply for entry clearance or, where appropriate, leave to enter for the whole family at the same time. He does not need to gain entry himself first.'

If the student was admitted for longer than a year, and the spouse arrives and is admitted when he or she has more than a year's time to run, the rules do not state anything about employment conditions, but the Home Office has confirmed that 'the conditions attached to stay will not restrict the right to take employment'. If students' spouses are allowed to work, and do so, this work does not give them any independent claim to remain in the UK in their own right. They are expected to leave with their student spouse.

The only other family members allowed are children aged under 18 on first arrival in the UK. The rules state they must be:

- coming to join a student or prospective student already admitted to or allowed to remain in the UK (but the Home Office has confirmed that the family may all travel to the UK together)
- unmarried and not have formed an independent family unit nor be leading an independent life
- maintained and accommodated adequately without recourse to public funds

They must also show that they will not remain in the UK beyond any period of leave granted to the parent. Again, the rules state that they should be prohibited from employment if given leave to enter or remain for less than 12 months but say nothing about employment if admitted for a longer period.

The families of students are entitled to state education, National Health Service medical treatment and any other benefit for which they meet the qualifying conditions. The benefits regulations debar them from several benefits, including income-based jobseeker's allowance, income support, housing benefit, council tax benefit and most disability benefits. There could be immigration consequences if they claimed other 'public funds' benefits ▶see chapter 10 for more information.

The Asylum and Immigration Act 1996 removed entitlements to child benefit and to council housing from certain categories of people. The Department of Social Security and the Department of the Environment produced Orders to implement these provisions, removing eligibility for both from most people with time limits on their stay, including international students and their families. Hard-to-let council accommodation leased by education institutions to students is not counted as recourse to public funds but they are no longer eligible for child benefit unless the claim began before 8 October 1996.

Applying for extensions

WHAT THE RULES SAY

The rules for students' extensions state that the students must still meet the requirements for leave to enter as a student and, if visa nationals, must have entered with student visas. All students must show:

- they are enrolled on a full-time course and, if the course has begun, must produce satisfactory evidence of regular attendance on it, or on any other course they have attended in the past
- evidence of satisfactory progress on the course, including the taking and passing of any relevant examinations
- they would not, if this extension were granted, have spent more than four years on courses of less than two years duration (or longer courses if broken off before completion)
- they have not come to the end of a period of a scholarship from a government or an international scholarship agency, or they have the written consent from such an agency for further studies, and can show sufficient sponsorship funding
- none of the general grounds for refusal apply ▶see pages 234–5.

From 25 November 1996, the Home Office made application forms compulsory, and stated that applications not made on the forms and not accompanied by all the documents specified on the forms, or acceptable explanations why they were not sent in and when they will be, were invalid. Student extension application forms are called FLR(S).

WHAT THE RULES MEAN

Full time studies; maintenance and accommodation

The Home Office requires evidence that students are still enrolled for a full-time course of study, that the money for maintenance and accommodation is still available and that they intend to leave the UK at the end of their studies. These can be shown in the same way as when the students first applied to enter, ▶see above.

Regular attendance

Students have to prove that they have been in regular attendance on the course they have been following. The Home Office can check their attendance records with their colleges. This has been done by a formal written questionnaire but the Home Office has also telephoned colleges and made decisions based on information given over the telephone, the source of which cannot later be traced. JCWI and UKCOSA advise institutions not to respond to telephone inquiries but to ask the Home Office to put the request in writing, so that the information can be checked by a person qualified to do so and so that the college will also have records of what it has told the Home Office. The student application forms include a section for completion by the college about the student's studies and attendance. The institution may also provide a letter confirming the student's satisfactory attendance. If students have not attended regularly for good reasons, for example illness, it is important that this should be explained to the Home Office and evidence be sent in, for example medical certificates for the relevant period that the students were unfit to attend classes.

The requirement that private education institutions 'maintain satisfactory records of enrolment and attendance' suggests that the Home Office also expects colleges to maintain written records, though it does not give details of what standard of records are expected.

Satisfactory progress

This was a new requirement in HC 395. In the past, the Home Office had refused to grant extensions to students who had failed examinations on several occasions, on the grounds that they did not appear able to follow their course, and to students who had not sat the examinations for which they were preparing, on the grounds that they did not appear to be attempting to bring their studies to an end or did not intend to leave the UK at the end of their studies. Thus if students applying for extensions are unable to take examinations for any reason, or need to stay in order to re-sit examinations, it will be important for the institution to confirm this explanation to the Home Office. The Home Office would expect the student to have a reasonable chance of success in the re-sit and would require evidence of support and accommodation.

Short courses

The rules state that extensions of stay should also not be granted to students who would be spending more than four years on short courses. Short courses are defined as courses of less than two years' duration, but include longer courses which were abandoned before completion. This is unnecessarily restrictive for some students whose planned courses are short or who may change their minds during courses; the Home Office has stated that it may be flexible about this in some individual cases. It is important to explain in the application the reasons for abandoning a particular course, or why the student is continuing on short courses, if possible with supporting letters from the institution(s) concerned, to show that this is part of a regular and coordinated plan of studies.

Before October 1994, the rules stated that the Home Office would refuse extensions of stay if students 'appear to be moving from one course to another without any intention of bringing their studies to a close'. This provision could be used against students who changed their career or study plans while in the UK. The Home Office prefers students who follow obvious study paths to an academic goal and is suspicious of those it believes may be 'perpetual students'. If students have a radical change of plans, it is still important to explain the reasons for it, if possible backed by letters from course tutors or lecturers supporting the change. This rule could also be used against students who started a new course after they had already been studying for many years as the Home Office might suspect that they are hoping to bring themselves within the ambit of the 'ten-year concession' (▶see pages 238–9) to be able to stay permanently.

How to apply for an extension

Students who wish to remain in the UK longer than the initial time they have been given need to apply to the Home Office for permission. It is very important to do this before the time given runs out – as long as the application is made in time, people are still legally in the country while the Home Office is considering it. Applications must be made on Home Office form FLR(S) and be accompanied by all the required documents, or explanations of why any documents are not available and when they will be sent. If the application is refused, there is a formal right of appeal against the refusal. If the application is made late, or not correctly on the form, the students are illegally in the UK even while it is under consideration and if it is refused, they have no right of appeal. It is therefore vital to apply in time even if not all the documents required for the application are available, as they can be sent later. ▶See chapter 11 for more information on making applications.

Applications can be made either by post or in person at the Home Office, or in person at one of the regional Public Enquiry Offices of the Home Office (▶see chapter 19 for addresses).

Permission to work

If students want to obtain part-time or holiday employment unrelated to their course, this may be possible. If the students' passports are stamped with a prohibition on working, they need first to apply to the Home Office for this to be varied to a restriction on working. This may be done if the Home Office is satisfied that the students do not need to work in order to be able to continue to pay for their studies. Students admitted for six months or less will not be allowed to work.

If a student's passport is stamped with a restriction on working (▶see chapter 13 for an example of this stamp) it is possible to get permission to do a particular job, as long as a complicated procedure is followed. Students wishing to undertake either part-time or vacation work must first get permission from their local Jobcentre. They must take their passport (and police registration certificate, if they have one) to their local Jobcentre, where the staff will check to ensure that they are not prohibited from working. The Jobcentre will give the student form OSS1, which is divided into three sections. Part 1 must be completed by the student, Part 2 by the prospective employer and Part 3 by the academic institution. When the form is completed it should be returned to the Jobcentre, to consider the application for permission to work. It is unlikely that permission will be granted for more than 20 hours per week in term time or 40 hours per week in holidays. The Jobcentre is more likely to grant the application if the job is related in some way to the student's course and if it has been advertised previously. It will refuse permission if it believes the work could be done by resident labour and the employer has not attempted to recruit locally.

It is very important that students who want to work during their studies, even when it is just a short-term holiday job, are advised to follow the correct procedure. Working without obtaining permission is a breach of conditions of stay and a criminal offence. Students who are found working illegally may either be prosecuted under section 24(1)(b)(i) of the Immigration Act 1971, or the Home Office may make its own administrative decision to deport them.

The consequences of working without permission have become more severe since the passing of the Immigration Act 1988, because there is now no full right of appeal against deportation for people who last entered the UK less than seven years before the decision to deport them. In most cases, therefore, students caught working without permission can only appeal on the facts of the case (which would mean arguing that the student had not been working, or had obtained permission to do the work). ▶See chapter 12 for more details of what to do when people are threatened with deportation.

Fees and grants

International students normally have to pay **full-cost fees** for their courses and are not normally entitled to local authority awards. Under the Education (Fees and Awards) Act 1983 and 1994 Regulations, differential fees can be charged to international students. In general, in order to qualify as home students, and therefore to be charged the lower level of home student fees, students must satisfy the education institution that:

- they have been ordinarily resident (▶see glossary) in the UK throughout the three-year period preceding 1 January, 1 April or 1 September closest to the beginning of the first term of their course and
- at no time during this period were they ordinarily resident wholly or mainly for the purpose of receiving full-time education.

Thus in most cases people who have been granted leave to remain as students, even if they have been in the UK for more than three years, will not qualify for home student fees. People who have been allowed to remain in the UK for another purpose, for example as the children of a work permit holder, or who are settled, but who happen to have been studying during that time, will qualify as home students.

In April 1996 the Department for Education and Employment announced plans for changing the regulations for eligibility for home fees, to provide that people must have indefinite leave to remain to qualify for home fees, as well as meeting the residence criteria. The Department stated that this change was connected to the 'Efficiency Scrutiny set up by the Home Secretary in 1993 on co-operation between government departments and agencies whose activities affect the enforcement of the immigration laws' ▶see chapter 10, but it is difficult to see the connection. This change is planned to come into effect from the 1998/99 academic year.

Some people, called 'excepted students', do not have to live in the UK for three years to be treated as home students for fees purposes. They are:

- people granted refugee status, people granted exceptional leave to remain after making a claim for asylum and their spouses and children. Once either of these statuses has been granted, the person must be assessed as a home student immediately. This does not apply to asylum-seekers waiting for a decision to be made on their case, who may be required to pay full-cost fees. However, as soon as they are granted refugee status or exceptional leave to enter or remain, they may be treated as home students, even in the middle of a course of studies.

People who claimed asylum more than three years before the start of the course should qualify for home fees on the ground that they have met the ordinary residence requirements. This is a difficult question to resolve and each case needs to be examined individually. Institutions may sometimes exercise discretion and reduce fees for asylum-seekers even if they have been in the UK for a shorter period.

- people who do not have the right of abode (see glossary) but who have been granted settlement in the UK during the three years before the start of the course and were not settled at a time before the beginning of the three-year period. This provision was intended mainly for families of those granted special quota vouchers for settlement (▶see page 332) but also applies to people granted settlement on other grounds, for example marriage to a settled or British person. Once settlement has been granted, the student will be eligible to pay home fees for any new course undertaken. This exception will probably be removed if the changed eligibility regulations come into force.
- people who have obtained the right of abode during the three years before the course but who have not been settled before and do not have the three years residence qualification. This applies mainly to people from Hong Kong who have qualified for registration as British citizens under the provisions of the British Nationality (Hong Kong) Act 1990 and who therefore only gained the right of abode with this citizenship change. In order to benefit from this exception, students have to show that they were settled in the UK by either 1 January, 1 April or 1 September preceding and closest to the start of the course. This exception will probably be removed if the changed eligibility regulations come into force.
- people who cannot meet the three year ordinary residence requirement only because they, their spouse or a parent were absent abroad for temporary employment reasons during all or part of the relevant period may also be excepted from the regulations and qualify as home students.
- EEA nationals who have been ordinarily resident in the EEA for the three-year period before the start of the course and at no time during this period wholly or mainly for the purpose of receiving full-time education and who have been migrant workers in the UK prior to the start of the course, and the children of such EEA migrant workers.
- EU nationals and children of EU nationals who have been ordinarily resident in the EEA for the relevant three-year period, and at no time during that period were they resident in the EEA wholly or mainly for the purpose of receiving full- time education.
- spouses of EEA migrant workers. If they are EEA nationals themselves, they must have three years' ordinary residence in the EEA not mainly for the purposes of education, see above. If they are not EEA nationals they only have to show one year's ordinary residence.
- students who are studying as part of a reciprocal exchange scheme, who normally do not have to pay fees.

The student **grants** regulations have similar requirements of three years' ordinary residence, not for the purpose of studies, so most students from abroad are not entitled to grants. In January 1996, the Department for Education and Employment consulted on a proposal that only settled people should be entitled to mandatory awards. Again, this was stated to be in connection with the Efficiency Scrutiny ▶see chapter 10. There are similar exceptions to the three years requirement although a student granted exceptional leave to remain will not be entitled to a mandatory award on that ground alone. Similarly, a student who has recently become settled will not automatically qualify for an award, and will still need to satisfy the three years' residence requirement. EEA nationals will only be eligible if they have been ordinarily resident in the UK for the three-year period and not for the purpose of receiving full-time education or have been migrant workers in the UK prior to starting the course. The eligibility of migrant workers and their spouses is particularly complex. British citizens who have been ordinarily resident in the EEA due to their own, or their parents' or spouse's, employment are also entitled to full mandatory awards. Applications should be made to the local authority in which the student is resident.

EU nationals who are eligible for home fees are entitled to a fees-only award, and should apply to the local education authority where the institution is situated. The application must be made not later than four months after the start of the course. If the fees are being paid or other finances are coming from the home government, students should ensure that this will continue for the full length of the course.

Student grants and fee reimbursements are not counted as 'public funds' for immigration purposes. If a student is receiving a grant, this will be acceptable to the Home Office as evidence of financial support.

▶Eligibility for home fees and for grants or fee reimbursements can be complex; UKCOSA (see glossary for address) is able to advise in detail on this.

Studies including training

Some studies normally include a large amount of practical work, for example nursing or accountancy. Such students are not treated consistently under the immigration rules. Nursing students are counted as students for immigration purposes, even if they are paid by health authorities, or receive training bursaries. There are specific provisions in the rules for them, and for doctors and dentists wanting postgraduate training. Accountancy students and others who often study while working at a firm require training permits, which the employer has to obtain from the Department for Education and Employment under its Training and Work Experience Scheme, see pages 140–41 and 173–74.

Nursing and medical students

For the first time, HC 395 made provision for nursing students separately from other students. They have to show:

- they have been accepted for training as a student nurse or midwife, leading to a recognised British qualification, or are already qualified abroad and are enrolled for an adaptation course leading to registra-

tion in the UK under the Central Council for Nursing, Midwifery and Health Visiting, and did not gain this acceptance by misrepresentation
- they are able and intend to follow the course
- they do not intend to work or engage in business other than their nursing training
- they intend to leave the UK at the end of their training
- they have sufficient funds for accommodation and maintenance here; this can include funding from a Department of Health bursary.

People wishing to train as nurses may also enter as prospective students, in order to come for interviews at hospitals, and to finalise arrangements for their training. Visa nationals are not able to change status within the UK to become student nurses; they must enter with student or prospective student visas.

The requirement that nursing students and prospective students also have to show that they intend to leave the UK at the end of their studies is new. Historically, it has often been possible for student nurses to obtain work permits to work in National Health Service hospitals after qualification. Until 1 October 1994 there was an exception to the immigration rules to allow work permits for student nurses to be considered without them having to leave the UK. This has been removed, as cuts in NHS funding mean that there are no longer vacant jobs except in a few specialist shortage areas. It may be possible for private nursing homes to obtain work permits, as their wages and conditions of service mean there is less competition for jobs, but the Home Office would have to make an exception to the rules to allow a student nurse to stay to work after qualification.

There are also particular arrangements for postgraduate doctors and dentists who want to study and gain experience in the UK. They must be either graduates of UK medical schools intending to do their pre-registration house officer jobs for up to 12 months, or who have qualified abroad but are eligible for full or limited registration with the General Medical Council or General Dental Council and who intend to undergo post-graduate training in a hospital. They cannot spend more than one year as pre-registration house officers nor more than four years in aggregate in this capacity after registration, and they must intend to leave the UK at the end of their training period. They will normally be admitted for 12 months initially, and may be granted yearly extensions up to a maximum of four years.

Training and work experience

Most other students who are being paid and gaining practical experience must have approval from the Overseas Labour Service of the Department for Education and Employment, under its Training and Work Experience Scheme (TWES). This means that their employers must have obtained a training and work experience permit for them from the Department.

People admitted to the UK on any basis other than students or trainees will not be allowed to switch to this status in the UK, but will have to leave the country to obtain these permits. The immigration rules state that they must hold such a permit, be capable of undertaking the training or work experience and intend to leave the UK on its completion. They must show that this training will pay enough to support them and any other family members, and that they do not intend to take any other employment. People coming for work experience will be admitted for a year initially and may apply for an extension in exceptional circumstances; work experience may not continue for more than two years in total. Trainees may be given three years initially and may be granted an extension for a further three years. Their family members will normally be allowed to work.

Being granted leave to enter or remain as a trainee therefore depends on the Department for Education and Employment approving a trainee permit. The person has to find an employer willing to employ him or her and willing to go through the procedure of applying to the Department for a trainee permit. Thus, for example, accountancy students who want to study by training with a firm need trainee permits. Their firms need to apply to the Department for Education and Employment, on form OW5 or WP2, to obtain trainee work permits for them, showing that they will be following an organised training programme in order to obtain a recognised qualification. The Department may query the training and experience proposed, and the salary offered, before deciding to approve the training. If the qualification could be obtained through full-time study training will probably not be approved.

When a course involves a period of employment or practical training, including work, it is the responsibility of the college to negotiate permission with the Department for Education and Employment Overseas Labour Service for all the international students on the course to do this. This is important, otherwise a student on a sandwich course may find that he or she is working illegally. Before taking up work, students should check with the course tutor, or other person in the college responsible for permits, that this has been done.

Applying for extensions

Since October 1991, applications for leave to remain in the UK *as a trainee* must be made direct to the Department for Education and Employment, not to the Home Office. Since the employers normally make this application, it is important for the trainee to check that it has been done in time, in order to remain legally in the UK. Department for Education and Employment application forms, not Home Office ones, must be used. These tell people not to send passports with the application, but when it has been decided, to send them to the Home Office. If the Department for Education and Employment approves the continued training, it will inform the Home Office, which will consider granting leave to remain.

Most people given trainee permits progress through a series of examinations before qualifying. The Department for Education and Employment normally gives them three chances at every examination stage, but if they fail one paper three times, it will probably not renew their trainee permission. As long as the application for extension was made in time, there will be a right of appeal against any refusal, and the trainee may remain in the UK, and continue training, during the appeal period. If there is time to take the paper again successfully, the training permit may be renewed.

People who wish to do practical training in the UK in fields with less-established paths to qualifications will have to negotiate individual programmes with their prospective employers, who will then need to apply to the Department for Education and Employment to obtain trainee permission. These are considered on a case-by-case basis.

EEA students

EEA nationals are not subject to British immigration law and rules but to Community legislation (▶see chapter 6 for more details). This means that they do not require leave to enter the UK and are free to travel between EEA countries to work, to seek work, to do business or be self-employed or to provide or receive services. If they are engaged in any economic activity, they are able to obtain 'residence permits', documents which confirm their right to live in a particular EEA country.

From 30 June 1992 an EC directive on the freedom of movement of students (90/366/EEC) has been in force, and was amended by directive 93/96 in 1993. This provides for free movement for:

- students enrolled at recognised educational establishments for the principal purpose of following vocational training courses
- who have sufficient resources to avoid becoming a charge on public funds and
- who are covered by all-risk sickness insurance.

Thus students are entitled to residence permits because of their studies. The directive refers to 'vocational' courses, but this in practice means all courses. As EEA nationals, they are also free to work without needing separate permission from the Department for Education and Employment, and to obtain residence permits in that way, provided the work is not 'marginal and ancillary' but is a real job, undertaken for its own sake. Their earnings or potential earnings can be considered to show that they will be able to support themselves. They should be entitled to pay home fees and for fees-only awards, provided they satisfy the ordinary residence requirement, that is, three years' residence in the EEA, not wholly or mainly for the purpose of receiving full-time education. EEA students may also be entitled to full mandatory awards, if they:

- have been ordinarily resident in the EEA for the previous three years, not wholly or mainly for the purpose of education
- have been in employment since last entering the UK (but not simply in order to qualify for a grant)
- intend to study a vocational course related to their previous employment in the UK or intend to transfer to a new employment sector, in the case of involuntary unemployment
- meet all the other requirements of the Mandatory Awards Regulations.

Spouses of EEA migrant workers, whether or not they are EEA nationals themselves, are eligible for full mandatory awards on the same basis as the worker spouse, provided that they are installed together in the UK and the spouse has three years' ordinary residence in the EEA not wholly or mainly for the purposes of education.

Under the directive, students are entitled to have their spouses and dependent children with them in the UK, whatever the nationality of the family members. Neither the student nor the family can be restricted from working, however short the student's course.

Becoming a student when already in the UK

People who are not visa nationals and who have entered the UK for any purpose, for example as visitors, can apply to the Home Office, on application form FLR(S), to change their status to become students. If people apply to become students shortly after gaining entry in some other way, the Home Office may wish to ascertain that there has been a genuine change of mind to become a student, and that this decision took place after they entered. If at the time of their entry people had already considered studying, or had definite plans to do so, the Home Office could treat them as illegal entrants, on the grounds that they had deceived the immigration officers when they arrived in the UK. ▶See chapter 14 for more details about illegal entry and its dangers.

Visa nationals (▶see glossary for list) who entered for any purpose other than studies will normally be refused permission to change their status to become students. It is probable that they will have to leave the UK and apply at a British embassy or high commission abroad for a student visa.

Students changing their status

The immigration rules provide for some people who have been students in the UK to change their status and prohibit others from doing so. The rules allow students:

- to apply to stay and settle with some close relatives; for example, children studying in the UK whose parents later gain settlement may apply to stay and settle with them (▶see page 55 for details)

- to marry and apply to stay with their spouse (▶see chapter 2 on spouses and fiancé(e)s for more information)
- to apply for asylum (▶see chapter 5)

They should make applications to the Home Office before the time limit on their passport runs out, asking for a change of status and showing how they fit into the relevant parts of the immigration rules for their new status. ▶See chapter 11 for more details about making applications.

The rules do not allow students to stay:

- in order to work or to be self-employed
- in order to set up a business
- as working holidaymakers

This does not mean that they cannot apply for such changes, but that any application is likely to be refused, with no right of appeal. The Home Office would need to be satisfied that there were very exceptional reasons for considering them. People should be referred for specialist advice about the consequences of such applications.

From 4 April 1996, students with government or international agency scholarships need permission in writing from the scholarship agency for any change of status. Previously, this permission had only been necessary to stay on for studies after the scholarship had ended. The change raises concerns about the situation of scholarship students applying for asylum, if the situation in their home country has changed greatly during their studies, or students applying to stay with spouses after marrying in the UK.

Temporary stay

Students may wish to remain in the UK as visitors after their formal studies are over, perhaps in order to attend a degree-giving ceremony, or to continue to write up a PhD thesis after the formal period of study has ended. This may be possible, provided an application is made in time, on the form FLR(O), and with the support of the academic institution, and provided the student has the money to live in the UK for this additional period without needing to work or to have recourse to public funds. There may be difficulties if the student has been in the UK for nearly ten years, because the Home Office may believe that he or she does not intend to leave at the end of the studies; see pages 238–9 for further details about the 'ten-year concession'.

Working after studies

It is not usually possible for students to stay in the UK after completing their studies in order to work. If students have lived legally in the UK for more than ten years, the Home Office has stated that it will consider making an exception to the immigration rules to grant them indefinite leave to remain because of the length of time they have spent in the UK; ▶see pages 238–9 for more details of this 'ten-year concession'.

Normally, however, students wanting to work in the UK after their studies are over need work permits. Work permits are normally only issued to people who are outside the UK and whose prospective employer applies to the Department for Education and Employment for a permit. One of the criteria for the grant of a work permit is that the person should have had several years' experience of work in a similar job outside the UK, so it is rare for students to qualify. There are two exceptions to this:

Work experience

When students want to gain practical experience of working in their subject for a year or so, they may qualify under the Department for Education and Employment's Training and Work Experience scheme ▶see above. This is a scheme permitting employers to offer work experience and professional training, for a limited period, to non-EEA nationals. The employers need to obtain work experience permits from the Department, showing that a programme has been worked out for the student, who will be gaining useful experience, and that it is understood that this is not a long-term job and the student will leave the UK at the end of the period. Students with training or work experience permits will not normally be allowed to change to ordinary employment later.

Academics

Students who wish to continue with an academic career may be able to do so in the UK, if the academic institution is willing to apply for a work permit on their behalf. The research that they have been doing and the job the institution wants them to fill are likely to be highly specialised and it may be possible to show that there was no other suitable candidate.

There is also a concession, outside the immigration rules, to allow overseas academics to come to the UK as 'academic visitors' for up to a year, instead of only six months like other visitors. This is usually of use to academics with sabbatical years, who are still paid by the institution abroad but wish to do unpaid research, or perhaps some teaching on an exchange basis, in a university here. It is not normally possible to extend this for more than a year. Such people will find it difficult to change to student status at the end of the year, and the rules prohibit visa nationals from doing so.

Travel outside the UK

Students can travel outside the UK and return within the time limit stamped on their passports. They may expect to be readmitted until the same date, as long as they still satisfy the requirements of the immigration rules on students. Usually their passports will be stamped 'given leave to enter section 3(3)(b) until date' which is what this section of the Immigration Act 1971 means. Visa national students who have been given permission to stay for more than six months do not need a visa to re-enter the UK within the time they have been given. Visa national students coming for six months or less may have obtained multiple entry visas; if they did not, they will need to apply at the British post in the country which they are visiting for a new visa before they can return.

Students cannot obtain any formal assurance while in the UK that they are likely to be readmitted after any absence. They have to satisfy an immigration officer when they re-enter that they still qualify to enter. It is therefore sensible for them to take letters from their college confirming their studies, and proof of their financial support, with them to show to the immigration officers on their return.

If a person has a valid visa and is then refused re-entry to the UK, usually on the grounds that there have been changes in circumstances since the visa was issued, or full facts were not given in order to obtain it, there is a right of appeal against the refusal and the person is able to remain in the UK while that appeal takes place. Students who are refused permission to re-enter and who do not have visas or other entry clearance have no right of appeal while they are in the UK. This is the case even when they had leave to enter or remain at the time they left the UK, which would still have been valid at the time of their return. Students enrolled on courses of more than six months will be able to appeal from abroad, but as this may take many months, it is unlikely to be of much use to them. Others have no right of appeal at all.

If students travel out of the UK when an application for an extension of stay is pending, the application automatically lapses. They may expect immigration officers to question them in detail on return before deciding whether to grant entry. For further consequences of requesting passports back from the Home Office in order to travel ▶see pages 239–241.

SECTION 6: BENEFITS

10 Immigration, benefits and other state provisions

The purpose of this chapter is briefly to explain the connection between immigration status and entitlement to some welfare benefits. It is not intended to give detailed advice on benefit entitlements or on which benefits people may be able to claim. The regulations on entitlement to many benefits have been amended to reflect immigration status, and the two are becoming ever more closely interlinked.

PUBLIC FUNDS

'Public funds' are defined in HC 31, para 1 as:

- **housing** under Part II or III of the Housing Act 1985, Part I or II of the Housing (Scotland) Act 1987 or Part II of the Housing (Northern Ireland) Order 1981 or Part II of the Housing (Northern Ireland) Order 1988
- **attendance allowance, severe disablement allowance, invalid care allowance** and **disability living allowance** under Part III, **income support, family credit, council tax benefit, disability working allowance** and **housing benefit** under Part VII and **child benefit** under Part IX of the Social Security Contributions and Benefits Act 1992, and the equivalent Act in Northern Ireland
- **income-based jobseeker's allowance** under the Jobseekers Act 1995

The Home Office first listed 'public funds' in 1985, when they were income support, housing benefit, family credit and housing as homeless persons only. Council tax benefit was added from 1 April 1994, attendance allowance, severe disablement allowance, invalid care allowance, disability living allowance and disability working allowance from 4 April 1996 and 'Part II' housing, child benefit and income-based jobseeker's allowance from 1 November 1996.

When the immigration rules state that a person must satisfy an immigration official that he or she can be supported and accommodated without recourse to public funds, this is the complete list of benefits and services that are meant.

Any other benefit not listed, for example contribution-based jobseeker's allowance, is not public funds and claiming it cannot affect anyone's immigration status. Any other parts of the welfare state – for example, NHS medical treatment, children receiving free state education – are not public funds. Claiming anything other than the benefits listed can have no direct immigration consequences for a person legally in the UK.

Under immigration law people may be admitted to the UK subject to the requirement that they do not have recourse to public funds. The box shows which benefits count as public funds.

Before 8 November 1996, there was never any endorsement on people's passports to show that they were subject to the public funds requirement. Moreover, there was often no way that the people themselves could be aware of this, unless they had a detailed knowledge of the immigration rules. Immigration officers did not tell a husband coming in to the UK to join his wife, for example, whether he might claim any benefits. Schedule 2, para 1 of the Asylum and Immigration Act 1996, which allows the Home Office to impose a formal condition on people's stay that they maintain and accommodate themselves and any dependants without recourse to public funds, came into force on 1 November 1996. The immigration authorities used new passport stamps from 8 November, including this requirement. Whether or not this is stamped on the passport does not determine people's eligibility to claim any benefit. However, breach of this formal condition is a criminal offence; see chapter 14 for more information.

Who is not affected by the public funds requirement?

- British citizens
- Commonwealth citizens with the right of abode (see glossary)
- people who are settled (allowed to stay permanently) in the UK. It does not matter why settlement was granted; once a person has been allowed to stay permanently, he or she has full entitlement to claim any benefits, subject only to any qualifying condition attached to that benefit.
- people who have refugee status
- people granted exceptional leave to enter or remain (see chapter 5)

Who is affected by the public funds requirement?

The immigration rules state in many places that people must satisfy an entry clearance or immigration officer that support and accommodation is available to them. A frequent wording is that they must show 'there will be adequate accommodation for the parties and their dependants without recourse to public funds, in accommodation which they own or occupy exclusively; and the parties will be able to maintain and accommodate themselves and any dependants adequately without recourse to public funds'. They may be refused permission to enter or remain in the UK if the officer is not satisfied. These groups of people are:

- people given limited leave to enter as spouses, to join a British or settled partner, before they are granted settlement
- children given limited leave to enter to join a British or settled parent, before they are granted settlement
- fiancés and fiancées

- students and members of their families
- visitors
- working holidaymakers
- au pairs
- people given permission to enter or remain as work permit holders, business people, self-employed people, workers who do not need work permits (permit-free employment) and retired people of independent means, and people admitted as members of their families

These people will be refused entry clearance overseas, or entry to the UK, if they cannot convince an official that they will not need to claim public funds.

EEA nationals *may* be affected by the public funds requirement.

Their position is confusing in law. Under Community legislation, EEA nationals are free to move between EEA countries to take or seek work, to set up in business or self-employment and to provide or receive services. They do not require leave to enter or remain under British immigration law and do not have to show that they can support and accommodate themselves without recourse to public funds. They are therefore able to claim benefits if they qualify under the benefits regulations.

Section 7(1) of the Immigration Act 1988 was passed in order to bring British law into conformity with Community legislation but it was not brought into force until July 1994, six years later. This was done through the Immigration (European Economic Area) Order, which was published in March 1994, and came into force on 20 July 1994; ►see chapter 6 for more details. The Home Office and the Department of Social Security have also attempted to cut down entitlements of EEA nationals to benefits by introducing a 'habitual residence' test for eligibility for income support, housing benefit and council tax benefit and by requiring EEA nationals to leave the UK if they claim income support ►see pages 189–90 and chapter 6 for further details.

Sponsorship

People coming to visit or study in the UK, or to join a relative in order to settle permanently, will have had to show that support and accommodation without recourse to public funds is available. The person providing this support is known as a 'sponsor'. Sponsorship is proved by the person concerned confirming in writing his or her willingness to provide the support required, and evidence that this can be done. For example, a person sponsoring a student must have a recent bank statement or recent pay slips or other evidence to show the money that is available to pay the college fees and to support the person while he or she is studying.

It is possible for people to fill in a 'sponsorship form' which will provide the necessary information and send this together with the evidence to the British embassy or high commission. Sponsorship forms are optional; they are merely a convenient way of recording information which may be required by the British authorities. Some advice agencies prepare their own to help the sponsor in the UK compile information but the information required is also listed on the entry clearance application forms at the British posts abroad. Sponsorship forms do not need to be in any particular format nor to be witnessed or attested by a solicitor.

Undertakings

The immigration authorities can also ask people to sign 'undertakings' to confirm that they will support the person (see appendix for copy of undertaking). These undertakings can be required under the Social Security Contributions and Benefits Act 1992 and the Immigration Act 1971, but should not be signed unless they are specifically requested. They are most commonly required for elderly relatives. Where an undertaking has been signed, after 23 May 1980, the DSS has the authority to claim back any income support (but not any other benefit) that the sponsored person has been paid. Action would be taken through the Benefits Agency local office.

Sponsored people who are in the UK with a time limit on their stay are not entitled to receive any income support, because under the income support regulations they do not qualify. Before 5 February 1996, a sponsored person who had indefinite leave to remain could claim, even when an undertaking had been signed. It was government policy that if sponsors' financial circumstances changed and they were no longer able to sponsor the person from abroad, they would not be required to repay benefit. The Benefits Agency might interview the sponsor, in the same way that other 'liable relatives' were pursued or people assessed by the Child Support Agency, to see whether the changes in financial circumstances were good enough reasons for the failure to maintain.

Since 5 February 1996, eligibility regulations for income support, housing benefit and council tax benefit were changed to debar people about whom such undertakings were signed. This embargo continues for five years after the person entered the UK or after the undertaking was signed, whichever is the later. The only exception is if the sponsor dies, when the person may be able to claim urgent cases rate income support ▶see pages 192–3. People who were sponsored but did not have undertakings signed about them remain eligible to claim benefits and people who had claimed and received income support before 5 February 1996 may still be considered under the old regulations.

Because this is so new a restriction on eligibility, it is important to monitor how the DSS deals with such applications. JCWI's concerns include who the DSS decides to interview about undertakings, whether the DSS recognises the difference between undertakings and sponsorship declarations, or whether there is any difference in effect between those undertakings signed before 5 February 1996 and afterwards. It is important that people should seek specialist benefits advice. Please inform JCWI of any problems or assurances from the DSS about its practices.

Possible effects of claiming

If people are admitted with limited leave subject to the requirement that they can support and accommodate themselves without recourse to public funds, and then receive one of the public funds benefits, and if the Home Office finds out, this may affect their immigration status. A claim for a public funds benefit may result in:

- leave being curtailed
- an application for a variation or extension of leave, or for settlement, being refused
- temporary rather than indefinite leave being given
- the possibility of being refused entry to the UK when attempting to return after previously having claimed public funds.

Advisers are often therefore reluctant or unsure whether to advise a person whose immigration status is subject to the public funds requirement to claim benefit because of the possible immigration consequences. There are close links between the Home Office and the DSS and established procedures for reporting claims for income support to the Home Office, because of the long-standing links between immigration status and eligibility. From April 1994 onwards eligibility for other benefits has increasingly been linked to immigration status, therefore checks in connection with these benefits can be made. The judgement in *R v Secretary of State for the Environment ex parte London Borough of Tower Hamlets* in April 1993 (▶see pages 201-2) gave council homeless persons' units the right to check up on the immigration status of applicants for housing and to tell the Home Office if they believe that people are in the UK illegally.

From 5 February 1996, the eligibility regulations for family credit, attendance allowance, severe disablement allowance, invalid care allowance, disability living allowance and disability working allowance have incorporated an immigration requirement – that claimants are settled. This was added as a condition for child benefit from 7 October 1996. The Asylum and Immigration Act 1996 and the Housing Act 1996 add restrictions on access to all social housing for people who are not settled. People recognised as refugees, those with exceptional leave and EEA nationals and their family members are excepted from this requirement. There is thus a close connection between immigration status and all eligibility regulations for 'public funds' benefits. There may still be some room for manoeuvre in those benefits administered by local authorities (housing benefit, council tax benefit and housing) as their local practices may vary.

It is important to be clear that there are two different authorities and sets of regulations involved in assessing whether someone can or should claim a public funds benefit:

i) **Home Office immigration rules** may lead to a refusal of entry or a refusal to extend someone's leave to enter or remain if public funds have been claimed and are thought likely to be needed again

ii) **DSS benefit regulations** bar some people who have limited leave to enter or remain from some benefits on the ground that they are 'persons from abroad'. This includes, for example, spouses of British citizens who have not yet been granted settlement.

Advisers will therefore need to assess whether people, or their family members on their behalf, *can* claim a particular benefit and also whether they *should* do so, if this might jeopardise their immigration status.

Home Office practice

The Home Office does not always enforce the full extent of the legal requirement not to have recourse to public funds, nor follow particularly harsh decisions of the Immigration Appeal Tribunal. It has been normal practice to ignore short periods of reliance on public funds. The Home Office has stated, in a letter from the then Minister, David Waddington, to Max Madden MP in December 1985: 'We would not use this power [to refuse] if a person had become dependent on public funds for a short time through no fault of his own. Moreover, if a sponsor here is dependent on public funds the relevant question will be whether *extra* funds were necessary to support the applicant' (our emphasis). This is still the practice, although it is now rare for a person subject to the public funds requirement to be eligible to claim under benefits regulations.

The courts and the Tribunal have developed the law on public funds beyond the Home Office's interpretation. In *Chhinderpal Singh* (1989 Imm AR 69) two boys were not permitted to come to join their parents because they would initially have been supported here on money their father had saved from supplementary benefit (now income support) and the boys would be indirectly reliant on public funds. Home Office practice has not followed this decision. On 5 October 1994 Nicholas Baker MP wrote to Sir Giles Shaw MP: 'with regard to public funds there is no objection to other residents in the same household receiving public funds to which they are entitled in their own right. The question is whether additional recourse to public funds would be necessary on the applicant's arrival here. The sponsor's means, including any public funds to which they are entitled in their own right, must therefore be sufficient to provide adequate maintenance and accommodation for the applicant and their dependants (if any).' The Tribunal recently and unwillingly confirmed that this Home Office interpretation of the rules should be followed in the case of *Scott* (13389).

For example, a British woman and her children who have been rehoused under the homelessness provisions of housing law require the same sized accommodation as a woman and man with children. Thus if the husband applies from abroad to join the family, he will be able to show that there is adequate accommodation for him because it was not provided for his needs but for the rest of the family. Once the husband has been allowed in, under the social security regulations he is not eligible to receive any income support, housing benefit or council tax benefit (see below for further explanation). The wife is eligible to claim for herself but will not receive anything for her husband. Under the immigration regulations, if the wife claims income support for herself and receives money, this could be used by the Home Office to refuse her husband permission to remain on the grounds that the couple cannot support themselves without recourse to public funds though it is current stated policy not to do so. If at all possible, it is advisable not to be claiming a benefit classed as public funds for immigration purposes at the time of an application for settlement.

If the extension or settlement application is refused on public funds grounds, and the spouse is able to appeal against the refusal, he or she may remain in the UK while the appeal is pending and normally is not restricted from working. An employer does not commit an offence employing a person who is appealing against a refusal if the person had been permitted to work before the refusal. If the person later finds work and is able to stop claiming, the Home Office should be informed, with proof of the other source of money, and it is likely that leave to remain would then be granted and the person be asked to withdraw any immigration appeal. It is unusual to be refused leave to remain on public funds grounds; 59 husbands and wives were refused on grounds including public funds in 1995. However, the number of spouses being refused entry clearance on these grounds is rising, especially in Pakistan and Bangladesh. In general, the safest advice that can be given is that where a person is subject to the public funds requirement, claiming a public funds benefit should be a last resort and the claimant should be aware of the possible immigration consequences.

Eligibility to claim

There is a general test, the habitual residence test, which nearly all applicants for income support/income-based jobseeker's allowance (JSA(IB)), council tax benefit and housing benefit must meet, regardless of immigration status. People who fail this test are also ineligible for consideration for council housing, whether as homeless people or for any other reason, from 20 January 1997. The only people exempted from this test are certain asylum-seekers ►see page 193, recognised refugees, people granted exceptional leave and EEA workers and business people. The latter category includes EEA nationals who have ever worked in the UK, unless the work was solely intended to make them eligible for benefits. EEA nationals who have been 'required to leave' the UK may also be ineligible for benefits. In speeches and press releases, Ministers made it clear that the habitual residence test was aimed against EEA national 'benefit tourists' who are alleged to be coming to the UK with no intention of working but mainly to claim benefits.

The 'habitual residence' test

From 1 August 1994 people claiming income support/income-based jobseeker's allowance (JSA(IB)), housing benefit and council tax benefit have to show that they are 'habitually resident' in the Common Travel Area. The Common Travel Area is the UK, the Republic of Ireland, the Isle of Man and the Channel Islands. This means that British and Irish citizens are least likely to be adversely affected by the change. The income support application form asks if people have come to live in the UK in the past five years; those who state that they have will be interviewed about habitual residence.

Commissioners' decisions

The interpretation of the term 'habitual residence' has been developed in case law. The first Social Security Commissioner's decision on it was made in October 1995. Commissioners' decisions are not reported under the name of the people concerned, but the reference is CIS/1067/1995. This decision concerned a British citizen who had spent most of her life in Burma and whose adult children still lived there. It set out several useful points to be considered in establishing habitual residence. These were developed and expanded in another decision, CIS/2326/1995, which concerned a Bangladeshi widow with the right of abode who had recently come to the UK for the first time and was being supported by relatives. The main points to consider are:

- **the Benefits Agency must be satisfied that a person is *not* habitually resident** before benefit is refused. It is not up to claimants to prove that they *are* habitually resident.
- **there is no legal definition of 'habitual residence'** and it must be decided on the facts of each case
- residence means more than just physical presence in the UK; a short-stay visitor is not resident and a person must be 'seen to be making a home here, even though it need not be his or her only home, nor need it be a permanent one, provided it is genuinely home for the time being'.
- the most important factors in deciding habitual residence are the **'length, continuity and general nature of actual residence, rather than intentions as to the future'**. Though it is possible to lose habitual residence in one place overnight, that does not mean that people automatically become habitually resident somewhere else until an 'appreciable period of time of actual settled residence' has passed. This time varies with the facts of each case, but must show a 'settled and viable pattern of living here as

a resident'. CIS/2326/1995 held that 'viable' does not necessarily mean without relying on public funds, but the decision should include consideration of all the reasons why a person lived here, for example, an elderly person living with family members.
- habitual residence may be attained after only a **short period of actual residence**. CIS/2326/1995 states 'there is no minimum period which is necessary to establish the acquisition of a new habitual residence. The question in each individual case must be whether, in all the circumstances, including the settledness of the person's intention as to residence, the residence has continued for a sufficient period for it to be said to be habitual'.
- people who are habitually resident in a country do not lose this by **'temporary or occasional absence'**. The absences may be of long or short duration but do not annul previous habitual residence. In one case known to JCWI, the absence was 15 months but a Social Security Appeal Tribunal case was successful.
- in deciding on habitual residence, the authority deciding must look at the situation **at the date of its decision**. Thus a person might not be habitually resident at the time of the original Benefits Agency decision but have become so before the date of a Tribunal or Commissioner's hearing.

CIS/2326/1995 is under appeal at the time of writing, so interpretation may change in future.

Benefits Agency guidelines

When the test was introduced in 1994, guidelines to Benefits Agency staff listed factors they should consider, based on a European Court of Justice case, *Di Paolo* (C–76/76). The Commissioners' decisions discussed above have made this case less relevant, as it was mainly concerned with questions of work. However, Benefits Agency staff may still give these ideas undue weight in deciding on habitual residence. The factors were:

- **where is the person's centre of interests?** This is a vague concept, and people who have recently arrived, have no immediate family or other ties in the UK and have spent most of their lives in another country may not be considered to have a centre of interests in the UK.
- **stable employment**
- **nature of the occupation**. This is connected to the previous factor, in that, for example, a person who is an au pair, exchange language teacher, on a fixed short-term contract, or a seasonal worker may not qualify.
- **why did the person come to the UK?** This is aimed against the government's bugbear of 'benefit tourists' from EEA countries, and if people are in the UK on holiday, or are students in their country of origin, they will not qualify.
- **length and continuity of residence elsewhere**. If people have not had long absences from their country of origin, and have had stable employment and

have family there, and have recently arrived in the UK, it is likely they will be considered habitually resident in that country, at least for an initial period.

- **what are the claimant's intentions?** People stating that they intend to stay or take permanent work may be accepted but their past history is also relevant. However, intentions may be overtaken by events and habitual residence may change.

In practice, the requirement affects those who are not EEA nationals more severely. From August 1994 to December 1996, of the UK nationals interviewed, 132,330 passed the habitual residence test and received benefit while 15,496 failed. 18,433 EEA nationals passed and 17,351 failed. Of 'other' nationals interviewed, 20,674 passed while 18,613 failed the test and were denied benefit.

EEA nationals

Requirement to leave

As explained in chapter 6, EEA nationals may move between EEA countries to work or to seek work. Work-seekers in the UK are entitled to claim income support/JSA(IB) while looking for work. The case of *Antonissen* in the European Court of Justice (C–292/89) decided that six months was a reasonable period in which to look. Before the 'habitual residence' test ▶see above was introduced, work-seekers were normally able to claim for six months or more, but this is no longer automatic.

The Home Office, the DSS and the Employment Service have combined in order to discourage EEA nationals from claiming income support while looking for work in the UK. From 12 April 1993, the Employment Service was instructed to use a different check on EEA nationals who have been seeking work for more than six months. To qualify for income support/JSA(IB) people have to show that they are available for work, are actively seeking work and have a current Jobseeker's Agreement. The conditions are interpreted to mean the person must have 'a reasonable chance or opportunity of obtaining work' – that there are jobs available in their field, even though the numbers of applicants may make it statistically unlikely that they will be selected. For EEA nationals, Employment Service staff are now instructed to decide whether they have 'a genuine chance of finding work', which is a higher standard to meet, as there has to be some correlation between the individual and the jobs available.

If the Employment Service decides that people do not have a 'genuine chance' of work, staff are instructed to report this to the Home Office. The Home Office will then inform the person that he or she is 'considered no longer lawfully present in the UK' and will tell the Benefits Agency this and that the person 'has been required to leave the UK'. A person subject to a requirement to leave the UK is defined as a 'person from abroad' under social security regulations (see below) and is therefore not entitled to income support/JSA(IB). The EEA national may therefore be refused further benefit and be threatened by the Home Office, although as soon as he or she finds any job, starts a business etc. the threat must be withdrawn and a residence permit granted. There is the right to appeal to a Social Security Appeal Tribunal on whether the person does have a 'genuine chance' of work.

The Home Office does not take any immigration action to make the person leave the country and indeed has no power to do so. The legality of this whole process was challenged in judicial review, arguing that these Home Office letters are not a 'requirement to leave' as it would take no action to enforce the requirement. The Court of Appeal rejected these arguments and confirmed the 'person from abroad' classification, in the cases of *Wolke* and *Remelien*, but an appeal to the House of Lords was pending at the time of writing, to be heard together with *Castelli* and *Tristan-Garcia* ►see chapter 6.

Habitual residence

It has been argued that the habitual residence test might be illegal under Community legislation, which prohibits discrimination on grounds of nationality between EEA nationals who have moved for a purpose covered by the Treaty of Rome, since the requirement is met more easily by British and Irish citizens than others. The argument failed in the Court of Appeal in the cases of *Sarwar* and *Getachew* on 24 October 1996. The judge followed the European Court of Justice case of *Raulin* (C–357/89) which held that, in establishing whether people are EU workers, only work in the country where they are now living is relevant. Thus an EU national who has worked in other EU countries but not in the UK does not qualify to be treated as an EEA 'worker' but as a 'work-seeker'. There is no right to equality of treatment in non-contributory benefits for work-seekers (though if they have paid enough contributions in another EEA country, they may be able to claim contribution-based JSA, previously unemployment benefit, for three months).

Rights of residence directives

Since 1 August 1994, income support regulations also differentiate between EEA nationals who are workers and those who have entered under the three Directives in force from June 1992, on rights of residence for students, retired people and others ►see page 115. Those Directives provide that people have to show they will not need to claim 'social assistance' benefits, which the British government has defined as means-tested benefits, including income support. It is debatable whether these Directives do restrict people from claiming benefits later, if their circumstances change, for example, if a student becomes a work-seeker. People in this category who experience difficulties in claiming benefits should seek advice.

'Public funds' benefits

Income support and income-based jobseeker's allowance

Benefit regulations

There are more detailed regulations about eligibility for income support than any other benefit. From 7 October 1996, people who were required to be 'available for work' to receive income support now receive income-based jobseeker's allowance (JSA(IB)) instead. At the time of writing, the DSS had proposed stricter regulations for making all applications for income support/JSA(IB), which were due to come into force in April 1997. The proposal was that 'a fully completed claim form and all of the evidence specified on the form' must be received before an application will be accepted and considered.

Although income support is intended as a safety net, not all people in the UK are entitled to receive it. The income support regulations list people who are not eligible for normal income support, who are called 'persons from abroad', and explain when they may be able to receive a reduced rate of benefit. 'Persons from abroad' do not have to be 'available for work' so even if they are permitted to work, they should continue to claim income support, rather than be pressed into JSA(IB). There are the same 'persons from abroad' exclusions from JSA(IB).

Paragraph 21(3) of the income support regulations lists 'persons from abroad'. They are:

- people who have limited leave subject to a requirement not to have recourse to public funds (▶see list on pages 181–2 for categories of people who come under this heading)
- people on temporary admission (▶see glossary)
- people who have remained in the UK beyond the time allowed them (overstayers)
- people subject to a deportation order
- people who the Home Office alleges are illegal entrants
- EEA nationals who have been 'required to leave' by the Home Office (from 1 April 1993) ▶see above and chapter 6
- asylum-seekers (from 5 February 1996)
- people about whom an undertaking of support has been signed and who have been here for less than five years (from 5 February 1996)
- people who are not 'habitually resident' in the Common Travel Area (from 1 August 1994) ▶see above.

The DSS tells the Home Office about claims from people who it believes may be 'persons from abroad' and the Home Office may follow up this information. It is therefore dangerous for people in the UK without

ENTITLEMENT TO INCOME SUPPORT

Immigration status	Immigration rules	Benefits regulations
settled person (for whatever reason)	full entitlement	normal qualifications *unless* undertaking signed
spouse (1 year's stay)	public funds requirement	not eligible to receive benefit
British citizen or settled person with spouse with 1 year's stay	able to claim	claim for self only – partner not eligible to receive benefit
student	public funds requirement	not eligible to receive benefit *except* for six weeks with temporary disruption of funds from abroad
visitor	public funds requirement	not eligible to receive benefit *except* for six weeks with temporary disruption of funds from abroad
refugee/exceptional leave to enter or remain	able to claim	normal qualifications
application pending to Home Office for leave e.g. fiancé(e) to spouse	public funds requirement	not eligible to receive benefit
application pending to Home Office for asylum:		
– application made at port	able to claim	urgent cases rate only
– application made after entry to UK	—	not eligible to receive benefit
appeal against any Home Office refusal	—	not eligible to receive benefit

permission to apply for benefits. Almost certainly they will not qualify, and the Home Office will be informed about their presence.

People in the country legally, but with a requirement not to have recourse to public funds, who apply for benefits may receive warning letters from the Home Office and their leave to remain may be curtailed, or any extension refused. From 1 November 1996, schedule 2 para 1(1) of the Asylum and Immigration Act provides that the public funds requirement can be imposed as a condition of stay, and therefore that breach of it is a criminal offence.

Urgent cases rate income support

'Persons from abroad' can qualify for this, lower, rate of income support if they meet one of the conditions listed in income support regulation 70(3), as amended by the Social Security (Persons from Abroad) Miscellaneous Amendments Regulations 1996. The parts relating to asylum-seekers were brought into force by Schedule 1 of the Asylum and Immigration Act 1996. People must show either:

a) they have entered the UK in a category which refers to there being no recourse to public funds and their funds which come from abroad are temporarily disrupted. Provided they have been self-supporting during their stay and there is a reasonable chance that their funds will be resumed, they can get income support for up to 42 days (six weeks) in any one period of leave granted. When this applies, even students can also claim housing benefit, for the whole of their 'eligible rent' under housing benefit regulations, and council tax benefit, for this six-week period.

b) they are people about whom an undertaking has been signed, but the sponsor who signed it has died. The claimants will be entitled to income support at the urgent cases rate only, for five years after the undertaking was signed or after they entered the UK, whichever is later. After the five-year period has elapsed, they may claim full-rate income support under the normal rules.

c) they are asylum-seekers who applied for asylum on arrival in the UK

d) they are asylum-seekers who applied for asylum within three months of the Home Secretary making a declaration that their country of origin has undergone a serious upheaval and who were present in Britain on the date the declaration was made. No such declarations had ever been made at the time of writing.

In situations (c) and (d), people are entitled to benefit until the Home Office makes a decision on their asylum claim. If it is granted, they can qualify for normal income support/JSA(IB). If it is refused, they have no right to receive benefit while appealing against the refusal of asylum. There are transitional provisions for asylum-seekers who were claiming on 5 February 1996, ▶see below.

The regulations with respect to asylum-seekers originally came into force from 5 February 1996. JCWI and a Zairean asylum-seeker, Ms B, applied for judicial review of the *vires* of the regulations and were successful in the Court of Appeal on 21 June 1996. This meant that people who had applied for asylum and claimed benefits after 5 February 1996 were able to apply for backdated payment. However, the Secretary of State for Social Security, Peter Lilley, announced that an amendment would be made to the Asylum and Immigration Bill to reverse the court's decision and this came into force from 24 July 1996. A further legal challenge failed, so the 5 February changes were reinstated. People who applied for asylum after entry to the UK since 5 February or were refused asylum and lodged appeals after that date have no current entitlement to income support.

Benefits Agency practice

When the Benefits Agency considers a claim under income support regulation 70(3), *all* capital and income will be taken into account. People will be paid only 90% of the basic income support personal allowance though children's personal allowances, any extra premiums to which the claimant is entitled, and housing costs under income support regulation 17(e) (mortgage interest) will be met without the 10% deduction. However, personal allowances and premiums which relate solely to any 'person from abroad' family member will not be met. The Benefits Agency has no power to recover benefit from the claimant or anyone else, but it is always paid at this reduced rate.

If a British or settled person has a partner and/or children who are 'persons from abroad' benefit is modified for the family. The settled partner can claim but the income support/JSA(IB) applicable amount will be for a single person, plus any additions for children who are not 'persons from abroad'. Thus the 'person from abroad' effectively has no 'applicable amount' and will receive no money. However the family's joint resources will be assessed, including those of the 'person from abroad', in deciding the amount payable. The presence of the partner from abroad means that the settled or British partner is not entitled to lone parent premium or one-parent benefit even though they do not receive full benefit for the family.

Most settled people are entitled to claim income support/JSA(IB), with no immigration consequences. However, if a sponsor signed an undertaking in respect of a person (►see page 183) the person will not be entitled to claim income support, housing benefit or council tax benefit for five years after the undertaking was signed. After the five years, if the person does have an entitlement to income support, the DSS may try to reclaim the income support from the sponsor. The Benefits Agency therefore has to check whether such an undertaking was signed, through its central records or through the Home Office. Such checking may also discourage people with an entitlement to benefit from claiming, if they are not secure in their knowledge of their position.

Asylum-seekers

There are transitional provisions for asylum-seekers who were in receipt of income support on 5 February 1996. They are entitled to continue to receive it until the next negative decision on their case. Thus, for example, people who were refused asylum in January 1996 and who appealed against the refusal and were claiming income support on 5 February will continue to receive it throughout the appeal period. If they stop claiming for any reason, for example because they find work, they may be entitled to income support/JSA(IB) again if the job comes to an end if there has been no new negative decision on their asylum claim. It is possible that some people refused asylum in early 1996 were not told of the refusal at the time, but only after 5 February. People who suspect this may be the case should get specialist benefits advice.

People who applied for asylum between 5 February and 21 June could make applications for backdated income support payment. These claims should have been made by 24 July 1996.

People who apply for asylum after entry to the UK, who are therefore not eligible for benefit while the case is pending, but who are later recognised as refugees, and all those who appeal against asylum refusals and win their appeals, are entitled to backdated benefit, at the urgent cases rate, for the period of their application or appeal. They must make all the benefit backdating claims within 28 days of receiving the refugee status decision from the Home Office. This does not apply to those granted exceptional leave to enter or remain, who are not able to make such backdating claims.

Over the past three years, some people recognised as refugees argued that they should be entitled to back payments of the full income support amount for the period they were asylum-seekers and receiving money at the urgent cases rate. The argument was that refugee status is something which exists because of a person's situation and fear of persecution and which is later recognised by the Home Office, rather than a status which is granted on that date. However Commissioner's cases CIS/564/94 and CIS/7250/95 on this point, decided on 11 November 1996, accepted the definition of asylum but not that this entitled people to full rate income support.

Immigration consequences

Since August 1993, people applying for variation of their leave to enter or remain are no longer eligible to claim income support/JSA(IB). However, the Benefits Agency has official instructions to inform the Home Office about claims made by people subject to immigration control, whether or not they are entitled to the benefit. For example it has to inform the Home Office about income support claims made by:

- citizens of countries which have signed the European Convention on Social and Medical Assistance (Cyprus, Iceland, Malta, Norway, Switzerland, Turkey and all other EU countries)
- asylum-seekers, most of whom are not entitled to normal income support but some may qualify for the urgent cases rate (see above). Claiming benefit does not affect their asylum case.

The Benefits Agency may also ask questions about people's immigration status and then contact the Home Office to confirm what the claimants have said. If the Home Office cannot trace the person's file or confirm status, this may delay the claim, or initiate immigration inquiries. The income support application forms ask if the claimant or a person for whom he or she is claiming has come to live in the UK within the last five years or came here under a sponsorship agreement. If the answer is yes the claimant will be interviewed by the Benefits Agency and this is a licence to ask immigration questions and to pass information to the Home Office.

The Home Office forms for applying for leave to remain also ask about any benefit claims made. When people apply to remain on compassionate grounds, outside the immigration rules, their ability to support themselves may be a relevant consideration for the Home Office. An application for an extension of stay or for settlement might be refused.

People with limited leave to remain whose funds from abroad have been temporarily disrupted may claim urgent cases rate income support for up to six weeks. This in itself should not affect their immigration position, but will mean that the Home Office will inquire more closely into financial support in dealing with any application for an extension of stay.

Housing benefit and council tax benefit

Benefit regulations

From 1 April 1994, eligibility for housing benefit and council tax benefit has been connected to immigration status. Housing benefit regulation 7A and council tax benefit regulation 4A define 'persons from abroad', who are not eligible to receive these benefits. The definition is slightly different from that of the Benefits Agency in relation to income support/JSA(IB). For council tax benefit and housing benefit, the definition is:

- people who are not habitually resident in the Common Travel Area (▶see above)
- EEA nationals 'required to leave' the UK
- people with limited leave and a public funds restriction (unless they are EEA nationals or nationals of Cyprus, Malta, Switzerland or Turkey, which are signatories to the 1953 European Convention on Social and Medical Assistance). Some Turkish nationals who have worked in the UK may have extra rights to benefits and should seek specialist advice.
- overstayers
- people subject to a deportation order
- people alleged by the Home Office to be illegal entrants
- asylum-seekers (from 5 February 1996)
- people about whom an undertaking of support has been signed (from 5 February 1996) for five years after the date of the undertaking or the date of arrival in the country, whichever is later

However, there is also a list of exemptions from the 'persons from abroad' definition. People in these categories are entitled to claim housing benefit or council tax benefit in the normal way. These are:

- people who are in receipt of income support/JSA(IB)
- people with limited leave and a public funds restriction whose funds from

abroad have been temporarily disrupted – but only for a maximum period of 42 days (six weeks) in any period of limited leave, including any extension
- people about whom an undertaking has been signed, but the sponsor who signed it has died
- asylum-seekers who applied for asylum on arrival in the UK
- asylum-seekers who apply for asylum within three months of the Home Secretary making a declaration that their country of origin has undergone a serious upheaval and who were in the UK at the time the declaration was made. No such declarations had ever been made at the time of writing.
- people with refugee status or exceptional leave to remain
- EEA nationals who are 'workers' or 'economically active'.

There are no transitional provisions for asylum-seekers whose claims began after 5 February 1996. People who were claiming on 5 February remain eligible until their asylum claim or appeal is determined. Asylum-seekers who were not eligible while their applications were being considered, or while they were appealing against a refusal, but who are later recognised as refugees may make claims for backdated payment within 28 days of receiving the Home Office decision on refugee status.

Immigration consequences

These benefits are administered by local authorities, whose practices may vary. They have instructions on dealing with applications for benefit and on establishing the rights of claimants. Some authorities may suggest that applicants should obtain independent immigration advice before pursuing a claim. However, there is as yet no formal duty on a local authority to inform the immigration authorities of the status of claimants or recipients of benefit. But the Home Secretary's policy statement of 18 July 1995 and the Home Office circular to local authorities of 24 October 1996 ▶see below set out a framework for more formal contacts.

If the Home Office is aware that people subject to a public funds requirement have obtained housing benefit, this could lead to an extension of stay being refused. For example, a husband from Malta, a Convention country, might be entitled under the benefit regulations to obtain housing benefit but might have his application for settlement refused by the Home Office, on the grounds of inability to support himself without recourse to public funds.

National Assistance Act 1948 and Children Act 1989

After the government removed eligibility for these basic benefits from asylum-seekers and others, alternative sources of finance were investigated. The National Assistance Act 1948, although largely repealed, states in section 21(1) that 'a local authority may with the approval of the

Secretary of State, and to such extent as he may direct shall, make arrangements for providing: (a) residential accommodation for persons aged 18 or over who by reason of age, illness, disability or any other circumstances are in need of care and attention which is not otherwise available to them'. Asylum-seekers therefore made claims to local authority Social Services departments for assessment under this and the Community Care Act 1990, and received responses varying from payments up to the income support urgent cases amount to accommodation in an old people's home. The DSS and three local authorities, Hammersmith, Lambeth and Westminster, argued that this duty should not apply to those excluded from income support. The Divisional Court decided on 8 October 1996 that, 'if Parliament really did intend that in no circumstances should any assistance...be available to those asylum-seekers, it must say so in terms. If it did, it would almost certainly put itself in breach of the European Convention on Human Rights and of the Geneva Convention'. The local authorities' appeal against the judgement was heard on 15 January 1997 and dismissed on 17 February, so asylum-seekers may still receive this support at the time of writing.

When there are children involved, local authorities also have a duty under the Children Act 1989 to provide for the children. The ethos of the Children Act is to keep children with their families wherever possible, so this may mean providing for the adults of the family too. These provisions may also be helpful for people who are not asylum-seekers, for example a wife who is not yet settled fleeing with her children from a violent husband.

Family credit

Benefit regulations

Eligibility for family credit depends, in addition to the financial requirements, on the claimant having responsibility for a child, being in paid work for at least 16 hours a week, the claimant and heterosexual partner (if any) being ordinarily resident in the UK and obtaining at least some of their income from work in the UK. From 5 February 1996, people must also have no time limit on their stay, or be refugees or have exceptional leave, or be EEA nationals or nationals of countries with which the EC has an association agreement ▶see glossary for lists, or members of the family of such nationals.

There is no specific residence period required. If one member of a couple is abroad but intends to come to the UK, and they have lived together abroad in the past, the claimant in the UK may be refused benefit on these grounds and should seek specialist benefits advice. If benefit is paid, the amount of money received is the same for a single adult claimant as for a couple.

Immigration consequences

When one partner is subject to the public funds requirement and the other is not it may be possible for the settled partner to make a claim without affecting the immigration status of the other. Although the woman is normally the claimant, if she is the person from abroad, the man may claim family credit for the family.

Disability benefits

Benefit regulations

From 4 April 1996 attendance allowance, severe disablement allowance, invalid care allowance, disability working allowance and disability living allowance are defined as public funds for immigration purposes, in the immigration rules. They all have the same restrictions on immigration status. To qualify for these benefits, people must have no time limit on their stay, or be refugees or have exceptional leave, or be EEA nationals or nationals of countries with which the EC has an association agreement ▶see glossary for list, or members of the family of such nationals. Disability working allowance has the same definition of 'ordinary residence' for the claimant and spouse as family credit.

Immigration consequences

It is only the claimant who must meet the requirements, not any other family members. Settled people are eligible to claim these benefits, regardless of the grounds on which they were granted settlement or whether or not an undertaking was signed about them.

The linking of eligibility to immigration status will add to complications and mistakes made by the benefits authorities as well as discouraging claiming. As people who are claiming come to the end of their current periods of entitlement, they may be asked to show again that they qualify. Revealing to the Home Office that they have claimed may lead to difficulties in gaining extensions of leave to remain.

Child benefit

Benefit regulations

From 7 October 1996, the child benefit regulations include an immigration requirement. People 'subject to immigration control' are not entitled to child benefit unless they 'satisfy prescribed conditions' listed in an Order from the DSS. This list of people who are still eligible comprises refugees, people with exceptional leave to enter or remain, EEA nationals, nationals of countries which have Association Agreements with the EC ▶see glossary for list, or members of their families, people with indefinite leave (settled) and nationals of countries which have reciprocal agreements with the UK. This means that immigration and nationality questions can now be asked in relation to this previously universal, non-means-tested benefit.

People who were claiming before 7 October 1996 may continue to do so until their claim is reviewed. However, many existing claimants are also receiving queries about their national insurance numbers; if they do not have numbers, the whole claim may be reviewed. If another child is born to the family after 7 October 1996 and a claim for child benefit made and refused, this should not be considered a 'change of circumstances' leading to a review of older children's benefit. People whose child benefit is questioned or removed should seek specialist benefits advice.

Immigration consequences

The compulsory Home Office forms for applying for extensions of leave to remain routinely ask whether people have claimed public funds. People who were entitled to child benefit in the past, for example international students, may continue to receive it. Routine reviews of child benefit entitlement may be infrequent and people may not know of any change in the regulations. They may therefore face problems when they apply to extend their permission to remain. Home Office practice in such areas should be monitored.

Council housing and homeless persons' accommodation

Housing regulations

The Asylum and Immigration Appeals Act 1993 changed the rights of asylum-seekers and their dependants to access to housing under the provisions of Part III of the Housing Act 1985, dealing with homelessness. If they had any accommodation, 'however temporary', they might not be considered as homeless under the terms of housing law. If the local authority did accept them as homeless, it might not provide permanent accommodation while the asylum application was being considered. As in other parts of the Asylum and Immigration Appeals Act, 'dependants' were defined as only the spouse and children under 18 of an asylum-seeker, when they are not British citizens and do not have indefinite leave.

The Asylum and Immigration Act 1996 removed rights to consideration for housing from asylum-seekers altogether and restricted the rights of other groups of people 'subject to immigration control', listed in an Order. This section came into force from 19 August 1996. It is part of the government's policy to 'align a specified person's entitlement to housing assistance with his entitlement to social security benefits' so that councils do not have a duty to provide accommodation for people who are unable to pay for it as they do not qualify for benefits.

The Order specifies the people 'subject to immigration control' who still qualify for ordinary council accommodation as:

- people recognised as refugees
- people granted exceptional leave
- people with any other limited leave not subject to a support and accommodation requirement
- people with indefinite leave to enter or remain
- international students living in hard-to-let council accommodation which has been let in bulk to their education institution.

For accommodation as homeless people, the Order specifies:
- people recognised as refugees
- people granted exceptional leave
- people with any other limited leave not subject to a support and accommodation requirement
- people with indefinite leave to enter or remain
- people who applied for asylum on arrival in the UK, or within three months of the Home Office declaring that their country of origin has undergone an upheaval, and whose applications are still pending
- people who were asylum-seekers, or appealing against refusals of asylum, and entitled to housing benefit, on 4 February 1996, and no further decision has been made on their case.

People qualify for consideration only from the date on which the Home Office makes its decision to grant them the relevant leave. It is therefore vital that housing departments should be informed immediately when refugee status or exceptional leave is granted to someone who needs accommodation, so that the process begins as soon as possible. EEA nationals and their families are not subject to immigration control and therefore are not affected by this change.

Local authority housing departments

Before 1996, housing law did not mention people's immigration status as a criterion for eligibility. However, local authority homeless persons' units have been able to question many applicants for housing in detail about their immigration status. The 7 April 1993 Court of Appeal decision in *R v Secretary of State for the Environment ex parte London Borough of Tower Hamlets* (1993 Imm AR 495) held that there is no duty on councils to house people illegally in the UK and that there is a duty to inform the Home Office about them. The Court of Appeal stated: 'there is nothing in either of the Acts or the rules to prevent the housing authority making enquiries as to what statements, representations or undertakings were given in relation to accommodation by or on behalf of the applicant but it is its duty to do so... if as a result of these enquiries the housing authority suspects that the applicant is an illegal entrant not only is there nothing to prevent the authority from informing the immigration authorities... but it would be its duty to do so.'

The case arose because Tower Hamlets council had applied for a judicial review of the guidance issued by the Department of the Environment on dealing with applications for housing as homeless people. This guidance stated that any information received about applicants' immigration status was to be treated as confidential. Tower Hamlets, concerned about the shortage of housing stock in the borough, initiated court cases in order to try to limit the council's housing responsibilities. It suggested that family members from abroad who had come in to join a settled person must have shown that there was adequate accommodation available for them; if this was not the case, incorrect information must have been given for the family to gain entry to the UK and therefore they had entered illegally. The council argued that people who were not legally in the UK were not entitled to housing and therefore that the Housing Department should make inquiries into immigration status and that it had a duty to report information to the Home Office, and the court upheld this decision.

The Department of the Environment published amendments to its Code of Guidance for homeless persons' units workers in the light of this judgement, and the provisions of the Asylum and Immigration Appeals Act, in March 1994. The guidance stated: 'Authorities cannot refuse to rehouse an applicant on the grounds that s/he (or those who reside with him/her) are immigrants, provided they are in this country legally. Authorities should handle applications from immigrants in exactly the same way as they handle applications from local people.'

However, it continues: 'It is open to an authority to consult IND [the Immigration and Nationality Directorate of the Home Office] about any case where it believes that an applicant may be an illegal entrant or overstayer. Although it is under no duty to do so, an authority may also wish to advise IND if it is considering an application from someone whom it believes to be a "no recourse to public funds entrant". Where an authority reaches its own conclusion that an applicant is an illegal entrant or overstayer, it should also inform IND of this.' These notification arrangements are still in force.

Immigration consequences

There were no immigration consequences for asylum-seekers applying for or being provided with accommodation as homeless persons, while they were entitled to obtain it. But there is a strong likelihood that homeless persons' units will pass on information to the Home Office about their claims for housing.

If people subject to the public funds requirement are rehoused as homeless they could be refused permission to remain longer if they make an application for an extension of stay to the Home Office. It has been rare for the Home Office to inquire how they have obtained council property, but this is likely to change. The Home Office has also stated that when a couple are in homeless accommodation it is only concerned with whether that accommodation had to be provided in order to meet the needs of a person from abroad. For example, if a British mother and her children are in homeless accommodation, this would not preclude her foreign husband coming to join them, as the same size accommodation would be necessary whether or not the husband were living there.

The Department of the Environment guidance includes standard forms to be sent between the local authority homeless persons' unit and the Home Office requesting and receiving information and provides that all enquiries should go through a named postholder. Housing officials may also question other people applying for housing about their immigration status. Consequently these people may be deterred from claiming housing to which they are entitled, or be wrongly refused housing. The way that different local authorities operate these guidelines should be monitored in order to see what effects they have and to ensure that people entitled to housing obtain it and that the way in which their entitlement is established is fair and non-discriminatory.

The Housing Act 1996

This Act came into force on 20 January 1997 but had been planned for some years before. It repeats the exclusion from both council housing and homelessness provisions of people subject to immigration control, with the same exceptions as listed above. But it also excludes another group from all types of housing – people who fail the habitual residence test ▶see above.

These changes therefore restrict people's chances to obtain housing, and may keep families apart for longer periods if they are unable to satisfy the housing requirements of the immigration rules, and reduce asylum-seekers to destitution. They mean that all local authority housing officials now have a reason for asking for immigration information and for referring queries to the Home Office. As information may well be complex and many long-settled people will not have passports or other proof from the Home Office of their settled status, further discrimination and wrong refusals of housing may be expected. It is important to monitor the operation of housing authorities, to ensure that people are able to exercise whatever rights to housing they still have and that the restrictions are not operated in a racially discriminatory way.

Deciding whether to claim

It is important to weigh up the financial and the immigration consequences of claiming or not claiming a 'public funds' benefit. Often when people seek advice on benefits they will be in dire financial straits. Some people now have no entitlement to any 'public funds' benefits at all, or indeed to any other benefits, but others may still have a chance of claiming. It is important that they understand any immigration implications of claiming, as financially they may have no choice but to try to do so, at least in the short term. The following checklist may be helpful in deciding how a claim can most safely be made:

- **Can the partner claim instead?** This will mean that no public funds are paid for these claimants themselves, although they may be able to benefit from their partner's entitlement. The Home Office has confirmed that 'there is no objection to other residents in the same household receiving public funds to which they are entitled in their own right.' Thus if a settled or British partner claims a public funds benefit for him- or herself only, this would not normally be used as a reason for refusal of settlement for a partner from abroad. Not-yet-settled people have been progressively excluded from eligibility for benefits: from income support since 2 August 1993, from housing benefit and council tax benefit since 1 April 1994, from family credit, attendance allowance, invalid care allowance, disability living allowance, disability working allowance and severe disablement allowance since 4 April 1996 and from child benefit since 7 October 1996.

- **Is there a financial alternative?** Clearly this needs to be immediate; other funds, for example, charities, sponsors' friends, student welfare organisations, any Social Services provisions under section 17 of the Children Act or for other vulnerable people under the National Assistance Act or the Community Care legislation or any embassy welfare provisions might be possible.

- **Will the claim be for a short or long period?** Short-term recourse to public funds can possibly be explained by 'mitigating circumstances'. Claiming income support, housing benefit or council tax benefit for up to six weeks, on the grounds that funds from abroad have been temporarily disrupted, ▶see page 193, should not directly affect immigration status. However, it could mean that the Home Office will ask for more detailed evidence of support in future applications for extensions of stay. The Home Office has indicated that when considering applications for family settlement a short-term claim may not prejudice the application.

- **Will the Home Office find out?** If the benefit claimed is income support, the Benefits Agency will report the claim or attempted claim to the Home Office. If it is a benefit administered by the local authority, policies on confidentiality and on contacting or informing the Home Office vary. Housing departments generally have arrangements on how to do so and other departments are setting them up. Local advice centres may have information.

- **Will a sponsor be pursued?** If the claim is for income support, sponsors might well be contacted about the claim and should be advised. If the relationship between the sponsor and the sponsored person has broken down, or if the sponsor no longer has the money, it is unlikely that the Benefits Agency will take action against a sponsor. If the claim is for any other benefit, there is no liability for the sponsor. If the undertaking was signed, or the person came to the UK, less than five years ago, he or she will not qualify for income support, housing benefit or council tax benefit unless the sponsor has died or until the person has been in the UK for more than five years.

Benefits which are not 'public funds'

All other welfare benefits are not classed as 'public funds' for immigration purposes and therefore have no direct effect on immigration status and on applications to remain.

There are reciprocal arrangements about eligibility for some limited benefits between the UK and Australia, Barbados, Bermuda, Canada, the Channel Islands, Cyprus, Israel, Jamaica, Malta, Mauritius, New Zealand, the Philippines, Switzerland, Turkey, the USA and the countries of the former Yugoslavia. The benefits authorities may ask for evidence of the nationality of a claimant, but this should be only in connection with establishing whether the person is eligible under any bilateral reciprocal arrangements. The relevant embassy or high commission may be able to give details of individual agreements. The Benefits Agency Overseas Branch, Newcastle-upon-Tyne NE98 1YX, produces leaflets on some reciprocal arrangements and can give more information.

Residence requirements

Most benefits are subject to a residence test, either directly or indirectly. National insurance benefits – for example, unemployment benefit (now contribution-based jobseeker's allowance) – require contributors to pay into the scheme for approximately two years before they qualify for benefits. Non-contributory non-means-tested benefits are often paid only where the claimant has been in the UK for a specified period, six months.

There are no residence requirements for means-tested benefits, other than the habitual residence test ▶see above. People may also be excluded because they are not eligible for income support, which is a requirement for benefits such as free school meals for children.

National Health Service

Immigration status and eligibility to use the National Health Service are not directly related. The Health Service was set up in 1949 to be available to all those 'ordinarily resident' in Britain, and this was confirmed in the NHS Act 1977. However, from 1 October 1982 people defined by the NHS as 'overseas visitors' can be charged for their NHS hospital medical treatment. This does not mean that all people from overseas are liable to pay for their NHS treatment; there are many exemptions from this. In particular, anyone who is ordinarily resident (▶see glossary) in the UK, or is allowed to stay permanently or intends to stay permanently, is exempt from charges. Hospitals interpret the regulations in their own ways, most commonly that people who intend to remain for less than six months are liable to be charged. Deciding on whether a person is ordinarily resident may also be complicated and hospitals may tell people they are liable, or send out bills, when this is not correct. When bills are challenged, hospitals may correct them.

Exemptions from charges

Certain sorts of medical treatment are exempt from charges:

- treatment in casualty and accident and emergency departments, including dental and ophthalmic emergency departments (but as soon as an emergency patient is transferred to an ordinary ward, liability to pay may begin)
- the diagnosis and treatment of certain diseases (including food poisoning, malaria, measles, TB, whooping cough and sexually transmitted diseases). This includes having a test for the HIV antibody, and counselling connected with the test, but not any further treatment if the test is positive.
- compulsory psychiatric treatment (ie detention under the Mental Health Act or treatment conditional on a probation order)

Some people are exempt from charges:

- anyone who has been in the UK for at least 12 months regardless of immigration status
- anyone who has come to the UK with the intention of remaining permanently. If an application for settlement is pending with the Home Office, the person is exempt.
- anyone who has come to the UK for the purpose of working
- refugees, people with exceptional leave to enter or remain and asylum-seekers. This includes all asylum-seekers, whether they applied on entry or after arrival, though there are concerns that this exemption may be changed.
- people in prison or detained by the immigration authorities
- members of HM Forces, other Crown servants and British Council staff recruited in the UK but serving overseas who have come back for treatment
- students who are on courses which last at least six months
- people working overseas who have had at least 10 years' residence in the UK and have either been working abroad for less than five years, or have been taking leave in the UK at least once every two years, or have a contractual right to do so or a contractual right to a passage to the UK at the end of their employment
- seafarers on UK-registered ships and offshore workers in UK territorial waters
- war disablement pensioners and war widows
- certain UK pensioners living overseas if they had lived in the UK for at least 10 years or been 10 years in Crown service

- the spouses or children, up to the age of 16, or 19 if still in full-time education, of any of these people
- citizens of the EEA and of other countries with which the UK has reciprocal medical treatment agreements. These are Anguilla, Australia, Barbados, British Virgin Islands, Bulgaria, Channel Islands, Czech Republic, Falkland Islands, Hong Kong, Hungary, Isle of Man, Malta, Montserrat, New Zealand, Poland, Romania, Russia, St Helena, Slovak Republic, the countries of the former Soviet Union except Latvia, Lithuania and Estonia, the Turks and Caicos Islands and the countries of the former Yugoslavia. Nationals of signatories to the European Social Charter with which the UK does not have a reciprocal agreement also qualify; these are currently Cyprus and Turkey.

These agreements vary: most only cover treatment for conditions which have arisen during the visit, or when people have been specifically referred to the UK for treatment for a particular ailment. People from these countries who do not fit in to any of the other exemptions may therefore be charged for medical treatment for a pre-existing condition. The full details of individual agreements should be checked with the consulate of the country concerned.

Liability for charges

People who do not fit into any of these exemptions and who cannot argue that they are 'ordinarily resident' in the UK are liable to be charged for hospital treatment. This applies mainly to visitors, to students who are attending courses of less than six months' duration and to people who already had the medical condition for which they require treatment before they came to the UK and who are not otherwise exempt.

Ordinary residence in this context means that people are legally in the UK, for a settled purpose, as part of the regular order of their lives for the time being. This was defined by the House of Lords in the case of *Shah and Akbarali v. Brent London Borough Council* (1983 2 AC 309), which decided that overseas students were ordinarily resident in the UK for the period of their studies. It is not directly connected to immigration status; a person who has entered as a visitor, for example, but who has applied to the Home Office for permission to settle, has shown his or her intention to remain permanently in the UK and is therefore ordinarily resident in the country and not liable to NHS charges.

Many hospital administrators have a rule of thumb that people intending to stay in the UK for less than six months are liable to pay for treatment. However, people in the UK for less than six months may be ordinarily resident, if they are in the country for a settled purpose. A student enrolled on a three-month course of studies, for example, may argue that, because of this purpose of the stay, he or she has become ordinarily resident and therefore not liable to be charged.

Procedures

People who come to a hospital for treatment for the first time should be asked up to three brief questions to determine whether they are eligible for free treatment or not. If they answer yes to either of the first two questions, they have shown that they are entitled to free treatment. The questions are:

- Have you (or your husband or wife, or parent for a person under 16) been living in the UK for the past 12 months?
- Are you/spouse/parent going to live in the UK permanently?
- On what date did you/spouse/parent arrive in the UK?

Hospital administrators are not supposed to ask to see passports at this stage, unless they have any reason to believe that they have not been told the truth. There are however many reports that requests for passports are routine.

Only if the patient has answered no to the first two questions should any further questioning be carried out. Hospitals call this Stage 2 questioning and the NHS *Manual of guidance on health service charges* gives complicated flowcharts for administrators for use in establishing whether people are exempt from charges. Instructions say that it is only at this stage that people's passports may be requested and then, because 'much of the information contained in passports cannot be correctly interpreted without specialised knowledge', only to check whether they are citizens of a country with which the UK has a reciprocal agreement on treatment. Other documents suggested to prove a person's exemption include rent books, mortgage documents, fuel or phone bills (paid!), used single tickets to the UK, TV licenses and life insurance policies.

The charges levied on people are the normal private rates for treatment, without any extra consultants' fees. The Department of Health publishes a list of the fees for particular treatments, drugs and operations as well as boarding fees. These vary according to the type of hospital, with prestigious teaching hospitals being more expensive.

Hospitals have no authority to charge anyone except the patient from overseas for medical treatment. They have no statutory authority to ask the relatives or friends of a visitor to pay or to underwrite payment for medical treatment and any requests for such guarantees should be resisted. Some health authorities have stated it is not worth their while pursuing debts abroad.

Private medical treatment

There are provisions in the immigration rules for visitors to come to the UK for medical treatment, but this treatment has to be private, and people have to show that they have the means to pay for it and to support themselves without working or having recourse to public funds and that they intend to leave the UK at the end of their treatment ▶see chapter 8. Having come to the UK for medical treatment does not stop people from becoming exempt from charges after being in the country for a year. They will then be eligible for free NHS treatment, but any application to the Home Office for permission to remain in the UK for NHS treatment would be outside the immigration rules, at the discretion of the Home Office. The chances of success would depend on the seriousness of the illness and the necessity of the treatment.

General practitioners

The NHS regulations do not apply to treatment from GPs. GPs are technically self-employed and have their own discretion about accepting or refusing any patient on to their lists. Department of Health guidelines suggest that they should accept people who are in the UK for less than six months only as private patients. Some GPs ask to see passports when registering new patients and this has inhibited many people from abroad from registering with a GP and obtaining a NHS number. However, visitors and other people in the UK for short periods are entitled to register with GPs and to receive a GP service through the NHS, if they can find a doctor who will register them.

Asylum-seekers may have particular difficulties in registering, due to unfamiliarity with the system or language problems, but they are entitled to GPs' care. If they are not entitled to income support, they are also not automatically entitled to free NHS prescriptions, sight tests or dental treatment. They have to fill in form AG1, obtainable from doctors, dentists, hospitals and Benefits Agency offices, to apply for a certificate of exemption from these charges. As this takes some time to process and is only valid for six months, people should not wait until they are ill before applying.

People with AIDS or HIV infection

The immigration rules state nothing about particular illnesses or conditions, but there are internal Home Office instructions. Stonewall (▶see chapter 19 for address) obtained the instructions on dealing with people with AIDS (BDI 3/95). These stated that allowing a person to remain must always be exceptional. AIDS in itself is not a reason either to refuse or to grant an application; the main consideration is whether someone fits into the immigration rules. If a person is applying for leave to remain, the Home Office requires a letter from his or her consultant confirming that the person has AIDS or is HIV-positive, the person's life expectancy, details of the treatment he or she is having, and whether the person is fit to travel. Where the absence of treatment abroad would 'significantly shorten the life expectancy' of the person, leave to remain would normally be appropriate. Home Office staff are reminded that the medical position may look very different in a few months, after a person has appealed against a refusal, and if the person is then too ill to travel.

Carers

Carers of people with AIDS, and other serious illnesses, might be admitted as visitors, but extensions beyond the normal six-month period are exceptional. BDI 2/95, the internal instructions on carers, states that applications from *relatives* who have entered as visitors for an extension to continue caring for a person with any terminal illness 'should normally be granted' for three months, while applications from *friends* should normally be refused, except in emergencies. The Home Office requires evidence of the person's illness and treatment, and why nobody else is able to be the carer, as well as evidence of support and accommodation. Even if successive extensions are granted to a carer, the person will not qualify for settlement and will be expected to leave when the patient dies or recovers, or if alternative arrangements for his or her care, such as admission to hospital, have been made.

State education

Educating children of compulsory school age (5 to 16) at state schools is not counted as recourse to public funds. International students, work permit holders, business people and any others who are subject to the public funds requirement are entitled to send their children to state schools. The 1994 immigration rules state that working holidaymakers should not have children over the age of five; the rationale for this can only be because older children would clearly be entitled to state education. The rules also state that visitors must not 'intend to study at a maintained school' but the decision on whether to admit a child is the school's.

Advice from the Department for Education and Employment (Annex B of circular 11/88, revised in March 1992) suggests that a school is entitled to refuse admission to a child who is only going to be in the UK for a short time (undefined), on the grounds that the disruption caused to the child and to the rest of the class is disproportionate to the benefit gained by a few weeks' schooling. However, if the parents are planning to remain longer the school should accept the child; immigration status in itself is not an adequate reason for refusing admission to school.

At the time of writing, this guidance was being revised, in the light of the Home Office and Cabinet Office 'efficiency scrutiny' ▶see below. A draft issued in December 1996 repeated this advice, but was written in a more restrictive manner, suggesting that in the event of an appeal against refusal of admission to a school the Secretary of State would only direct admission if the authority had acted unreasonably. More worryingly, it states that 'occasionally, however, admission authorities receive applications which give rise to concern that the applicant may be in the UK without permission. In such circumstances consideration should be given to writing to the Immigration Status Enquiry Unit [of the Home Office]. Disclosure of information to prevent or detect an offence is permitted under the provisions of the Data Protection Act 1984. This covers offences under the immigration laws. Contact with the Enquiry Unit will, however, only be appropriate where reasonable suspicion is aroused during the course of normal admission procedures.' The draft circular itself gives rise to concern, as it inappropriately draws schools into immigration control mechanisms.

A child will not be granted leave to enter or remain in the UK as a student in his or her own right in order to attend a state school. Children may come to the UK as students, but they have to be attending private fee-paying schools and have the money available for this, and arrangements have to be made for their care, either living with foster-parents or at a boarding-school with adequate arrangements being made for school holidays. If a child who has been granted leave to remain as a student is transferred from a private to a state school, any application for leave to remain for that purpose is likely to be refused.

The 1994 immigration rules also stressed the need for students to be paying for their studies when at a publicly-funded college. The DfEE changed the regulations about part-time courses in 1995, to provide that colleges can charge full-cost fees to part-time students from overseas. There are proposals to restrict student grants and loans to settled people. All these measures could have serious effects on asylum-seekers, who have been able to study before they were allowed to work, and others who have leave to remain on a different basis but have been following part-time or evening studies as well, or who have qualified as home students or for grants.

Status checking

Home Office efficiency scrutiny

Connections between the immigration authorities and other central and local government departments have increased, as a matter of government policy. The Cabinet Office, Home Office and DSS set up a three-person 'efficiency scrutiny', which carried out investigations between October 1993 and April 1994. The results of the investigation have not been made public, but on 18 July 1995 the Home Secretary, Michael Howard, put out a press release based on it. He stated he planned a 'clampdown on abuse of social security benefits, student awards, health and social housing by illegal immigrants and temporary visitors'. On 24 October 1996, Ann Widdecombe said that the scrutiny process was complete, and had 'successfully created a coherent legal framework which bars immigration offenders and temporary visitors from access to important and expensive benefits.' This chapter has discussed the proposed and actual changes created.

Home Office aims

The Home Office issued a circular to local authorities about this on 24 October 1996. The circular stated the proposals 'were designed:

- to ensure that people who were here unlawfully or as temporary visitors did not receive benefits to which they should not be entitled, including social security, social housing, free NHS treatment and student awards
- to ensure that officials responsible for providing benefits and services were given the necessary training, guidance and information to identify claimants who were ineligible by reason of their immigration status;
- to strengthen the arrangements for officials responsible for providing benefits and services to pass information about suspected immigration offenders to the immigration authorities.'

The intention was thus to formalise arrangements to enlist other government departments and local authority employees into acting as immigration officials. Such arrangements have already been in operation for years, for example in the relationship between the DSS and the Home Office which ensures that income support claimants who have come to the UK in the past five years will be questioned about their immigration status. Queries are referred to the Home Office, and claims reported to it. The new arrangements need to be monitored and resisted.

Access to benefits

Changes to benefit entitlements brought into operation by regulation and by the Asylum and Immigration Act 1996 mean that the criteria for eligibility for family credit, child benefit and most disability benefits also now include immigration status; these are discussed above. Advisers may need to be vigilant that people are not wrongly refused benefit on the grounds of misunderstanding of their immigration status.

Eligibility for child benefit was linked to immigration status from 7 October 1996. The DSS legal department showed its lack of understanding of immigration law when it first produced an Order on child benefit which would have meant that settled people were no longer able to claim for their children. JCWI pointed out the error and the Order was quickly amended. However, the episode shows the problem of officials of other departments not understanding immigration matters and suggests that training proposed for them may not have been effective.

Since 1993, staff in council homeless persons' units have been obliged to ask applicants about immigration status. The Asylum and Immigration Appeals Act 1993 restricted asylum-seekers' housing rights and the Asylum and Immigration Act 1996 and the Housing Act 1996 removed such rights altogether from most asylum-seekers. With effect from 20 January 1997, people not yet settled or not 'habitually resident' are not eligible for any council housing. Thus housing staff now need to ask further questions to determine eligibility and are encouraged to report suspicions to the Home Office. Insensitive and inept questioning will lead to complaints of racial discrimination and to people being refused housing to which they may be entitled.

Information-gathering and sharing

There are serious questions about confidentiality of information being given to one government or local authority department and being passed on to another. The Home Office affects not to recognise this, stating that 'government is unitary' and therefore information can be passed on. However this argument does not make sense when it comes down to the level of a single school or hospital or workplace. The requirement on employers from 27 January 1997 to see documents relating to new employees and to keep evidence of this as a defence against being charged with employing them illegally raises similar questions.

When housing authorities were first found to have a duty to pass on information to the Home Office, complex arrangements were set up to ensure that a named postholder in the local authority should communicate with a named person at the Home Office and all queries should be routed through this. The arrangements have been extended, so all local authority enquirers should go through either the newly-created Immigration Status Enquiry Unit or the Asylum Screening Unit to make their enquiries, which should be in writing or by fax. As a minimum safeguard, it is vital that all authorities ensure that this is done, to protect information being used in an incorrect or malicious way.

National Insurance numbers

People are often asked to show their passports when they are applying for a national insurance number. If they are not working, the Contributions Agency may ask why they require a NI number. It will be given if they have proof of identity and can 'demonstrate satisfactorily' that they are seeking work or claiming benefits and therefore need a NI number, but otherwise it may be refused. As people born in the UK are allocated a NI number automatically, it is assumed that anyone who needs to apply will be subject to immigration control and must be checked. Contributions Agency officials are not always aware of the meaning of immigration stamps and they have no authority to demand passports, though in practice there may be complications and delays for the claimant if this is refused.

Register offices

There has been an established link between register offices and the Home Office for some time. When people want to get married and signify their intentions to the marriage registrar, he or she is required to be satisfied as to their identity, their age and that they are free to marry and therefore may request sight of a passport. This has understandably caused worries for people who are in the UK without permission.

In general, the registrar is looking at the passport for evidence of identity and age and nationality. A minority of registrars also act as immigration officials and attempt to check immigration status. This practice is becoming more prevalent. Registrars also have to be satisfied that the planned marriage is genuine and not being undertaken for immigration purposes, and if they have suspicions to pass them on to the Registrar-General, who may alert the Home Office. JCWI knows of arrests in connection with weddings at Wolverhampton, Westminster and Hackney (where an investigation into alleged marriages of convenience was run by the *News of the World*) and of inquiries relating to immigration status being made in Southwark and Haringey (the latter denied that this was policy).

In November 1993 officials at the Registrar General's department and the Home Office agreed together to pass information about some couples applying to divorce to the Home Office. When this practice became known it was disowned by the departments concerned and stopped in February 1994. It was stated that no use had been made of the information collected and that it had been destroyed.

Opposition to status checking

Community groups have often taken up the issue of internal immigration checks and controls in particular areas. Examples include the No Pass Laws Here! group which was active from 1979 to 1987, the Hackney Anti-Deportation Campaign which produced a useful booklet on internal checking in Hackney and the Committee for Non-Racist Benefits, which has produced practical leaflets for claimants. Public service unions have also expressed opposition to checks.

The effect of checks is often to discourage people who have every right to claim but who are worried about their status, rather than to find or arrest people who may not be entitled. The trend towards aligning entitlements to benefits and services with immigration status, the requirement on employers to check employees' nationality or immigration status and to keep a document relating to it and the increased police powers to raid premises all mean that these developments can only increase. Immigration questions are being raised in ever-wider contexts and more authorities believe they need to make immigration inquiries or to check with the Home Office. The effects of this on access to benefits and services and on increased race discrimination and injustice must be monitored, challenged and opposed.

SECTION 7: TRAVEL

11 Coming, going and staying: the practicalities of travel

This chapter discusses the practicalities of travel to the UK, both when entering the UK for the first time and travelling in and out of the country after having been given permission to remain. People who are not EEA nationals need leave to enter the UK, so immigration officers still check all entrants. There is an argument that people travelling from within the area of the EEA should not be examined, but the British government does not accept this interpretation of Community legislation. The chapter also covers the practical details of making applications to the Home Office for variation and extension of leave for different purposes.

Entry clearance

Entry clearance is permission from a British embassy, high commission or consulate to travel to the UK. It may be called either a visa, when it is compulsory, or an entry certificate. People applying for entry clearance have to satisfy officials at a British post that they qualify under the immigration rules to enter the UK in the category in which they are applying.

People who need entry clearance

There are three groups of people who need to obtain entry clearance before travelling to the UK. They are:

- **people who are visa nationals** (▶see glossary for list) who must have entry clearance before travelling to the UK for any reason *except* when they are returning residents ▶see page 229, or had permission to stay for more than six months and are returning within that time and for the same purpose ▶see page 228

- **people who are coming intending to stay permanently**: this usually means people coming to join relatives in the UK, for example spouses, children or parents

- **people who are coming in order to work or to do business**, including working holidaymakers, all the categories of permit-free employment in the immigration rules (▶see chapter 7), self-employment and diplomatic work, *except* EEA nationals.

How to apply for entry clearance

People apply for entry clearance to the British embassy, high commission or consulate in the country in which they are living before travelling to the UK. The Foreign and Commonwealth Office produces a list of these 'designated posts' where applications for entry clearance must be made. Most will deal with all types of entry clearance applications, but some are restricted to dealing with particular types of applications ▶see appendix for details. When there is no designated post in their country, visit visa applicants may apply at a designated post in any other country. People applying for other purposes normally must apply at a post in a specific country.

People have to fill in the official application form IM2A (▶see appendix for example) and any other form relevant for their application. Form IM2B is for people applying for settlement, Form IM2C for people applying to work, Form IM2D for people claiming the right of abode and Form IM2E for anyone who has previously applied for entry clearance and been refused or been refused entry on arrival in the UK. Form IM2F must be filled in by anyone who has had previous immigration problems in the UK – being removed or deported, or threatened with removal or deportation. People who have ever 'received social security benefits or been a charge on public funds', or who have criminal convictions must also state these and people who have worked in the UK are asked to 'explain the circumstances' on this form.

The forms are obtained from the British post. They can also be obtained from the Migration and Visa Department of the Foreign and Commonwealth Office in the UK, and a relative in the UK may fill them in on behalf of the person abroad. However, the person abroad should sign the forms and take or send them, with the fee, to the British post. The fee (▶see appendix) is payable in local currency and is not refundable. The Foreign Office states that settlement entry clearance fees are likely to be increased in April 1997, and the intention is to achieve 'full cost recovery for entry clearance services'.

The application is made on the day the British post receives the form and the fee; if the fee has not been paid, the application is not considered to be valid. The date of application is particularly important in children's settlement applications, as they must be under 18 at the date of application. In some countries, the application will be dealt with straight away. In others, for example the countries of the Indian subcontinent, the Philippines and Thailand, there are long delays for people applying for settlement and may be delays for visitors.

Applications for settlement

The entry clearance officers at the British post interview almost all people applying to come to the UK for settlement with family members, except children under 10. Children between 10 and 14 should be interviewed only in the presence of an adult, preferably a parent or guardian, or other adult associated with their family. The Foreign Office states that 'questions should be confined to relatively simple matters and details of immediate family.' All applicants have to satisfy the entry clearance officer that they are related as claimed to the person they are applying to join, and that there is adequate support and accommodation for them.

The officers may use interpreters for the interview. Usually the interview will start with a standard initial question to confirm whether the interviewee is tired or unwell and can understand the interpreter. Few people express any worries on this score, as the result is likely to be the stopping of the interview and long delays in continuing the case. If there are problems, it is helpful to raise them as soon as possible in as much detail as possible, so that they can be investigated and consideration of the case be continued quickly.

The entry clearance officers will make their own notes for their records of the interview, and to use in preparation for any appeal against refusal. In a letter of 12 May 1993 to APART ▶see chapter 19 for address, the Home Office confirmed its refusal to allow applicants to tape record their interviews, but added that 'there is no objection to an applicant taking verbatim notes and/or to having an independent witness present at interview. There is no objection to an applicant being accompanied at interview by his or her own interpreter for verification purposes.' The Foreign Office confirmed this to JCWI on 26 September 1996: 'it is still policy to allow requests from MPs, solicitors and other representatives to attend an applicant's interview as an observer. There is no objection to this provided that the applicant concerned has no objections [and] the representative clearly understands that, as an observer, he/she must not intervene while the interview is taking place. But at the end of the interview, the observer may then make comments on the case to the ECO. These ground rules should be spelled out in advance, in writing if necessary, and if the observer fails to abide by them, the interview may be terminated.'

The British High Commission in Dhaka, where delays for settlement applicants had always been among the longest, introduced a new system in 1994, based on the provision of documents. By summer 1996, they did not interview about 60% of applicants – and 50% of husbands and 25% of wives were refused.

Documents required

The British post requires some standard information, both about the applicant and about the person he or she is coming to join (the sponsor). This includes:

- **photocopies of the sponsor's passport**. If she or he is a British citizen with a maroon British passport, the last page is enough; if the sponsor has an old blue British passport, the first five pages. If the sponsor is not a British citizen, copies of all the pages with personal details and all the pages with any immigration officers' stamps on them are required. Because passports should not be sent through the post between countries, British posts will accept photocopies, but they must all be certified by a solicitor as genuine copies; the solicitor should write on each photocopied page 'I certify this is a genuine copy of...', sign the statement and add an official stamp. In general, the immigration authorities will not accept photocopies of documents, on the grounds that a photocopy might not reveal a forged or altered document, unless the copies have been certified by a solicitor in this way.

- **the sponsor's birth certificate** if he or she was born in the UK
- **evidence of adequate financial support in the UK**. If the sponsor in the UK is working, this could be recent pay slips, or a letter from the employer confirming the job and salary, or recent bank statements covering at least the past three months showing money coming in and out. If other friends or relatives will be supporting the applicant, a letter from them will be necessary, confirming that they are able and willing to do so and similar evidence to the above that they are able to do so. If the sponsor in the UK is running a business, the business accounts or bank statements could be sent.

A spouse from abroad applying to come to join a British or settled spouse in the UK may also provide evidence of his or her own means or plans, for example a letter from an employer offering a job when the spouse arrives. Support from people other than the sponsor, for example parents-in-law supporting a married couple, will normally only be acceptable for a limited period, at the discretion of the entry clearance officer. Other relatives must show that the sponsor is able to support them.

There is no separate immigration law definition of what 'adequate' support is; as long as the money coming in is above the level of income support that would be payable to the household, this should be considered adequate. However, the Immigration Appeal Tribunal has held in one case (*Azem* 7863) that the level of support should be above the basic income support level, because a person on income support receives other things free, such as prescriptions and eye tests and free school meals for children, therefore income support cannot be considered adequate total support.

The immigration rules require people to show that adequate maintenance without recourse to public funds is available. The Home Office interpretation of this is that no 'additional' public funds must be needed to support the person concerned, but that sponsors in the UK can continue to rely on any public funds they are claiming in their own right. The Tribunal in *Clevon Scott* (13389) reluctantly confirmed the 'lamentable state of affairs' that 'it is quite clear that, from at least 28 September 1989, it has been the stated policy and practice of the UK government

that, where reliance upon public funds is in issue, only *additional* reliance upon such funds is objectionable.'
- **evidence of accommodation.** Accommodation does not have to be owned; council or privately-rented accommodation is quite satisfactory. If it is being bought on mortgage, a letter from the building society or other organisation giving the mortgage, confirming the ownership of the accommodation and the number of rooms available should be adequate. If it is council accommodation, a letter from the council confirming the tenancy, the size of the accommodation, and that there is room for the extra person to live there will be necessary. Such letters can be difficult to obtain from overworked council housing departments which may take a long time to provide letters that they do not see as immediate emergencies.

If the accommodation is privately rented, a letter from the landlord confirming the size and tenancy and that he or she has no objection to the extra person coming should be sent. Entry clearance officers may want to see the terms of any lease or tenancy agreement for rented accommodation, to be sure that sub-letting is allowed, or the numbers of people permitted to live in the accommodation. Their instructions state that one room in a joint family household might be acceptable accommodation for a married couple, if this arrangement is short-term. When landlords are unwilling to write, or when the accommodation is owned outright, some council environmental health departments are prepared to write to confirm that accommodation is adequate.

There are no special immigration law standards for the adequacy or size of accommodation. The standard laid down under the Housing Act 1985, now repeated in the Housing Act 1996, has applied – that is, that two people, of the opposite sex and at least one of them over the age of 10, and who are not married or living in a relationship similar to marriage, should not have to share the same room to sleep in. The number of rooms includes bedrooms, living-rooms and kitchens, but not bathrooms and toilets. However, the immigration rules in force from 1 October 1994 state that in most cases the accommodation must be 'exclusively' available to the parties concerned. This could be interpreted to mean that it would no longer be possible to satisfy the requirement of the rule by living in a joint family household and sharing some facilities, as the whole of the accommodation would not be 'exclusively' occupied by the people concerned. However, there have been Immigration Appeal Tribunal determinations and a High Court decision (*Iftikhar Ahmed*, 1 November 1993) under the old rules, holding that as long as there is at least one room for the 'exclusive' occupation of the parties concerned, this is adequate.

The Home Office has confirmed, in letters to Sir Giles Shaw MP of 5 October 1994 and to UKCOSA of 12 October 1994, that it does not intend to alter its present interpretation. The UKCOSA letter states: 'There is no objection to accommodation, i.e. a house or flat, being shared provided an applicant and his spouse have at least a small unit of accommodation, i.e. a bedroom for their exclusive use. The accommodation must, however, be either owned or legally occupied by the sponsor. It must not contravene public health regulations and be capable of accommodating the applicant and any dependants without causing overcrowding as defined in the Housing Act 1985. Arrangements whereby the applicant joins his or her spouse in an established household with other residents are acceptable provided the aforementioned requirements are fulfilled.' It is not clear why the Home Office changed the wording of the rule and it is important that any refusal cases taken to the Tribunal under the new wording are strongly argued, in the terms of housing law, to ensure that this definition is confirmed.

- **the applicant's current passport.** If the person has travelled to the UK before, he or she may also be asked for old passports, to show that he or she did leave the UK as required.

In addition to the general requirements, there are further requirements for people applying to come for particular reasons. They are listed in the relevant chapters.

Applications to work

The British post will need evidence of the work offered. For most employment, the employer in the UK has to obtain a work permit for the person from the Department for Education and Employment in the UK and the British post will need to see this. As the Department for Education and Employment only issues permits when it is satisfied about the pay and conditions offered for the job, and that the employers could not find a suitable worker already resident in the UK, the British post will not normally make further checks. If the employment does not require a permit (▶see chapter 7) the British post will need a letter of confirmation from the employers about the job and the pay and conditions offered in order to consider whether it meets the requirements of permit-free employment.

If the application is for business or independent means, full details of the money and business proposals are necessary. The British posts frequently refer business applications to the Home Office Business Group, at Lunar House, for decision, so that it can check on the feasibility of the enterprise. This may add months of delay to the application.

Applications for temporary stay

People who are not visa nationals and who are not coming to settle, work or do business in the UK do not need to get entry clearance before travelling. They have the choice of applying for entry clearance abroad, or of travelling to the UK without it and seeking entry from the immigration officer they see at the port of entry. There are advantages and disadvantages in applying for entry clearance when it is optional, but the final decision on whether it would be wise to do so depends on the person and the facts of the case.

Advantages and disadvantages of applying for optional entry clearance

The advantages are:
- people know in advance whether they satisfy the requirements of the immigration rules and therefore they are unlikely to have problems or delays when they arrive in the UK
- if they are refused entry clearance, they will have spent money only on the entry clearance fee, not also on the ticket to the UK
- if they get entry clearance but are nevertheless refused entry when they arrive in the UK, they can appeal against the refusal and remain in the UK while the appeal is pending, and give evidence at the appeal hearing

The disadvantages are:
- in some countries there are delays in considering applications and there may be further delays if the applications are referred to the Home Office
- there is a fee for entry clearance, which is not returned if the application is refused, and an application may involve more than one long journey to the nearest British post
- the refusal rates for entry clearance overseas are much higher than those at ports of entry in the UK
- if entry clearance is refused, the person's passport will be marked to show this and information about the refusal may be passed on to the authorities in the UK, so that travel to the UK (and to some other countries) will be more difficult in future.

If the application is successful

If the entry clearance officer is satisfied, the person will be given entry clearance. There are different names for this depending on the nationality of the person applying ▶see chapter 13 for examples. If they are visa nationals, they will be given a visa. Others will get an entry certificate. Both these are multi-coloured watermarked stickers placed in passports; the entry clearance officers call them 'vignettes'. Most of these stickers also include the statement 'valid for presentation at a UK port within 6 months'. This does not mean that people will be admitted to the UK for a six-month period. It means that they must travel to use the clearance within six months. If they do not travel within this time, they will need to get a new clearance, as the old one will no longer be valid.

GENERAL GROUNDS FOR REFUSAL of entry clearance/leave to enter

Reasons which 'should normally' lead to refusal: where there is discretion

- not giving all the required information to the immigration officers
- seeking leave to enter as a returning resident after being away for more than two years (though the specific rules on returning residents say that people may still be admitted, for example if they have lived here for most of their lives)
- travelling on a passport issued by a state which is not recognised by the British government, for example the Turkish Federated State of Cyprus. In practice, people who otherwise qualify for entry may be admitted on an immigration service form IS 87.
- having previously overstayed or broken other conditions on stay
- having previously entered by deception, or been granted an extension of stay by deception ►see chapter 14
- if people cannot show they will be allowed in to the country to which they intend to travel after a time-limited stay in the UK (this does not apply to people with entry clearance for settlement or as spouses leading to settlement)
- refusal by a sponsor to sign an undertaking of support if requested
- false information having been given in relation to a work permit application, whether or not the person knew about this
- children seeking entry for any reason except to join their parents or legal guardians without written consent from the parents or legal guardians. This does not apply to child asylum-seekers.
- refusal of a medical examination when required. This does not apply to people settled in the UK.
- having been convicted of an offence which, if committed in the UK, could be punished with imprisonment for 12 months or more. This can be waived if there are strong compassionate reasons to allow entry.
- if the immigration officer believes refusal is justified on public good grounds ►see chapter 14.

The rules state that immigration officials must refer asylum applications to the Home Office, but not any others. Entry clearance officers are instructed to refer in some other cases, including business applications, adoption of children and people who do not qualify under the rules if there are strong compassionate or other reasons for referral, or where the Home Office has papers on the person in relation to previous immigration applications. When the case has been referred, representations may be made to the Home Office.

If the application is refused

If the entry clearance officer is not satisfied, or believes that one of the general grounds for refusal applies ►see boxes above/below, the application will be refused. This must be done in writing and the person must be informed of any right to appeal against the refusal.

People refused entry clearance as visitors, as prospective students and

> **GENERAL GROUNDS FOR REFUSAL** of entry clearance/leave to enter
>
> **Reasons for mandatory refusal**
>
> - where 'entry is being sought for a purpose not covered by these rules', which makes it clear that immigration officers should not make exceptions. No set of rules can cover all aspects of human life, therefore discretion is important.
> - being subject to a current deportation order
> - not having a valid passport or identity document
> - people seeking to enter the UK or coming through the Channel Tunnel with the intention of continuing to Ireland when the immigration officers are not satisfied that they are acceptable there
> - not having a visa where that is necessary
> - where the Home Secretary has directed exclusion on grounds of public good ▶see page 270
> - on medical grounds, where the Medical Inspector has confirmed it is undesirable to admit the person. People who are settled, or where there are strong compassionate reasons for admission, may be allowed to enter in spite of medical grounds which would otherwise lead to refusal.
>
> These grounds relate to all applications and therefore appear to lessen the discretionary powers of immigration officers to make exceptions to the rules. They must be monitored carefully.

students coming on courses for six months or less have no right of appeal. Ways of contesting refusals are discussed further in chapter 12. People refused entry clearance for any other purpose, such as settlement or a working holiday, may appeal. Any appeal must be received by the British post which refused within three months of the date of refusal; see chapter 16 for more information about appeals.

Arrival in the UK

On arrival at a UK air-or sea port, people who are subject to immigration control must be examined by an immigration officer to see whether they satisfy the requirements of the immigration rules for leave to enter in a particular category, including that none of the general grounds for refusal apply to them ▶see boxes above. If they are granted leave, immigration officers stamp their passports with a square stamp showing the date and port of entry, and the time limit and any conditions on their stay (▶see chapter 13 for examples). The time limit is from the date on this stamp, the date on which the person was granted permission to enter, not from the date on which any entry clearance was granted. For example, a person granted visit entry clearance on 3 January who was admitted to the UK on 30 March for six months is permitted to stay until 30 September. Before 30 September, the person should either leave the UK or apply to the Home Office for permission to remain longer. It is worth keeping a record of the date separate from the passport, so that if the passport is lost, the person knows the date to which he or she is allowed to remain and can make any application to remain longer in time, before permission runs out.

If immigration officers put a time limit on a person's stay in the UK, they may also impose other conditions, either a restriction or a prohibition on employment, and/or a requirement to register with the police. From 1 November 1996 a requirement that people maintain and accommodate themselves and any dependants without recourse to public funds can also be imposed. The significance of these conditions is that breach of any of them is a criminal offence and can also lead to deportation.

If people are refused entry to the UK, they may be able to contest this refusal. See chapter 12 for more information.

Illegible passport stamps

When people are admitted as visitors for six months, the stamp put on their passports is usually a standard rubber stamp stating 'leave to enter for six months employment prohibited' or, since 8 November 1996, 'leave to enter for six months: employment and recourse to public funds prohibited'; ▶see chapter 13 for examples. If the immigration officer does not press hard enough, or does not have enough ink on the inkpad, the stamp may not be legible. The Immigration Act 1988, in force since 1 August 1988, provided that where an entry stamp is illegible, the person is deemed to have been granted leave to enter for six months, with a prohibition on employment.

Before 1 August 1988, an illegible stamp was deemed to have granted the person indefinite leave to enter. This was because the Immigration Act 1971 provides that people must be given notice in writing of the time limit and conditions on which they have been granted entry. When these could not be read, it was decided that no valid time limit or conditions had been imposed on the person's stay. Thus people who last entered the UK before 1 August 1988 and had no legible time limit placed on their stay may apply to the Home Office to confirm that they are settled in the UK. They should obtain specialist advice before approaching the Home Office.

Entry through Ireland

The UK and the Republic of Ireland, together with the Isle of Man and the Channel Islands, form a Common Travel Area. This means that there are no immigration controls between the two countries and most people do not require leave to enter when travelling from one to the other. People's passports are not usually stamped as they are not examined by immigration officers. Irish citizens entering the UK automatically become settled on arrival, as do British citizens entering Ireland. The Prevention of Terrorism Act, used to control the movement of British citizens between Britain and Northern Ireland, is beyond the scope of this book.

The Immigration (Control of Entry through Republic of Ireland) Order 1972 applies to most people who are not Irish citizens. It provides that, although not requiring leave to enter, people subject to immigration control who enter the UK through Ireland for the first time are deemed to have been granted leave to enter for three months, with a prohibition on employment and business. Nothing will be stamped on their passports and there will usually be no evidence of their date of entry other than their travel ticket, if they have kept it. If they wish to remain in the UK for more than three months they should apply to the Home Office for an extension of this stay, with any evidence they have of the date of arrival (so they will not be treated as overstayers) and showing how they fit into the immigration rules to remain longer.

Both the UK and Ireland have their own lists of countries whose citizens require visas to enter and there is not a common visa for both countries. Visa nationals intending to travel to both countries should obtain visas from both the embassies concerned before setting out. This is necessary even though it is unlikely that passports will be checked while travelling. A visa national who has been given a visa endorsed 'short visit' to enter the UK from a British embassy or high commission and who enters through Ireland is deemed to have been given a month's leave to enter, with a prohibition on employment and business and a requirement to register with the police. People with visas for any other purpose are deemed to have been given three months.

People who have limited leave to remain in the UK and who travel between the UK and Ireland and return to the UK within the currency of their leave still have the same length of time left. People who are granted leave to enter the UK for a limited period, who travel to Ireland and return after that leave has expired are deemed to have been granted seven days' leave to enter the UK again.

The Immigration (Control of Entry through Republic of Ireland) Order does not apply to visa nationals who do not have visas, illegal entrants and overstayers in the UK who cross to the Republic from the UK and then return to the UK, people who have been deported from the UK, or people who, on their most recent attempt to enter the UK, were refused leave to enter. It also does not apply to people who arrive by air in Ireland and simply transit by air to the UK, or to those whose exclusion the Home Secretary has directed is conducive to the public good. They still require leave to enter. If they enter without seeing an immigration officer to grant this leave, they are deemed to have entered in breach of the immigration laws and can be treated as illegal entrants (▶see chapter 14). Even though they have not been examined by an immigration officer, and did not know that they should have been, the Court of Appeal decided in the case of *Bouzagou* (1983 Imm AR 69) that people in this situation are illegal entrants. They are liable to removal with no right of appeal until after they have left the UK.

Travelling in and out of the UK

The immigration rules provide for people who have been granted leave to enter or remain in the UK to return after being abroad during this time. The provisions are different for three groups of people – those with leave to enter or remain for six months or less, those with leave to enter or remain for more than six months but who still have a time limit on their stay, and those with indefinite leave to enter or remain. There are also provisions for people who are applying to the Home Office for leave to remain at the time they want to travel. People with the right of abode always qualify to re-enter but those not travelling on British citizen passports should obtain a certificate of entitlement to the right of abode before travelling.

People who always qualify to re-enter

People with the right of abode

These people are not subject to immigration control and therefore can enter the UK at any time. People who are British citizens and are travelling on British passports are able to enter just by showing this document. Immigration officers only have to be satisfied that the person travelling is the rightful holder of the passport. Occasionally they make more detailed checks when they suspect that a person is travelling on a forged passport or on a passport issued to someone else, and people can be refused entry for this reason. It is up to the immigration officers to prove their case that a person travelling on a full British passport is not entitled to do so, and the person travelling has the right to appeal against refusal and to remain in the UK while the appeal is pending.

British Visitor's passports

All kinds of British nationals (see chapter 17) who were resident in the UK used to be able to obtain travel documents through the Post Office. These were called British Visitor's passports and were normally valid for one year and for western European countries, Turkey and Bermuda only. Because the Post Office did not usually demand evidence from people to show that they were British, but issued these documents on request, immigration officers did not necessarily accept a British Visitor's passport as proof that a person was British or was entitled to re-enter the UK.

On 20 December 1994 the Home Secretary stated that British Visitor's passports would be discontinued from 1 January 1996. The reasons the Passport Agency gave included that 'it does not provide definite evidence of national status or identity...it is used in the evasion of immigration controls and...by criminals, terrorists and football hooligans' and the Spanish authorities had stated they would no longer accept them after October 1995. British Excursion Documents, valid only for short-term visits to France, were discontinued from 1 March 1995. Thus the only documents British nationals may travel on now are full British passports.

Certificates of entitlement to the right of abode

People born in the UK before 1983 are automatically British citizens, as are people born in the UK from 1983 onwards if either parent was a British citizen or was settled in the UK at the time of their birth. They may also be entitled to another nationality by descent from a parent and therefore may be travelling on the passport of the other country. This may be when the other country, for example Malaysia or Nigeria, does not allow dual nationality or places restrictions on the stay of people using non-national passports. These people with the right of abode need to have their passports stamped with a 'certificate of entitlement to the right of abode' (▶see chapter 13 for example) as proof of their status in order to qualify to enter the UK. These certificates of entitlement can be obtained either from the Home Office, if the person is in the UK, or from a British embassy or high commission if the person is abroad. There is a fee payable (▶see appendix for amount). Difficulties sometimes arise in countries where the British authorities are suspicious of documents shown.

Other Commonwealth citizens with the right of abode also need certificates of entitlement before travelling to the UK. They may have the right of abode through the birth of a parent in the UK or through a marriage, before 1 January 1983, to a man with the right of abode (▶see glossary for further explanation and remember that to qualify for the right of abode people must have been Commonwealth citizens in 1982/83, thus Cameroonians, Mozambicans, Pakistanis and South Africans do not qualify as their countries were not then in the Commonwealth). They also need to show original documents to prove their claim to the right of abode. In some countries where there may not be contemporaneous birth or marriage certificates to prove the relationship people may have difficulties in convincing the British authorities that they qualify.

Certificates of entitlement are valid for the same length of time as the passport on which they are stamped. When people renew their passports they can then apply to the British authorities for a new certificate of entitlement.

People with leave to enter/remain for six months or less

Most people with leave to enter or remain for six months or less are visitors, but some students on short courses may be admitted only for the period of the course and others coming for short-term work, like summer agricultural work, may also be given less than six months stay. When they are given leave to enter at a British air- or sea port, they have permission to stay for the time stamped on their passports. If they travel out of the UK, the leave they have been given lapses, that is, has finished. If they return, immigration officers will treat them as new arrivals and question them again to decide if they qualify to enter.

Thus people given leave to enter for six months as visitors, for example, who travel to mainland Europe after two months and then seek to re-enter Britain a month later cannot assume that they will be given the further three months leave left to run. They must again satisfy the immigration officers of their claim to enter as a visitor. If they are admitted, they will probably be given leave to enter for another six months. But they may be refused permission to enter if the immigration officer is not satisfied, and can then face removal to the country from which they have travelled, rather than to their country of origin.

Visa nationals need a visa for every entry to the UK. Visa national visitors who are planning to travel out of and into the UK during their visit need a valid visa for each entry. They should therefore apply initially for multiple-entry visas, not single-entry visas, so that they will be able to return. Once people with single-entry visas have travelled to the UK and been admitted, the visa is no longer valid. If they want to return, they need a new visa.

Until May 1991 it was possible for such people to apply to the Passport Office in London for re-entry visas, which were either for multiple or single entry, while they were in the UK on holiday, and then travel out of the UK and return. Re-entry visas were abolished on 16 May 1991 and visas can now only be obtained outside the UK. Thus visa national visitors with single-entry visas who want to travel out of the UK and return must apply to the British post in the country to which they have travelled for another visa before returning to the UK. If they return without a new visa, they are liable to be refused entry just for this reason. Immigration officers do have the discretion to readmit people who they believe genuinely did not know about the visa requirement (and may then mark their passports with a large 'W' to show they have been warned about this) but it is not safe to count on it.

There are current proposals for the creation of a 'Eurovisa', a single visa allowing visits for up to three months to all European Union countries. This had not been agreed at the time of writing, although the countries whose nationals need visas for all EU countries were agreed from April 1996.

People with leave to enter/remain for more than six months but with a time limit

Since May 1991, people who have been granted leave to enter or remain for more than six months can travel and return to the UK and expect to be allowed in again for the same purpose for the rest of that time without detailed questioning by immigration officers on their return. This is because paragraph 1 of the Schedule to the Immigration Act 1988 came into force on that date. It provides for leave to enter to continue after an absence. As long as people coming back are still doing the same thing for which they were originally granted entry, they should not have difficulties on return. Thus, for example, a student who is still following the same full-time course of studies and who still has the financial support available to do this should be readmitted for the same time as he or she had before leaving. If the student has stopped studying, or has married a settled or British person and seeks entry as a spouse, he or she could be refused entry because the entry sought would be in a different category and a new entry clearance would be necessary.

Visa nationals returning within the time given do not need visas. They are exempt from requiring visas if they return during a period of leave of more than six months. This applies to all visa nationals in these circumstances, so visa exemption stamps are no longer used. This means that people have nothing in writing to show that they do not require visas. They may therefore have problems in convincing other authorities, for example airline staff, that it is safe to allow them to travel and that they do not need visas (as airlines can be fined £2000 if they bring in someone who needs a visa and does not have one).

People returning in these circumstances do not have any right of appeal in the UK if they are refused entry. Even though they had leave to remain when they left, they do not have entry clearance on arrival, so if the immigration officers believe there has been a change of circumstances they can be refused with no redress. If they are applying to enter as a visitor, a prospective student or a student enrolled on a course for six months or less they have no right of appeal at all. People applying to enter for other purposes have a right of appeal after they have been sent back; see chapter 16.

People who have indefinite leave to enter/remain: the returning residents rule

People who are settled (have indefinite leave to remain) in the UK are free to travel out of and into the UK, provided they do not stay out of the UK for more than two years. This is called the returning residents rule. Visa nationals are exempt from requiring visas if they return within this time.

WHAT THE RULES SAY

The immigration rules state that people must satisfy an immigration officer that:

- they are returning for the purpose of settlement
- they had indefinite leave to enter or remain in the UK when they last left the country
- they did not have assistance from public funds towards the cost of leaving the UK
- they have not been away for longer than two years.

WHAT THE RULES MEAN

Returning for the purpose of settlement

This means that immigration officers have the power to question people returning to their homes in the UK about the purpose of their travel. Although this may not happen each time they travel, there is always the possibility that they may be asked personal and intrusive questions about their intentions. In order to retain their settlement rights, people who have lived in the UK must satisfy the immigration officers that they are intending to remain indefinitely on this particular occasion.

In the years before 1 May 1990, settled people returning within two years of departure were automatically admitted again for settlement. It did not matter how long or short a period they had remained in the UK on their last entry and immigration officers did not have the power to inquire into their intentions. Returning to the UK for short periods in order to retain settlement rights is now more difficult, because immigration officers are more likely to question people who have spent long periods outside the UK about their current intentions.

Indefinite leave when they last left the country

People who once had indefinite leave to remain but lost it because they returned and were granted only limited leave now have no way under the immigration rules to qualify again for settlement. Even if they have spent most of their lives in the UK, by being admitted for a limited period any application to settle again is considered at the discretion of the Home Office. They might also qualify under some other part of the rules, for example as the spouse of a British citizen if the whole family has returned after some years away.

Young people who have spent most of their lives in the UK but who have gone abroad for postgraduate study, for example, may wish to return to their homes during summer holidays. Strictly speaking, they would not be returning 'for settlement' as they plan to leave the UK at the end of the holiday to continue studies, before returning to stay permanently at the end of the course. Women with indefinite leave whose husbands have been refused permission under the primary purpose rule to live in the UK with them may spend long periods abroad with them and may intend to go abroad again but also return to the UK to see their parents and other relatives living in the country. If questioned by immigration officers, they would explain this – and could then be admitted as visitors, rather than for settlement. The next time they returned it would be for settlement – but they would not then fit into the rules as returning residents as they would not have been admitted with indefinite leave on their last entry. It is therefore important that returning residents should always make it clear that they intend to continue to live in the UK, and this country is their home.

Not had assistance from public funds to leave

This does not mean people who had claimed welfare benefits during their previous stay in the UK, but refers to the tiny number of people who have been repatriated. Section 29 of the Immigration Act 1971 provides for financial help towards fares for people who are settled in the UK but want to return to their countries of origin. See page 283 for more information.

Not been away for more than two years

This is a clear requirement and is strictly interpreted. Settled people who have been out of the UK for nearly two years and who are unable to return within this time should apply to the British embassy or high commission in the country they are in for entry clearance as returning residents. There is a fee for this; see appendix for the amount. If the application for entry clearance is made before the two-year period is finished, and the people explain the reasons for the delay in travel, it is likely to be granted.

People who have been away for more than two years before returning or applying for entry clearance to return are in a more difficult position. The immigration rules state that an application may still be granted in certain circumstances, for example if people have 'lived here for most of their lives'. Thus people who came as young children to join their parents and were educated in the UK but who have then spent three or four years abroad without returning home may be able to qualify because of the length of time they have spent in the UK and their strong family ties.

The rules do not give any other examples of exceptional circumstances which would allow people to return to their homes. The courts have decided in the case of *Khokhar* (1981 Imm AR 56n) that being too ill to travel at the relevant time (when detailed medical evidence has been provided) and in the case of *Armat Ali* (1981 Imm AR 51) that having the passport detained by the authorities in connection with legal proceedings have been strong enough reasons. It is important for people to explain in full, with evidence, the reasons why they have not been able to return to the UK within two years and why they are doing so at the time of application.

If the application is successful

If people are applying abroad they will be granted entry clearance as returning residents and this will be endorsed on their passports. They must travel to the UK while the entry clearance is still valid, usually within six months. On arrival at the port of entry, they will be given leave to enter for an indefinite period. If people are applying at a port in the UK, they will be admitted for an indefinite period.

If the application is refused

People who have applied for entry clearance as returning residents have the right to appeal against any refusal. The entry clearance officers have to give them a letter giving brief reasons why the application was refused and forms to fill in to appeal against the refusal. The forms must be returned to the entry clearance officers within three months of the date of refusal. People who apply for entry at a sea- or airport have a right of appeal but if they did not have entry clearance they can only appeal after they have been sent back. People who are given limited leave when they enter can challenge this by applying as returning residents after entry. If they are refused, they should have a right of appeal as long as a valid application was made before their leave to remain ran out. However, there is no provision in the immigration rules for people to be granted returning resident status after entry to the UK, so these appeals are unlikely to succeed. See chapter 16 on appeals for more details.

Applying to the Home Office

People who have been allowed to enter or remain in the UK for a certain period or under certain conditions may apply to the Home Office to extend the time or to change the conditions.

Applying in time: valid applications and application forms

If at all possible, **people should apply to the Home Office in time**, before their present permission to stay runs out. From 25 November 1996, the Home Office demanded that such applications should be made on its official application forms.

All applications must be made on the forms *except*:
- extensions of stay for work permit and training and work experience permit holders (which are made to the Department for Education and Employment, not to the Home Office)
- claims for asylum
- those from nationals of EEA countries and their family members

The forms state they should be returned to the Home Office 'not more than one month' before leave runs out. If an application is not on the correct form, or does not include all the documents requested on that form, or an explanation why each particular document is unavailable and when it will be sent, the application is not valid. Thus if a person writes a letter to the Home Office but does not use the form, or sends the form without all the documents requested and without a satisfactory explanation of why a document is not there, the Home Office does not consider it to be a valid application.

The Home Office has set up a Document Reception Centre at Lunar House, whose work is solely to decide whether or not applications are valid. When they are not, the parts which are not 'satisfactory' are marked in red pen and the entire form and documents returned to the applicant. The Home Office states that this will be done by return of post. From the Home Office point of view, no application has been made. If the person later corrects or amplifies the form and returns it to the Home Office, it is the date of return which counts as the date of application. There is thus a serious possibility that applications originally sent in time will not be counted and that they will be returned after the person's leave to remain has run out. This means the loss of any right of appeal against refusal.

It is therefore vital that the form and all the documents, or an explanation and a timescale for any documents which are not there, are sent to the Home Office before the time stamped on a person's passport runs out. When such an application for an extension is made before the time runs out, the person is still legally in the UK while the Home Office considers the application, however long this takes. During this time, any conditions imposed on the person's stay still apply. If the application is refused, there is normally a formal right of appeal against the refusal.

If people want an answer quickly, they may decide to go to the Home Office to apply in person. They still need to fill in a form and take it and the documents with them. The application may be decided on the day, but this is not always possible if the Home Office staff are too busy or there are special circumstances in the case. Otherwise, it is normally best to write to the Home Office, particularly if there are any unusual circumstances in the case. The application should be sent by recorded delivery post and the person should keep a copy.

The application forms

The Home Office states that one reason for the introduction of compulsory forms is to reduce delays in dealing with applications. At the end of June 1996 there were 21,500 immigration applications outstanding. The average time for the Home Office to decide on student applications was 14 weeks, on marriage applications for a year's leave, 29 weeks, and nine weeks in most other cases.

There are six separate application forms. People must fill in the correct form for the type of application they are making, or the application is not valid. The forms are also time-limited; the first forms state that they are valid only until 14 April 1997. People applying after that date will need to use different forms to make valid applications. The Home Office has set up an Application Forms Unit, telephone 0181 760 2233, which will send out application forms on request.

All application forms include the sentence 'We reserve the right to consider and decide your application on the evidence provided one month after the application has been made.' The Home Office states that it does not normally intend to send people reminders about providing any further information or evidence, as it has done in the past, so applications may be decided without information which could be sent later.

The forms, at the time of writing, and at least until 14 April 1997, are:

FLR(M) for people applying for a year's leave to remain on the grounds of marriage, and their children

SET(M) for people applying for settlement on the grounds of marriage, after having had one year's leave, and their children

FLR(S) for students and student nurses applying for leave to remain, and their spouses and children

FLR(O) for people applying for further leave to remain for any other reason, for example for permit-free employment, as an au pair or for an extension of exceptional leave to remain, and their spouses and children

SET(F) for people applying for settlement for family reasons, other than spouses, for example elderly parents, or children joining parents already settled

SET(O) for people applying for settlement for any other reason, for example after four years' work or business.

Applying after leave to enter or remain has expired

If the person's permission to remain has already expired it is often still worth applying to the Home Office, particularly if the person fits into the rules apart from the overstaying, or has a strong compassionate case. If an application is made late, it must still be made on the relevant application form. It is important that the person has advice and makes as full a case as possible for the Home Office to consider. It is usually best to make the application through an advice agency, so the Home Office knows that the person is receiving competent advice.

If the application is made late, after the time stamped on the passport has run out, the person is in the UK without permission while the application is under consideration and there is no right of appeal against any refusal. While the application is under consideration, the person is still an overstayer and thus liable to deportation and detention. However if the police or immigration service come across the person, the fact that an application has been made gives some protection. It is unlikely that further action against him or her will be taken while the Home Office is dealing with the application. If the application is refused, although there is no formal right of appeal against the refusal, further representations may be made to the Home Office.

General grounds for refusal of leave to remain

HC 395 lists ten grounds on which an extension of stay 'should normally be refused' ▶see box opposite and one where it 'is to be refused'. The latter is 'the fact that the variation of leave to enter or remain is being sought for a purpose not covered by these Rules'. This is very worrying; it

> **GENERAL GROUNDS FOR REFUSAL** of leave to remain
>
> **Reasons when applications for leave to remain 'should normally be refused': where there is discretion**
>
> - making false representations or failing to disclose a material fact when applying for leave to enter or remain in the past
> - breaking a condition imposed on previous leave to enter or remain, for example overstaying or working without permission
> - if people have not been able to support themselves or family members without recourse to public funds
> - if a person's character, conduct or associations make it undesirable to allow him or her to remain, or if there is a threat to national security
> - if a sponsor refuses to give an undertaking of support, or has not complied with such an undertaking in the past
> - if people have not complied with any undertaking or declaration about the length or purpose of their stay
> - if people cannot show that they will be allowed into another country at the end of their stay (except those who qualify for settlement, or spouses of settled people)
> - if people do not produce documents or information demanded by the Home Office in a 'reasonable time'
> - if people fail to attend an immigration interview without a reasonable explanation
> - if a child is applying to remain not in conjunction with his or her parents or legal guardians and does not have the written consent of the parent or guardian to do so. This does not apply to child asylum-seekers.
>
> Many of these reasons existed under previous rules, but were not listed in this way. If any of these factors might apply to a person, it may be important to explain in any application why they should not be used as a ground of refusal and how the person otherwise qualifies for further leave to remain. The Home Office procedures outside the rules, for example the 'fourteen-year concession' and the 'ten-year concession', are expected to continue. Home Office practice should be monitored and refusals contested ▶see chapter 16.

suggests that applications made outside the rules, asking the Home Office to use its discretion, will not be successful. However it would seem to be contradicted by the fact that the Home Office continues to operate many of its established practices outside the rules, such as allowing children to come in for adoption ▶see page 61, the relaxation of the primary purpose rule for certain couples ▶see page 13 and its long residence concessions ▶see below. It could also mean the Home Office telling more people that they have no right of appeal against refusal as they have applied for something not permitted under the immigration rules. It is important to monitor Home Office practice in this respect and to contest cases where it is alleged there is no right of appeal.

Dealing with the Home Office

It is important to remember that the Home Office Immigration and Nationality Directorate exists to carry out the immigration law, not to give advice, either to advisers or individuals. If advisers want further information before being able to advise someone, they should not ask the Home Office first, but should get in touch with an independent specialist source – JCWI, IAS, the Refugee Legal Centre, a local specialist centre such as the Greater Manchester Immigration Aid Unit or the Independent Immigration Support Agency in Birmingham, or a local law centre or citizens' advice bureau – where information will not be recorded for use against the person later, and which will give independent advice.

When people use Home Office application forms, all the information or evidence the Home Office may require should be sent with the form, or forwarded later in accordance with any explanation given on the form. If the Home Office asks for further information on the telephone, there is no need for advisers to give it; they may ask for the request to be put in writing.

Do not assume that everything the Home Office says is correct. Staff turnover at Lunar House, which deals with most immigration and asylum work at the Home Office, is high. Advisers are likely to know just as much about the law as many Home Office staff do. Home Office threats are not always carried out. For example, a standard Home Office reminder letter stated that if information was not received within two weeks, the application might be refused. This rarely happened, particularly if the person or the adviser remained in touch with the Home Office explaining the reason for any delay in providing evidence. The Home Office application forms state that it 'reserves the right' to decide an application within a month whether or not further information or evidence is submitted and that it will no longer send out routine reminder letters. Advisers may wish to monitor practice on this.

Do not give up just because the Home Office has refused, or has sent out threatening letters. Even when people have been told to leave the country without delay, under threat of deportation, decisions can still be altered.

Home Office discretion

The Home Office and the immigration authorities have the power to make decisions outside the immigration rules, if they are satisfied that there is sufficient reason to do so. When a person has strong compassionate or other reasons for needing to remain in the UK, but does not fit into the immigration rules, an application for treatment outside the rules may be made. Full details should be given of the reasons why the person needs to remain, together with any available evidence to support this.

Although the rules state that applications outside them should be refused, this does not take away the power to make exceptions. It may mean that

CHANGES OF STATUS allowed under the immigration rules

This table lists changes which are specifically allowed under the rules. **This does not mean that an application will automatically be granted; people have to satisfy the Home Office that they qualify.** See relevant chapter for details. Other applications may be made, but they are outside the immigration rules, at the discretion of the Home Office. For example, there is no provision in the rules for a person in the UK to become a fiancé(e), but such applications may be granted when there are strong reasons for delaying the marriage. BUT applying to change status may cast doubts on the person's original intentions; ▶see chapter 14.

1 visitor
can change to 8, 9, 10
can change to 2 if *not* a visa national
cannot change to 3, 4, 5, 6, 7, 11
cannot extend 6 months stay as 1

2 student
can change to 8, 9, 10
can apply to extend stay as 2 until end of studies
can change to 1 for short period after end of studies
cannot change to 3, 4, 5, 6, 7, 11

**3 work permit holder
permit-free employment**
can change to 8, 9, 10
can change to 11 after four years in approved employment
can change to 2 if *not* visa national
can change to 1 for short period after end of work
cannot change to 4, 5, 6, 7

4 working holidaymaker
can change to 8, 9, 10
can change to 2 if *not* visa national
can change to 1 for short period at end of stay
cannot change to 3, 5, 6, 7, 11

5 business, self-employed, independent means, investor
can change to 8, 9, 10
can change to 11 after four years residence
can change to 2 if *not* visa national
can change to 1 for short period at end of stay
cannot change to 3, 4, 6, 7

6 au pair
can change to 8, 9, 10
can change to 2 if *not* a visa national
can change to 1 for short period at end of stay
cannot change to 3, 4, 5, 7, 11

7 fiancé(e)
can change to 8 after marriage
if marriage plans fail, can change to 1, 9, 10
can change to 2 if *not* visa national
cannot change to 3, 4, 5, 6, 11

8 spouse with one year's leave
can change to 11
if marriage fails, can change to 1, 9, 10
can change to 2 if *not* visa national
cannot change to 3, 4, 5, 6, 7

9 refugee
can change to 11 after four years
can change to 8

10 asylum-seeker granted exceptional leave to remain
can change to 11 after seven years
can apply for 9
can change to 8

11 settled – indefinite leave to remain
no immigration applications necessary
may be able to apply for British citizenship

the person will not be able to appeal against any refusal, or that any appeal would be unsuccessful.

If the person has already been through the formal processes of dealing with the Home Office – making an application, appealing against a refusal, losing the appeal – it may be worth making any further application through the local Member of Parliament. It is important to write to the MP with full details of the case and ask him or her to send that letter on to the Home Office Minister, with any further covering letter. If an MP takes up a case, this means that the correspondence and the file will be dealt with by the office of the Minister responsible for immigration rather than at Lunar House. MPs' intervention is most useful as a last resort; if they intervene while an appeal is pending, for example, they will usually be told that their representations will not be considered until after the appeal has been decided. It is now Home Office policy rarely to make exceptions or to agree to representations unless new information is put forward.

The Home Office has stated some circumstances in which it will exercise discretion, outside the immigration rules, in a particular way. The 'under-12 concession' (►see page 52) has been in existence since 1976 but has never been put into the rules. The granting of exceptional leave to remain instead of refugee status to asylum-seekers (►see chapter 5) is outside the immigration rules. There are also policies about granting indefinite leave to remain to people who have lived in the UK for a long period.

The 'ten-year concession'

The Home Office has stated that if people remain in the UK legally (that is, with Home Office permission) for more than ten years they will normally be allowed to stay permanently. They will be granted indefinite leave to remain in the UK and thus become settled. Both the period and the legality of residence are interpreted strictly. Being in the UK with permission means precisely that; if a person was late in applying for permission, even if that permission was subsequently granted, the person was an overstayer for a period and therefore may not fit into the ten-year concession. The Home Office has stated that short periods between applications, when the application was subsequently granted, will not stop the ten-year period running. Time spent while waiting for an appeal against a Home Office refusal will only count towards the ten year period if the appeal was subsequently successful. If a person is waiting for an appeal at the end of the ten-year period, she or he will not be granted settlement then, but will have to wait for the outcome of the appeal and only if it is successful will settlement then be granted. Time spent exempt from immigration control, for example as a diplomat or other work for an embassy, counts towards the ten-year period, but the person would have to leave the job and cease to be exempt from control before the Home Office would consider any application.

The Home Office stresses that granting indefinite leave on this basis is always discretionary. It refers to '10 years or more continuous lawful residence' but has stated in a letter of 23 February 1994: 'In assessing whether a person has been continuously resident in the UK for 10 years or more, short absences abroad of up to 6 months may be treated as not breaking any ties with the UK. However, where there is evidence that the person did not intend to return to this country or had not established ties here, such an absence would be regarded as a breach of residence. Similarly a series of short absences during a period of a year or more which meant that the person was spending most of their time abroad could be regarded as breaking the continuity of residence. In all these cases the period of residence should be lawful.'

The people most commonly able to benefit from this policy are international students. However, as the immigration rules provide that students must intend to leave the UK at the end of their studies and as this 'concession' becomes more widely known, it is becoming more difficult for people who have been students for eight or nine years to obtain extensions of their stay. The Home Office is likely to ask ever more detailed questions about their plans and intentions after their studies and if they give any indication that they might want to apply to settle under this provision, they will be refused further student extensions.

The 'fourteen-year concession'

The Home Office has also stated that if people remain in the UK for over fourteen years, whether legally or illegally, this will also normally qualify them for settlement. In the letter quoted above, it confirms: 'Once a person has been here continuously for 14 years or more they would normally be granted indefinite leave to remain regardless of the fact that some of their residence was unlawful, provided that there were no strong countervailing factors such as an extant criminal record or a deliberate and blatant attempt to evade or circumvent control.' Thus a student or any other person who has been in the UK for over ten years, but who has spent some time without permission, will have to wait until fourteen years have passed before it is likely that settlement will be granted. In general, when a deportation decision or order has been made against the person earlier this 'stops the clock' and the Home Office may still carry out the order later. This policy was accepted by the courts in the case of *Ofori* (1994 Imm AR 581).

Requesting return of passports

While the Home Office is considering an application for an extension of stay or variation of conditions, it is normal for it to keep the applicant's passport. The passport can be requested back at any time, if the holder needs it, for example as proof of identity for a bank or to show to a marriage registrar. However there may be dangers in requesting a passport *in order to travel*.

The Home Office has stated in correspondence with JCWI that it will grant three months leave to remain in some circumstances when a passport is requested in order to travel. This is when the application to the Home Office is for an extension in the same capacity as that previously granted and it appears that the person qualifies for the leave requested but the Home Office has not yet had time to look at the application. When the person returns, he or she is likely to be readmitted for a period of two months in order to make a further application to the Home Office.

Variation of Leave Order

However it is more common for a different procedure to be followed. Under the Immigration (Variation of Leave) Order 1976, amended in 1989, when people have made valid applications for extensions to the Home Office before their leave to remain expires, this leave is automatically extended for the period the Home Office is considering the application. This leave to remain expires either 28 days after the date the Home Office decides the application or the date the application is withdrawn. The Home Office has stated that if people request their passports in order to travel this *automatically* withdraws the application for leave to remain longer.

In these circumstances, the Home Office will return the passport as requested but without any further endorsement. If the previous leave has not yet expired, it is still valid. If the previous leave has already expired, the Home Office will send a letter stating that the person must leave the UK within 28 days as the application for leave to remain has been withdrawn. This is a grace period within which the Home Office will not take any further steps to force the person to leave. If the person's plans change and he or she does not travel but instead returns the passport and application form to the Home Office to continue to apply to remain, the Home Office treats this as a new application, made on this date. Thus if the person's previous leave to remain had expired, this will be treated as a late application and there will be no right of appeal if it is refused. The person will also become an overstayer after the 28-day period is up, and therefore liable to arrest and deportation.

It is therefore very important that people who want their passports for any purpose other than travel should make this clear in their request to the Home Office. *An application is only withdrawn if the request for the passport is for the purpose of travel; it remains pending if the passport is taken away from the Home Office for any other purpose.*

Travelling before an application is decided

It is risky for people to travel and to expect to be able to return when the Home Office has not yet decided an application. They will be able to leave the UK without difficulty but when they return they will have to satisfy the immigration officers that they fit into the immigration rules. Their passports will show the previous leave to enter or remain, and the triangular stamp showing the date of departure from the UK. If there is a period of time between these two dates, immigration officers will ask why and will then contact the Home Office to check the position.

If the application to the Home Office was straightforward, and if people can satisfy the immigration officers that they qualify to enter, they may be granted leave to enter for the period they request. If the application appears more complicated but it seems likely that it would be granted, people may be admitted for two months and told to apply again to the Home Office within this time. If the application was for a change of status, especially if this was one for which entry clearance is necessary, people may be refused entry. For example, an international student who marries a British citizen in the UK, applies to remain as her husband but travels before the application has been decided, will not qualify to re-enter. He does not qualify as a student, because he no longer intends to leave the UK when his studies are completed; he does not qualify as a husband because he does not have entry clearance for that purpose.

People who need to travel while the Home Office is considering an application sometimes believe it would be easier to obtain emergency travel documents from their own embassies or high commissions and travel on these while the Home Office continues to consider the application. This is not a safe procedure. It is unusual for a travel document to be issued in these circumstances, but if one is, it does not alter the holders' immigration status – that an application for further leave to remain had been made, but not decided, when they left. When they return, immigration officers will see a departure stamp on the travel document but no other evidence of the person's status in the UK. They will certainly need to know what that was; when they know that an application was pending they will contact the Home Office about the reasons for the application and what is happening about it. It is not safe to expect leave to enter to be granted.

People who travel out of the country when they have an appeal pending against refusal of leave to remain are unlikely to be allowed back into the country, because the Home Office has already decided they do not qualify to stay. From 1 October 1996, leaving the country while an appeal is pending means that the appeal will be treated as abandoned.

SECTION 7: TRAVEL

12 Problems and emergencies

Many people find giving immigration advice very frightening, because of the possible consequences of making a mistake, especially in situations which require urgent action. However, it is not as complicated or difficult as it sometimes seems. It is largely a question of keeping within deadlines, knowing who to contact and being prepared to be persistent. This chapter discusses the main immigration problems in which urgent, or time-limited, action may need to be taken.

Refusal of entry clearance overseas

A relative or friend may seek advice on behalf of someone who has been refused a visa or entry clearance overseas. ▶See chapter 11 for more details about applying for entry clearance.

1 Find out what the person was applying for (e.g. visit, family settlement).
2 All people refused abroad should be given a written notice explaining the reasons for refusal and whether there is a right of appeal against refusal. All people *except* those applying as visitors, as prospective students and as students coming for courses for six months or less, and those whose refusals are 'mandatory under the immigration rules' (▶see pages 249–50) have the right to appeal against any refusal. People with a right of appeal will be given forms to fill in to lodge the appeal.
3 Ask whether the person in the UK has copies of these documents. If not, ask him or her to get copies and return with them.
4 Even before the removal of the right of appeal, some British embassies and high commissions had been discouraging people from applying for visit entry clearance. Where entry clearance was optional, people were often told that it was not necessary and that they should travel and apply for leave to enter at the airport in the UK. Where people were visa nationals, and the visa officers thought on superficial inspection that they were likely to be refused, they were told that if they withdrew their applications they would not have to pay the visa fee and there would be no record of any refusal. This of course also meant that they had no chance of appealing.
5 Thus if the person abroad has not been given written notice of refusal, he or she has not legally been refused. Unless the person wants to withdraw,

or not to pursue, the application, he or she should go back to the British embassy or high commission and insist that the application be formally considered and decided.

6   When there is a right of appeal, the notice of refusal will state (very briefly) the reason why the person has been refused (but this may be too vague or subjective to be very helpful).

7   The appeal forms must be filled in and returned within three months of the date of refusal. ▶See chapter 16 for how to fill in appeal forms. The 'representative in the UK' requested on the forms can be a friend or relative in the UK, or an adviser, and arrangements for someone to act as representative at the appeal itself can be made later.

8   Full details of the reasons for refusal (and possibly a record of the interview at the British embassy or high commission) will be sent to the appellant's representative after a few months. At this stage, if the person has not already arranged for someone to represent at appeal, this should be done. This might be a local law centre or other advice agency, the Immigration Advisory Service or a solicitor; ▶see chapter 16 for more information on appeals.

When there is no right of appeal

People refused entry clearance as visitors, as prospective students and students coming on courses for six months or less and those whose refusal is 'mandatory under the immigration rules' lost their right of appeal under the Asylum and Immigration Appeals Act 1993. People refused entry clearance for any other purpose, such as settlement or a working holiday, may appeal.

When the Act was being debated in the House of Commons, the Home Office recognised the strength of feeling against the loss of visitors' appeal rights by issuing a press release on 8 December 1992. This suggested that the right of appeal was not very important and listed 'protections for people wishing to visit relatives in the UK'. These included:

- giving the person more detailed reasons for refusal
- stating on the refusal notice that a past refusal would not prejudice a fresh application
- suggesting that applicants might get together further information to make a fresh application, which, wherever possible, would be considered by a different entry clearance officer
- where there appear to be 'exceptional compassionate circumstances, illogicalities or procedural errors' the Foreign and Commonwealth Office would ask the post to review the decision by a more senior official
- the Foreign and Commonwealth Office would amend and improve its information leaflets, particularly with regard to the information sponsors in the UK can provide.

Many of these procedures were already in existence and other suggestions are mainly cosmetic. For example, entry clearance application forms request details of any previous refusals and posts keep records of previous decisions. These are routinely consulted when a person applies again, and the person's passport is normally marked to show the refusal, so this information is known. These 'protections' are in no way a substitute for the right of appeal, or even for an independent review of an administrative decision.

Friends and relatives in the UK may therefore contact the Foreign and Commonwealth Office Migration and Visa Department direct ▶see chapter 19 for address, or through their Member of Parliament, with any further information or arguments on the visitor's behalf they wish to be considered. They may also put these direct to the entry clearance officer and it is possible for the case to be reconsidered.

An amendment to the Act from the House of Lords established a Home Office-appointed monitor of refusals of entry clearance (but not of refusals at British ports and airports) where there is no right of appeal, who must make an annual report to the Home Secretary. The government accepted this amendment, but made it clear that the monitoring would not be a replacement appeal process. Dame Elizabeth Anson DBE, JP, DL, a former immigration adjudicator, was appointed as the monitor in late 1993. As the Foreign Office explained, 'all refusals without the right of appeal from all Posts world wide were allocated consecutive serial numbers. A random series was then computer generated, so nobody knew in advance which cases would be selected. The file on the application which corresponded to the randomly chosen number was submitted by the Posts to Lady Anson for review. Even the smallest Posts have had at least one refusal chosen for examination.'

This system is wholly unsatisfactory. As there is no appeal for which the entry clearance officer would have to prepare, these files must contain little more than any notes of the officer's interview and a formal refusal notice. There is no chance for the refused person to put his or her side of the case to the monitor, or for this process to provide any redress for individuals wrongly refused. Lady Anson's first annual report, published in December 1994, appeared more concerned about illegible handwriting on refusal notices than the refusals themselves. She has now made three annual reports, and has criticised procedures and refusals, particularly for family visits, but has no power directly to affect refusals. The reports can be obtained from the Foreign and Commonwealth Office.

Problems on arrival in the UK

One of the most common emergencies is for advisers to be contacted on behalf of someone who has been refused entry on arrival. This situation most commonly arises when people coming for a temporary purpose, such as visitors or students, are unable to satisfy immigration officers that they intend to leave at the end of their stay. Advising them will almost certainly mean negotiating with immigration officers at the port or airport where the person arrived.

It is important not to be intimidated by immigration officers. They are ordinary people who are not all-powerful; a chief immigration officer may sound important but he or she is only the second tier of official with more senior inspectors and chief inspectors above. Be firm with immigration officers and assume that negotiation is possible. If they do not alter their decision, ask to speak to a chief immigration officer and then to an inspector to continue the negotiations.

1 **As soon as possible try to find out the following details about the person:**
- name (preferably as on his or her passport)
- nationality
- date of birth
- port of entry (including which terminal at Heathrow or Gatwick) and approximate time of arrival
- purpose of travel
- port reference number (if possible; this will be on any papers that he or she has been given by immigration officers)
- from which country and port or airport the person travelled (with flight details)
- does the person have entry clearance?
- what did the person say to the immigration officers?
- what evidence to support his or her statements was shown to them?
- what information have the immigration officers given about why they are not satisfied and what they are doing next?
- has the person been in the UK, or attempted to come to the UK, before? (with full details)
- what is the person's marital status? If married, what is the nationality, whereabouts and intentions of spouse and children?
- what does the person want to do now?

2 **Find out whether the person has been refused entry** or whether he or she is still being questioned before a decision has been made.

If the person is still at the airport or port, this can be found out by contacting the immigration service there. The immigration officer will need to know from where and when the person arrived, his or her name and nationality, and if possible date of birth. Immigration officers usually refer to the person as the 'passenger' or 'pax' for short.

If the person has been released from the port or airport, look at the documentation he or she has been given. If the reference number includes /RLE/ the person has been refused entry; if not, there has still been no final decision.

3 **If the person has not yet been refused entry**, it is much easier to try to convince the immigration officers to allow him or her in. Get as much information as possible from immigration officers about why they are suspicious and check this with the person him or herself or with the friends or relatives in the UK. If there are any obvious misunderstandings or errors which can be corrected, the immigration officers may be satisfied and may grant the person leave to enter.

4 **If the person is refused entry**, and if he or she had obtained a visa or an entry clearance before travelling, there is a right of appeal against refusal and the person can remain in the UK until the appeal has been decided. This means that, whatever the final decision, he or she will be able to stay for some time. Forms for appeal will be handed to the person at the same time as the refusal notice or before arrangements are made for his or her removal. They must be filled in and returned to the port or airport where the refusal took place within 28 days of the date of refusal. ▶See chapter 16 for more details about filling in appeal forms.

5 **If the person did not have a visa or entry clearance before travelling**, and if he or she was coming as a visitor, as a prospective student or as a student on a course lasting for six months or less, he or she has *no* right of appeal against refusal. The only remedies are negotiating with the immigration officers or (rarely) judicial review ▶see 7 below.

6 **If the person did not have a visa or entry clearance before travelling** but was coming for any other purpose, he or she has a right of appeal, *but only after being removed from the UK*.

7 **If there is no right of appeal, or only after removal**, the remedies available to people refused entry are very limited but should nevertheless be tried.

i) Obtain copies of any papers given to the person, with details of the reasons for refusal and immigration reference numbers. In spite of assurances, refusal letters written after the 1993 Act came into force have sometimes not contained more than the assertion that the officer is not satisfied that the person intends to leave the UK at the end of the period requested.

ii) Contact the immigration officers at the port or airport. Try to convince them that they have made a mistake. They are unlikely to change the decision, but it may be possible to negotiate an extension of temporary admission, if this has been granted, so that the person is able to stay for at least a week. If the person is detained, try to negotiate temporary admission. The person will need an address and sponsor. Immigration officers will need to be convinced that he or she will leave the UK when required. Detention has to be authorised by a chief immigration officer, so insist on speaking to him or her and if necessary go higher (to the inspector in charge of the port or airport terminal).

iii) See whether there are any grounds for involving an MP. MPs used to be able to intervene very effectively in port refusal cases and removal was always deferred while their representations were being considered. Since January 1989 this is no longer done. The Home Office will only defer removal if the MP is able to bring forward exceptional compassionate circumstances which the immigration officer knew about but did not properly take into account. If such circumstances have been put to an immigration officer and have not been properly considered, it may be worth involving an MP. Use the constituency MP of one of the friends or relatives the person is coming to be with. However, some MPs refuse to take on such cases at all now, or need a great deal of persuading to do so. MPs can be contacted at the House of Commons (0171 219 3000) which may also be able to give the number of the MP's secretary or constituency office.

iv) See whether there are any grounds for asking the courts for leave to apply for judicial review of the refusal. If it is a really strong or compassionate case, the passenger may wish to take legal advice about judicial review, but it is of little use in most refused visitors' cases. Before the Asylum and Immigration Appeals Act came into force on 26 July 1993, judicial review was rarely granted in port refusal cases, as the courts held it to be inappropriate because there was a right of appeal after removal. This argument is no longer valid, so the courts' views may change. However there are difficulties in obtaining legal aid, both because the person is abroad and because the Legal Aid Board may not accept that the benefit the person would achieve from success in the case would be proportionate to the money spent on it.

8 **If the person has applied for asylum** find out whether he or she came through a 'safe third country' or not. If people have travelled through an EU country, or Canada, Norway, Switzerland or the United States of America to reach the UK, they may be returned there to apply for asylum and have no right of appeal until after removal. It may be possible to apply for judicial review and people should consult the Refugee Legal Centre or other specialist organisation quickly for advice on this. If they have travelled direct to the UK from the country of persecution or have come through any other country, the asylum application will be considered in the UK and there will be a right of appeal if it is refused. This may take some time so the question of temporary admission or bail ▶see chapter 15 may be relevant.

9 **If the person is eventually removed**, and has the right of appeal make sure that he or she fills in and returns the appeal forms provided. The appeal must be received within 28 days of the date of removal. This is important, even if the person's planned stay has been ruined and he or she does not intend to try again immediately. If the refusal is not challenged, it

will form part of the person's immigration record. Refusals are marked on the passport (in the form of a cross through the square entry stamp, ▶see chapter 13 for example). This will mean that if people attempt to return to the UK, they are likely to be refused again. Other countries' immigration officials know what these marks mean – so they are likely to refuse a visit visa too. With the closer cooperation between EU governments, being refused one visit visa once does not only mean losing a particular visit, but may mean that the person will never be able to travel to Europe again.

Late applications to the Home Office

Often people come for advice about extending their stay either just before their existing leave to remain runs out, or after it has done so.

1 **If the person's leave is about to expire**, it is vital that he or she should apply for an extension *before* the existing leave runs out. An application should be posted (recorded delivery) or taken to the Home Office immediately. From 25 November 1996 all applications *except* those for asylum or for work permit extensions or for EEA nationals and their families must be made on an official Home Office application form. If they are not on the correct form, with all the questions answered and with all the documents listed on the form, or an explanation of why each document is not there and when it is expected, they are not valid applications. It is important that all the documents and evidence to support the application are sent on to the Home Office as soon as possible afterwards. The forms state that the Home Office may decide the application on the information available to it within 28 days.

An application is made in time provided it is posted to the Home Office on or before the date the leave runs out and is on the correct form, with all the documents required, or explanations why they are not available and when they will be sent. The person is then legally in the country while the Home Office considers the case. There will normally be a right of appeal against any refusal, and even if there is not, the person is given 28 days in which to make arrangements to leave. ▶See chapter 16 for more details.

2 **If the person's leave expired recently**, the Home Office may consider the application as though the relevant immigration rules applied (check the relevant chapter for a description of the rules and how they are interpreted). If the application is straightforward (for example, a student who is in the middle of a recognised course, has paid the fees and has adequate financial support), the person can make the application him- or herself, explaining and apologising for the lateness. The person becomes an overstayer the day after leave runs out. Any application to extend stay is completely discretionary, outside the immigration rules, and there is no right of appeal against a refusal. But if there may be problems fulfilling the other requirements of the rules, the person should seek further advice.

3 **If the person's leave expired some time ago**, there may be difficulties with the application. The Home Office may begin deportation action as

soon as it is contacted; or indeed may already have done so without the person knowing about it. Before advising the person to contact the Home Office, check:

i) whether he or she has been in the UK continuously for seven years or more. If so, there is a full right of appeal before deportation and the Home Office is likely to give the case more serious consideration.

ii) whether there are strong reasons for the person to stay (for example, marriage to a British or settled person, strong compassionate reasons). But see pages 21–23 on Home Office internal instructions on marriage and deportation.

iii) whether the person has received any threats of deportation from the Home Office.

If people decide to make an application to the Home Office it should be through an adviser, so that the Home Office knows that they will be properly represented if deportation action is threatened. The application should be made as fully as possible, with all the details of the person's case and history, and supporting evidence. The Home Office has to consider all information known to it in deciding whether to deport a person, but does not have to ask for any more details than those initially provided, so making a thorough case is important. ▶See chapter 14 for more information about the process of deportation and the ways to challenge it.

Refusals without right of appeal

People who apply late for an extension of leave to remain have no right of appeal against refusal. This includes people who made a request in time, but not on the correct form, or without all the documents or explanations required, or did not send the form in until after the leave had expired. If the Home Office refuses the application, it sends a letter stating this and telling the person to make immediate arrangements to leave.

Even when there is no formal appeal, it may be possible to make representations to the Home Office to urge that the refusal be reconsidered. This is usually only worthwhile if there is substantial new evidence available to support the previous application or there have been changes in the person's circumstances which the Home Office does not know about. The case should be put to the Home Office as fully as possible. It may also be helpful to write to the person's Member of Parliament to explain the case and ask him or her to take it up with the Home Office Minister. However, the person remains an overstayer while the Home Office is considering the case, and is therefore liable to arrest and deportation.

The Asylum and Immigration Appeals Act 1993 removed rights of appeal from people whose refusal was 'mandatory under the immigration rules' – where a person has applied for something not permitted under the rules. It lists these refusals:

- when 'a relevant document which is required by the immigration rules has not been issued'; these are defined as entry clearances, passports or other identity documents and work permits or permissions to work given after entry
- when people do not 'satisfy a requirement of the immigration rules as to age, nationality or citizenship'
- when people seek an extension of stay for a period longer than that permitted by the immigration rules
- if 'any fee required by or under any enactment has not been paid'.

The Home Office has stated that the age requirement does not apply to people applying to settle with family members, because there are provisions in the immigration rules to allow children over 18 to join parents, or parents under 65 to join children. Working holidaymakers or au pairs however must be between 17 and 27. At present, the only Home Office fee is for the issue of certificates of entitlement, but there is power under the 1988 Immigration Act to charge for granting settlement as well. Some examples of situations where people lose the right of appeal are:

- a visitor who has been in Britain for six months and applies for a further extension as a visitor
- a visa national who enters as a visitor and applies to remain as a student
- a non-Commonwealth citizen who applies to be a working holidaymaker
- a student who has attempted to get a work permit after his studies (who did not have entry clearance for this purpose).

However the Home Office has interpreted this provision broadly and has refused applications without the right of appeal even when there is no specific prohibition in the rules. For example, a British Overseas citizen applying to remain in the UK because she is a British national and has no right of re-entry anywhere else has been refused as though she had been applying as a visitor, with no right of appeal.

When people apply for variation of leave to remain but are asking for something that is not specifically provided for in the immigration rules, it is therefore important to stress that the application is made outside the rules, in order to try to retain a right of appeal. If no immigration rule applies to a situation, and an application is refused, it should then be possible to appeal. If the Home Office does not accept this, the person can appeal anyway, and the case be considered as a preliminary issue – see pages 300–301. If there is an appeal hearing the adjudicator can be asked for a recommendation that the application be granted or reconsidered outside the rules. However, the Home Office does not have to follow recommendations and stated on 23 July 1996 that it would not normally do so unless new exceptional compassionate circumstances had been raised at the appeal.

If applications are made before people's permission to stay runs out, they will be told of the refusal and that they have 28 days in which to make arrangements to leave. After the 28 days have elapsed, they become overstayers. It may be possible to contest such refusals by making representations to the Home Office, perhaps through the local Member of Parliament, explaining the compassionate or exceptional circumstances and asking the Home Office to reconsider the case, outside the rules. The Home Office may have disregarded important compassionate aspects; for example, a grandmother visiting to help care for her grandchildren at the time another baby is expected and is born may need to stay for more than six months. Knowing there will be no right of appeal against their decision, officials may not have considered the case fully.

Arrest and threatened deportation or removal

Advisers are often contacted on behalf of people who are being held by police or immigration officers, on the grounds that they are illegally in the UK, and threatened with deportation or removal.

As soon as possible, find out the following information:

- the detainee's name, date of birth and nationality
- the Home Office or immigration service reference number
- where the person is detained
- under what authority the person is detained – for example, as an alleged illegal entrant or because a deportation decision has been made
- are there any plans to send the person away, and if so, when
- has the person been given any papers and if so, what
- what the detainee wants – for example, to contest the situation in every possible way, to return to the country of origin as quickly as possible, to be released for a short period to make arrangements to leave.

Speak to the officer dealing with the case, at the Home Office or the immigration service office, to register interest in the case and ensure that you will be informed of any decision or action that is taken.

1 **Find out whether the person has been charged** with any criminal, or immigration, offence. If no charge has yet been brought, but is being considered, try to ensure that the person does not say anything, and certainly does not sign anything, until a solicitor or adviser can be present. The police may call on a duty solicitor, but some do not know very much about immigration law.

2 **If the person has not been charged**, find out whether he or she is being treated as an illegal entrant, or is threatened with deportation:

- alleged illegal entrants will have been given a form called IS 151A. They may have signed a 'confession' while in custody, possibly without understanding what this meant, and the decision on their status may be

based on this. Alleged illegal entrants will need legal advice if they wish to challenge this decision; ▶see chapter 14 for more details about illegal entry.
- people threatened with deportation will have been given a form called APP 104. This is a 'notice of intention to deport'; the person should also be given forms to fill in to appeal against it. The immigration officers may tell them about the possibility of voluntary or supervised departure, suggesting that any appeal may not succeed. If people agree to this, they may be asked to sign a form to waive their appeal rights. This can be reversed; people may change their minds, after further advice, and reinstate the appeal, provided this is done and the forms received by the Home Office within the 14-day period allowed. ▶See chapter 14 for more about the deportation process and possible action.

3 **Try to negotiate temporary release or bail**. The factors which the immigration service will consider include:
- does the person have a stable home? For example, how long has he or she lived at that address, is this with family or close friends with whom he or she would want to keep in touch?
- is the person in employment, and for how long?
- has the person abided by any immigration or bail conditions in the past?
- what incentive does the person have to keep in contact with the immigration service?
- how strong is the person's case?

It is less likely that a woman or child will be detained, but probable that a young man without close family ties, who has not lived at the same address for long and who does not have a strong immigration case, will be.

If the person is not released, *visit* as soon as possible, to find out exactly what he or she wants to do and to advise on whether this is feasible.

If there are plans to remove the person very quickly, and he or she wants to contest removal, speak to the chief immigration officer or the Home Office official dealing with the case. If there is new information or arguments which have not been considered before, for example marriage, a long-standing relationship, or an asylum claim, it is possible that the person's removal will be delayed while representations are considered.

If the person does not have a right of appeal against the immigration decision, representations from the MP for the area where he or she lives or works may delay removal. Under Home Office guidelines to MPs in force since January 1989, if the MP agrees to take up the case, he or she should contact the officer dealing with it to say so, and to give an outline of the 'new and compelling evidence' which will be put forward. The MP then has five working days in which to submit written representations. If nothing is received by that time, arrangements for the person's removal will proceed. If the MP makes initial telephone representations and thereby secures a delay in the person's removal, the adviser should write to the MP with full details as soon as possible. The MP will probably pass the adviser's letter on to the Home Office, with a covering letter, so the adviser should state all the relevant facts and arguments in the letter to the MP. If the person is detained, arguments for his or her release should be repeated, as the intervention of the MP may add further delays to the consideration of the case.

Appealing to the courts

When all attempts to make the Home Office reconsider a case have failed, it may be possible to apply to the courts. If the person has had a right of appeal and has been unsuccessful in an appeal hearing before the Immigration Appeal Tribunal, an application can be made to the Court of Appeal. If the person had no right of appeal, or had been refused leave to appeal to the Tribunal, an application can be made to the Divisional Court for judicial review. There are strict time limits for both these applications. Courts will only grant leave to appeal if they believe that the Home Office or the Tribunal was wrong in law, or that there were serious procedural defects in its practice. If the person wants to attempt to go to court, it is important that he or she is referred quickly to a solicitor who is experienced and knowledgeable in immigration law and who will advise honestly about the chances of success. Legal aid is available for court cases on immigration on the same basis as for any other legal matter – when the person meets the financial criteria and the Legal Aid Board is satisfied that there is an arguable case and that the cost is proportionate to the benefit gained.

SECTION 7: TRAVEL

13 Passport stamps and codes

This chapter gives examples of common passport stamps and codes used by the immigration authorities. It is intended for reference, to help advisers identify endorsements and make deductions from them and to familiarise people with Home Office practices.

Interpreting passports

The stamps which the Home Office and the immigration service put on people's passports or travel documents have specific meanings. The Home Office and the immigration service also have private codes which they use as well as the official stamps, so that an immigration official, whether from the UK or another country, often has more information than is known to the holder of the passport. It can be important for people to know what these codes mean as the endorsements on their passport may seriously affect their chances of being allowed into the UK again or of being granted an extension of stay, even when there is no apparent reason why they should face difficulties.

Entry clearance

British embassies and high commissions endorse passports when they deal with entry clearance applications from people wanting to come to the UK. When an entry clearance application is made, the entry clearance officer will want to see the passport and at that time it is likely that 'entry clearance applied for' and the date will be written on the first blank page of the passport.

An entry clearance passport endorsement is called either a visa or an entry certificate. Recently-issued entry clearances are certificates stuck into passports and then embossed with the post's official stamp. In the past they were sometimes inked stamps placed directly in a passport.

The entry clearance includes written information to show why it was granted, for example 'settlement to join mother' or 'visit'. A settlement entry clearance for a person who is given a year initially will normally be marked to state this, for example 'WYR' meaning 'wife – one year'. This is used to remind immigration officers that people should be given leave to enter for a year, rather than an indefinite period. The entry clearance also normally states 'valid for presentation at a UK port within six months of issue'. This means that the entry clearance is valid for six months from its date of issue and people should use it to travel within that time. If they are unable to travel during that time, they must apply to the British embassy or high commission to extend the validity of the entry clearance.

Entry clearances state whether they are valid for a single entry or multiple entries. A single-entry entry clearance may be used for only one journey to the UK; it is not valid for any subsequent re-entry. If the person is a visa national and wishes to travel out of the UK and to re-enter, a new visa is necessary.

A Entry clearance sticker

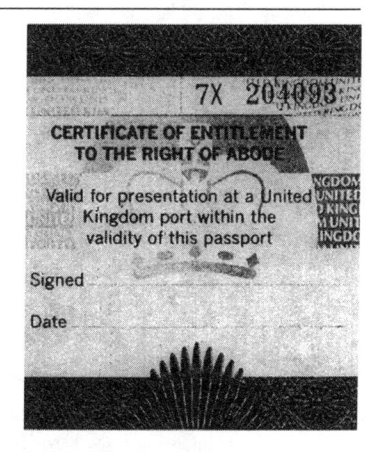

B Certificate of entitlement to the right of abode

Certificates of entitlement to the right of abode

People who have the right of abode (▶see glossary for definition) but who are not travelling on British passports need to get this right confirmed by the British embassy or high commission before travelling. They will be given a certificate of entitlement to the right of abode, which is a sticker like the entry clearance sticker. Before 1983, this was called a certificate of patriality, which means precisely the same thing. If people apply to the Home Office for confirmation of their right of abode, the Home Office can also give the certificate of entitlement.

Passport stamps at ports of entry

When a person subject to immigration control arrives at the borders of the UK and is admitted, the passport will be stamped with a square date stamp. This will have the date on which the person arrived, the name of the port, and the number (in brackets) of the individual immigration officer who dealt with the application. Any time limit stamped on the passport runs from the date of this square stamp, not from any date from which entry clearance was granted abroad.

C arrival stamp

> IMMIGRATION OFFICER
> * (369) *
> 10 DEC 1994
> HEATHROW (2)

Immigration officers may also impose conditions either prohibiting or restricting work or business. They may also require the person to register with the police and, from 1 November 1996, impose 'a condition requiring him to maintain and accommodate himself, and any dependants of his, without recourse to public funds'. If there is only a time limit on the person's stay, that means that there are no restrictions on what that person may do while in the UK for that time. If there is no time limit on a person's stay the person has indefinite leave to enter or remain (settlement) and there can be no other conditions either.

Visitors

It is usual for visitors to be admitted for six months, even if they only intend to stay for a shorter period. Most people admitted as visitors will have stamp **D** and the date stamp. If they entered before 8 November 1996, the public funds requirement will not be stamped on their passport, but this does not mean they are eligible to claim benefits; ▶see chapter 10.

If the immigration officer was not totally satisfied but did not have enough evidence on which to base a refusal, there will be a more detailed stamp **E** and a computer reference number. If the suspicions are particularly strong the time may be written as SIX (6) MONTHS, which will alert any immigration official dealing with that person in the future to ask more questions than she or he otherwise might to try to elicit evidence for a refusal. It does not appear to the person concerned that there is anything unusual.

> **D**
> LEAVE TO ENTER FOR SIX MONTHS
> EMPLOYMENT AND RECOURSE TO
> PUBLIC FUNDS PROHIBITED

> **E**
> Leave to enter the United Kingdom on condition that the holder maintains and accommodates himself and any dependants without recourse to public funds, does not enter employment paid or unpaid and does not engage in any business or profession is hereby given for/until
> SIX MONTHS
> AB   123   456

When a visitor is merely transiting through the UK, he or she will usually be admitted for 48 hours only. This will not be extended. When a person has requested a very short period as a visitor, occasionally the precise period may be given. Immigration officers may also give a shorter period than six months if they feel there is a particular reason for doing so, for example a person coming for a short course of medical treatment. Any shorter period will also alert another immigration official to something unusual about the applicant.

Students

The most common stamp on a student's passport is **F**, known as a 'restriction on working'. Although it is often fairly illegible, its conditions are still valid even if not known by the person. It means that if the student

F Leave to enter the United Kingdom on condition that the holder maintains and accommodates himself and any dependants without recourse to public funds, does not enter or change employment paid or unpaid without the consent of the Secretary of State for Employment and does not engage in any business or profession without the consent of the Secretary of State for the Home Department is hereby given for/until **TWELVE MONTHS**

wants to work in the weekends or evenings, the prospective employer must apply for a work permit to the Department for Education and Employment for the work to be legal (►see chapter 9). If the student wants to be self-employed, for example giving private coaching, she or he must approach the Home Office to request permission to do this.

Some students will have the same stamp as a visitor (►see **E**) with the time in handwriting, for example TWELVE MONTHS. This stamp is known as a 'prohibition on working'. If more than six months has been given initially, the person must have come in as a student, because a visitor will never be given more than six months. If a student has been admitted for six months or less, or as a prospective student, he or she may be prohibited from working.

It is possible for the student to try to alter this by applying to the Home Office to request that the stamp be changed to a restriction on working. It is important not to give the Home Office the impression that the student needs to work for financial reasons; ►see details of the support and accommodation requirements in chapter 9.

Students' spouses may be allowed to live in the UK with them while they are studying. HC 395 states that students' spouses are to be prohibited from working unless they are granted leave for 12 months or longer, and

G Leave to enter the United Kingdom is hereby given for/until **TWELVE MONTHS**

that they cannot be granted leave for a longer period than the student. Thus they are likely to have a stamp **G** or stamp **E**, depending on the length of time they have been given.

Stamp **G** means that people do not need to get permission from the Home Office or any separate work permits and if they find work they will be given a national insurance number on request. After 8 November 1996, it may also include a public funds requirement.

Workers and business people

H Leave to enter the United Kingdom on condition that the holder maintains and accommodates himself and any dependants without recourse to public funds, does not enter employment paid or unpaid other than with/as

and does not engage in any business or profession without the consent of the Secretary of State for the Home Department is hereby given for/until

People admitted with work permits or as business people or self-employed will have a stamp restricting employment (►see stamp **F**), with TWELVE MONTHS or FOUR YEARS in handwriting. People admitted to do specific work, such as ministers of religion, or specific types of work, such as working holidaymakers, may have a different stamp **H**. The spouses of work permit holders and business people will normally have no restrictions on working, merely the same time limit as their spouse. This means that spouses are free to work; there are no restrictions on what they can do in the UK during the time they have been admitted. They do not need to get permission from the Home Office or any separate work permit and they will be given national insurance numbers on request.

People admitted as persons of independent means, and their spouses and children, will have a prohibition on working (▶see stamp **E**) with the time, usually FOUR YEARS, in handwriting.

Refugees and those granted exceptional leave

Refugees' passports are not stamped, because they cannot use them without forfeiting their refugee status. They will be given a letter from the Home Office which explains their position as refugees and some of their rights in the UK and which states that they have been given leave to remain until a certain date. They may be given refugee travel documents, issued by the Home Office under the United Nations Convention relating to the Status of Refugees, and their leave to remain will be stamped on them. The travel documents are valid for all countries except the refugee's country of origin.

People granted exceptional leave to remain may use their national passports and will have leave to enter or remain stamped on them. If they cannot obtain passports, they may be given Home Office brown travel documents, but this is always discretionary. These will be endorsed with leave to remain without restrictions on employment or occupation (▶see stamp **G**). Leave is usually given for one year initially, then for two periods of three years and then settlement may be granted.

Registration with the police

After the time limit and conditions, some people will have an extra passport stamp **J**. This is a requirement which may be imposed on people who are not Commonwealth or EEA citizens, who are over 16 and who have been given leave to enter or remain in the UK for more than six months or who have come in to work for more than three months. It is normally imposed on students and workers of the relevant nationalities, and on refugees and people granted exceptional leave to remain, but not normally on people given leave to enter or remain as spouses. If the requirement to register with the police has not been stamped on people's passports, even in situations where it could have been, they do not have to do so. When the requirement is imposed, it should be taken seriously.

J The holder is required to register at once with the police.

'At once' means within seven days. The person should go to the Aliens Registration Office, 10 Lamb's Conduit Street, London WC1 3MX if he or she lives in the London Metropolitan Police area, or to the central police station of the town if living outside London. The police need the person's passport, two photographs of the person and the fee (▶see appendix).

The police record the person's full name, date of birth, address, marital status, occupation in the UK and immigration conditions in the UK and note all this in a green police registration certificate. A person required to register with the police must inform them of any change in any of these particulars within two months of the change occurring. When people are allowed to settle, they no longer have to register with the police and this is endorsed on their passports.

Family members

Most family members coming for settlement will be admitted for a year initially. Their passports will be stamped with leave to enter the UK for this period, with no conditions about employment (▶see stamp **G**) but probably with a public funds condition. They are free to work or to study or to do anything else they wish during that time.

Re-entering the UK

Section 3(3)(b)

People who have been granted more than six months' permission to enter or remain in the UK and who travel out of and into the UK within the period of time that they have been given may expect to be allowed in again for what is left of that time, on the same conditions. This will happen provided the immigration officers are satisfied that their circumstances have not changed to make them no longer qualify for leave to enter in that capacity. When they return, their passports are usually stamped as **K** and the same date as when their previous leave would have expired is in handwriting.

K Given leave to enter to [date] Section 3(3)(b)

3(3)(b) is the section of the Immigration Act 1971 which provides for readmission in these circumstances. It has applied automatically to people granted leave for more than six months since 16 May 1991.

Multiple-entry visas and visa exemption

Visa nationals allowed to remain for more than six months are exempt from requiring visas if returning to the UK within the time of their previous leave. This exemption is now universal, so the old visa exemption stamps are no longer used. Re-entry visas are no longer issued. Visas can only be obtained from British posts outside the UK.

Visa national visitors still need a visa each time they enter (as they have leave only for six months). They should therefore apply for multiple-entry visas before coming to the UK if they are considering visiting other countries and then returning to the UK. If they do not do so, and travel and intend to return to the UK during that time, they will have to obtain new visas from the British post in the country which they have visited.

Leave to remain

When the Home Office has any dealings with a person, the person is given a Home Office reference. This is a unique personal reference; it is normally the first letter of the person's surname followed by five or six numbers. If a woman marries, the Home Office changes her reference to that of her husband, if he already has a Home Office file, or gives her a new reference, from the first letter of his surname. For Arabic names, the Home Office uses the first letter of the first name. This reference should always be used in any correspondence and will help the Home Office to find any file. If the Home Office has ever held the person's passport, it writes the reference number on the passport, usually on the inside back cover, but on the inside front cover of passports with personal details at the back.

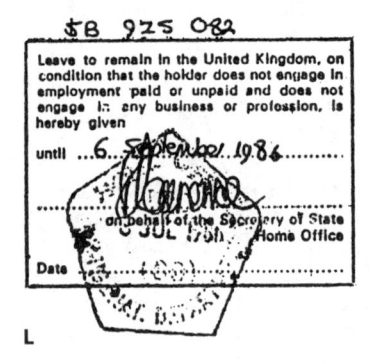

L

When the Home Office grants permission to stay, this is known as 'leave to remain', as the person has already entered the country. The Home Office uses larger stamps, with oblong borders, using broadly the same wording as immigration officers' stamps apart from the wording 'leave to remain' rather than 'leave to enter', as **L**. It is signed by the official who has granted the leave, then stamped 'on behalf of the Secretary of State, Home Office'. The Home Office date stamp is pentagonal, stating 'Home Office Immig & Nat Department', the date, and the number of the official in brackets.

Home Office-granted leave to remain may also have a requirement to register with the police.

Settled status

There are several different stamps a person who is *settled* in the UK may have on his or her passport. When a person has been granted entry clearance for settlement and arrives at a UK air- or sea port, the stamp put on the passport will state

M Given leave to enter the United Kingdom for an indefinite period

If people have already been granted settlement but have travelled and returned after a holiday, it is not necessary to repeat the stamp to enter indefinitely again. They will usually just be given the square date stamp, (▶see stamp **C**) showing when and where they returned. This means exactly the same thing; the person has been admitted with no time limit and no conditions on his or her stay.

When a person is travelling for the first time on a new passport, it is sensible to carry the old passport as well, so that the immigration officer can immediately see what the person's status is. When a person enters the country for the first time on a new passport, it is usual for the 'Given leave to enter the United Kingdom for an indefinite period' stamp to be given again, so that the person's status will be clear to other immigration officers in the future. When this has been done, there is no need to continue to carry the old passport as well as the new one when travelling, though it should still be kept, if possible, in case the evidence is ever required, for example if the person applies for naturalisation. When the Home Office grants settlement, it uses a sticker as **N**, showing that there is no time limit or conditions on the person's stay. Until 1992, indefinite leave was shown by a rubber stamp, the design of which was changed periodically, **O** being the most recent, rather than by a sticker.

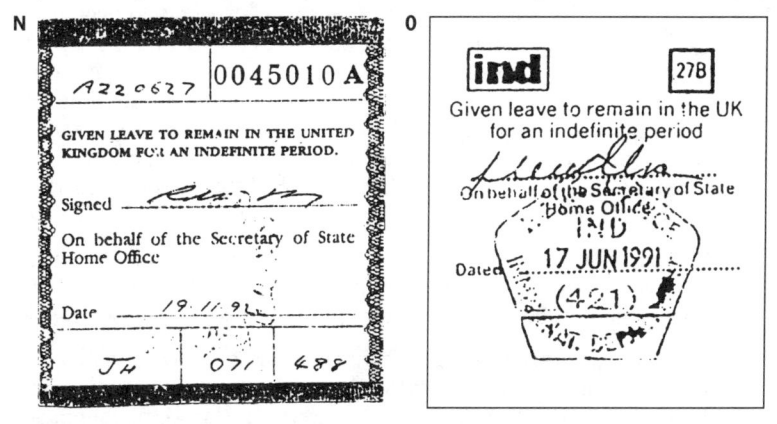

N
```
A22 0627   0045010 A
GIVEN LEAVE TO REMAIN IN THE UNITED
KINGDOM FOR AN INDEFINITE PERIOD.
Signed _____
On behalf of the Secretary of State
Home Office
Date   19.11.91
       JH    071    488
```

O
```
ind                          27B
Given leave to remain in the UK
for an indefinite period
_____
On behalf of the Secretary of State
            Home Office
Dated     17 JUN 1991
            (421)
```

When settlement has been granted, but the passport on which it was endorsed has run out, and the person obtains a new passport, this may be endorsed by the Home Office. Because the leave has already been granted, this will not be stamped again. The endorsement the Home Office then gives is either

P

| There is at present no time limit on the holder's stay in the United Kingdom | or | Holder's stay in the UK is no longer subject to a time limit |

These mean exactly the same as indefinite leave. Many people are worried by the 'at present' phrase. It does not mean anything more temporary, or that the Home Office could impose a time limit in the future. The Home Office uses this form of wording because retaining settlement is conditional on the person not being out of the UK for a period of more than two years and qualifying to enter under the returning resident rules (▶see page 229).

Visa nationals who are settled do not require visas to return for settlement within two years. If they have been away longer, it might be wise to apply for returning resident visas; ▶see page 229 for further details.

Leaving the UK

When people leave the UK, their passports are stamped with a triangular stamp, showing the date and port of exit and the number of the immigration officer as **Q**.

If there is a period of time between the expiry of the last leave to enter or remain granted and the date of departure, it will be clear that something unusual has happened. If the person tries to return in the future, the immigration officers may ask questions to find out the reason for this. It may be because an application for an extension had been made to the Home Office, but not decided when the person left, or an application had been refused and the person had appealed, or that the person has overstayed leave to remain. This will not affect the person when he or she leaves, as the passport is just stamped with the date of departure. However, the immigration officers will normally send a report to the Home Office of the person's departure, so that there will be a record should he or she attempt to enter again.

If the person is being deported or has been forced to leave under the supervised departure provisions (▶see chapter 14) the date will be underlined to show that the person left with some immigration problems.

If the immigration officers believe that the passport may be forged or there is some doubt about the person's immigration status, they will underline the immigration officer's number on the stamp. This will alert immigration officers in future should the person attempt to re-enter the UK.

Refusals and problems

When people apply for entry clearance abroad, the entry clearance officers write 'entry clearance applied for', followed by the place and date, on the first blank page of the passport or on the inside back cover. If the application is refused, they underline these words.

When people are refused entry to the UK, their passports are still stamped with the square date stamp but an ink cross is put through this to show the refusal of leave to enter.

When the Home Office refuses further leave to remain, it underlines the date to which the previous leave had been granted. This may not be noticed by the person but shows any other immigration official that there has been a refusal.

If the passport is a new one, with no leave to enter or remain stamped in it, the Home Office underlines the person's Home Office reference number, written on the inside back cover of the passport.

The Home Office may also write EMB by the side of the last leave to enter or remain granted, or on the inside back cover of the passport if there are no other British stamps on the passport. This means that when the person leaves, immigration officers are required to write a report to the Home Office to confirm the person's embarkation.

British passports

Since 1983, British passports have had the nationality status of their holders printed on the page with personal details, which is the inside back cover of new-style maroon European Union passports or the front page of old-style navy blue passports. This may state: British citizen, British Dependent Territories citizen, British Overseas citizen, British subject, British Protected Person or British National (Overseas). British citizens automatically have the right of abode and are not subject to British immigration control. All other British nationals are subject to immigration control and therefore their passports have immigration stamps on them showing any time limit and conditions on their stay.

People who are settled in the UK will be given an indefinite leave stamp. They may also have a stamp

T Holder has the right of readmission to the UK

which means that they are settled and can return after *any* length of absence. The normal two-year restriction on returning residents does not apply to British passport holders.

British passports issued before 1983 will state that their holders are: British subjects, citizens of the UK and Colonies; or British Protected Persons; or British subjects without citizenship. Page 5 of the passport may be printed

U Holder has the right of abode in the UK

which means that the person is a British citizen under the British Nationality Act 1981.

This printed phrase may have been crossed out, and page 5 of the passport may be stamped with stamp **T**, confirming that the person is settled in the UK and can return after any length of absence. If the passport was issued abroad, in a place which was a British colony at the time of its issue but is now independent, ▶see pages 321–2 for more information on whether the person is likely still to be British or to have the right of abode.

Alternatively British passports may be stamped

V Holder is subject to control under the Immigration Act 1971

which means that the person is not settled in the UK. The passport will have other immigration stamps giving limited leave to remain.

Special quota vouchers for settlement are stickers, like entry clearances, but have QV and a reference number written on them. The person should have been granted settlement on arrival (▶see stamp **M**).

SECTION 8: ENFORCEMENT OF CONTROLS

14 Deportation, illegal entry and removal

Immigration control is enforced by both criminal and administrative sanctions. People who fall foul of immigration law may be dealt with:
- either through Home Office administrative powers, which are extensive, and which lead to deportation or removal
- or through the criminal law and the courts.

Deportation means sending people away from the UK under an order signed by the Home Secretary and prohibiting their re-entry. The person will normally have entered the UK legally and been granted leave to remain; but then broken a condition of stay, for example by overstaying leave to remain or working without permission. If a person is convicted of any criminal offence, immigration or non-immigration, for which the punishment could be imprisonment, the court may recommend deportation as part of the sentence. Alternatively, the Home Office may start proceedings using its administrative powers. The person cannot return to the UK unless the deportation order has first been revoked.

Illegal entry means entering the UK, or seeking to enter, without gaining permission from an immigration officer (and therefore in breach of the immigration laws, which require all non-EEA nationals who do not have the right of abode in the UK to have such permission). People may be treated as illegal entrants if they bypass immigration control altogether, or enter in breach of a deportation order or deceive an immigration officer about their identity, their reasons for coming to the UK or anything to do with their entry. Entry by deception is an area of illegal entry which has been expanded greatly by immigration officers extending the definition of 'deception'. The word used for the process of making an illegal entrant leave the UK is **removal**, not deportation.

How people are traced

The Home Office may come to know of people in breach of the immigration laws in many ways. They may have been in contact with the Home Office themselves. For example, they may have applied for an extension of stay which was refused, or lost an appeal, and remained in the UK after this, trying to persuade the Home Office to allow then to stay. The Home Office response to further representations may be a decision to deport.

If the person has not been in contact with the Home Office, but has simply stayed beyond the leave granted or worked without permission, he or she may be traced through various sources. Many authorities, such as the Benefits Agency, local authority housing departments, employers and colleges may now check on immigration status and make inquiries from the Home Office. The police or the immigration service or both may have been sent information. The police frequently ask for evidence of identification and immigration status from black or 'foreign-looking' people they stop for other reasons – on suspicion of a traffic offence, at a demonstration, as a witness to an accident or crime. People may call the police because of a burglary or an assault and then be asked to prove their status. If it is then established or suspected that the person may be in breach of the immigration laws, the police can check with the immigration service or with the police national computer (which contains the names of people against whom deportation orders have been signed) to confirm their suspicions. They may then hold the person pending immigration officers coming to interview him or her and to take further action.

The police and the immigration service have powers, increased by the 1996 Asylum and Immigration Act, to make unannounced raids on premises to search for people. The police's powers of search and arrest in dealing with the immigration offences of illegal entry, obtaining leave to enter or remain by deception and breaking conditions of stay, are the same as those they have for dealing with 'serious arrestable offences' under the Police and Criminal Evidence Act. The Home Office stated on 27 April 1995 that 'every reasonable effort should be made to establish the names of people whom it is suspected will be found and to check them against immigration records.' Some employers therefore are prepared to collaborate with the immigration authorities. When they are not and the Home Office believes that 'efforts to enlist the co-operation of the employer would undermine the effectiveness of a planned operation, visits will be authorised where there is apparently reliable information that immigration offenders will be found. Particular account will be taken of whether there is a history of the premises being used by offenders.'

Although the Home Office states, 'Visits to private addresses will continue to be authorised only where there is good reason to suspect that an identified person is there in breach of the immigration laws' the police may raid a house looking for one person and then ask any other people at that address to prove their identity.

The Home Office and DSS Efficiency Scrutiny (▶see page 211) provides mechanisms to increase contacts between the Home Office and other government departments and authorities to establish people's immigration status. There are established channels of communication for local authorities to find out people's immigration status from the Home Office and therefore for the Home Office to know about their presence and to continue to make its own inquiries, which may lead to action to enforce their departure. The new criminal offence for employers of employing someone not permitted to work without having made certain specified checks on the potential employee may also lead to more information about individuals at risk being given to the Home Office. All this may lead to the police being informed about possible criminal offences or the Home Office taking administrative action to deport or remove people.

Deportation – through the criminal courts

Criminal offences under immigration law

When a time limit is placed on a person's stay in the UK it is an offence under section 24(1)(b)(i) of the Immigration Act 1971 for the person to remain beyond the time limit given. It is an offence under section 24(1)(b)(ii) to fail to observe a condition attached to leave to remain, for example working when forbidden to do so. These offences are usually known as overstaying and as being in breach of conditions. It has been rare for people to be prosecuted for them; there were 29 cases, and 6 people convicted, in 1994. Prosecutions for other offences, such as assisting illegal entry, or harbouring, have increased in recent years, with 38 people convicted in 1994.

Prosecutions for other immigration-related crimes have increased. In 1995, there were 450 convictions for fraud in connection with the use of false passports detected at Heathrow airport. Most people were asylum-seekers and those in transit to apply for asylum in Canada or the United States and their passports were checked by airline staff who passed information to the police. People were generally sentenced to imprisonment, then held under Immigration Act powers ►see chapter 15, and not permitted to continue to their destinations.

The Asylum and Immigration Act 1996 created new immigration criminal offences. With effect from 1 October 1996, seeking or obtaining leave to remain (in addition to leave to enter) by deception carried out by the person is a criminal offence. Those who assist people to obtain leave to remain, as well as leave to enter, by means which include deception also commit a criminal offence. The scope of this offence was extended to include assisting the entry of anyone who a person 'knows or has reasonable cause for believing to be an asylum claimant'. The offence of assisting asylum claimants does not apply to those assisting people after they have claimed asylum on entry, or to people acting 'otherwise than for gain, or in the course of their employment by a *bona fide* organisation whose purpose it is to assist refugees'. Neither of these exemptions is defined further; but the government has stated that community organisations, churches and charities would fall within the latter part of the definition, and that the offence is not meant to apply to solicitors.

Another new offence, with effect from 27 January 1997, is committed by an employer who, after that date, employs a person who does not either have leave to remain without a restriction on taking the relevant job or does not fall into a category specified in an Order from the Home Office listing those people permitted to work here, ▶see pages 144–5. Employers who check one of a list of specified documents and keep a copy of one of these documents relevant to the person's work will not have committed an offence, even if it is found later that an employee was not allowed to work. The listed documents include official records of a person's National Insurance number, such as a P45, a passport or an identity card showing the person is an EEA national, passports from other countries with British immigration stamps showing that the people can work and Home Office letters confirming a person can work. There are concerns that this requirement will lead to further discrimination in recruitment, contrary to the Race Relations Act 1976.

Overstaying

People are overstayers if they remain in the UK without permission after their immigration leave has run out. This includes people who applied to the Home Office after their permission to remain had run out, even if the application was only one day late and even though the Home Office is considering their application.

People who made valid applications for extensions (▶see chapter 11) before any previous leave ran out and who are still waiting for a reply from the Home Office are *not* overstayers while the application is pending. People who are appealing against a Home Office refusal are protected from deportation while the appeal is pending, even though their leave has expired.

Breach of conditions

A common condition, as well as a time limit, to be put on a person's stay is a prohibition or a restriction on working. It is then illegal for the person to do any kind of work, paid or unpaid, even helping out at a friend's shop or business for a couple of hours, without the employer obtaining permission in advance from the Department for Education and Employment. International students in particular often believe, erroneously, that they are permitted to work during their holidays, or for a specific number of hours a week, without seeking permission but this is not the case (▶see chapter 9 for details of how students may obtain permission to work). As the Home Office can take deportation action against a person found to be working without permission, it is important that students should not work without permission and without realising the seriousness of the possible consequences.

The other conditions which may be imposed are a requirement to register with the police and, since 1 November 1996, under the Asylum and Immigration Act 1996, a requirement on people to support themselves and any dependants without recourse to public funds. Breach of any of these conditions can lead to the Home Office making a deportation decision against the person or to criminal charges and convictions.

Criminal convictions for non-immigration matters

People convicted of immigration offences are likely to be recommended for deportation. Some people may also be recommended for deportation, as part of the sentence, if they are convicted of a non-immigration criminal offence. Anybody who is not:

- a British citizen
- a Commonwealth citizen with the right of abode (▶see glossary)
- a Commonwealth or Irish citizen who was settled in the UK on 1 January 1973 and who has lived in the UK for the last five years before deportation was contemplated

can be recommended for deportation if convicted of a criminal offence for which he or she could be sentenced to imprisonment. This includes people who are settled in the UK and are convicted of a non-immigration offence. In order to be recommended for deportation it is not necessary for people to receive a custodial sentence. It is enough that they are convicted of an offence for which imprisonment is a possible sentence.

EEA nationals are not subject to deportation in the same way as other non-British nationals. They can only be deported for reasons of public policy, public security and public health and the definitions of these concepts have been interpreted by the European Court of Justice. A court should therefore only recommend an EEA national for deportation after conviction for a very serious offence, or if a person has been convicted of a string of offences and appears likely to reoffend. If a recommendation is made, it is normal practice for the Home Secretary not to act on it but to issue a notice of intention to deport, on the grounds that the person's presence is not conducive to the public good ▶see below. This means that the EEA national has a right of appeal at which all matters can be considered, as required under Community legislation.

The court process

A police officer may arrest without warrant anyone he or she suspects to have committed an immigration offence and the person may be charged to appear before a magistrates' court. It is important that the person's legal representative should understand immigration law and the possible immigration consequences of conviction.

Overstaying is a continuing offence; people can be arrested for overstaying at any time after their leave has run out. If they are convicted of overstaying or working in breach of conditions they may be fined a maximum of £5000, imprisoned for up to six months, and recommended for deportation. People can only be convicted of the offence once during any one period of overstaying; if, after a conviction, the person still remains in the UK without permission, any further action would be under the Home Office's administrative powers.

If people liable to deportation are charged with any offence, including an immigration offence, for which they could be imprisoned, they must be informed of their liability to deportation and be given a standard information sheet, IM3, by the police or the Crown Prosecution Service explaining this. This sheet is written in legal language and may be frightening. It does not mean that people are to be deported, but that if they are convicted a recommendation for deportation is possible as part of any sentence. The case must be remanded for at least a week to enable them to seek advice and, if they allege they are not liable to deportation, to obtain evidence of this fact. The threat of deportation is particularly worrying to people settled or with close family in the UK. It is important that the legal representative in the criminal matter also knows about immigration law and the importance of arguing against a recommendation for deportation and appealing against any recommendation that is made.

Recommendations for deportation

The official handbook for magistrates, *The sentence of the court*, gives them guidance on making recommendations for deportation. The person or representative should be asked to address the court specifically on the question of a recommendation, and the court should also consider the effects of a recommendation on others, such as the person's family. The handbook states, 'Those who have committed serious offences or who have long records are suitable for recommendations, as are those who are convicted of immigration offences.' The court is reminded that people recommended will be detained unless the court directs release, and that 'detention in custody (as opposed to bail) pending criminal proceedings is not normally appropriate unless there is reason to suppose that the defendant would abscond or commit further offences.'

If people are recommended for deportation, the recommendation is part of the sentence and the only formal appeal against it is through the criminal appeals system against conviction or sentence. Appeals from a magistrates' court decision must be made within 21 days and from the Crown Court within 28 days. If no appeal is made, or if the appeal is unsuccessful, the Home Office then considers whether to carry out the recommendation.

It is important to remember that the courts cannot deport people; they only recommend to the Home Office that the person should be deported. The final decision rests with the Home Office, which has to consider any representations made as to why it should not carry out the court's recommendation. If representations are made to the Home Office, it is important to explain any special or compassionate circumstances, or why deportation should be delayed, for example to enable a person to complete a course of studies. However, in 1995 the Home Office decided not to deport only 50 court-recommended people and signed 260 such deportation orders. 10 people successfully appealed against recommendations. It is therefore probable that a recommendation will be carried out.

Deportation – Home Office administrative powers

The most common reason for deportation is that people have remained in the UK without permission. It is very much more frequent for the Home Office to use its administrative powers to force people out of the UK, rather than people being charged with a criminal offence and their case dealt with by the court system.

The Home Office follows a two-stage process: first it makes a formal decision to deport a person, against which there is a right of appeal. If the appeal is lost, or no appeal is lodged, the Home Secretary can sign a deportation order.

The Home Office may make an administrative decision to deport a person who it believes has breached the immigration laws ►see above; 5180 such decisions were made in 1995. If people have been in the UK for less than seven years, they have only a restricted right of appeal against deportation ►see below.

The Home Office may also decide to deport people whose presence it believes is not conducive to the public good; there were 90 such decisions in 1995. This reason is most commonly used against settled people who have been convicted of non-immigration criminal offences and the court has not recommended their deportation. It may also be used against people who have no criminal convictions, for example husbands alleged to have obtained settlement by deception about the state of their marriage. There is a full right of appeal against a decision made on these grounds, regardless of the length of time people have lived in the UK.

If the decision is on grounds of 'national security', there is no right of appeal and the Home Office does not have to give any further reasons. People may put their case before a panel of three 'advisers', who may make a recommendation to the Home Secretary, but both the panel hearing and the recommendation are secret and the Home Office does not have to follow it. Two EEA nationals' cases, *Radiom* and *Shingara*, (CO/477/93) have been referred to the European Court of Justice to decide whether this process is lawful for EEA nationals. The European Court of Human Rights held in the case of *Chahal* (70/1995/576/662) in November 1996 that this procedure is inadequate in asylum cases. People threatened with deportation on these grounds should get specialist advice.

The deportation process

If the Home Office already knows about the person, for example if an immigration appeal has been dismissed, it will normally send a standard letter to the person, stating that he or she has no further right to remain in the UK and should make arrangements to leave without delay (►see appendix). This is not a formal deportation notice or order, though many people think it is. If the person does not leave, or make any new application for leave to remain, the next letter from the Home Office will probably be another standard letter, reminding the person of his or her liability to deportation, and asking for a reply within 28 days stating any compassionate or other reasons why deportation should not be carried out. The immigration rules state that 'the Secretary of State will take into account all relevant factors known to him' before a decision to deport is made. It is therefore very important, if the person does intend to contest deportation, that all possible information on his or her behalf is given to the Home Office at this stage.

When the person is traced by chance, or through inquiries made by the police or other authorities, they may pass information to the Home Office. The person may be held by police in connection with an offence pending Home Office inquiries, or by the immigration service pending removal, or released and advised to make an application for leave to remain. Any information in support of the person's case to stay, or to show that he or she intends to leave the country very shortly, should be put to the Home Office to avoid deportation.

It is not automatic that the Home Office will make a decision to deport a person found to be in the UK illegally or working without permission. The person can put any arguments or representations to the Home Office about why he or she should not be deported. The Home Office wrote to JCWI on 18 July 1989 about deportation practice after the Immigration Act 1988, stating 'genuine students do not normally merit removal under the deportation powers unless their offences are serious or persistent'. Slightly differing statements have been made periodically since then, most recently on 22 July 1996 when the Minister, Timothy Kirkhope MP, stated, 'Each case where a student is found to be working without permission is considered on its individual merits. As required by the immigration rules, the case for deportation is considered in the light of all known relevant factors.'

Decisions to deport

When the Home Office makes a formal decision to deport it must be given in writing to the person. The Home Office standard letter stating the decision and the reasons for it includes an explanation of the person's right to appeal against the decision within 14 days of the date of the notice. The Home Office also sends appeal forms to fill in.

Until August 1988, decisions to deport had to be authorised by a senior official at the Home Office, acting on behalf of the Secretary of State. Since that date, the Home Office authorised immigration officers, of the rank of inspector, to make deportation decisions. This devolution of power to a quite different class of official was contested, but in October 1990 the House of Lords decided, in *Oladehinde* and *Alexander* (Imm AR 1991 111), that it was lawful for immigration officers to take these decisions. However, the House of Lords suggested that the procedures were of great concern. The Home Office agreed to ensure that there are written records of the decision-making process and that instances where there are any compassionate aspects or where the person has been in the UK for a long time must be referred to the Home Office for decision.

The immigration rules state that when the Home Office considers whether to deport people it must take into account 'all relevant factors known', including the person's

- age
- length of residence in the UK
- strength of connections with the UK
- personal history, including character, conduct and employment record
- domestic circumstances
- the nature of any offence of which the person was convicted
- previous criminal record
- compassionate circumstances
- any representations received on the person's behalf.

Home Office internal instructions on deportation (▶see pages 21–23) give an indication of the weight the Home Office may give to some of these points. The instructions, revised in March 1996, state that if a marriage has lasted for more than two years before action to enforce a person's departure was started and if 'it is unreasonable to expect the settled spouse to accompany his/her spouse on removal' deportation action should not 'normally' be initiated. However it is still important to draw these factors to the Home Office's attention. What it considers 'unreasonable' includes when the settled spouse:

- has very strong and close family ties in the UK such as older children from a previous relationship who form part of the family unit; or
- has been living in the UK for at least 10 years; or
- suffers from ill-health and medical evidence conclusively shows that his/her life would be significantly impaired or endangered if he/she were to accompany his/her spouse on removal.

Having children born in the UK is also important, but the Home Office considers that children under 10 may 'reasonably' be expected to adapt to life overseas and to leave with their parent(s). When children are aged 10 or over, the Home Office should also consider the length of the parents' stay without permission, whether they have made protracted representations to delay their removal, whether returning to the parents' country of origin would cause 'extreme hardship to the children or put their health seriously at risk' and, bizarrely, whether the children were conceived at a time when either parent had leave to remain.

After the Home Office makes a decision to deport people, it can also decide to detain them pending deportation or any appeal. ▶See chapter 16 for more details of the appeal process. If no appeal is lodged within the 14 days, or if the appeal is dismissed, the Home Secretary can then proceed to the second stage and sign a deportation order against the person. It is also possible to make written representations to the Home Office again at this stage, if there is relevant information which has not yet been considered.

Before 1986, the Home Office had a practice of making decisions to deport or deportation orders, and 'serving them on the file' at the Home Office without the person concerned being aware of it. If records of the person's arrival at the airport and admission had been sent to the Home Office but were not followed by records of the person's departure or by any application for further leave to remain, the Home Office then assumed that the person had remained without authority. This also happened when a person moved and the Home Office was unable to find the new address and assumed that the person had not left. As there is only a right of appeal against a deportation decision within 14 days of the decision, people may lose their right to appeal. If a decision is served some time later, when the person is traced, he or she may apply for leave to appeal out of time but it will be a matter for the appellate authorities whether the appeal can still be heard. If a deportation order has already been signed, there is no appeal against the decision to make it. The Home Office now normally waits until a person has been traced and dates decisions to deport when they are sent to the person.

It is the person's legal responsibility to keep the Home Office informed of his or her address. It is Home Office practice to send decisions to deport to the last known address that it has been given, even when the person has a representative. If the person wants papers to be sent to the representative, he or she may have to sign a formal letter to the Home Office asking that this be done. Because of the strict time limits for appeals, this may be important when people are living in temporary accommodation and there is a chance that they will not receive letters.

Rights of appeal against decisions to deport

People who have been in the UK less than seven years

The Immigration Act 1988 removed full rights of appeal against deportation for people who have been in the UK for less than seven years at the time of a decision to deport them on grounds of overstaying or breach of conditions. Although they can still appeal, the appeal can only be won if the facts on which the Home Office based its decision to deport were not correct. The only arguments that can be considered at the appeal are whether the person was an overstayer or not, or whether the person had been working or did not have any restrictions on doing so. No other arguments against deportation, such as information about ties with the UK, family, marriage or other compassionate circumstances can be put at the appeal.

The only exception to this is if a person claims to be a refugee and therefore has rights of appeal to a special adjudicator under the Asylum and Immigration Appeals Act 1993 ▶see chapter 16 for further details. In any other case, the appeal will automatically be dismissed if the Home Office had its facts right. It may still be worth lodging an appeal, for example to give the person more time to make preparations for leaving, or, if the person is detained, to make it possible to apply for bail (▶see chapter 15). It may also be possible to try to persuade the adjudicator to make a recommendation to the Home Office that the person be allowed to remain, if there are strong compassionate but not legal grounds. The Home Secretary stated on 23 July 1996 that he will no longer normally act on recommendations ▶see page 295. It is important, therefore, that the person realises the reasons for lodging an appeal and that a restricted appeal of this type cannot succeed.

People who have been in the UK for more than seven years

When people have been in the UK continuously for more than seven years at the time the Home Office makes a decision to deport them, the appeal can consider all the factors of the person's situation. Arguments can be put forward to show why the Home Office should have exercised its discretion differently and should not have made the decision. Any family, compassionate or other reasons can be argued. Witnesses can be called to testify to the suffering that would be caused or the loss to the community that would be sustained by the person's deportation as well as details about the individual's life. A campaign may gather support and momentum in the time that an appeal is pending, and show its support by being present at the appeal. There is thus a possibility of the appeal succeeding and the adjudicator reaching a different decision from the Home Office about whether a person should be deported. There are other details about the appeals process in chapter 16.

When a deportation order has been signed

If an appeal against a decision to deport has been lost, or if no appeal has been lodged within the 14-day period, the Home Office may proceed to sign a deportation order. After an order is signed, there is no further appeal against deportation; the person only has the right to appeal against destination. This is also the case if an order has been signed after a court recommendation.

The Home Office normally deports people to their country of nationality, or to the country which has given them a travel document, because they will be readmitted there. If people want to appeal against destination, this should be stated at the time of lodging the appeal. In order to succeed in this part of the appeal, the person has to have proof that another country will allow him or her to be deported there. It is rare for this to be granted unless a person has very strong ties with another country.

It is possible to urge the Home Office to revoke a deportation order while the person is in the UK, but the application is only likely to be considered if the deportation order was signed a long time ago, there have been changes in circumstances since the order was signed and the person has only recently been traced. All the changes in the person's circumstances or any compassionate or family reasons, unknown to the Home Office at the time the order was signed, should be put forward.

Alternatives to deportation

Leaving the country quickly

Where there are no legal challenges and no strong compassionate circumstances to put forward, and particularly where the person is detained or threatened with detention, he or she may not wish to contest refusal but instead to leave the country as soon as possible. This may be arranged without going through the whole deportation process, if the person formally renounces rights to appeal against the deportation decision and confirms his or her willingness to leave the country. Immigration officers may try to persuade people they have arrested to renounce their appeal rights and to say that they want to go. People may agree to this if they are detained and scared and have not had advice from anyone other than an immigration officer. They may then sign disclaimer forms, stating that they do not want to appeal. Even when this has been done, people may change their minds, and lodge an appeal, as long as it is within the 14 days allowed. Even when the appeal cannot succeed, the fact that it has been lodged means the person is able to apply to an adjudicator for bail, and the immigration service may reconsider temporary admission.

If people genuinely wish to leave, and are not detained, they may do so voluntarily, by buying their own ticket and leaving. It is worth informing the Home Office of travel plans, so that it is less likely that a deportation order will be signed against the person before he or she leaves. There may still be evidence that the person was in fact forced to leave, as his or her passport may have been endorsed 'served with form APP 104' (the notice of the Home Office's decision to deport and the right of appeal against it) but if there is no deportation order there is no formal prohibition on the person's return.

Supervised departure

Supervised departure is when the immigration service pays for the ticket of a person against whom a decision to deport has been made, but the person has shown that he or she is willing to leave and has signed a formal disclaimer of any appeal rights. Again, the person's passport will be endorsed 'served with form APP 104' to show that a deportation decision has been made. The 1990 immigration rules contained a formal power for the Home Office to prohibit the person's re-entry. This power did not appear to be used and was omitted from the 1994 and subsequent rules changes.

Until 1988, supervised departure was rare; it could only be used for people recommended for deportation after a court conviction, and was supposed to be restricted to 'young and first offenders'. Since 1988, it can be used for anyone threatened with deportation and has become more common. In 1987, 779 people were deported and 147 left under the supervised departure procedure; in 1995, 660 people were deported and 860 left under supervised departure. The contrast was even greater in the early 1990s.

Enforcement of deportation

If any appeals against deportation and destination are lost, or if no appeal is lodged, the Home Office can proceed to make a deportation order. This has to be signed by the Home Secretary, or by another Secretary of State from a different department on his behalf. The immigration service then has to make the practical travel arrangements, for which the Home Office will pay; there is no advantage to the deportee in paying his or her own fare. If people have no money at all for their journey, the Home Office states it will give those being sent to a European destination £5 and £10 to those being sent outside Europe. There is the power to demand the fare from a deportee but the Home Office rarely does so. The immigration service will make sure that the deportee has a valid passport or travel document.

The police or private security firms may be used in enforcing deportation. The immigration service may call in reinforcements when it believes that the person may resist arrest and removal. After the death of Joy Gardner on 29 July 1993, as a result of the police restraint used on her, the Home Office and police carried out a review of procedures in deportation cases where the police were involved. The review decided that all immigration requests to the police for assistance should be made in a standard way to ensure that all relevant information was passed on. People should not usually be taken direct from their homes to an airport for departure on the same day, but the police should still be used for escort and support duties. It also stated that the use of mouth restraints was permanently suspended.

People may be detained pending travel arrangements being made; the immigration service will usually hold their passports or travel documents and will give them to the captain of the plane to hold and to pass to the national authorities. The passport will be marked, by the date of the triangular departure stamp being underlined (►see chapter 13, stamp **Q**), so that it will be difficult for the person to use that passport in future travel. The deportation order will be logged on the port computer system, so that if the person tries to return, immigration officers will know about the deportation. The Home Office has stated that passports may be returned to deportees on the plane if this is requested through their advisers in advance of travelling. This is important for citizens of countries which may impose further penalties on their nationals if deported, or when people have applied for asylum in the UK, so that their deportation will not immediately be clear to the authorities of the country to which they are returning. It is difficult to check whether this is in fact done.

When people have left the UK with deportation orders signed against them, they cannot return while the order is still current. If they do gain entry while there is still a valid deportation order against them, they have entered illegally and can be arrested and removed as illegal entrants (see below). The order must be revoked before they can apply to return.

Returning to the UK

Revocation of deportation orders

It is possible to apply at any time for a deportation order to be revoked. If the person is abroad, he or she may apply either by letter or in person to the British embassy or high commission in that country, or by letter to the Home Office. Anybody else may write on the person's behalf to the Home Office. The immigration rules state that an order will not normally be revoked until the person has been out of the UK for at least three years. If an application is made sooner, it should contain full details of the exceptional circumstances justifying revocation earlier than normal. Having a spouse and children settled in the UK, who have reasons for being unable to join the deportee abroad, for example, may be strong enough compassionate circumstances.

It may also be possible to argue that the continued separation of a family is contrary to Article 8 of the European Convention on Human Rights, which deals with respect for family and private life. Any disruption of family life must be 'proportionate' to the object served by the officially-sanctioned disruption, so it is arguable, for example, that the continuing enforced separation is a disproportionate penalty for the person and family when the sentence of the court has been served. However, when people have been deported after criminal convictions, the order is unlikely to be revoked before the conviction has become spent under the Rehabilitation of Offenders Act. This is ten years for a sentence between six months and 2½ years, seven years for a sentence of up to six months, and five years for a fine. If revocation is refused, there is a right of appeal against this refusal.

If a deportation order is revoked, this does not give the person the right to come back to the UK. It merely means that there is no legal obstacle to him or her applying for permission to return. The person will still have to fit in to all the requirements of the immigration rules in the category in which he or she is seeking to return. The Home Office is likely to consider the application in great detail, so even if the person is not a visa national it is advisable to apply for entry clearance rather than simply travelling to the UK, in order to minimise the risk of refusal at the airport.

After supervised or voluntary departure

Although there is no formal bar, returning is difficult. If people apply for entry clearance it is likely that the application will be referred from the British post abroad to the Home Office and therefore that the details of their past immigration history will be known. This can be considered in deciding whether it is likely that they will abide by any conditions put on their stay in the future. The Home Office has stated that information about people removed under the supervised departure process is available to immigration officers and to entry clearance officers in the country concerned.

Illegal entry: Home Office administrative powers

The Home Office can force alleged illegal entrants to leave the UK under its administrative powers. Illegal entry means entering the UK in breach of the immigration laws. There are three ways in which people can enter illegally:

- without seeing an immigration officer at all or by failing to obtain leave to enter when this was required
- entering the UK while there is still a valid deportation order signed against them
- by deceiving an immigration officer as to their identity or nationality, or about something considered relevant to their claim to enter the UK

The concept of illegal entry was originally designed to cover people in the first two categories but the definition has been greatly expanded by the Home Office and the courts. If the Home Office alleges that people are illegal entrants, it can immediately make arrangements for their return to their country of origin and detain them pending their removal. Unless they are asylum-seekers, there is no formal right of appeal until after they have been sent back. Representations can be made to the Home Office but the only formal process for contesting removal before departure is to apply for a judicial review of the decision to treat the person as an illegal entrant. It is rare for the courts to reject the reasons for the Home Office's decision and overrule it.

Entering without leave

Without seeing an immigration officer

This is what was originally understood by illegal entry – for example, a small boatload of people arriving at midnight on a deserted beach, or people hidden in the backs of lorries, coming into the country. This is still rare, but asylum-seekers may have no alternative to trying to smuggle themselves in to claim asylum ▶see chapter 5. If a person confesses to having entered by avoiding examination by an immigration officer there is no way of arguing that he or she is not an illegal entrant, but it is still possible to make representations to the Home Office to urge that the person should not be removed. If there are exceptional compassionate circumstances, for example a person who has been living in the UK for many years or who is married with children, he or she may still be allowed to remain.

Without obtaining leave from an immigration officer

Immigration officers are required to examine people subject to immigration control when they enter the UK, in order to decide whether to grant them leave to enter or not. If they fail to examine people subject to control and pass them through into the UK without stamping their passports with leave to enter, those people can also be treated as illegal entrants because they have not obtained this leave. This was confirmed in the case of *Rehal* (1989 Imm AR 576). Mr Rehal was a British Overseas citizen whose passport was not stamped on entry because the immigration officer mistakenly assumed he was a British citizen and therefore not subject to immigration control. The court accepted that Mr Rehal had not deceived an immigration officer, but decided nevertheless that he was an illegal entrant.

Entry through Ireland

It is also possible for people who enter through Ireland to be treated as illegal entrants. There is no immigration control between the two countries, and normally people do not require leave to travel within the Common Travel Area (the UK, Republic of Ireland, Channel Islands and Isle of Man) so they do not have to see an immigration officer; ▶see page 224. However, some people do require leave, and if they enter without it, they have entered illegally. They are:

- visa nationals who do not have visas to enter the UK (even if they did have visas to enter Ireland)
- people who have previously been refused entry, or entered illegally, or have overstayed in the UK or in Ireland
- people against whom there are current deportation orders
- people who were only in transit in Ireland
- people who have been excluded from the UK on public good grounds.

Records are not generally kept of people entering through Ireland, so such people are only likely to be treated as illegal entrants if they apply to the Home Office for an extension or a change of status and the Home Office then makes checks on their entry.

In breach of a deportation order

If a person enters the UK while there is a deportation order signed against him or her that has not been revoked, the entry is illegal. It would be rare for a person travelling in his or her true identity to be readmitted, so there may also be another problem connected with this entry, such as obtaining a false passport. The only right of appeal is concerning the person's identity – arguing that he or she is not the person named on the deportation order. The person may remain in the UK to fight this appeal, unlike all other illegal entrants.

'Deception' of an immigration officer

Most people treated as illegal entrants are so treated because the Home Office alleges they have entered by deception. People who appear to have been legally allowed into the country and who have stamps on their passports granting leave to enter may be treated as illegal entrants by deception. The Home Office or the immigration service may allege that they told lies or deliberately hid information when applying for permission to enter.

Alternatively, the authorities may claim that the person did not give information which, if the immigration officer had known it, would have meant that the person did not qualify to enter and would have been refused. There is often no evidence to support the Home Office's view and the only way that the allegation can be substantiated is through the 'confession' or admission of the person concerned.

Entry by deception has been the subject of many court cases. The most important is *Khawaja and Khera* (1982 Imm AR 137). The House of Lords decided that the Home Office has to prove, on the balance of probabilities, that people accused of illegal entry have made false representations to the immigration authorities and that they were granted leave to enter on the basis of that false information. Mr Khera was found not to be an illegal entrant. He had applied as a child to come with his mother to join his father but had married in India while the application was still under consideration. He did not know that this made any difference and was not asked whether he was married, so it was accepted that he had not deceived the immigration authorities. Mr Khawaja was held to be an illegal entrant; he had entered as a visitor saying that he would spend a week with his cousin but applied to the Home Office shortly afterwards to remain as a husband, having married his wife in Belgium before travelling to the UK and married her again in the UK during his visit. He was held to have deceived the immigration officers on arrival and therefore to be an illegal entrant.

More recently, court decisions appear to be widening this definition. It has been held in the cases of *Durojaiye* (1991 Imm AR 307) and *Akinde* (1993 Imm AR 512) that merely showing a passport with a previous immigration stamp of leave to remain to an immigration officer can count as deception if the reason for which the previous stamp was given is no longer current. For example, a student who is no longer studying but has several months' extension of stay and who travels out of and returns to the UK within this time could be considered to have deceived the immigration officers on return, because he was no longer a student. Entering or seeking to enter by means which include deception is also a criminal offence under the Asylum and Immigration Act 1996. It is important to monitor these developments and to consider referring people for legal advice on possible judicial reviews of illegal entry decisions.

Establishing illegal entry

It is quite common for the Home Office to treat people as illegal entrants when they might instead be treated as overstayers, or are legally in the UK as visitors or students. For example, if a man who was given entry as a visitor is subsequently found working, it is likely that he will be questioned by immigration officers about his intentions when he first came to the UK – had he really intended just a visit? had he always wanted to work here? did he know before he came that he would work? had he always intended to stay longer than he said? If the answer to any of these questions is 'yes', immigration officers may allege that he had concealed his true intention, of coming to the UK to work, from the immigration officers. If this had been revealed, it would have resulted in refusal of permission to enter, therefore entry was gained by deception as he was never really a genuine visitor.

Most people are questioned by immigration officers shortly after arrest, or after being detained in a police station for some hours, and have not received advice. They do not know the reasoning behind the questions or what the officer is trying to make them say and are unaware of the crucial difference between remaining in the UK 'illegally' after any leave has run out and being an 'illegal entrant'. They may make admissions in response to questions about their original intentions, believing they are talking about their current situation.

The Home Office has the power to detain people alleged to be illegal entrants pending their removal from the UK and this is frequently done; ▶see chapter 15 for more information. Continued detention may also be used as a threat against people who are being interrogated, to urge them to admit to illegal entry, after which their release will be considered.

Advising alleged illegal entrants

Because the Home Office has powers to remove illegal entrants very quickly, usually with no right of appeal until after they have left, it is necessary to act promptly; ▶see chapter 12.

It is important to ask the immigration office concerned for a copy of its notes or tape recording of the person's interview, which may clarify what the person has said and whether the responses have been misunderstood. Interviews carried out at police stations are normally tape recorded, while those at immigration offices may not be. It may then be possible to write to the relevant immigration authorities to explain such misunderstandings, or give new evidence, and to urge that the person is not in fact an illegal entrant. These arguments may be accepted; if not, it may be possible to refer the person to a solicitor experienced in immigration work to apply to the courts for a judicial review of the decision, showing that there is inadequate evidence to support the illegal entry allegation. While a judicial review is pending, arrangements for the person's removal will be delayed.

When there are strong compassionate or family reasons why the person should be allowed to remain, representations can be made to the Home Office to treat him or her exceptionally and grant leave to remain, even if there is no way of contesting the illegal entry decision. Internal instructions to Home Office officials in March 1996 (▶see pages 21–23) stated that if before removal action was considered a person had been married for more than two years to a person settled in the UK, or a British citizen, and it is unreasonable to expect the settled spouse to leave the UK, removal action should not normally go ahead.

It is important to give all the relevant details and information to the Home Office as quickly as possible. Representations may also be made through the local Member of Parliament; if an MP takes up a case at this stage, any arrangements for the person's removal will be delayed while the Home Office considers the MP's representations.

Removal

If people alleged to be illegal entrants do not contest this allegation, or their removal, they can be sent away very quickly, because there is no formal right of appeal before removal. The airline or shipping company which brought them to the UK is liable to pay for their return but if negotiations about this appear to be protracted, the Home Office may pay instead.

Illegal entrants who are not detained may leave the country voluntarily by buying their ticket and leaving. Those who do not wish to contest removal may explain this to immigration officers, who will arrange for their 'voluntary' departure, without setting formal directions for their removal. They have to sign a disclaimer, Form IS 101, renouncing their right of appeal after removal. Illegal entrants may be removed either to the country of their nationality, the country which gave them a travel document, the country from which they embarked for the UK, or to any other country where there is reason to believe they will be admitted. It may be easier to persuade another country to accept them than deportees, since there is no formal deportation order against them.

The immigration authorities are likely to hold the person's passport, which they may return as he or she passes through immigration control on exit from the country, or give to the crew of the plane. It is likely to be marked to show that the person was removed. The Home Office has stated that if a specific request is made for the person to be given the passport on embarkation, this can be done, to avoid the authorities of the country of origin knowing of the basis on which the person is leaving. It is difficult to verify whether this happens.

Returning to the UK

After a person has been removed as an illegal entrant, there is a right of appeal from abroad, but only on the grounds that the person was not an illegal entrant. As the appellant must be outside the country while the case is being fought and it is always difficult to prove a case in contradiction to the explanatory statement prepared by the immigration service in the UK, such appeals are rare and are very rarely successful.

There are no formal procedures laid down to restrict people who have been removed as illegal entrants applying to return. They may apply immediately, but will have to show that they satisfy the requirements of the immigration law and rules for the category in which they are seeking to return to be successful. Because of their past immigration history in the UK, it is likely that the application will be referred to the Home Office to consider whether any exceptional or compassionate aspects of the case outweigh the illegal entry. Having a spouse and children settled in the UK, who have reasons for being unable to join the removed person abroad, for example, may be strong enough compassionate circumstances. The Home Office is likely to consider the application in great detail, so even if the person is not a visa national it is advisable to apply for entry clearance rather than simply travelling to the UK, in order to minimise the risk of refusal at the airport. Details of the previous removal are likely to have been entered on the port computer system.

Repatriation

Section 29 of the Immigration Act 1971 provides for the payment of fares, and a small baggage allowance, for settled people who wish to return to live permanently in their countries of origin. This is only payable under very restrictive conditions, normally to people from outside Europe, who are reliant on income support and when the DSS believes that their leaving the country will result in a long-term saving to public funds. The scheme is administered through International Social Service (▶see chapter 19 for address) and the government does not intend to publicise it. Small numbers of people have left under this scheme each year, over half of them returning to Jamaica. In 1994/95, 154 of the 226 people who inquired about the scheme were helped, with an average amount of £1711.

SECTION 8: ENFORCEMENT OF CONTROLS

15 Detention

The Home Office and the immigration service have wide powers to detain people for immigration reasons. It has been Home Office policy for the past decade to increase the use of detention, particularly for asylum-seekers. The number of people detained is rising, to 1033 in total on 31 October 1996. On 19 July 1993 there were 317 detained asylum-seekers; on 28 October 1994 there were 702 and on 1 October 1996, 864.

People may be held either in an immigration detention centre, a prison or a police station cell, solely on the basis of their immigration status and the Home Office or immigration service's view that they might try to evade immigration control if they were freed. The decision to detain them is made by an immigration official, who rarely has to justify this decision before any court. When people are detained pending criminal proceedings, they have a right to apply to a court for bail (release from detention, on conditions imposed by the court, usually that they live at a particular address and return to court on a specified date and that they, and at least one other person, promises to pay a sum of money to the court as a 'surety' if the person breaks the bail conditions). The Bail Act 1976, which applies to criminal proceedings, contains the presumption that people should be released unless there are strong reasons against this.

When people are detained for immigration reasons, they often have no realistic chance to apply for bail and there is no time limit laid down for their detention. In these circumstances, detention or release is entirely a matter for the discretion of the Home Office and it is not necessary for it to give any substantive written reasons for continuing detention. When people are able to apply for bail, often this is to an immigration adjudicator, not to the courts, so the provisions of the Bail Act do not apply.

Reasons for detention

People may be detained in several different circumstances:

- **People arriving in the UK** may be detained while their application is under consideration or after they have been refused entry and before they are returned to their country of origin. This includes people seeking asylum in the UK and those appealing against refusal of entry or refusal of asylum.
- **People who are suspected immigration offenders** can be held by the

police while waiting for the immigration service to come to interview them, or after a decision to deport or remove them has been made and an immigration detention order served. If they are held in a police station and interviewed there, the interview is subject to the safeguards of the Codes of Practice of the Police and Criminal Evidence Act.

- **People who are charged with an immigration offence** to appear before a magistrates' court may be detained either pending the case coming to court or pending Home Office administrative action. They can apply to the court for bail in the normal way, but it is quite common for the police or immigration service to object to bail on the grounds that the person may abscond.

- **People who have been recommended for deportation** by a court will be detained while the Home Office considers the recommendation, even if no custodial sentence was imposed, unless the court also specifically directs that they should be released. It is possible to ask the Home Office to grant temporary release but this is totally discretionary.

- **People who have been sentenced to imprisonment** and recommended for deportation may be detained after the sentence is over, while arrangements are made for deportation. They may be moved from the prison where they were held to an immigration detention centre.

- **People against whom a decision to deport has been made** may be detained on the order of the Home Office or by the immigration service, even if they are appealing against the decision.

- **People against whom a deportation order has been signed** may be detained while travel arrangements are made, or any further representations considered.

- **People alleged to be illegal entrants** may be detained while their case is considered or pending removal from the UK.

In most of these circumstances, it is the Home Office's discretionary decision whether or not to detain the person. Instructions to the immigration service of 20 September 1994 state that detention should be authorised 'only when there is no alternative' and that 'the overriding consideration is whether the person is likely to comply voluntarily with any restrictions imposed, including any arrangements for removal'. Other factors considered include any compassionate circumstances, the likely length of detention, whether a person has a settled address and family ties and the person's immigration history. This would include any evidence that people had previously absconded or failed to comply with conditions and whether they are likely to do so again, whether they had used false documentation, and their expectations of the outcome of the case.

The instructions suggest that asylum-seekers should not be detained unless there are 'strong countervailing factors' against them, for example cases considered to be 'without foundation and [which] fall to be considered under fast-track or accelerated procedures' or people subject to deportation action, or those who had entered clandestinely. Further internal instructions, DP10/92, state that it is normally 'inappropriate' to detain unaccompanied children, the elderly, pregnant women, people suffering from serious medical conditions or physical disabilities or mentally disturbed, or people with suicidal tendencies. 'Determined absconders' and 'those with a violent or serious criminal background' should be in a secure prison regime, rather than an immigration detention centre.

Further amplification of these instructions, DP13/95, repeats the need to review detention regularly and states, 'the longer the person has been detained, particularly if it is as a result of a failure on behalf of the Department to resolve the case, the greater is the onus on us to justify the continuation of detention'. Officers are told 'it is not an effective use of detention space to detain people for lengthy periods' and that people with appeals pending have an incentive to comply with restrictions. In practice, it is often hard to see how these instructions are followed in relation to individual cases. Decisions also seem to depend on the detention space available.

The Home Office states that it informs detainees on a monthly basis about the progress of their immigration cases. When this happens it is usually on a very general basis, for example: 'You are detained as the subject of a deportation order, pending consideration of your claim for political asylum. You will be advised of a decision on this application in the near future.' This does not greatly alleviate detainees' uncertainty.

Conditions of detention

Immigration detainees may be held in police cells, for up to five days, before being transferred to a prison or detention centre. If they are to be removed within two more days, they may be kept in the police cell for that time. Airport detention centres, such as Queen's Building at Heathrow airport, are also intended for short-term detention and people must be transferred after five days.

Immigration detention centres have a more relaxed regime than prisons, with easier access for visitors and longer hours of association (when detainees are able to mix with each other, rather than being locked in cells). But as privately-run institutions, the regime is generally less professional and structured, with poorer staff training, education and library facilities and without a formal complaints procedure. The standards to which the private security firms are contracted to run the centres are not published therefore it is difficult to monitor them, or to influence their procedures and practices.

However the ethos of the prison service is geared towards a punitive regime designed to address offending behaviour, rather than dealing with immigration detainees. The effects of budget cuts and serious overcrowding are felt by all inmates. Those in remand prisons may have visits five days a week, but many immigration detainees have nobody in the UK to visit them. Because remand prisoners are intended to be there only for a short period, remand conditions are generally poor.

A problem in both types of institution is the lack of information available to detainees. The Home Office or immigration service officials who make the decisions about detention are not there to assess its effects on individuals, and are not obliged to give written reasons for continuing detention. Regimes emphasise the need for security and control rather than the therapeutic needs of detained asylum-seekers, who may have suffered detention and torture before. Hunger-strikes, for example, may be seen as a disciplinary matter, meriting transfer from a detention centre to a prison, rather than a desperate reaction to an impossible situation. There is no independent scrutiny of the effects of immigration detention; even those in prison are not within the remit of the Prisons Ombudsman.

Places of detention and visit facilities

From June 1994, it has been Home Office policy to concentrate immigration detainees in specific prisons: Rochester, Kent; Winson Green, Birmingham; Holloway, London (for women) and Haslar, near Gosport, Hampshire, as well as immigration detention centres. Initial plans for Doncaster to be used in this way have been changed and another prison for the north of England is being sought. Most immigration detainees are held either at these prisons, or at the immigration service detention centres of Campsfield House, Kidlington, near Oxford, Harmondsworth, near Heathrow airport, or the new Meadvale and Tinsley House near Gatwick airport. A building programme for immigration detention places is continuing; there are plans to replace Harmondsworth and detention accommodation at Stansted has also been expanded recently.

People are also detained in other prisons; in 1993 and 1994 Pentonville prison held the second largest number of immigration detainees and people from other parts of the country were sent to their local remand prison. Although the numbers in local prisons are decreasing, on 1 October 1996 there were 71 asylum-seekers detained in other prisons, the largest number in Wormwood Scrubs, and 33 in police cells.

Immigration service detention centres are precursors of other privatised prisons in the UK. Detainees at Harmondsworth are guarded by the security company Group 4. The firm has a contract with the Home Office to operate the centre and to escort detainees to immigration interviews and courts. Detainees are able to move around the communal areas of the detention centre during the day and social and legal visiting hours are between 2 pm and 8 pm, with no limit on how long a single visitor may stay. Visitors may be asked to provide proof of identity, and frequently passports, before they are permitted to go in and see people in the visiting area. Tinsley House at Gatwick, opened in spring 1996, is run by Wackenhut security firm, again under a contract which has not been made public.

Campsfield House is a converted youth custody centre, which holds 200 people, mainly asylum-seekers, and was opened in November 1993. It is several miles outside Oxford and is difficult to reach by public transport. Detainees are guarded by Group 4 employees and are able to have unlimited legal and social visits between 8 am and 8 pm – but Group 4 may arbitrarily refuse certain visitors, allegedly those on its videos of demonstrations outside the centre. People sleep in unlocked dormitories, and are able to associate together during the day in television and games rooms. There is a small library.

Haslar prison used to be a young offenders' institution but has been an immigration holding centre since July 1989. Up to 100 detainees are held in four large dormitories, where they can receive and make telephone calls. Rochester holds 200 people, mainly asylum-seekers who have been arrested at the Channel ports or the airports and who are often held for long periods there. They are run by the prison service, under the same conditions as those which apply to remand prisoners, and are the main detention centres for men arrested in London and south-east England.

As in other remand wings and prisons, there are time limits on legal visits, which must be in the sight, but not the hearing, of a prison officer. The visitor normally has to book in advance, to be sure that one of the limited number of legal visit rooms is available, and will have to show proof of identity on arrival. Social visits are restricted to a quarter of an hour a day for detainees and there is no privacy for discussion. Detainees are given the minimum prison allowance of £2.50 per week for things like phone cards, stamps etc; as most of them are not permitted to work, they are unable to supplement this money as other prisoners can do. Few have friends or relatives in the UK who can provide extra money or resources.

Getting people out of detention

Bail

Almost all people detained under Immigration Act powers now have the right to apply to an adjudicator or the Tribunal for bail. They are:

- people who have lodged appeals against a decision to deport or against destination after a deportation order has been signed. If no appeal has been lodged, they are not able to apply for bail.
- people refused entry to the UK who have a right of appeal before departure (because they had obtained a visa or entry clearance before travelling) and who have appealed
- people seeking entry to the UK, whose cases have not been decided after seven days
- people refused asylum on entry, who always have a right of appeal before removal.

From 1 September 1996 the Asylum and Immigration Act extended the right to apply for bail to:
- people held as alleged illegal entrants
- people who are applying for leave to appeal to the Immigration Appeal Tribunal, or waiting for a Tribunal appeal hearing.

There are specific bail application forms which ask for details of where the person would live if granted bail, the amount of money the detainee him or herself could offer as recognisance and for details of two other people prepared to stand as sureties. Bail forms should be returned to the immigration office dealing with the case; it will inform the immigration appeals authorities and the hearing will probably be listed within a few days. Notification of the date is usually by telephone, not in writing.

Although this is not a legal requirement, large amounts of money are now usually demanded from the sureties; one adjudicator states that he would normally request £5000–£10,000 and £2000 has become routine for many. If such an amount of money is not available, it may still be worth applying for bail, if there is a stable address where the person can live. The Bail Act does not apply to immigration detention and it is therefore necessary to argue the case for bail in principle, showing why it is not necessary for the person to be detained, or that any reasons the Home Office has given for detention are inadequate.

Anyone may represent a bail application to an adjudicator; it does not have to be a solicitor or barrister. It is usually necessary for the people standing surety to go to the bail hearing, with evidence of identity, nationality or immigration status and of the money that they are prepared to put up, such as their own bank statements or savings books, and of their standing, such as evidence of their house ownership, or job details. They may also be asked what their connection with the detainee is and how they can ensure that the detainee complies with his or her bail conditions.

People who have been recommended for deportation after a criminal offence and detained, but are appealing against the conviction or any part of the sentence, may be released on bail by order of the court dealing with the appeal. This is always discretionary and is rare because it is thought that people have a high incentive to abscond.

Temporary release

It is always possible to ask the Home Office or the immigration service to consider the temporary release of a person detained under Immigration Act powers, even when there is no formal right to appeal or to apply for bail, or the person has no prospect of finding sureties for bail. This includes:

- people detained on arrival in the country, when no decision has been made on their case, for example, asylum-seekers

- people who have been refused entry, but have some time before their removal directions
- people detained as alleged illegal entrants
- people held pending deportation.

It is best to speak on the telephone, if possible to the official dealing with the case (▶see chapter 19 for details of Home Office groups and telephone numbers and chapter 12 for more information on dealing with immigration officials) addressing the issues listed in Home Office guidance and to follow up the request by fax or in writing. The Home Office states that the use of detention is reviewed initially on a fortnightly basis, and then monthly, for all those detained, and at an increasingly higher level, so it is possible to request temporary admission repeatedly and for it to be reconsidered over a long period of detention. It is usually important that the detainee should have a stable address to go to. New factors, like the distress caused to the detainee and his or her family, and medical evidence of deterioration, or a new address becoming available, may all be useful.

Habeas corpus and other legal remedies

Habeas corpus is a legal process when a person can challenge the legality of his or her detention in the courts. It is unusual for immigration detainees to be able to apply for *habeas corpus* because the powers of detention are so wide and this form of action in the High Court can only succeed if there is in law no power to detain. However, this may be possible when people have been detained pending removal for a long time after they have been refused, or an appeal has been lost, and no action has been taken to remove them, or it is not clear to which country they can be removed. It is worth discussing the cases of people in such situations with a solicitor experienced in immigration and detention work to see if *habeas corpus* might be possible. The main court case on this is *Hardial Singh* (1983 Imm AR 198). In that case, the Home Office believed that Mr Singh was an Indian citizen and wanted to deport him to India. He had no documents to prove his identity and the Indian authorities would not give him a travel document. The court held that people cannot be detained pending deportation if it is not feasible or practicable to deport them and that if no travel document was issued shortly Mr Singh should be released. The case was followed in *Wasfi Mahmod* (1995 Imm AR 311) when the Home Office was unable to negotiate with the German authorities to accept back a man who had refugee status in Germany but had been convicted of drugs offences in the UK, and he had been detained for ten months after he was eligible for parole.

In two other cases, *Khan* (1995 Imm AR 348) and *Samateh* (1996 Imm AR 1), it was argued that there was no power to detain pending removal alleged illegal entrants or deportees who had applied for asylum because they cannot be removed while their applications are under consideration. Both applications failed in the Court of Appeal. The case of *Chahal*

(70/1995/576/662) in the European Court of Human Rights suggests that detention can be challenged when the person has strong grounds under Article 3 of the European Convention on Human Rights, that he or she would face inhuman or degrading treatment if returned.

When the reasons given for maintaining detention are inadequate, it may be possible to apply for judicial review of the immigration authorities' decision, or an adjudicator's decision to refuse bail. In granting leave for judicial review in one detained asylum-seeker's case in June 1996, CO-2053-96, McCullough J. stated, 'I am not happy that this is an adequate statement of reasons for continuing [detention]. There is no balance in the document. It simply sets out arguments for continued detention. It does not acknowledge that there were other arguments raised against continued detention and that the two had to be considered together and balanced before a decision was reached. I am also unhappy about some of the individual reasons advanced...the special adjudicator, in refusing bail, was asked to give reasons. He replied... 'I think there is a chance the appellant will not attend court.' A chance, not a probability, not a substantial risk, but a chance' which the judge clearly thought to be inadequate. This may be helpful in making the Home Office state real reasons for continuing detention.

Resistance

After actions by detainees, the Home Office may decide to release people. For example, there were mass hunger strikes by detainees, mainly asylum-seekers, in early 1994, which resulted in some people being released, but had less impact later in the year. On 4/5 June 1994 there was a disturbance at Campsfield House, caused because of the removal of an Algerian asylum-seeker, which resulted in substantial damage to parts of the centre. Several smaller-scale revolts have taken place at Rochester, which has also seen many hunger strikes by individuals and groups.

There are support groups for detainees, organised groups of visitors and campaigning groups against detention ▶see chapter 19 for details. Several of these groups combined to produce a Charter for immigration detainees in May 1994, demanding that detention be kept to a last resort and listing safeguards for detainees. Copies can be obtained from JCWI.

SECTION 9: APPEALS

16 The immigration and asylum appeals systems

The appeals system exists in order that administrative decisions made by the Home Office, the immigration service and British posts abroad can be reviewed by an independent judicial body. It is separate from the Home Office and independent of it. Its personnel are now appointed by the Lord Chancellor's Department but until 1987 they were appointed by the Home Office. The immigration appeals system was set up under the Immigration Acts and the practical details of its operation are laid down in the Immigration Appeals (Procedure) Rules 1984. There are two levels of appeal:

- appeals are heard first by an **adjudicator**, who sits alone to decide a case
- the losing side then has the right to apply for leave to appeal to the higher level, the **Immigration Appeal Tribunal**, to review the case. This is a three-person panel, and will grant leave to appeal when it believes that there is a legal point at issue, or if there are other special circumstances which it believes justify a further appeal.

The Asylum and Immigration Appeals Act 1993 set up a separate system for appeals against refusal of asylum, with separate Asylum Appeals (Procedure) Rules and **special adjudicators** who hear only asylum appeals. This system applies to all asylum refusals made on or after 26 July 1993. It was altered by the Asylum and Immigration Act 1996 and new Asylum Appeals (Procedure) Rules 1996. All refused asylum-seekers have some right of appeal, but some are not able to remain in the UK while the appeal is pending, and not all people have the right to apply to the Tribunal.

When the appeals system was set up in 1969, it was accompanied by a change in the immigration rules which required people coming to join relatives for settlement to obtain entry clearance from the British high commission or embassy in their country of origin before travelling to the UK. As all appeals are heard in the UK (the idea of having them abroad was rejected as too expensive) the people appealing (the appellants) often cannot be present at the appeal to give evidence or to explain their own case.

Appeal hearings are open to the public, unless any party to the appeal specifically requests that it should be in private. Decisions of the Tribunal,

IMMIGRATION APPEALS AND TIME LIMITS

Decision	Notes	Time limit to appeal to adjudicator	Time limit to apply to Tribunal
refusal of entry clearance/visa	appellant outside UK	3 months	42 days
refusal of entry to UK	appellant in UK if had visa/entry clearance	28 days	14 days
	appellant outside UK if no visa/entry clearance	28 days	42 days
refusal to vary or extend leave to remain	appellant in UK if made valid application in time	14 days	14 days
	if applied late/ 'out of time'/ application not valid	no appeal	—
decision to deport	full appeal if in UK over 7 years	14 days	14 days
	on facts of case only, if in UK less than 7 years	14 days	14 days
– on national security grounds	no appeal – review by panel only	—	—
court recommendation for deportation	appeal through courts system only	—	—
deportation order signed	only against destination	14 days	14 days
removal as illegal entrant	appellant in UK, only on identity grounds	28 days	14 days
	after removal	28 days	42 days
refusal to revoke deportation order	appellant outside UK	28 days	42 days

and of higher courts, may be quoted by the appellant or the respondent (the representative of the immigration authority which made the decision appealed against) in support of their arguments. Selected decisions of the Tribunal, and of the courts, are published quarterly by the appellate authorities in *Immigration appeals: selected determinations of the Immigration Appeal Tribunal on appeals under the Immigration Act 1971 and selected reports of decisions of the House of Lords, the Court of Appeal and the High Court* (usually cited as Imm AR), known as the 'green books' because of the colour of their covers.

It is generally helpful for people to be represented at appeals, provided they have a competent representative. Representatives do not have to be solicitors or barristers; anybody may appear at an appeal, with permission from the adjudicator or Tribunal, to represent the case. The Home Office set up the Immigration Advisory Service to provide free representation at immigration appeals, and the Home Office and the UN High Commission for Refugees fund the Refugee Legal Centre to give free representation to asylum-seekers. Local law centres and other advice agencies may also have the specialist knowledge to be able to represent and will not charge for doing so. In London, the Free Representation Unit has been able to represent some cases.

Legal aid under the green form advice and assistance scheme (pink form in Scotland) is available for the preparatory work for an appeal but not for representation at the hearing itself. In asylum cases, solicitors may act in conjunction with the Refugee Legal Centre, with the RLC carrying out the actual appeal representation, so the asylum-seeker need not be charged. Full legal aid is available for applications for judicial review and to the Court of Appeal.

Powers of adjudicators

An adjudicator normally only has the power to consider whether a decision made by the Home Office, an entry clearance officer or an immigration officer was in accordance with the law and the immigration rules; an appeal can normally only be successful on those grounds. The standard of proof is the balance of probabilities, at the lower end of the scale for asylum appeals. When the application made to the Home Office was a request to exercise discretion, within the rules, for example a conflict about the weight to be given to particular compassionate circumstances, it is possible for an appeal to be allowed on the grounds that the discretion should have been exercised differently. Where a decision is not in accordance with a published Home Office policy outside the rules, people may argue that discretion has been exercised unlawfully, as it is not in accordance with principles of fairness, or the person's legitimate expectation. The scope of this power, and the consequences of allowing such an appeal, remain unclear. When there is no immigration rule which deals with a particular situation, the appeal must be dismissed.

Recommendations

If the adjudicator or Tribunal believes the decision was correct, but that there are strong compassionate or other reasons why the authorities should have acted differently, in certain circumstances they can make a recommendation to the Home Office to make an exception in this case. The government referred to this power in debate on the 1988 Immigration Act, in response to criticism about loss of real appeals against deportation decisions. Not all adjudicators make recommendations but until July 1996 the Home Office stated that it would normally consider them if they were made.

As the immigration rules become more precise and the scope for appeals shrinks, more people lodge appeals in order to argue for recommendations, as they have no other way to contest their case. However, on 23 July 1996, Michael Howard stated, 'Henceforth I will act on adjudicators' recommendations in dismissed or withdrawn appeals only where the written determination discloses clear exceptional compassionate circumstances which have not been previously considered and which would merit the exercise of my discretion outside the immigration rules.' This greatly reduces the power of adjudicators and the significance of appeals as a method of contesting executive decisions, in particular against deportation and against refusal of asylum.

When people can appeal: immigration refusals

There are very strict time limits laid down under the Immigration Act 1971 with regard to lodging appeals. This means that the person appealing may have to act very quickly initially, but there are then no time limits within which the Home Office or British post abroad has to respond, or by which the appellate authorities have to act. The box on page 297 explains when there is no right of appeal against an immigration decision. ▶See chapter 12 for how to contest such decisions.

Appeals from abroad

When entry clearance is refused by a British embassy or high commission abroad, there may be a right of appeal against that decision. The appeal forms have to be returned to the entry clearance officers at the British post within *three months* of the decision. See box on page 297 for people with *no* right of appeal.

Appeals against refusal of entry

When people are refused entry at a British air- or sea port there may be a right of appeal. See box on page 297 for people with *no* right of appeal. If people obtained entry clearance they must appeal within *28 days*, and can remain in the UK while the appeal is under consideration. If they did not have entry clearance, they can only appeal after they have been sent back and the appeal forms must be returned to the immigration service at the port where they were refused, to reach the port within *28 days* of the removal from the UK.

Appeals against refusal to vary stay in the UK

When the Home Office refuses people permission to stay longer in the UK, or refuses to alter their conditions of stay, there may be a right of appeal against the decision. However, a valid application must have been made in time, on the correct Home Office official application form, before their leave ran out. The appeal forms must be received by the Home Office within *14 days* of the date of refusal. See box on page 297 for people with *no* right of appeal.

Appeals against deportation and removal

When the Home Office makes a decision to deport a person, there is a right of appeal. The appeal forms must be received by the Home Office within *14 days* of the date of the decision. However, if the person has been in the UK for less than seven years at the date of the decision, the appeal can only challenge whether the facts on which the Home Office made its decision are correct; see pages 273–4 for further details.

When a deportation order has been signed against a person, there is a right of appeal against destination (the country to which the person is to be deported) only. The appeal forms must be received by the Home Office within *14 days* of the date on which the notice was served on the person, and must include the name of the country to which the person wants to be sent. The appeal can only be won if it can be shown that another country will accept the deportee.

When a person is alleged to be an illegal entrant, there is a right of appeal only after the person has been removed to his or her country of origin. The only exception to this is where the Home Office alleges the person has entered while there is a deportation order in force against him or her, and the person claims it is a case of mistaken identity. The appeal forms must be received by the immigration office which dealt with the case within *28 days* of the person's removal.

When an application to revoke a deportation order is refused, an appeal can be made to the authority which refused the application. The appeal must be received by the Home Office within *28 days* of the refusal.

Mixed appeals

When people have rights of appeal against both an immigration decision and an asylum decision, both appeals will be dealt with together, under the asylum appeals procedure ▶see below.

When people can apply to the Tribunal

When an appeal is lost before an adjudicator, there is the right to apply for leave to appeal to the Immigration Appeal Tribunal. If the appellant is in the UK, the appeal forms must be received by the Tribunal within *14 days* of the adjudicator's decision. If the appellant is abroad, the forms must be received within *42 days* of the adjudicator's decision. If the appellant wins the case before an adjudicator, the Home Office can apply to the Tribunal. Only if leave is granted will the Tribunal hear the case.

When there is no right of appeal

People who are late in applying to the Home Office for permission to remain, after their previous permission has run out, have no formal right of appeal against any refusal. It does not matter for how short a time the

WHEN THERE IS NO RIGHT OF APPEAL

1 People who apply to the Home Office late (after their previous permission has run out) for permission to remain longer have no right of appeal against refusal.

2 From 25 November 1996, people who do not apply on the correct Home Office application forms, or do not send all the documents required or explanations of why the documents are not there and when they will be supplied, are not considered to have made valid applications and have no right of appeal.

3 The Asylum and Immigration Appeals Act 1993 removed rights of appeal against refusal of entry clearance, or refusal of entry at a port when people do not have entry clearance, from

- visitors
- students coming for courses lasting for six months or less
- prospective students.

4 It also removed rights of appeal from people whose refusal was 'mandatory under the immigration rules'; that is, where a person has applied for something not permitted under the immigration rules. It lists these refusals as:

- when people do not hold 'a relevant document which is required by the immigration rules'; these documents are defined as entry clearances, passports or other identity documents, and work permits or permissions to work granted after entry; or
- they do not satisfy a requirement of the immigration rules as to age, nationality or citizenship; or
- they are seeking entry, or an extension of stay, for a period longer than that permitted by the immigration rules.

These refusals may be either refusals of entry clearance, or refusals of leave to enter or remain. Also, in refusals to vary leave to remain only, there is no right of appeal if

- 'any fee required by or under any enactment has not been paid'.

person had overstayed, or whether he or she knew that the application was late, the right of appeal has still been lost.

The way in which applications are made to the Home Office is important. From 25 November 1996 all applications, except those for asylum and for extensions of stay as work permit holders and those from EEA nationals and their families, must be made on the correct Home Office application form, and be accompanied by all the required original documents, or explanations of why the documents are not available and when they can be expected, in order to be valid applications. ▶See chapter 11 for more details about making valid applications.

If people's circumstances change while an application for leave to remain is pending at the Home Office and they write to give new information or explain changes of circumstances, *it is important to stress that this new information is in continuation of the first application.* For example, a woman may apply for an extension of stay as a student using application form FLR(S), her leave as a student may expire while she is waiting for an answer, but she may marry her British boyfriend during this time. When she applies to remain with her husband she should not withdraw her student application, as this would leave her without any legal basis for her stay in the country. She should write to the Home Office in continuation of the previous application, explaining her change of circumstances and asking for leave to remain as a wife. She will also need to fill in a new application form, FLR(M).

The Asylum and Immigration Appeals Act 1993 removed several rights of appeal. Visitors, prospective students and students coming for courses of six months or less have no right of appeal against being refused entry clearance or against being refused entry at a port if they have no entry clearance for these purposes. Also when a refusal is 'mandatory under the immigration rules' there is no right of appeal. A mandatory refusal is defined in the 1993 Act as when people do not have a document specified under the rules, (listed as entry clearance, passports or other identity documents, work permits or permission to work granted after entry), when they do not meet a requirement of the rules such as age, nationality or citizenship, and when they apply to remain longer than permitted under the rules. In some cases when people are told they have no right of appeal, they may wish to contest the Home Office interpretation of this and send off an appeal anyway, which they hope will be considered as a 'preliminary issue' ▶see below. ▶See chapter 12 for more details of how to contest refusals without rights of appeal.

There is no right of appeal if the Home Office makes a decision to deport on national security grounds. The person can ask a three-person panel to review the decision, but is not told the details of the allegations against him or her and the Home Secretary does not have to follow the panel's decision. In November 1996 the European Court of Human Rights held in the case of *Chahal* (70/1995/576/662) that this procedure is inadequate when people have applied for asylum.

How to appeal

Forms and time limits

When people are refused by the immigration authorities, they must be given notice in writing of the decision and the reasons for it. This is a standard printed letter, with a space at the top for two or three written lines explaining why the application has been refused. The printed part explains the right of appeal and the time limits for appealing. It may be handed to people who are applying in person at the Home Office or a

British high commission or embassy abroad, or may be posted by recorded delivery post (in the UK) or registered post (abroad).

The refusal letter sent to people in the UK may be confusing, as it explains that if they do not appeal they have 28 days in which to make arrangements to leave. People sometimes misunderstand this to mean either that they have 28 days in which to appeal, instead of 14, or that they should leave within 28 days even if they appeal. The letter informs people of the possibility of consulting the Immigration Advisory Service or the Refugee Legal Centre (►see chapter 19) for free advice and representation at the appeal. The authorities also send appeal forms to be filled in and returned, with the address to which they must be sent.

These time limits are extremely important because the right of appeal can be lost if the forms are not received in time. Thus if a person seeks advice on an appeal the first thing to check is the date of refusal, to make sure any appeal is still in time. In order to ensure that there is proof the forms have been returned, they should be sent by recorded delivery post to addresses in the UK and by registered post abroad. If it is nearly the end of the period, the appeal forms should be filled in and returned to the Home Office or British post abroad straight away, by fax or telex as well if it is too late to be sure the post will arrive in time. The form asks if people will require an interpreter at the appeal; if they have any worries about understanding and speaking English, an interpreter should be requested, in view of the importance of the issues involved. It is the responsibility of the appellate authorities to find an interpreter in the correct language and only their approved interpreters will be used.

Grounds of appeal

The section on 'grounds of appeal' does not have to be completed in detail at the time of lodging the appeal. It is sufficient to state 'The decision is not in accordance with the immigration law and rules applicable. Further grounds will follow' in order to lodge a valid appeal, if there is not time to obtain the full facts or to refer the person to a specialist agency. Further grounds can be sent after the person has received more detailed advice.

The appeal can only determine whether the Home Office or other immigration authority has interpreted the law or exercised any discretion correctly. Thus, in preparing detailed grounds of appeal, it is important to look at the reasons given in the refusal letter, to see whether they can be refuted, or whether further arguments or evidence can be put to show that the reasons are wrong. The decision may be based on a simple factual error – for example, students being told 'You have applied for further leave to remain as a student but the Secretary of State is not satisfied that you are enrolled on or attending a full-time course of studies' when in fact they are attending a full-time course but had not been doing so at the time of the application, or could not obtain a confirmatory letter from a college until the end of the summer holidays, and the Home Office had not waited for it, or had not known that they had to send fresh evidence.

If the refusal was made on the basis of wrong or out-of-date information, it is important to lodge a formal appeal and to return the forms in time, to protect the person's stay in the UK. A new application should also be made, with the fresh evidence, either together with the appeal forms or afterwards. If the refusal can easily be shown to be wrong, the Home Office may change its mind and decide to grant fresh leave to remain. If the decision is changed, the Home Office will write to state this and will also send another form for the person to withdraw the appeal. Once the Home Office has confirmed that leave will be granted, it is safe to withdraw the appeal.

It may not be possible to argue in detail against the reason for refusal at this stage. For example, a student refused entry because the immigration official is 'not satisfied you intend to leave the UK at the end of your studies' will have no indication about why the officer was not satisfied. A husband refused entry clearance to come to the UK to join his wife, because the entry clearance officer 'is not satisfied that the marriage was not undertaken primarily to obtain admission to the UK' will not be told fuller reasons for this belief, which will be based on an interview between the officer and the husband, at the time of refusal. Usually all that can be stated on the form is the assertion that the student intends to leave on completion of studies or the marriage was not undertaken primarily to gain admission to the UK. It can be useful to ask the person concerned to write down as much as he or she can recollect about the series of questions and the answers given, as soon as possible after the interview at the British post. There will then be some record to compare with the detailed report prepared later by the entry clearance officer.

Appealing 'out of time'

There are very limited provisions for appealing to an adjudicator after the time limit given. When people have been refused an extension or variation of leave in the UK, they have 14 days in which to lodge an appeal, but are also given 28 days in which to make arrangements to leave the UK if they do not appeal. If they miss the first 14-day deadline, but send an appeal which reaches the Home Office within the 28 days, the Home Office has discretion to allow the appeal to proceed because it is 'just and right' to do so.

If the Home Office refuses to accept the appeal, it has to refer the case to the appellate authorities to decide, as a preliminary issue, whether the reasons for the appeal being late are such that it would be just and right to allow it to proceed. The appellant or representative has the chance to write to explain the reasons for lateness. It has been decided that if the notice of refusal was sent to the wrong address, because the appellant had not told the Home Office of any change, or if the Post Office could not deliver the recorded delivery letter and it was not collected in time, or if the person did send an appeal, but by ordinary post and it was not received by the immigration authorities, these are not strong enough reasons to overlook the appeal being late. It is therefore very important that the Home Office always has a correct address for an applicant, or that representatives have formally told the Home Office that they are representing, and keep in touch with the applicant.

Waiting for an appeal hearing

After an appeal has been lodged, the person appealing will receive an acknowledgement letter from the authority appealed against, to confirm that the appeal has been lodged. When the person is in the UK, this acknowledgement is proof of his or her immigration status, and confirms that he or she can remain in the UK while the appeal is under consideration. This letter supersedes the refusal letter, as it shows that the person may stay in the UK beyond the 28 days then stated, for however long it may take until the appeal is heard. During this time, there are normally no restrictions on an appellant working in the UK; any restrictions on working lapse at the end of the 28 days' leave granted.

The Home Office acknowledgement is sufficient evidence for the Benefits Agency that the person is free to work and can therefore be issued a national insurance number. Whether working is advisable or not depends on the person's case. For example, if the appellant is a student who has been refused because the Home Office was not satisfied about financial support without working or recourse to public funds, working during the appeal time could be used by the Home Office in the future to show that there was inadequate support. It could also make the employer liable to prosecution, ▶see pages 144–5.

It is not safe to travel out of the UK during this time and expect to be allowed back in. When the person returns, the immigration officers would see that he or she had been refused and would need to be satisfied that those reasons for refusal no longer applied, and that the person qualified under the rules for leave to enter. Also, from 1 October 1996, if a person leaves the country while an appeal is pending the appeal is taken to have been abandoned and there is no way to continue to contest that refusal.

The appeal process

The immigration authorities next prepare a detailed statement, known as an explanatory statement, amplifying the reasons for the refusal. Any other documents on which the officials have relied are attached to the statement.

If the appeal is against a refusal of an extension of stay, the explanatory statement will go into some detail about the person's immigration history in the UK, from the Home Office point of view. There will be details about the application that has been refused, the checks carried out by the Home Office, the information it has gathered and the reasons why it believes that the person does not qualify. The Home Office will annex any documents in support of its case to the explanatory statement, as well as copies of correspondence. There are frequently delays of several months before the statement is prepared.

If the appeal is against refusal of entry at a port or airport, the explanatory statement is prepared by an immigration officer and is usually much shorter and prepared more quickly.

If the appeal is against refusal of entry clearance, the explanatory statement is normally prepared by an entry clearance officer at the overseas post, probably not the person who made the decision. It frequently includes a report, in question-and-answer form, of the interview between the entry clearance officer and the appellant, and anyone else who was interviewed, and then an explanation of the reasons for the refusal. Many posts have their own forms for asking details of the appellant's family tree in family settlement cases; this is also attached to the statement. The time taken to prepare the statement varies between posts. Where there is little immigration work it may be only a few days or weeks but it may be much longer from countries where there are delays, for example in the Indian subcontinent, when statements may only be prepared in a few of the less busy months of the year. If the post referred the case to the Home Office for decision, the explanatory statement is written by the Home Office.

If the appellant is in the UK, the statement and documents are sent to the immigration appellate authorities in the UK and distributed to the appeal hearing centre nearest to the appellant's or representative's address. The appellate authorities then arrange when the case can be listed for hearing before an adjudicator. When this has been fixed, they send copies of the documents to the appellant, or to the representative if one is known, with notification of the date of hearing. Usually at least six weeks' notice is given for the hearing date but in London delays at the time of writing were over a year. If the appellant has not yet sought detailed advice about the case it is sensible to do so now, rather than appearing unrepresented.

If the appellant is abroad, the immigration appellate authorities send the papers to the named representative in the UK, who may also be the sponsor. No date of hearing is fixed at this stage. The representatives are asked to contact the appellate authorities when they are completely ready to proceed with the case and the appellate authorities will then fix a date, again with long delays in London.

Appeals listed 'for mention'

When a case has been pending for some time, but is still not ready for hearing, the appellate authorities may list it for a 'pre-hearing review' or 'for mention'. This means that the representative is expected to go to the court on that date to explain whether or not the case is ready to proceed. If it is, a date of hearing will be fixed later; if it is not, another 'for mention' date, usually about three months ahead, will be fixed. The appellate authorities use this procedure when the Home Office is reconsidering a refusal on the basis of further information, so the appeal may not be necessary, or when other evidence, such as a DNA test about the relationship of the appellant to the sponsor (►see box on page 48), is awaited.

How to prepare for an appeal

The appellants or sponsors in the UK should seek specialist advice when they receive the explanatory statement, if they have not done so before. Although people do not have to be lawyers to represent at immigration appeals, appeals are becoming more specialised and rely on legal precedents, so it is important that the representatives understand and have experience of the system. If people need an interpreter but have not yet requested one, this should be done now.

The basis of the appeal is the explanatory statement. This is normally accepted by the adjudicator as a statement of fact, rather than what it is, a statement prepared by one of the parties to a case. If it is argued that the statement is not correct, it is important to have evidence to show what actually happened. For example, if it is alleged that a student did not attend her course regularly but the student contends that she did, it is important to have a letter from the course tutor, college registrar or someone else in authority to confirm her attendance. If it is alleged that a husband cannot adequately support his wife it is important to have pay slips, bank statements or other evidence of the financial support available.

It is important that the person concerned has read through the explanatory statement carefully, so that he or she can explain anything that is not correct. If the appellant is abroad, it is also important for the representative in the UK to have received comments on the statement from him or her. This may be a letter or may be in the form of a sworn affidavit. Documents from abroad may be used at the hearing by submitting them in advance, or may be used by the sponsor in the UK to help in giving evidence about the appellant's intentions. Other evidence from abroad, such as letters between a husband and wife or an engaged couple, or other documents to prove a relationship or a situation, will also be helpful. Documents which are not in English should be translated and the originals and translations sent to the appellate authorities, preferably at least three weeks before the date of hearing, to give them time to check the translations.

If a date of hearing has been given but the appellant is not ready to proceed with the case, for example if important evidence is needed from abroad and has not yet been received, representatives can request an adjournment of the appeal. They should first discuss this with the Home

Office presenting officer dealing with the case, to see if he or she supports the request, and then write to the immigration appeals authorities, requesting an adjournment and explaining the reasons for it, and what the response of the Home Office has been. This should be done as far in advance of the hearing date as feasible, so that the appellate authorities can reschedule their timetable. If the application in writing is refused, it can be repeated orally at the hearing and might be granted then.

At the time of writing, legal aid for advice and assistance (green form, pink form in Scotland) is available for preparation of cases for appeal but not for representation at the hearing. People may therefore receive bills from solicitors for representation at the hearing, who have been acting on legal aid up to this time. People who may have difficulty in paying should obtain an estimate of cost as early as possible, so they will not need to change their representative shortly before the appeal. The Immigration Advisory Service, the Refugee Legal Centre, JCWI, law centres and some other advice centres do not charge for representing at appeals but may not be able to take a case on at short notice.

Withdrawal of appeals

When people receive the explanatory statement for their appeal and discuss the case with their advisers, they may not wish to continue with it. This may be because they have already spent the time they needed in the UK, because circumstances have changed so much since the appeal was lodged that it is no longer relevant, or because it is clear that an appeal cannot succeed. If the person plans to leave the UK before the date of hearing it is worth writing to the appellate authorities and to the Home Office just before the person leaves, giving travel details and stating that the appeal is being withdrawn. If the Home Office then checks departure records and sees that the person did indeed leave, this will be recorded in the Home Office file. It will therefore be clear what happened at that time if the person should seek to return to the UK in the future.

If the appellant is in the UK and wants to remain longer but on a different basis from that of the application that has been refused, the person's new situation cannot be considered at the appeal hearing. For example, someone who appealed against a refusal of an extension as a student and who subsequently married a British citizen cannot put that new fact to the appellate authorities. Instead, the person may make a new application to the Home Office for leave to remain as a spouse, using the Home Office application form FLR(M), and ask the appellate authorities to adjourn consideration of the appeal against the previous refusal while the Home Office considers a fresh application.

In order to safeguard the person's position in the UK, this new application should be made before the date of hearing of the appeal. A copy of the application should be sent to the appellate authorities with a request for the appeal to be adjourned while the Home Office considers the new application. Adjudicators may grant an adjournment on those grounds. If the Home Office decides the new application favourably, it will respond to say that further leave has been granted and will ask the person to withdraw the appeal.

If an appeal is simply withdrawn before the Home Office has made any decision to grant fresh leave to remain, the person immediately loses the protection against deportation which the appeal had given and is in the UK without authority. This is a vulnerable position and should be avoided if possible by keeping the appeal pending while any fresh application to the Home Office is under consideration.

Appeals on the papers

The appellant can choose whether to ask for an oral hearing of the appeal, or to request that it be decided on the papers available and any further written representations. Most people want to have an oral hearing, so that they can see what is happening and put their case in their own words. This is usually helpful, particularly when the case depends on the credibility of the persons involved, for example a primary purpose marriage refusal. Sometimes, however, when the case depends purely on points of fact and there is adequate written evidence, or when the person is afraid of speaking out in a formal setting, or when the main point of the appeal is to gain time, it may be better to ask for the appeal to be decided on the basis of written representations. It is still important to go through the explanatory statement with the appellant to check all possible inaccuracies, to write with evidence to correct them, and to give all the arguments on the person's behalf. A letter asking for the appeal to be decided in writing should reach the appellate authorities several days before the date fixed for hearing, to give them time to rearrange other hearings on that date.

An appeal may be lodged mainly in order to enable the person to gain more time in the UK, for example a student who applied to remain to finish studies part-time and has been refused. It is not possible to win such an appeal because the immigration rule is specific about full-time studies, so it is not necessary to argue the case in detail.

Normally nothing will happen on the date that had been designated for the hearing; the adjudicator will send his or her decision in writing some time afterwards. The appeal is still pending, and the person may remain in the UK, while waiting for the decision.

Oral hearings: at the appeal

Appeals are supposed to be an 'informal process' but there are formal operating procedures. The adjudicator often sits with a clerk, who is there to carry out any clerical duties such as photocopying required during the appeal. The appellant and representative sit at one side of the room, usually the left, and the Home Office presenting officer, representing the official who made the decision, sits at the other. If there is an interpreter, he or she will usually sit with the person giving evidence to do the interpretation. The case is started by the appellant's representative, who is able to call witnesses (including the appellant if he or she is in the UK) and to go through the case and the evidence with them, asking questions to draw out the information required. It is important for the appellant and any other witnesses to be confident about what they are saying and to have organised their thoughts in advance.

The Home Office representative may then cross-examine the witnesses, and the appellant's representative can ask further questions to clarify any points. At any point the adjudicator may intervene to ask questions of the witnesses. When all the evidence has been heard, the Home Office representative and then the appellant's representative sum up their respective cases. The adjudicator may give a decision orally at the end of the hearing, but it is more common for the decision to be 'reserved' and sent in writing to both the representatives some time later.

In 1995, adjudicators decided 14,770 immigration appeals. Just over 10% were allowed; the proportion of successful appeals against refusal of entry clearance was 20%, but around 5% for other types of appeals.

Appeals to the Tribunal

With the determination of the case, the losing side also receives an application form to apply for leave to appeal to the Tribunal. The form must be received by the Tribunal within 14 days of the decision being sent out when the appellant is in the UK and within 42 days when the appellant is abroad.

These time limits for applying for leave to appeal to the Tribunal are very strict and the time begins to run from the date of the adjudicator's decision. There are no provisions for an application which is received late to be considered; even when the Home Office made an application which was received late the courts confirmed that the appeal could not be considered. The forms can be returned without detailed grounds of appeal being stated, in order to preserve the right to argue the case further after deciding whether there are grounds to do so. Statements such as: 'the adjudicator erred in law in his decision' or 'the adjudicator failed adequately to consider the evidence about...' are sufficient to lodge a valid application for leave. When the Home Office loses cases, it commonly puts in these brief applications and then does not pursue the matter further. The Tribunal will acknowledge the application and indicate a date by which all the grounds must be in. More detailed grounds must be submitted before then for the application to have any chance of succeeding.

Most applications for leave to appeal to the Tribunal are unsuccessful. While an application to the Tribunal is pending, the Home Office will not take any action to try to make the person leave.

If leave to appeal is granted, it will be some months before a date will be fixed for hearing. A Tribunal hearing is more formal than one before an adjudicator. There is a panel of three members hearing the case; it is normally based on legal, not factual, arguments and it is rare for the Tribunal to hear witnesses. Fresh evidence can be put before the Tribunal, although it should be identified in the grounds of appeal and preferably submitted at the same time as the grounds. The hearing is usually based on legal argument, first from the appellant and then from the respondent, and the decision will usually be sent out to the representatives in writing some months after the hearing. The Home Office will not take any action to deport the person while a Tribunal appeal is pending or while waiting for its determination.

Appeals in the courts

From 26 July 1993, the date the Asylum and Immigration Appeals Act 1993 came into force, any further appeal from a Tribunal decision is to the Court of Appeal, or the Court of Session in Scotland, on legal grounds only. The application for leave to appeal must be made in the first instance to the Tribunal, within 14 days. If the Tribunal refuses leave to appeal, it may be made again to the Court of Appeal itself, within 28 days. The grounds of appeal should identify all the legal points the appellant wishes to raise. At this stage, full legal aid may be available. If the case appears to have a new dimension to it, not previously considered by the courts, or is contesting a Home Office reinterpretation of the rules, or is on a new point which will be of significance to many people other than the appellants involved, it may be worth doing, but leave is rarely granted.

If the Tribunal refuses leave to appeal, an application for judicial review may be made to the High Court, as there is no appeal to the Court of Appeal against the refusal of the Tribunal to grant leave to appeal. The determination of the Tribunal refusing leave to appeal will state that it is not a 'final determination' by the Tribunal and that any application to challenge the refusal of leave must be made through judicial review. The application must be made promptly, in any event within three months.

While any court proceedings are pending, the Home Office is unlikely to try to make the person leave the UK. Once the proceedings are over, as the person is an overstayer, he or she is liable to arrest or deportation. Further representations, outside the immigration rules, can be made to the Home Office even after appeals have been dismissed, urging that a different decision be made.

When no formal appeal is pending, the person is not legally protected against the Home Office making a decision to deport, or signing a deportation order, just because a fresh application for leave to remain has been made to the Home Office and representations are under consideration. It is possible to request an assurance from the Home Office that if representations are being made, the representative should be informed of their rejection before a deportation order is signed, but no guarantees can be offered in advance.

This is a difficult situation in which to advise, particularly after an appeal against a decision to deport has been lost. The person may wish to wait if there is the slightest chance of a change in the Home Office's decision, but risks a deportation order being signed and therefore being prohibited from return to the UK for a prolonged period until the order has been revoked. Representations can still be made after a deportation order has been signed and before the person has left the UK, but are rarely successful.

When people can appeal: asylum

People refused asylum before 26 July 1993 had rights to appeal against the refusal under the immigration appeals system ▶see above. People refused asylum on or after 26 July 1993 have appeal rights under the asylum appeals system set up by the Asylum and Immigration Appeals Act 1993. This Act created a new system of 'special adjudicators' who deal only with appeals involving asylum. Because the Act created new rights of appeal without adequate resources, immediately long delays sprang up and the new time limits were impossible to keep.

In 1994, the Home Office commissioned KPMG Peat Marwick, management consultants, to report on the system's operation and make

ASYLUM APPEALS AND TIME LIMITS

Asylum refusal	Time limit to appeal to adjudicator	Time limit to apply to Tribunal
at port	7 working days	5 working days
at port AND case 'certified' AND the person is detained AND given refusal notice personally	2 working days	—
at port, person removed to 'safe third country'	28 days	14 days
in country, application made in time	7 working days	5 working days
decision to deport, after asylum application refused	7 working days	5 working days
refusal to revoke deportation order, after refusal of asylum	7 working days	5 working days
removal directions made, after refusal of asylum	7 working days	5 working days

* BUT there is no right to apply to the Tribunal if the case is 'certified' by Home Secretary suggestions for change. The report was made public on 9 February 1995 and some of its suggestions were incorporated into the 1996 Asylum and Immigration Act and the Asylum Appeals (Procedure) Rules 1996, which explain the detail of the system. On 18 December 1996, the Home Secretary stated that he and the Lord Chancellor again intended to review the system to decide 'whether it provides adequate rights of appeal consistent with the costs to public funds and the impact upon the operation of the immigration control' so further changes may be proposed.

The procedure rules provide that the UK representative of the UN High Commission for Refugees may become a party to any asylum appeal, on request. This may be useful if the UNHCR has evidence about the situation in a particular country of danger, or the asylum procedures in a third country, and can put this to the special adjudicator. UNHCR normally only intervenes in cases where there are important standard-setting principles which will have an effect on the procedures as a whole or on the wider development of UK law.

Nearly all people refused asylum in the UK have some kind of appeal:

- people refused leave to enter the UK at an airport or sea port on asylum grounds have the right to appeal against that refusal
- people who have leave to remain in the UK on another basis, who apply for asylum while that leave is still current and are refused, have the right to appeal
- people who apply for asylum when they have overstayed previous leave to remain and are refused have the right to appeal, on asylum grounds, if the Home Office makes a decision to deport them. If the Home Office makes a decision to deport, people may appeal against it on asylum grounds.
- if arrangements have been made to remove people from the UK as illegal entrants, there is a right of appeal on asylum grounds before removal
- if a deportation order has been signed against them, they had not had the right to appeal against the decision to make it and the Home Office refuses to revoke it they have a right of appeal on asylum grounds against removal

BUT people who did not exercise their right of appeal against a deportation decision cannot appeal against a deportation order if it is made.

People who apply for entry clearance for the purpose of asylum do not have a right of appeal under this Act. They have a formal right of appeal under the 1971 Immigration Act, but as there are no provisions in any Act or rules for entry clearance for asylum, such an appeal could never be successful.

People applying for entry clearance to join a family member who has been granted asylum or exceptional leave to remain also have a formal right of appeal. However they are unlikely to win it because the person they are applying to join is not settled in the UK and there is no specific provision in the immigration rules for family members of refugees and those with exceptional leave to join them. This was confirmed in the case of *Dhudi Abdi* (1996 Imm AR 148), which reiterated that there is nothing in the UN Convention relating to the Status of Refugees about refugee family unity. Because this case concerned Somali families, where the Home Office had stated a specific policy, more generous than the immigration rules, the appeal could decide whether it had adhered to its own policy.

Appeals procedure and time limits

The Asylum Appeals (Procedure) Rules provide the practical regulations for appeals. Some key provisions are:

- time limits for appealing against adverse decisions are within *two working days* of the date of the decision (or the next working day if this ends at a weekend or bank holiday) in cases which are:
  - 'certified' by the Home Secretary as falling within section 1 of the 1996 Act ▶see below, previously known as 'without foundation' cases; and
  - when people have applied for asylum on entry to the UK; and
  - are detained; and
  - are handed the refusal decision personally.
- when people appeal from abroad ▶see page 312 the time limit is *28 days* after departure from the UK
- in other cases, people have *seven working days* in which to lodge appeals. The procedure rules say that these deadlines may be extended, but do not specify how.
- all appeals must be lodged on the official forms, signed by the person or by his or her representative.
- all grounds of appeal must be included with the application
- if asylum-seekers contest a refusal of asylum, they lose any separate rights of appeal on any other matter (for example against a refusal to remain on grounds of marriage, or against a deportation decision). All these matters will be dealt with by the special adjudicator at the same time as the asylum appeal.

All appeals to the Immigration Appeal Tribunal must be made within *five working days* of receipt of the special adjudicator's decision and there is no provision to extend this time.

Claims 'certified' by the Home Secretary

The point of 'certifying' claims for asylum is so that the people concerned do not have a full right of appeal to both a special adjudicator and to the Immigration Appeal Tribunal, and their cases must be decided within shorter time limits. The 1996 Act greatly extends the situations in which people only have this **'fast-track' appeal**. In fact it is quite hard to see any asylum applicant whose case the Home Office could not bring within this provision and it must be monitored closely. It came into force on 21 October 1996.

People who have only this short form of appeal

- people who are to be sent back to a country in which it 'appears' to the Home Secretary that 'there is in general no serious risk of persecution' (known as the 'white list' countries). In January 1997 these countries are Bulgaria, Cyprus, India, Ghana, Pakistan, Poland and Romania, but others could be added at any time. Countries are listed in an Order; the first Order was debated by Parliament on 15 October 1996 and agreed but new Orders listing any changes can come into force immediately, though they may be debated later.
- people who arrived in the UK without passports and did not give a reasonable explanation for this, or who had invalid or forged passports and did not explain this to the immigration officers
- people whose fear of persecution is not for one of the five reasons listed in the UN Convention on Refugees: race, religion, nationality, membership of a particular social group or political opinion. No specific mention is made of the UK's obligations under other Conventions, such as the European Convention on Human Rights or the UN Convention against Torture.
- people who have shown a subjective fear of persecution for a Convention reason, but the fear is considered 'manifestly unfounded or the circumstances which gave rise to the fear no longer subsist'. These are two widely different circumstances put together. As the majority of asylum appeals are decided on special adjudicators' views of the applicant's credibility, it begs the question of how the Home Office makes any decision that the fear is 'unfounded', or what assessment it makes of the circumstances abroad.
- people who apply for asylum after they have been refused leave to enter the UK, or have had a decision to deport them or to remove them as illegal entrants, or have been recommended for deportation by a court. There are often good reasons why no asylum claim is made until later, due to people's lack of understanding of the British system, fear of authority, ignorance, lack of English or other reasons. It is wrong to penalise them still further.
- people whose claim is 'manifestly fraudulent, or any of the evidence adduced in its support is manifestly false'. If a claim is otherwise strong, but one false document has been submitted, perhaps unknown to the applicant or to any representative, it is wrong to negate the whole case because of this.
- finally, if a case is 'frivolous or vexatious'. This provision existed in the 1993 Act, and was hardly used for cases other than those where people had been through another country on the way ▶see below. This shows that, despite Home Office assertions, there are very few 'bogus' claims for asylum.

People in all these circumstances have only a 'fast-track' appeal. The Home Office must send its appeal papers to the appellate authorities within *42 days* and the appellate authorities must send out notification of the time and place of hearing within *five days*. The special adjudicator must decide the case within *10 days*. If he or she agrees with the Home Office certification and dismisses the appeal, the decision must be given orally at the end of the hearing and sent out in writing within five days. There is no right for the appellant to apply for leave to appeal to the Tribunal, though the Home Office may do so if it loses.

The 1996 Act does not make the effect of winning such an appeal clear. The 1993 Act provided for the case to be referred back to the Home Office for reconsideration, but this provision (in Schedule 2, para 5(6) of the 1993 Act) has been repealed. People may therefore have to argue their full asylum case only days after their refusal, with no chance to prepare the case properly. The consequent legal challenges will add greatly to the government's administrative costs in implementing the Act.

However, people do *not* have a fast-track appeal when 'the evidence adduced in support [of the claim] establishes a reasonable likelihood that the appellant has been tortured in the country or territory to which he is to be sent'. Even if any of the other conditions apply, they will have a full appeal. Thus quickly providing medical evidence to support any claims of torture is particularly important in establishing people's appeal rights.

Appeals from abroad

People who have come through another country on the way to the UK to claim asylum can have their claims refused, unconsidered, on the grounds that they would not be in danger of persecution for a Convention reason in the country to which they are being sent. They can be removed to the country from which they travelled if the Secretary of State is satisfied that that country is 'safe', and would carry out its obligations under the Convention, without reference to the authorities of that country.

Most asylum-seekers come from countries whose nationals are required to obtain visas before coming to the UK – indeed, once a country begins to produce refugees, a visa requirement is swiftly imposed (for example, Turkey in 1989, Uganda in 1991, most of former Yugoslavia in 1992, Ivory Coast and Sierra Leone in 1994, Tanzania and Kenya in 1996). The immigration rules make it clear that asylum applications will not be granted unless the person reaches the UK. Asylum-seekers who are overseas therefore cannot get visas as refugees and airlines carrying them direct to the UK face fines under the Immigration (Carriers' Liability) Act. They are usually forced to flee via a third country; the decision on whether that country is 'safe' for them as individuals or at a particular time is not one that can or should be taken summarily or arbitrarily.

If the country is a European Union country or Canada, Norway, Switzerland or the United States of America, there is no appeal against refusal of asylum until they have been sent back there. In this case, the appeal must be lodged within 28 *days* of the person leaving the UK, and the other time limits are the same. In appeals under the 1993 Act, Belgium, France, Germany and Spain were accepted at different times not to be safe countries for people of particular nationalities. People threatened with removal before their appeal should be referred for advice on a possible judicial review of their case. At the time of writing, this had been successful in relation to France and Belgium.

The appeal from abroad will be almost worthless. People will have to argue that the facts on which the Secretary of State based his decision were wrong, or have subsequently changed. The practical difficulties of pursuing such an appeal, from an unfamiliar country, with no fixed abode and no resources, do not need to be spelled out. It is important to try to monitor what happens to people removed before their appeals.

If people came through other countries not on this list, their claims are likely to be 'certified' so that they have only a fast-track appeal, but they will be able to remain in the UK while the appeal is pending and to argue that it is not safe for them to be returned to the other country. This may be either because that country itself is not safe (for example, Kenya for Somalis) or because that country cannot be guaranteed to consider their asylum claim rather than returning them to yet another country which would not be safe.

Refused claims which are not 'certified'

In all other situations listed on pages 309–10, refused asylum-seekers have *seven working days* to lodge appeals. This is still an unreasonably short time; in court proceedings, appeal periods are more often 21 or 28 days.

In these asylum appeals, a date for hearing must be fixed within five days and the appeal determined within 42 days of receipt of notice of appeal. The written determination must be sent out within 10 days. These are clearly inadequate times for such serious issues to be decided, as often evidence and information will be required from abroad, and people need time to be able to give full details of traumatic experiences. There is the power for the Home Office and the appellate authorities to extend these times and this is generally done. In June 1996, the average time for the appellate authorities to deal with any asylum appeal was 8.2 months and the period was lengthening.

Asylum appeal hearings

The Asylum Appeals (Procedure) Rules state that 'the overriding objective shall be to secure the just, timely and effective disposal of appeals'. The special adjudicators and the Tribunal may therefore make 'directions' to either the Home Office or the asylum-seeker about how they must deal with the appeal. For example, both sides may be required to make:

- a written statement of the evidence they want to bring to the appeal
- a bundle of all the documents they want to produce, with page numbers and index
- a skeleton argument (summary) of the points that they want to argue at the hearing

and the special adjudicator may limit the amount of time allowed for examination of witnesses or making submissions (summarising the case and the arguments). If the asylum-seeker does not comply with directions, the appeal can be treated as abandoned; if the Home Office does not comply, its decision to refuse asylum can be treated as withdrawn. The special adjudicator has the power to hear the appeal without the asylum-seeker being present, for example if the person cannot be contacted and has no representative.

The Home Office does not usually prepare explanatory statements for asylum appeals, but relies on the full records of an interview with the asylum-seeker and on its detailed refusal letter, which states the reasons why it was not satisfied the person qualified for asylum. When the asylum-seeker or representative has put forward other information and representations these may also be copied for the appeal.

The Home Office has prepared 'country reports' as background on several countries from which asylum-seekers come, and expects these to be accepted as evidence in the case. Many of them have been disputed, in particular its report on Nigeria which painted a very rosy picture of that country. It is often important to draw the adjudicator's attention to other reports and evidence from the country concerned as general background; ▶see pages 98–99 for details of other organisations which may be able to provide useful information.

Deciding asylum appeals

In asylum appeals, unlike immigration appeals, the special adjudicator is not limited to considering facts at the date of the Home Office's decision. The appeal must decide whether, if the person were removed, this would be in contravention of the UN Convention on Refugees, which 'manifestly looks to the future'. Thus the appellate authorities must look at the facts in the country of origin at the time of the appeal hearing and assess the likelihood of future persecution as well as past events. This was stated in the case of *Rajendrakumar* (1995 Imm AR 386) 'I cannot believe that the appellate authorities should do anything other than ascertain...whether the appellant with whom they are dealing is then and there a person with a well-founded fear of persecution' and confirmed in *Sandralingham and Ravichandran* (1996 Imm AR 97).

Asylum appeals frequently depend mainly on the 'credibility' of the asylum-seeker. The procedure at the hearing is similar to immigration appeals, with the appellant giving evidence and explaining his or her past history and reason for fearing persecution now. It is thus very important to prepare people for detailed questioning, probably even more specific than in their initial interview with the Home Office or the immigration service, and to explain the importance of being absolutely accurate. When an interpreter is used, it is important that he or she always gives a full translation of what is said and understands the detail of the situation the appellant is explaining, to avoid misunderstandings. When the response is more detailed than the initial interview, this may be a cause for suspicion that the story has been embellished and expanded, and therefore is not 'credible'. If new information is put forward at the appeal, again it may be queried why it was not provided initially, and the special adjudicator may disregard it.

Standard of proof

The standard of proof in asylum cases is at the lower end of the civil standard of proof of the balance of probabilities: that 'there has to be demonstrated a reasonable degree of likelihood that [the person] will be persecuted for a Convention reason if returned to his own country'. This was decided by the House of Lords in the case of *Sivakumaran* (1988 Imm AR 147), which concerned six Sri Lankan Tamils who had been refused asylum and returned to Sri Lanka.

The definition of the standard of proof was developed in the Tribunal case of *Koyazia Kaja* (11038, 1995 Imm AR 1), where the Tribunal stressed that a lower standard of proof is required in asylum cases; 'a lesser degree of likelihood...reasonable chance, substantial grounds for thinking, a serious possibility' are all ways of expressing that there is a reasonable degree of likelihood that a person would face persecution. It also stated that it was important for the adjudicator in any determination to make it clear '(i) that the assessment of whether a claim to asylum is well founded is based on the evidence as a whole (going to past, present and future) and is according to the criterion of the reasonable degree of likelihood (ii) the evidential foundation for the decision (iii) how the adjudicator moves from the evidential foundation to the conclusion.' If the process of reasoning and the standards used are not set out in the determination, these are grounds for an application for leave to appeal to the Tribunal. During 1995/96 the Tribunal remitted many cases for re-hearing by a different special adjudicator for this reason.

In 1995, special adjudicators decided 7035 asylum appeals. 80% were dismissed, 3% allowed and the rest withdrawn or referred back to the Home Office for reconsideration. The backlog of cases awaiting hearing is growing steadily, reaching 20,455 at the end of December 1996.

Applications to the Tribunal

The losing party to the appeal may apply for leave to appeal to the Immigration Appeal Tribunal, within *five days* of receipt of the determination and the Tribunal must decide within five days whether to grant or refuse leave. It is not possible for these times to be extended. If leave is granted, a date for hearing must be fixed within another five days and the appeal must be decided within 42 days of the Tribunal's receipt of the notice of appeal. It must send out its written determination within *10 days*.

If the Tribunal refuses leave to appeal, the decision could be contested by judicial review. This may also be possible when there was no right of appeal to the Tribunal, or when the case was on a point not covered in British immigration law, such as Article 3 of the European Convention on Human Rights. If the Tribunal grants leave, and the appeal is dismissed, the person can apply for leave to appeal in the first instance to the Tribunal itself and, if the Tribunal refuses, to the Court of Appeal, or the Court of Session in Scotland, for leave on a point of law. It is beyond the scope of this book to discuss appeals in the courts in detail.

SECTION 10: NATIONALITY

17 British nationality

Some information about the historical background to British nationality law and its interrelation with immigration law is essential to understanding the present situation. This chapter gives a brief outline of how the law developed, with an illustrative flowchart on page 318, and then explains the different kinds of British nationality in existence at present.

The historical background

Before 1948

The 1948 British Nationality Act first defined UK citizenship. Before then, people born in, or with a connection with, the UK or a British colony or dependency had the status of **British subject**, which described the allegiance of an individual to the British Crown. The status of a British subject born in the UK was identical in UK law to that of a British subject born in India, Hong Kong or the Caribbean: this included the right of entry to the UK itself and the right to vote and hold public office once in the UK. People who were not British subjects were classified as **aliens**, and their right of entry to the UK was restricted during the twentieth century by various Aliens Acts.

In addition to subjects and aliens, there was also a group of people called **British Protected Persons**, who were born in or had a connection with British protectorates, protected states or trust territories, rather than with a colony. (Many British territories were under such protection, for example, Tanzania, the princely states in India, part of Kenya, northern Nigeria). Technically, they fall between subjects and aliens; under international law they are British nationals, but in UK law they were treated as aliens.

1948–1962

The British Nationality Act 1948 created the status of **citizen of the United Kingdom and Colonies** (CUKC). This was acquired by people born in, or with a connection with, the United Kingdom itself or any territory which was still a colony. Former colonies had generally evolved into self-governing Dominions and the Act recognised them as independent Commonwealth countries with their own citizenships. But it also retained

THE DEVELOPMENT OF IMMIGRATION & NATIONALITY LAW

RIGHT OF ENTRY TO THE UK | NO RIGHT OF ENTRY

BNA 1948

BRITISH SUBJECTS → CITIZENS OF UK & COLONIES (CUKCs) / CITIZENS OF INDEPENDENT COMMONWEALTH COUNTRIES (e.g. India, Australia, Ghana, Jamaica) / BRITISH SUBJECTS WITHOUT CITIZENSHIP (BSWCs)

BRITISH PROTECTED PERSONS (BPPs) → BPPs

ALIENS → ALIENS

IAs 1962–1971

'PATRIAL' CUKCs | 'PATRIAL' C'WEALTH CITIZENS | 'NON-PATRIAL' CUKCs | 'NON-PATRIAL' C'WEALTH CITIZENS | BSWCs | BPPs | ALIENS

BNA 1981

BRITISH CITIZENS | C'WEALTH CITIZENS PATRIAL ON 31.12.82 | BRITISH DEPENDENT TERRITORIES CITIZENS (BDTCs) | BRITISH OVERSEAS CITIZENS (BOCs) | C'WEALTH CITIZENS NOT PATRIAL ON 31.12.82 | BRITISH SUBJECTS | BPPs | ALIENS

BNA (FI) 1983

BDTCs with Falklands connection become BRITISH CITIZENS

HKA 1985

BDTCs with Hong Kong connection may become BRITISH NATIONALS (OVERSEAS) (BN(O)s)

1997

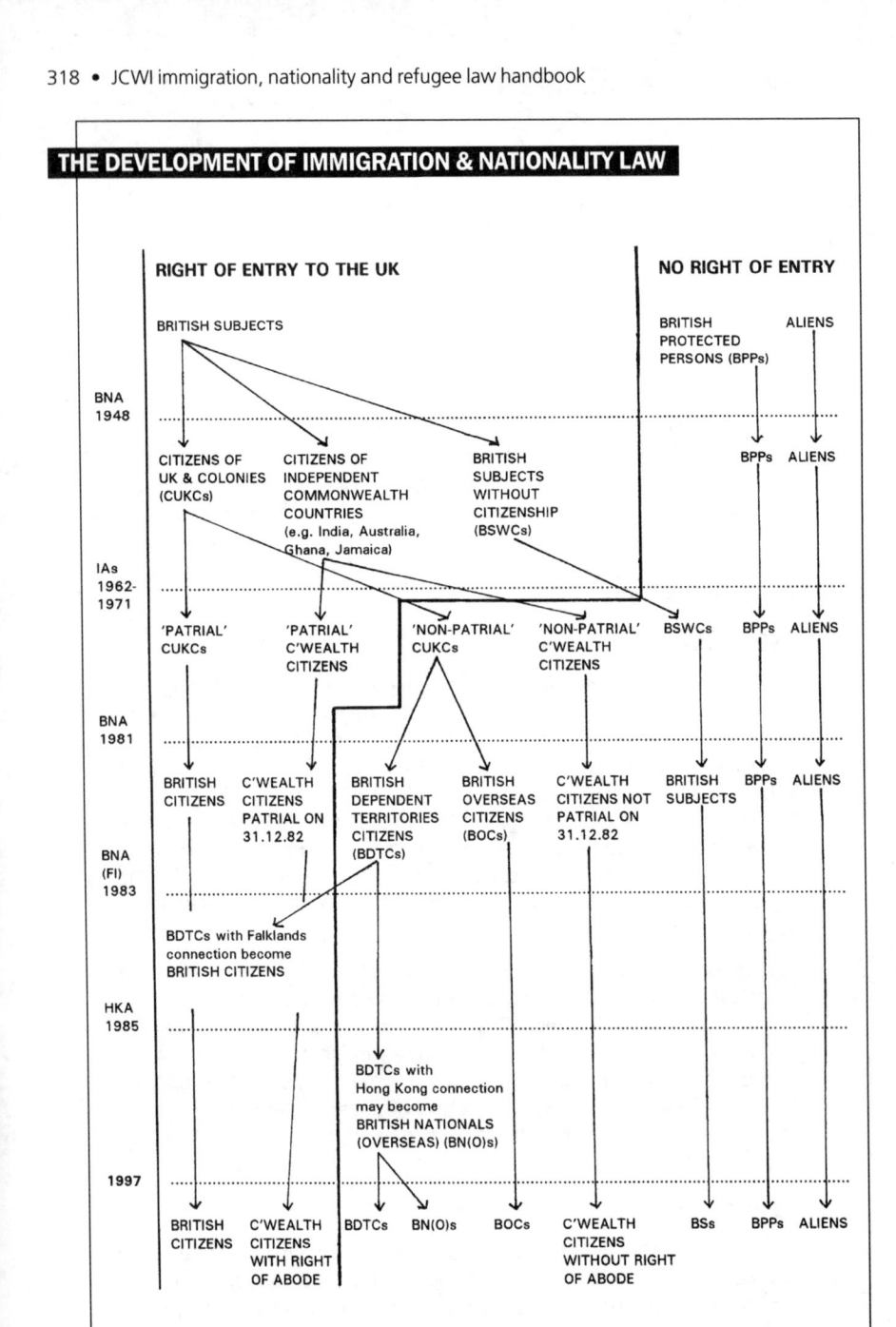

BRITISH CITIZENS | C'WEALTH CITIZENS WITH RIGHT OF ABODE | BDTCs | BN(O)s | BOCs | C'WEALTH CITIZENS WITHOUT RIGHT OF ABODE | BSs | BPPs | ALIENS

the status of **British subject**, which was held by all citizens of the UK and Colonies *and* all other Commonwealth citizens – almost like a dual nationality. Once again, all British subjects, whether they were CUKCs or Commonwealth citizens, had the same rights, principally the right of abode in the UK without being subject to any immigration requirements. **British Protected Persons** retained their peculiar in-between status, but were still free from immigration controls.

The 1948 Act also created the status of **British subject without citizenship** for pre-1949 British subjects who when the Act came into force were still awaiting citizenship laws to be made in their own country. This mainly affected people from India and Pakistan.

As more colonies became independent after 1948, the normal procedure was for people in those countries to lose their CUKC status, provided that they gained citizenship of the newly independent country, but to retain their status as British subjects. In British nationality and immigration law, they were classified as **Commonwealth citizens** *and* **British subjects**. These terms had been made interchangeable in the British Nationality Act 1948. As British subjects, they had full rights of entry and abode in the UK.

1962–1981

Between 1962 and 1971, the main body of British immigration law was developed, and for the first time restricted the immigration rights of British subjects. Those laws did not do so by distinguishing between British subjects who were CUKCs and British subjects who were citizens of independent Commonwealth countries. Instead, they withdrew the right of abode in the UK from some people in both categories. The right of abode means not being subject to British immigration control. It was also called patriality from 1973 to 1982 inclusive and was developed to differentiate between people with the same nationality status.

CUKCs who had acquired their citizenship in the UK (through birth or by registration or naturalisation), who had a parent or grandparent who had similarly acquired CUKC status in the UK, or who had themselves lived in the UK for five years or more, kept the right of abode in the UK. Other CUKCs, for example people of Asian origin in East Africa and people from existing colonies such as Hong Kong, lost that right. **Commonwealth citizens** who had a parent born in the UK, or who were women married to a man with right of abode, were also able to retain or gain right of abode in the UK; other Commonwealth citizens were not able to do so. It was no longer possible to tell from people's nationality status whether or not they were free from immigration control: CUKC passports were endorsed on page 5 if the holder had right of abode.

The British Nationality Act 1981

The British Nationality Act 1981 came into effect on 1 January 1983. It changed the way people can acquire British nationality, by birth, descent or grant (▶see chapter 18). It also abolished CUKC status and created three new citizenships, which came into existence automatically on 1 January 1983:

- **British citizenship** for people who, at 31 December 1982, were CUKCs with right of abode in the UK
- **British Dependent Territories citizenship** for people who, at 31 December 1982, were CUKCs by virtue of a connection with a territory which was still a British dependency (for example Hong Kong)
- **British Overseas citizenship** for other CUKCs, without right of abode or a connection with a British dependency (such as East African Asians).

The citizenship status of Commonwealth citizens was unchanged and those who had the right of abode retained it. However, since 1 January 1983 it has not been possible to acquire the right of abode except by becoming a British citizen.

The Act also abolished the status of British subject as a unifying status for British and Commonwealth citizens: citizens of independent Commonwealth countries, together with all kinds of British nationals except British Protected Persons, are now simply known as Commonwealth citizens. It also changed the name of those people defined in the 1948 Act as British subjects without citizenship: confusingly, they are now called **British subjects**. The status of **British Protected Person** survived untouched. (Both these latter categories, and British Overseas citizenship, will die out over the passage of time as there are no provisions for their automatic acquisition.)

Since 1983, there have been two changes to the structure set out in the 1981 Act. People from the Falkland Islands, who were classed as British Dependent Territories citizens, were made into full British citizens after the Falklands war under the British Nationality (Falkland Islands) Act 1983. People from Hong Kong, who are also British Dependent Territories citizens, were given the opportunity to acquire yet another new British status, **British National (Overseas)**, under the Hong Kong Act 1985, to prepare for the return to China in 1997: this status does not carry the right of abode in the UK.

There are now six different groups of people who may hold current British passports:

British citizens	British subjects
British Dependent Territories citizens	British Protected Persons
British Overseas citizens	British Nationals (Overseas)

Only the first category, British citizens, have the right of abode in the UK and are not subject to immigration control. Other kinds of British nationals need to fit in to the immigration rules as described in the other chapters of this book; they may therefore have permission to be in the UK (for example as students, visitors or spouses) but they have no automatic right by virtue of their British nationality – they are treated like any other foreigner applying to enter Britain (except for British Overseas citizens eligible for special quota vouchers: ▶see page 332).

Establishing citizenship

In some cases, the passport will indicate the exact status of the holder. ▶See chapter 13 for examples.

Passports issued before 1 January 1983

Most British passports issued before 1 January 1983 describe the holder, on page 1, as a 'British subject: citizen of the UK and Colonies'. If this is the case, turn to page 5 of the passport. This usually says 'holder has the right of abode in the UK'. If this is in the passport, and has not been crossed out, it is almost certain that the holder is now a **British citizen**. She or he would automatically have become a British citizen on 1 January 1983 without needing to do anything about it.

If the wording on page 5 has been cancelled, then it is likely that the holder is now a **British Dependent Territories citizen** or a **British Overseas citizen**. This will mean that he or she does not have right of abode in the UK and will need to fit into the immigration rules, or to get a special quota voucher (▶see page 332) to come to or stay in the UK. But it is still worth checking the points below in case this status has changed since the passport was issued, or it was issued in error.

The status of **British Protected Person** and **British subject** was not changed by the British Nationality Act 1981. A few British subjects (usually married women) have right of abode in the UK; if so, it will be signalled on page 5 or as a stamp called a certificate of patriality. But the majority of British subjects and all British Protected Persons do not have right of abode in the UK and will need to fit into the immigration rules or get a special quota voucher (▶see page 332) if they wish to come to or stay in the UK.

Points to note

- Check that nothing has happened to change the person's status since the passport was issued. A passport is not proof of present nationality; it is only evidence that a person had that status when the passport was issued. This is particularly relevant for people from Commonwealth countries who hold British passports which were issued before their countries became independent. At independence, most people from that country automatically lost their British nationality and gained nationality of the newly independent country; but their British passports were not recalled and they were usually not even told about their change of nationality. For people born outside the UK, without parents or grandparents born in Britain, it is therefore worth checking the date of issue of the passport against the date of independence of their country of origin (▶see glossary) especially if the passport is no longer current.

- **People from Caribbean countries which gained their independence from 1981 onwards** gain citizenship of the new country but also, if they had lived in the UK for more than five years and were settled before independence, keep their British citizenship. This applies so far to people from Belize, St Kitts-Nevis and Antigua and Barbuda.
- **Some people from Hong Kong** are not any kind of British national, though they have travel documents issued by the Hong Kong government or the British Home Office. They are people born in the People's Republic of China, who emigrated to Hong Kong and may subsequently have come to the UK. They travel on brown documents called certificates of identity (or CIs in Hong Kong). They are in effect stateless people (save for having Chinese nationality) and have no special rights in British immigration and nationality law. In the past they could apply to naturalise to become British Dependent Territories citizens after five years legal residence in Hong Kong, or three years legal residence there and marriage to a British Dependent Territories citizen. These applications had to be received by 31 March 1996.

Passports issued on or after 1 January 1983

These passports should describe people's nationality status on the page with their personal details: 'British citizen', 'British Overseas citizen', 'British Dependent Territories citizen', 'British subject', 'British Protected Person' or 'British National (Overseas)'.

Points to note

- There is now no endorsement on British citizen passports stating that the holder has the right of abode: that is automatic because of the holders' status as British citizens. This worries some people, when they get a new passport, in case their right of abode has been withdrawn. They should be reassured that this is not the case.
- No other British nationals have the right of abode in the UK, except for a few British subjects (usually married women). They should have passport endorsements called 'certificates of entitlement to the right of abode', (▶see chapter 13 for examples) which have replaced the old certificates of patriality, issued before 1 January 1983.
- All British passports issued now are the uniform EU passports, which are maroon-coloured and computer-readable. Some people, wrongly, believe that they are of lower status than the old blue passports.

British citizens

Checking for British citizenship

If people have current passports which describe them as 'British citizens', then it is clear that they are British citizens. But some people do not have passports (for example, children born in the UK), or may have changed their status since their British or foreign passport was issued. The flowcharts will help to identify other people who are British citizens.

Points to note

1. It is not definite that people are *not* British citizens just because they do not fit into the flowchart; there are other, somewhat rare, ways of acquiring British citizenship.
2. The flowcharts deal only with *British citizens* and not other kinds of British national.
3. 'Parent' or 'father' applies to men only if they were legally married to the child's mother. If the parents married after the child's birth it depends on the law of the country where the marriage took place whether the marriage automatically 'legitimates' the child (if so, this makes him or her a British citizen), or whether any special procedures have to be followed.
4. British citizens are divided into those who acquired their citizenship 'by descent' (that is, through a parent or grandparent) and those who acquired it 'otherwise than by descent'. (Page 328 explains how to tell, and what difference it makes.)

People born or adopted in the UK

Before 1983

Prior to 1 January 1983, everyone born in the UK and all children adopted in the UK by a British father were British citizens. The only exception was the children of diplomats. The British Nationality Act 1981 did not change the status of people born before 1 January 1983; and therefore all those born in the UK before that date (except diplomats' children) are British citizens automatically.

Since 1983

One of the major changes in the British Nationality Act 1981 was the provision for acquiring nationality by birth in the UK. People born in the UK on or after 1 January 1983 become British citizens at birth only if one of their parents either is a British citizen or is settled (allowed to stay permanently) in the UK at the time of the birth.

Children adopted in the UK become British citizens if either adoptive parent is British at the time of adoption.

WHO IS A BRITISH CITIZEN? People born before 1 January 1983

Where born? ——— UK ——▶ British citizen

NOT UK ↓

Where was father born? ——— UK ——▶ British citizen

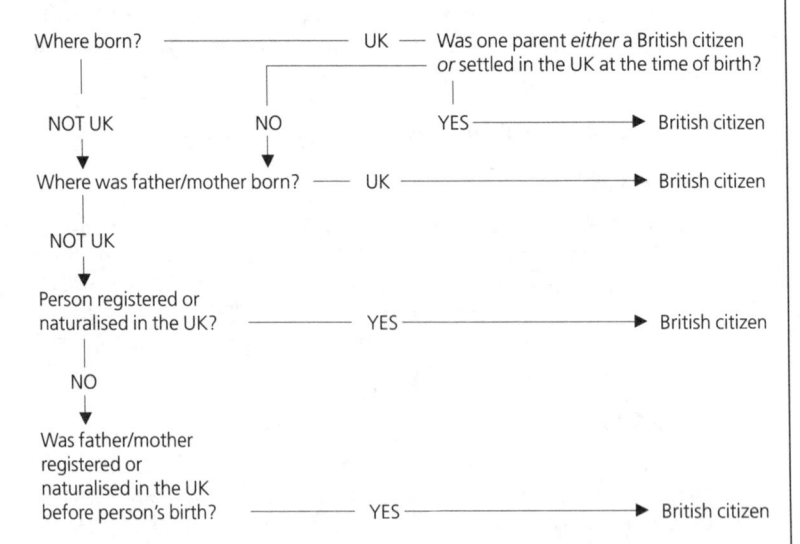

NOT UK ↓

Person registered or naturalised in the UK? ——— YES ——▶ British citizen

NO ↓

Was father registered or naturalised in the UK before person's birth? ——— YES ——▶ British citizen

WHO IS A BRITISH CITIZEN? People born on or after 1 January 1983

Where born? ——— UK ——— Was one parent *either* a British citizen *or* settled in the UK at the time of birth?

NOT UK ↓   NO ↓   YES ——▶ British citizen

Where was father/mother born? ——— UK ——▶ British citizen

NOT UK ↓

Person registered or naturalised in the UK? ——— YES ——▶ British citizen

NO ↓

Was father/mother registered or naturalised in the UK before person's birth? ——— YES ——▶ British citizen

You cannot be sure that someone is *not* British on the basis of these flowcharts

Throughout, father = father who is married to mother

Most children born in the UK after 1 January 1983 are still born British, even if their parents are not British, because the vast majority of foreign nationals living in the UK have settled status.

Points to note

- The people whose children are likely *not* to be British are foreign nationals who are in the UK as students, visitors, au pairs, work permit holders during their first four years, refugees within their first four years, and people granted exceptional leave to remain within their first seven years. Children of overstayers and of people treated as illegal entrants are not born British citizens.
- The Home Office had accepted that children of European Union nationals born in the UK were born British, because EU nationals have no time limits on their stay under British immigration law, since it does not apply to them. However the Tribunal decided in the case of *Gal* (10620) that because the EU national's stay depends on continuing in a particular activity, there is in practice a time limit and therefore a child born in the UK is not automatically born British. The Home Office view remains that if the EU national parent is in the UK for a Treaty purpose (▶see chapter 6) that is the equivalent of settlement for nationality purposes, and the child is born British. If the British-born child of an EU national is refused citizenship, it is worth seeking advice and contesting the case.
- 'Parent' in nationality law does not include the father of a non-marital child. In order to gain any benefit from a father's nationality or immigration status, the parents must be married (in the UK, this can be either before or after a child's birth).
- Some children born in the UK after 1 January 1983 are born stateless, if they cannot obtain nationality from their parents' country of origin or if the parents do not want to claim that nationality for them (for example, because they have asylum in the UK). In such cases, the Home Office should provide travel documents (▶see pages 344–5 on passports and travel documents).
- Children born in the UK and not born British do not have any immigration status. They cannot therefore overstay a leave to remain, as they do not have, or need, leave, so long as they remain in the UK. However, if their parents are deported as overstayers, non-British-citizen children can be deported as part of the family unit. Otherwise, the children (though not necessarily their parents) can remain in the UK indefinitely. However, if they leave the UK, they will not automatically be able to return. If they are travelling with parents who have leave to remain in the UK (for example as students or refugees) the children will usually be readmitted for the same time period and on the same conditions as their parents; they will then be subject to the usual sanctions if they overstay that leave.

If the parents do not become settled their children have no claim to British nationality through birth until they have lived in the UK for ten years. If the parents want to travel and to take the children, the children have no claim to a British passport. They may be entitled to the nationality of either parent, depending on the nationality laws of their country and may be able to get a passport from the relevant high commission or embassy, or a parent may be able to have the children's names inserted on his or her passport. If the children are not able to get a passport, the parent should try to obtain the refusal in writing, or confirmation that the children are not regarded as citizens of the country. It may then be possible for the parent to obtain stateless travel documents for the children from the Home Office.

- Children born in the UK and not born British may be able to register as British citizens after their birth *either* if their parent becomes settled *or* if they live in the UK for ten years. ▶See chapter 18 for further details.

People born overseas

People born before 1 January 1983 with a British parent

Before 1 January 1983, British nationality could pass only through fathers; children born overseas to British mothers and foreign fathers were not born British.

Children born outside the UK to British fathers automatically became CUKCs with the right of abode, and therefore British citizens, if their father had that status in one of the following ways:

1 by being born, or being adopted by a UK citizen father, in the UK
2 by being registered or naturalised in the UK before the child was born.

Both conditions are very important. Registration outside the UK would give the father (and possibly the child) some other kind of British nationality (see above) and not British citizenship. If the father became British after a child's birth, this did not retrospectively make the child British.

It is also important to remember that *father* in British nationality law applies only to men who were legally married to the child's mother; marriage certificates or some very clear proof of marriage will be required in order to prove the citizenship of people born overseas. The authorities are likely to demand a higher standard of proof than that required for family reunion under immigration law, although the standard of proof is theoretically the same.

Children born outside the UK before 1983 to British *mothers* could not inherit their mother's citizenship. However the Home Office has stated that if British-born mothers apply for their minor children born outside the UK to be registered to become British citizens, this will be granted, provided the father (if the parents are still married) has no well-founded objection and provided that the child is still under 18 at the time of application. This will therefore come to an end at the end of 2000. There is no special provision for people who are now adults born abroad to British mothers to become British citizens.

There are some circumstances in which having a British *grandfather* could result in a child born overseas before 1 January 1983 being a British citizen now. This applied if:

- the grandfather in question is the father's father *and*
- the grandfather acquired his citizenship in the UK by birth, registration or naturalisation *and*
- the child was born in a non-Commonwealth country (▶see list in glossary for Commonwealth countries) *and*
- the child's birth was registered at a British consulate within a year of the birth.

People born on or after 1 January 1983 with a British parent

Since 1 January 1983, women as well as men have been able to pass on British nationality to children born overseas. Children born abroad on or after 1 January 1983 are therefore British citizens automatically if either their father or mother is a British citizen who acquired citizenship in the UK as in (1) or (2) above, or is a British citizen otherwise than by descent in some other way. Once again, the father's status only counts if he was married to the mother and can prove this to be the case.

This provision is not retrospective: in other words, there will be families of British women living overseas where some children (born before 1 January 1983) are not British citizens while their siblings born on or after 1 January 1983 are British citizens.

From 1 January 1983, any British citizen who acquired his or her citizenship *otherwise than by descent* (see below) is able to pass on that citizenship to children born abroad. Thus there is a further category of people whose children born abroad from 1983 onwards are British citizens: people who themselves were British otherwise than by descent and who had gained the right of abode by living in the UK, as a UK and Colonies citizen, for five years or more, and being settled in the UK, before 1 January 1983 and before the child's birth. The parent must have been British during the five-year period and must have remained so at least until the child's birth. If the child was born before 1983, he or she will not be a British citizen. Thus there are families in, for example, Hong Kong, where the parents are British citizens because they were born in Hong Kong and are therefore British by birth and they lived in the UK for more than five years before 1983, thus gaining the right of abode. Their older children born in Hong Kong before 1983 are British Dependent Territories citizens and their younger children, born after 1983, are British citizens *and* British Dependent Territories citizens. After 1 July 1997, they will all lose their British Dependent Territories citizenship, but those who are British citizens will keep British citizenship.

The provisions for acquiring British citizenship for subsequent generations are set out in the flowchart on page 329.

People without a British parent

People born overseas who do not have a British parent or grandparent can normally only obtain British citizenship by living in the UK and meeting the residence and other requirements for registration or naturalisation (►see chapter 18).

British citizenship by descent

People born overseas who acquire British citizenship only because one or both of their parents is a British citizen are classified as **British citizens by descent**.

People who acquire British citizenship by birth in the UK, by registration/ naturalisation in the UK or by being UK and Colonies citizens with five years' residence and settlement in the UK before 1 January 1983 are classified as **British citizens otherwise than by descent**.

The only difference between the two kinds of British citizens is that those who are citizens by descent cannot automatically pass on citizenship to their children born abroad.

Before 1 January 1983 British men who had children in *non-Commonwealth* countries could pass on British nationality through numerous generations, provided that the children's births were registered at a British consulate. This would not usually make the children full British citizens after the second generation born abroad (that is, if they did not have a grandfather born, registered or naturalised in the UK). Such children would not fulfil the requirements for patriality under the Immigration Act 1971 (►see glossary for definition of patriality) and would therefore normally have become British Overseas citizens on 1 January 1983.

Children born in *Commonwealth* countries did not acquire any form of British nationality if their father was British by descent.

After 1 January 1983 the British Nationality Act 1981 removed the difference between Commonwealth and non-Commonwealth countries but restricted the automatic transmission of British nationality to one generation. Children born abroad to a parent who is a British citizen otherwise than by descent are automatically born British. However, if the British citizen parent is a citizen by descent, a child born abroad will not be born British. This means that British citizenship can pass automatically only for one generation to a child born abroad to British parents. However, the Act included provisions for some second-generation children to be registered abroad as British citizens.

These provisions mean that a child born overseas has the right to be

CITIZENSHIP BY DESCENT

For children born outside the UK to a British parent on or after 1 January 1983

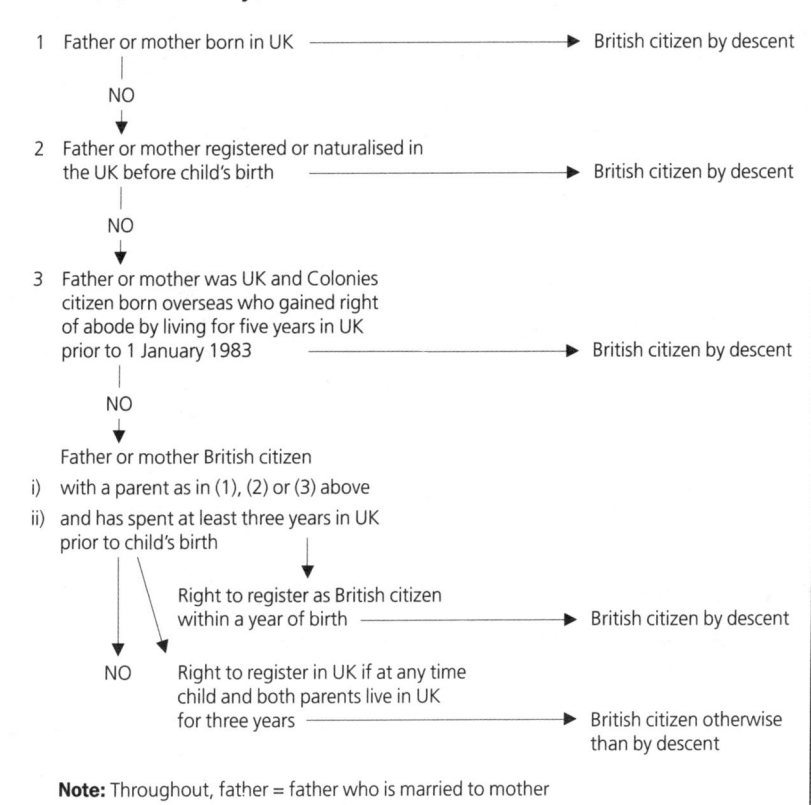

1. Father or mother born in UK ──────────▶ British citizen by descent

   │
   NO
   ▼

2. Father or mother registered or naturalised in the UK before child's birth ──────────▶ British citizen by descent

   │
   NO
   ▼

3. Father or mother was UK and Colonies citizen born overseas who gained right of abode by living for five years in UK prior to 1 January 1983 ──────────▶ British citizen by descent

   │
   NO
   ▼

   Father or mother British citizen
   i) with a parent as in (1), (2) or (3) above
   ii) and has spent at least three years in UK prior to child's birth

   Right to register as British citizen within a year of birth ──────────▶ British citizen by descent

   NO

   Right to register in UK if at any time child and both parents live in UK for three years ──────────▶ British citizen otherwise than by descent

Note: Throughout, father = father who is married to mother

---

registered at the British consulate as a British citizen within a year of the birth provided that:

- one of the parents is a British citizen by descent
- the British parent has a parent who is or was British otherwise than by descent
- the British parent had at some time before the child's birth lived in the UK for a continuous period of three years, not being absent for more than 270 days in that period.

A registration form (MN1) must be completed and a fee is payable. The child will become a **British citizen by descent**.

If the child and its parents do not fulfil all the above requirements, it is not possible for the child to be registered as a British citizen overseas. A third-generation child born overseas will never have a right to registration under the provisions above, because she or he will never be able to fulfil the second requirement (▶see chart above). The only exception to this is if a parent is in 'designated service' (see below).

However, there is a fallback provision if the child and both its parents return to live in the UK. Any child born overseas to a British citizen by descent parent has a right to be registered as a British citizen in the UK provided that the child and both parents (unless they are divorced or one is dead) live in the UK for a continuous period of three years. In that case, the child will have a right to register as a British citizen and moreover will become a **British citizen otherwise than by descent**.

It is possible to use this last provision as an alternative to registration abroad; for example, if the parents have missed the one-year deadline or if they would rather wait and register the child in the UK so that the child will be able to pass on its own British nationality later without any problems. Once a child has been registered abroad as a citizen by descent, it is not possible to alter this to become a citizen otherwise than by descent, even if the family comes to live in the UK for more than three years.

There are further details about other registration and naturalisation provisions in chapter 18.

Citizenship through Crown or designated service

There are special citizenship provisions for people doing certain government service jobs abroad. The work must be either Crown service (that is, working at a British embassy or high commission abroad, or serving in the British armed forces abroad) or designated service (working outside the UK in a defined list of jobs for the British government, for example working for the British Council, the British Tourist Authority or the Medical Research Council, or working abroad for an EU or international institution, for example the United Nations). People in these jobs are considered as working in the UK for the purpose of passing on citizenship. A child born outside the UK to a parent who is a British citizen (by descent or otherwise than by descent) working in Crown or designated service at the time of the birth will be born a British citizen otherwise than by descent.

British nationals who are not British citizens

British Overseas citizens, British Dependent Territories citizens, British Protected Persons and British Nationals (Overseas) do not have the right of abode in the UK. Nor do British subjects, except for a very few who had a UK-born mother and a very small number of women who were married before 1 January 1983 to men who had the right of abode in the UK. Pages 321–2 explain how to identify these categories of people.

For these people, their British status amounts to little more than a travel document facility. It does not give them the right to live anywhere. Most British Dependent Territories citizens, however, will have the right to live in the territory where they or their parents were born, ▶see glossary for list of British dependencies, but this will depend on the immigration ordinance or regulations of that territory. If the territory becomes independent, they can expect to be granted citizenship of the newly independent country. The special arrangements for Hong Kong are discussed below.

Right of readmission

British Overseas citizens who have been admitted for settlement to the UK have a right to be readmitted for settlement at any time. They may obtain a passport endorsement from the Home Office, 'Holder has the right of readmission to the UK'. This means that even if they stay away from the UK for more than two years at a time they cannot be refused indefinite leave to remain when they return. They are not, therefore, subject to the requirements of the returning residents rule (▶see page 229). In practice, this also normally applies to other British nationals except BDTCs.

Passing on nationality to children

British Overseas citizens, British Protected Persons, British subjects and British Nationals (Overseas) cannot pass on their citizenship to their children. Apart from the special provisions for Hong Kong, it is no longer possible to acquire BOC, BPP or BS status through birth or descent, so these nationalities will die out with their present holders.

British Dependent Territories citizens (BDTCs) can pass on their status to their children in exactly the same way as British citizens. Children born in a dependent territory will become BDTCs at birth automatically provided that they have one parent who is either a BDTC or is settled in the territory (▶see glossary for list of dependent territories). Children born in a dependency who do not automatically become BDTCs at birth will have a right to register as BDTCs if either of their parents become settled in the territory or if the children remain in the territory for ten years.

A BDTC parent who has a child born outside a dependency is able to pass on his or her BDTC status in exactly the same way as a British citizen parent can pass on British citizenship to a child born abroad (see above for details).

There are some provisions to protect the children of British nationals who would otherwise be **stateless**, but these are very restrictive. Children born to a British national, other than a British Protected Person, in the UK or a dependency have a right to acquire their parent's status by registration if they would otherwise be stateless. Children born outside the UK or a dependency to such a British national parent only have a right to registration if they become settled in the UK or a dependency and have lived there for three years.

There are general discretionary provisions for the Home Secretary to register minors as British subjects, British Overseas citizens and British Dependent Territories citizens. The qualifications for this are not defined and the provisions are very rarely used.

British nationals with an East African connection

The special quota voucher scheme

In the late 1960s, British nationals living in East and Central Africa, most of whose families originated from the Indian subcontinent, faced pressure to leave some of the newly independent countries, particularly Uganda and Kenya, and to go to the country of their nationality. It was because of this pressure, and the fear that more such British nationals might come to the UK, that the Commonwealth Immigrants Act 1968 was passed. This prevented the entry of citizens of the UK and Colonies (as they were then called) who had not acquired their citizenship in the UK, or who did not have a parent or grandparent who had acquired citizenship in the UK.

At the time the 1968 Act was passed, the UK government announced the creation of the special quota voucher scheme to admit a small number of these British nationals who were under pressure to leave the countries where they were living each year. In 1972 there was a large-scale expulsion of British nationals of Asian origin from Uganda. Many of the people concerned found it difficult or impossible to enter the UK and often sought temporary refuge in India to wait for a voucher under this scheme. Some people made complaints to the European Commission of Human Rights, which found the UK guilty of 'inhuman and degrading treatment' of its own nationals. As a result, it agreed to increase the number of vouchers issued every year; the nominal annual quota is now 5000.

However, people in India found that they were waiting longer and longer for vouchers to be issued. The British government refused to say how many of the 5000 'global quota' were allocated to India, and how many to East Africa (where demand and supply soon met, because most of the people who needed to leave had already done so). In 1982, it emerged that only 600 of the 5000 vouchers were allocated to India, and most of the rest of the notional quota remained unallocated. As a result, in the mid-1980s the queue for issue of a voucher in India reached eight years. By 1994, the waiting period in India had gone down to three months and there were no queues by 1995. In that year, under 320 vouchers were issued worldwide, 180 in India and 120 in Kenya.

Qualifications for obtaining a special quota voucher

The voucher scheme is completely outside the immigration rules and is administered at the discretion of the Home Secretary. Vouchers are issued only to British nationals, with no other nationality, who are:

- 'under pressure' to leave the country in which they are living
- and who are 'heads of households'.

British nationals with no other nationality: this includes British protected persons and British subjects as well as people who are now British Overseas citizens, but not British Dependent Territories citizens. However, it does not apply to any of these people if they have access to another nationality, even if they do not want to take up that nationality. This means, for example, that most people whose families originate from Pakistan will not be considered eligible for vouchers, because Pakistan allows dual nationality (whereas India does not).

Under pressure to leave: this means people living in the countries of East and Central Africa (Uganda, Kenya, Tanzania, Malawi, Zambia) and people who left those countries to go to India and wait for admission to the UK. Vouchers are not normally issued to people from East Africa who went to live in other countries (for example to work in the Gulf States) or to British nationals living in other countries in the world, even if their immigration or other status is very insecure.

Heads of households: under the voucher scheme, married women are not regarded as 'heads of households'. Therefore, British national women married to Indian men, for example, cannot qualify for vouchers unless they can show that their husband is physically or mentally incapacitated and cannot be considered the 'head of household'. Divorced or widowed women are eligible for vouchers if they fulfil the other requirements. An attempt to challenge this blatant sex discrimination in the British courts (*Amin*, House of Lords, 7 July 1983) failed.

Admission of dependants

Voucher-holders' immediate family may qualify to accompany or join them in the UK. This includes spouses and dependent children up to the age of 25 (this upper age limit was introduced because the eight-year queue in India meant that children who were nearly 18 when their parents applied would reach 25 before the application was considered). In order to remain dependent, however, children must be unmarried and financially dependent on their parents (that is, not working). Entry clearance officers may also investigate to decide whether they are dependent 'by necessity' or whether they have chosen to remain or become dependent in order to qualify to accompany the family. Young men who take up employment or marry will normally be able to apply for a voucher in their own right once they reach 18, if they are also British nationals. However, young women who marry non-British men will cease to be eligible for a voucher as they will not be considered 'heads of households'.

Voucher-holders do not have to fulfil the public funds requirement (▶see box on page 180) but their families do. The 1994 immigration rules state that support and accommodation must be provided by the voucher-holder. It is not clear if this means that the family could not come if they were to be partially reliant on the earnings of the non-British-national wife, or if there are friends or relatives able and willing to give a family initial support, or whether the voucher-holder will have to go first to the UK to find accommodation and a job to support his family.

How to apply for a voucher

Applications for special quota vouchers are made to the nearest British high commission. There is no special form for the voucher applicant, but his or her dependants will have to fill in the usual forms for people seeking settlement in the UK, IM2A and IM2B. Voucher applicants do not have to pay a fee, but their dependants have to pay the usual settlement fee at the time they apply.

Voucher applicants and their dependants then wait for an interview which will usually take place within a few weeks. If there are young adult children, particularly daughters, decisions may be held up after interview, pending further enquiries to check whether or not they are married.

If a voucher is issued, the voucher-holder has to travel to the UK within six months and will be admitted for an indefinite period (settlement). If entry clearance is issued to his or her dependants, this also has to be used within six months of issue and they will be admitted for a year initially.

People who do not have vouchers

Any other British nationals have to fit in to the immigration rules to come into the UK for any other purpose ▶see the relevant chapter for details. People who enter as visitors and then apply to remain longer, because their citizenship does not entitle them to live in any other country, may be refused under the strict letter of the immigration rules. The Home Office has also made decisions to deport them, usually to the country in which they were living immediately before coming to the UK, and has then put pressure on the authorities of that country to admit them. Deportation orders have been enforced against two BOCs in 1994-96, but the Home Office has not stated to which countries they were sent. Immigration officers have completed application forms for visas to other countries for British Overseas citizens who have made it clear they do not wish to travel there. It is important to monitor this Home Office harassment of British Overseas citizens and to challenge attempts to deport them.

British nationals from Malaysia

Besides East Africa, the other country where there are many British Overseas citizens is Malaysia. Three areas of Malaya – Penang, Melaka and Singapore – were ruled directly by Britain as the Straits Settlements and Malayan independence law provided that people who were born or whose father had been born in those areas before independence (31 August 1957) would retain their citizenship of the UK and Colonies. When

Singapore became independent separately from Malaysia, this provision was lost for Singaporeans, but it still exists for people from Penang and Melaka. They are British nationals, but unless they have lived in the UK for five years and became settled before 1983, they are not British citizens, but British Overseas citizens. Since they have no connection with East Africa, they do not qualify for special quota vouchers. Malaysia does not permit people to gain any advantage from holding another nationality without forfeiting their Malaysian nationality and many Malaysians do not know that they have British nationality. People with this connection with Penang or Melaka who wish to claim their British nationality should obtain specialist advice.

British nationals from Hong Kong

Most British nationals from Hong Kong lost the right to live in the UK under the Commonwealth Immigrants Act 1962. The only citizens of the UK and Colonies (as they then were) from Hong Kong who retained the right of abode, and who still have the right of abode now, are:

- people who were born, registered or naturalised in the UK
- people who had at any time before 1983 spent five years continuously and legally in the UK and were settled in the UK at the end of that period
- people with a parent or grandparent who was born, registered or naturalised in the UK
- women married to a man who fulfilled any of these conditions.

This means that most people of Chinese or other Asian origin in Hong Kong lost the right of abode in the UK. However, some of these people lived in the UK as students or workers in the 1950s or 1960s. At that time, people from Hong Kong and other Commonwealth countries were technically 'settled' in the UK, because no conditions could be put on their stay if they were admitted. It is therefore worth checking if Hong Kong British nationals have lived in the UK. If they lived in the UK for more than five years, before 1983, and had no time limit on their stay at the end of that five year period, they gained the right of abode and are therefore British citizens now.

British Nationals (Overseas): the Hong Kong Act 1985

In 1985, Britain and China signed an agreement for the return of Hong Kong to China on 1 July 1997. They agreed that the status of British Dependent Territories citizen would no longer apply to people from Hong Kong after that date. Instead, it was agreed that they would be able to apply for a new status, called British National (Overseas). This does not carry the right of abode in the UK. The Chinese authorities do not regard this as a citizenship, merely as a travel document facility.

BDTCs from Hong Kong can apply for British National (Overseas) passports until 1997. An Order in July 1993 provided that, for administrative convenience, people born between certain dates had to apply at certain times. The deadlines for most people have now passed; people born before 1947, for example, had to apply before 30 June 1995. Children born in 1996 had to apply before 31 March 1997 and those born between January and June 1997 must apply before 30 September 1997. Late applications could be accepted if 'special circumstances' applied, but in general anyone who had not applied by the relevant date will lose British nationality altogether when Hong Kong returns to China.

Most BDTCs from Hong Kong are also considered by the Chinese authorities to be Chinese citizens and will have Chinese citizenship after 30 June 1997. People who are not of Chinese ethnic origin may not be Chinese citizens, for example people of Indian origin who have lived in Hong Kong for many years or generations. If they have no other nationality, they will become British Overseas citizens after 30 June 1997. However, they will not qualify for special quota vouchers ▶see above, and have no claim under immigration law to come to the UK. Government assurances that 'if, against all expectations, they come under pressure to leave Hong Kong and have nowhere else to go, the Government of the day would consider with considerable and particular sympathy their case for admission' to the UK have not allayed all worries. The Labour Party stated in June 1996 that it would 'remove the need for special circumstances to arise before those members of the ethnic minorities gain admission and right of abode.' Michael Howard stated on 4 February 1997 that he would 'make provision enabling them to apply for registration as British citizens' but did not explain how.

British citizenship: the British Nationality (Hong Kong) Act 1990

After the events in Tiananmen Square in June 1989, people in Hong Kong became very alarmed about their future and the emigration rate from the territory increased. There was great concern that this might endanger the financial and social stability of Hong Kong. After representations from the Hong Kong government and others, the UK government agreed to provide up to 50,000 full British citizen passports for BDTCs from Hong Kong in certain specified categories.

Applications were decided on a points system, based on the so-called 'emigrateability rate' of the groups of people concerned (their age, qualifications and the actual emigration rates of people in their profession). There were also special categories for people in 'sensitive services' (for example key civil servants or people in the security services), for 'disciplined services' (for example police, immigration and prison officers) and for a small number of 'entrepreneurs'. Applications for the first tranche of 43,000 places had to be returned by 28 February 1991. There were fewer than anticipated – only 65,623 – some categories were under-subscribed and not all places were filled. The second tranche of applications had to be made by 31 March 1994, and 41,588 people applied for 13,156 places.

These applications were decided during 1996. This scheme provided the only route to right of abode in the UK for most Hong Kong BDTCs.

People from Hong Kong who are living in the UK

The following checklist will help to decide the status of someone from Hong Kong who is living in the UK:

- **Does the person have a (brown) certificate of identity?**

  If so, the person is not a British national of any kind. He or she was born in mainland China and is probably entitled to Chinese citizenship. He or she may be able to obtain British citizenship by naturalisation if he or she fulfils the requirements; ▶see chapter 18.

- **Does the person have a British passport?**

  – does the passport state 'holder has the right of abode in the UK' on page 5, or 'British citizen' on the inside back cover or on page 1? If so, the person is a British citizen, with the right of abode in the UK.

  – did the person, at any time before 1 January 1983, live legally in the UK for at least five years, without any conditions on his or her stay at the end of the period? If so, and provided that the person can prove this, he or she is a British citizen with the right of abode in the UK.

  – was the person born in the UK before 1983? was the person born in the UK on or after 1 January 1983 to a parent who was British or was settled in the UK at the time of the birth? If so, the person is a British citizen.

  – was the person born in the UK on or after 1 January 1983, and is a BDTC by descent? If so, the person has the right to register as a British citizen after living continuously in the Uk from birth for over five years.

  If none of these apply, check the immigration stamp on the passport (▶see chapter 13 for examples of different passport stamps). This will show under what conditions, if any, the person has been admitted or allowed to remain. Only people with indefinite leave can apply for British citizenship (▶see chapter 18). Students, visitors and work permit holders cannot apply and should not do so as this may prejudice future applications to remain here or return here. Some students who have been in the UK for ten years or more may be able to obtain indefinite leave (▶see pages 238–9).

SECTION 10: NATIONALITY

18 How to become British

There are two ways in which people of other nationalities can obtain British citizenship:

- **naturalisation** is the way almost all adults (people aged 18 and over) can become British. It is always discretionary and can be refused with no reason given. There is no right of appeal against a refusal of citizenship.
- **registration** is the way all children (people under 18) and a very small number of adults (see below) can become British. It is sometimes a right which cannot be refused, but in most cases is discretionary, without the need to give reasons and without a right of appeal.

Points to note

- All adults applying for British citizenship *must* be settled (have indefinite leave to remain) in the UK at the date of application. Sometimes people who are in the UK for a limited period (for example as students) mistakenly believe that an application for citizenship will be a means of being able to stay in the UK permanently. Quite the reverse is true: they do not qualify for citizenship, and the Home Office is likely to interpret a citizenship application as evidence that they do not intend to leave the UK at the end of their studies and therefore may refuse an extension of leave as a student.
- Applications for citizenship will probably lead to an investigation of the whole family's immigration status. If there is any irregularity in the applicant's status or that of a close family member (for example if they are overstayers) they should seek advice about regularising their status before making a citizenship application.
- The Home Office now retains the whole of the citizenship fee, even if the application is unsuccessful (▶see appendix). It is therefore very important for people to check before applying that they at least fulfil the objective criteria (that is, residence, language) rather than risk losing money.

Naturalisation

Requirements for naturalisation

- residence and settlement in the UK
- language
- good character
- intention to live in the UK

The requirements (and the fees) are slightly different for people who are married to British citizens and people who are not married to British citizens. The former will usually find that it is easier and cheaper for them to become British. The requirement of marriage is a requirement at the time of application. However, if a couple separate or divorce after the application is made but before it is granted, the Home Office should be told of the state of the marriage. If the couple are divorced, it is likely that the application will be refused. The person may be asked whether he or she wants to apply instead on the basis of residence, by paying the extra amount of money.

Residence and settlement

People who are not married to British citizens must have been living legally in the UK for five years continuously, and must have been physically present in the UK on the date five years before they apply. They must not have been absent for more than 450 days in total and not more than 90 days in the year immediately before they apply. They must have been settled (have had indefinite leave to remain in the UK) for at least a year before they apply.

People who are married to British citizens must have been living legally in the UK for three years continuously, and must have been physically present in the UK on the date three years before they apply. They must not have been absent for more than 270 days in total and not more than 90 days in the year immediately before they apply. They must be settled (have indefinite leave to remain in the UK) at the time they apply.

Language

People who are not married to British citizens must show that they have a 'sufficient knowledge' of English, Welsh or Scottish Gaelic. They do not need to be literate in the language, but should be able to converse in it. This test is assessed by the immigration service in London and by police forces in other areas. It is usually done by means of a visit or an interview, occasionally by a telephone call to the applicant. It is very unsatisfactory as the people making the assessment are not trained to do so and the people being assessed may be shocked by the arrival of a police officer, or have difficulties with telephone conversations. In theory, elderly or infirm applicants can be excused the language test, but this is at the discretion of the Home Office.

People who are married to British citizens do not need to pass a language test.

Good character

All applicants must show that they are of 'good character'. This is very ill-defined. Unspent criminal convictions are taken into account (applicants have to list these, including motoring offences, on the application form). Checks are also usually made on financial solvency. The Special Branch is also usually asked to comment on any alleged security risk. In addition, the local police force (or, in London, the immigration service) may be asked to run checks on the applicant, which may include an interview. This is the most subjective of the tests and the one where the Home Office is least likely to give the reasons why it has refused.

Intention to live in the UK

People who are not married to British citizens have to show that they intend to continue to live in the UK if the application is granted. Ministers have said that they want to be sure that applicants are really committed to the UK and do not simply want 'the convenience of a British passport'. It is therefore unwise, for example, to seek to speed up the processing of an application giving as a reason that there is likely to be a prolonged absence abroad.

Technically, applicants can travel overseas for as long as they like after the application has been submitted (the residence requirements refer to the period before the application was made). However, if it is clear that an applicant is no longer living permanently in the UK while the application is being considered (for example, if it is impossible for a police interview to be arranged) the Home Office may consider this as evidence of a lack of intention to live permanently in the UK. It may then require evidence that the stay abroad is only a temporary one (for example, contractual employment, study or caring for a sick relative) and that connections with the UK are maintained, indicating a return in the near future. People who have submitted naturalisation applications remain in any case subject to the returning residents rule (▶see page 229) and will need to return within two years to secure their settled status in the UK.

People who are married to British citizens do not have to show that they intend to continue to live in the UK.

The process of application

Applicants have to fill in Form AN, available from the Home Office Nationality Directorate (▶address in chapter 19). They need to send the fee (▶see appendix) at the same time as the application. A married couple applying together pay only one fee between them. From March 1991, the Home Office retained most of the fee if the application was unsuccessful and since April 1996, all of it.

Naturalisation applications have been taking a very long time to process. In December 1996, the average waiting period was 12–15 months. The Home Office has stated that it will consider representations to expedite consideration in particular cases when there are exceptional circumstances.

Applicants do not need to send their passports with the application form, because it takes so long to deal with applications. The Home Office will ask to see the passport when it is needed.

Refusals of applications

The Home Office is not obliged to give reasons for refusal. If the refusal is because of a technicality (for example, a failure to meet the residence requirements, an assessment that the applicant's language skills are inadequate) the Home Office will usually indicate this. In other cases, an MP may be able to elicit more information about the reasons for the refusal. If the Home Office refuses to give any details, this is usually because the refusal has been made under the 'good character' test and may well be connected with political activity or allegations of financial impropriety. The Al Fayed brothers, the owners of Harrods, were refused naturalisation with no reasons given; they were successful in their application to the Court of Appeal on 13 November 1996 to require the Home Office to 'inform an applicant of the nature of any matters weighing against the grant of the application in order to afford the applicant an opportunity of addressing them.' This did not require the Home Office to give reasons for the decision, but to indicate *before* a decision what sort of concerns it had so that the applicants had an opportunity to meet those concerns.

Although there is no right of appeal against refusal, it is sometimes possible to challenge refusals which are manifestly wrong. This should be done through the applicant's MP. JCWI has successfully challenged refusals on language grounds where it has been perfectly obvious that the applicant can communicate effectively in English. It is also possible to argue against a Home Office assumption that an applicant who has spent long periods abroad since applying does not intend to make his or her home in the UK.

Crown service

A person who is not British but who is working in Crown service overseas may apply for naturalisation on the ground of a period of work rather than of residence in the UK. Crown service involves working for the British government abroad, but no length of service is stipulated. The Home Office interprets the term as people in fully-established permanent positions, whose salaries are paid directly from government funds, for example people in the armed forces, the civil service and the diplomatic service. The other requirements for naturalisation must be met, including the intention to continue in the service of the British government, rather than to live in the UK. It is rare for naturalisation to be granted on this basis.

Registration

Registration of adults

There is one small group of adults able to obtain British citizenship by registration. Their applications cannot be refused.

British nationals who are not British citizens

British nationals who are not British citizens (British Overseas citizens, British Dependent Territories citizens, British Protected Persons, British subjects and British Nationals (Overseas) ▶see chapter 17 for definitions) have a right to obtain British citizenship by registration if they gain settlement rights in the UK. It is very difficult for most of these people to gain settlement rights in the UK as they are subject to immigration control.

They have to fulfil the following requirements:
- they must have lived in the UK legally for at least five years, and have been physically present in the UK on the date five years before they apply, and not have been absent for more than 450 days, not more than 90 of those days in the year immediately before applying
- they must have been settled (have had indefinite leave to remain in the UK) for at least one year.

The process of application

Applicants have to fill in Form B, available from the Home Office Nationality Directorate (▶address in chapter 19). Applicants need to send the fee (▶see appendix) at the same time as the application. In December 1996, the average waiting period for registration of adults was 6–9 months.

Registration of children
Children with a right to register

Children under 18 always obtain British citizenship by registration. Two groups of children have a right to register as British citizens. They are:

a) Children born in the UK since 1 January 1983 and not born British

Children who were born in the UK but who did not acquire British citizenship at birth because neither of their parents was a British citizen or settled in the UK have a right to register as British citizens if:

- one of their parents becomes settled (is given indefinite leave to remain) in the UK or
- the children remain in the UK for the first 10 years of their life and are not outside the UK for more than 90 days in any of those years.

b) Children born overseas to parents who are British citizens by descent

Children who are born overseas to a parent who is a British citizen by descent do not acquire British citizenship automatically. Some of these children have a right to register overseas within a year of their birth, while others will acquire a right to register if they and their parents live for three years in the UK. For details of the requirements, ▶see the section on British citizens by descent in chapter 17.

Children who can apply to register at discretion

All other children can register only at the discretion of the Home Secretary. There are no specific qualifications in the British Nationality Act 1981, which simply says that the Home Secretary can register a minor child as a British citizen. In theory, this means that any child, anywhere, could be registered as British. In practice, it is rare for registration to be granted to a child living outside the UK (except those children with a right to register, described above). The Home Office has also stated that children born outside the UK before 1983 to British-born mothers (who would have automatically been born British by descent if they had been born after 1 January 1983) will be registered if the mother applies for this before the children are 18, and, if the parents are still married, if the father has no well-founded objection.

In other cases, if children are living in the UK, there are no specific residence or other requirements. The Home Office has given little guidance on the factors it examines, only that 'consideration is given to' the following:
- the child's connections with the UK (for example, whether the child is settled)
- where the child's future is likely to be
- the views of the parents
- the nationality of the parents.

In the case of 'older children, particularly those approaching 18', the Home Office will also take into consideration:
- whether the child is of good character (▶see above for definition of this)
- the length of time the child has lived in the UK.

Because the qualifications are so unclear, it is very difficult to be sure whether a child's registration application will succeed. In practice, if one or both parent(s) is or are British or applying to become British, the Home Office will usually register young children, and older children who have lived in the UK for some time (this is undefined, but would certainly include children who have been living in the UK for five years or more and usually includes those here for the last two years). If neither parent is British, or intending to become British, there may be some difficulty in fulfilling the requirements. The Home Office would not normally register a child whose parents were not settled in the UK, unless the child had been taken into local authority care and it was clear that there was no prospect of the parents regaining custody.

The process of application

Parents or guardians normally apply on behalf of a child. If an older child makes an application him- or herself, the reasons for this should be explained to the Home Office. When an application is made for children on their own, it is normally on form MN1, available from the Home Office Nationality Directorate (►address in chapter 19). Parents who are applying for registration of their children at the same time as for naturalisation for themselves may add the children's names to their own AN forms. Children born in the UK who have lived here for over 10 years may apply on Form T. A single fee covers all the children in the same family if they apply at the same time either on their own or with their parent(s). Whether or not the application is successful, the Home Office retains the fee. In December 1996, registrations of children took an average of 6–9 months to process.

Passports and travel documents

When the Home Office grants an application for British citizenship, it sends the person a certificate to confirm the grant of citizenship. This certificate is then evidence of the person's citizenship status.

In order to obtain a British passport, people need to apply to the office of the Passport Agency nearest to where they live (►see chapter 19 for addresses). They can get application forms for British passports from any large Post Office; there are separate forms for adults and children. The forms must be filled in and sent together with the citizenship certificate, any other documents requested and the fee (►see appendix) to the Passport Agency. At present, the time this takes varies with the season but the Passport Agency has a target time of issuing passports in a few days at any time of year. All newly-issued passports are now the uniform European Union machine-readable maroon-coloured British passports, rather than the old blue British ones; the colour of the passport makes no difference to the person's status and rights.

Stateless people living in the UK, for example some children born in the UK but not born British, apply to the Home Office Travel Documents Section for travel documents. They fill in a form TD112 and return it to the Home Office with the fee (►see appendix). The Home Office normally requires evidence that the person cannot get a travel document from any other country which might be expected to provide it, for example, a letter from the embassy of their parents' country confirming that the child does not have that nationality, before issuing a travel document. When it is hard to obtain this evidence, or when the parents are not prepared to contact the embassy, for example if they have been granted exceptional leave to remain, this should be explained to the Home Office and the application submitted anyway. In February 1997 the Home Office stated that applications which are in order should be dealt with in eight weeks, but it is sensible to allow more time.

Deprivation of citizenship

The Home Office has the power to make an order depriving a person of citizenship. It can do this if the citizenship had been obtained by fraud, or if the person is convicted of an offence and sentenced to imprisonment for a year or more within five years of citizenship being granted, and the Home Office decides it is not conducive to the public good for the person to remain a citizen.

This power under the 1981 British Nationality Act has never yet been exercised. It was discussed in 1993, in the case of *Naheed Ejaz* (1994 Imm AR 300). She had naturalised on the grounds of her marriage, but it later emerged that her husband had never been a British citizen himself. The Home Office therefore stated that she also had never been a citizen, and tried to remove her as an illegal entrant. The Court of Appeal held that because Mrs Ejaz had not been involved in any deception the Home Office could not simply strip her of citizenship but would have to go through the formal process of deprivation. The Home Office did not do so, and she remains a British citizen.

SECTION 11: USEFUL INFORMATION

19 Useful addresses and telephone numbers

Home Office Immigration and Nationality Directorate
Lunar House,
40 Wellesley Road,
Croydon CR9 2BY.

Main telephone number:
0181 686 0688,
fax 0181 760 1181
policy 1197

The Public Enquiry Office at Lunar House is open from 9am to 4pm, Monday to Friday.

Direct telephone lines to the groups dealing with individual cases are organised initially by the last two numbers of the Home Office reference for the case. They all start 0181 760, followed by the direct number.

Group	Reference	Extension	Room
1	01–10	2194/2188/1343	824
3	11–15	2284/2285/1117	1002
4	16–20	2333/2172	1002
5	21–25	2176/2173	1002
6	26–30	1120	722
7	31–35	2158/1350	732
8	36–40	1353	731
9	41–45	2615/2686/2147	721
X	46–65	1354/1128/4729/ 2085/4711/1700	901
14	66–70	1779/1357	713
15	71–/5	1359/4520	707
16	76–80	2727	701
17	81–85	1145/2256/2397	703
18	86–90	2066/1364	734
19	91–95	2566/2030	919
20	96–00	1163/2789	741

Business, sole representatives, persons of independent means

| 21 | All | 2328 | 735 |

Settlement groups

26	01–17	1362/1562/2790	815
27	18–34	1196/1533	819
28	35–51	2900/2955	801
29	52–68	2861/2925	801
30	69–85	1552/1491	801
31	86–00	2752/1727	801

EEA section 8517/8398/8376, room 1204, fax 8521

BOCRA (British Overseas Citizens and Right of Abode)
All   2641/1260   931

Appeals groups

40	01–22	2691/2453	923
41	23–44	2446/2461	925
42	45–66	2444	928
43	67–88	2947/2657	930
44	89–00	4565	924
45	All	1713/1301	926

Useful addresses and telephone numbers • 347

Home Office continued
All telephone numbers start 0181 760

Deportation groups

Group	Reference	Extension	Room	fax
D1	general	8419/8421	311	8400
D2	01–25	8432/8433	212	8259
D3	26–50	8455/8456	210	"
D4	All removals	8469/8483	209	"
D5	51–75	8496/8497	204	"
D6	76–00	8694/8695	202	"

Illegal entry groups

IES1   All those detained, temporary release
8–9, 13–18, 20–21, 23–24, 43–44, 46–47, 65–68, 87–90
extension 8635/8636, room 305, fax 8621/8177

IES2   Temporary release
00–7, 10–12, 19, 22, 25–42, 45, 48–64, 69–86, 91–99
extension 8652/8654, room 307, fax 8637

Document Reception Centre Room 828, 0181 760 2275
Application Forms Unit 0181 760 2233
Employers' information line 0181 649 7878

Asylum Directorate
Most asylum cases are dealt with at
Quest House,
11 Cross Road
Croydon CR9 2BY
and are divided by the geographical region from which the asylum-seeker comes.
Numbers all start 0181 760.

Teams 1 and 2   Americas, former Soviet Union, Bahrain
                 Caribbean, China, Cuba, Haiti, Hong Kong
                 Mongolia, Saudi Arabia, Virgin Islands
                 tel 1077/2441/1703/2942, fax 1591

Team 3   Algeria, Egypt, Iraq, Tunisia, Morocco
         tel 4698, 1298, fax 2389

Team 4   Iran, Israel, Jordan, Kuwait, Libya, Lebanon, Oman
         Qatar, Palestine, Syria, United Arab Emirates, Yemen
         tel 1636, 1687, fax 2389

Team 5   Turkey tel 4541/1528, fax 2389

Team 6   Afghanistan, India, Cambodia (Khmer Republic)
         Laos, Pakistan, Vietnam
         tel 1527/2473, fax 1216/2882

Team 7   Australia, Bangladesh, Burma, Indonesia, Kampuchea
         New Zealand, Sri Lanka and the rest of Asia not listed
         tel 1544/1073, fax 1322

Team 8   Eastern Europe not listed
         tel 1502/2997, fax 2437/2871

Team 9   Angola, Botswana, Burundi, Lesotho, Namibia
         Rwanda, South Africa, Uganda, Zaire, Zimbabwe
         tel 4802/4452, fax 4496

Team 10 Benin, Burkina Faso, Cameroon, Cape Verde, Central
          African Republic, Chad, Congo, Equatorial Guinea
          Gabon, Gambia, Guinea, Guinea Bissau, Ivory Coast
          Niger, Nigeria, Sao Tomé e Principe, Togo
          tel 4917/4436, fax 4756/4973

Team 11 Comoros, Ghana, Liberia, Madagascar, Mali, Mauritania
          Mauritius, Senegal, Sierra Leone, Tanzania
          tel 4454/4840, fax 4944

Team 12 Djibouti, Eritrea, Ethiopia, Kenya, Malawi
          Mozambique, Seychelles, Somalia, Sudan, Swaziland
          Zambia
          tel 4485/4807, fax 4833

Home Office Asylum Directorate continued
Appeals Support Section
tel 4722/2334/1701, fax 1036
Asylum Screening Unit
tel 1303/1728, fax 2820
Travel Documents Section
tel 2345, fax 1036
Unaccompanied Children's Module
tel 4458, fax 4833

Nationality

Nationality Directorate, Home Office,
3rd floor, India Buildings, Water Street
Liverpool L2 0QN
tel 0151 237 5200, fax 0151 237 5385

Home Office regional Public Enquiry Offices

Belfast
Olivetree House, Fountain Street
Belfast BT1 5EA
tel 01232 322547

Birmingham
Immigration Office (Cargo Terminal)
Birmingham Airport, Birmingham B26 3QN
tel 0121 606 7345

Glasgow
Admin Block D, Argyll Avenue
Glasgow Airport, Abbotsinch, Paisley
Renfrewshire PA3 2TD
tel 0141 887 2255

Liverpool
Graeme House, Derby Square
Liverpool L2 7SF
tel 0151 236 8974

Ports of entry Immigration service and detention centres

London Heathrow
Terminal 1
 casework 0181 745 6808
 arrivals control 0181 745 6800
 fax 0181 745 6814
Terminal 2
 general 0181 745 6850
 casework 0181 745 6862
 fax 0181 745 6877
Terminal 3
 general 081 745 6900
 casework 0181 745 6932
 fax 0181 745 6943

Heathrow Terminal 4
 switchboard 0181 745 4700
 casework 0181 745 4724
 fax 0181 745 4705
Queens Building detention centre
 0181 564 9726/7 (detainees)
 0181 745 6484 (Group 4)
Harmondsworth detention centre
 Building JA 0181 262 1223
 Building DA 0181 261 1220
 0181 564 7790 (detainees)
 0181 759 9727 (Group 4)

Belfast city office 01232 322547
 fax 01232 244939
 airport switchboard 01849 422500
 immigration ext. 4093

Birmingham International Airport
 0121 606 7357/8
 fax 0121 782 0006

Midland Enquiry Unit
 0121 782 0771
 fax 0121 782 2901

Bristol 01275 472843
 fax 01275 474434

Cardiff 01222 764474
 fax 01222 764014
 airport 01446 710485, fax 710606

Cheriton (Channel Tunnel) 01303 282600
 fax 01303 282610

City Airport (London) 0171 474 5555
 immigration 0171 474 1395
 fax 0171 511 2363

Dover East immigration 01304 244900
 fax 01304 213594

South-East Ports Surveillance Team
 01304 216405

Detention holding area 01304 215395

Dover Harbour police station
 01304 206260

Dover Hoverport 01304 240246
 fax 01304 215343

East Midlands Airport 01332 812000
 fax 01332 811569

Edinburgh 0131 344 3330
 fax 0131 335 3197

Gatwick South
 switchboard 01293 502019
 casework 01293 502627
 fax 01293 553643

Useful addresses and telephone numbers • 349

Gatwick North switchboard 01293 892500
  casework 01293 892520
  asylum 01293 892515
  fax 01293 892560
Tinsley House detention centre
  01293 434800
Meadvale Buildings detention centre
  01293 569772
Glasgow 0141 887 4115
  fax 0141 887 1566
Gravesend, Apex House 01474 352308
  fax 01474 534731
Harwich immigration 01255 504371
  fax 01255 240233
  detention 01255 241326/252176
Hull 01482 223017
  fax 01482 219034
Leeds/Bradford 0113 250 2931
  fax 0113 250 5716
Liverpool 0151 236 8974
  fax 0151 236 4656
Luton 01582 421891
  fax 01582 405215
Manchester casework 0161 489 2657
  enforcement 0161 489 2367/8/9/2677
  detention 0161 437 2994
  fax 0161 489 2370
Newcastle 0191 286 9469
  fax 0191 214 0143
Ramsgate 01843 594716
  fax 01843 587605
Sheerness 01795 667733
  fax 01795 661509
Stansted 01279 680118
  enforcement 01279 680691
  detention 01279 681548
  fax 01279 680041
Waterloo International Terminal
  0171 919 5910/5900
Campsfield House 01865 845700
  detainees 01865 377712
  fax 01865 377723
Haslar Holding Centre 01705 580381
  fax 01705 504432
  fax to IOs 01705 528631
  Dormitories
  A 01705 528604, B 01705 510653
  C 01705 510599, D 01705 510362

Rochester 01634 830300
  fax 01634 826712
Winson Green 0121 554 3838
  fax 0121 554 7990

Immigration service offices

Becket House
66–68 St Thomas' Street
London SE1 3QU
tel 0171 238 1300
0171 238 1331/2 (asylum)
fax 0171 378 9107 (duty officer)
casework fax 0171 378 9110

Status Park Enforcement Section
Status 3, Status Park, Nobel Drive
Harlington, Middlesex UB3 5EY
tel 0181 745 2400/2462
fax 0181 745 2474/2407

Immigration appeals offices

Thanet House, 231 The Strand
London WC2R 1DA
tel 0171 353 8060
fax 0171 583 1976
Immigration Appeal Tribunal cases are
heard at Thanet House and at Glasgow.

2nd floor, Sheldon Court, 1 Wagon Lane
Birmingham B26 3DU
tel 0121 685 3300, fax 0121 742 4142

1st floor, 2 Park Street
Cardiff CF1 1ET
tel 01222 376439/40

c/o County Court, 35 Parsons Street
Banbury, Oxon
tel 01295 269230
Part–time hearing centres, administered
from Birmingham

7th floor, Lancashire House
5 Linenhall Street
Belfast BT28 9AA
tel 01232 332344

York House, 2–3 Duke's Green Avenue
Feltham, Middlesex TW14 0LS
tel 0181 893 1000, fax 0181 831 3500

4th floor, Coronet House, Queen Street
Leeds LS1 2SH
tel 0113 244 9898, fax 0113 244 6260

3rd floor, Aldine House
New Bailey Street, Manchester M3 5EU
tel 0161 837 1000, fax 0161 839 3793

Immigration appeals offices, continued
5th floor, Portcullis House
21 India Street, Glasgow G2 4DZ
tel 0141 221 3489, fax 0141 221 3532

26 King Street, Gravesend, Kent, DA12 2DU
tel/fax 01474 334349

Lincoln House, 75 Westminster Bridge Road
Waterloo, London SE1 5HZ
tel 0171 450 4360, fax 0171 401 9073

654 Lordship Lane, Wood Green
London N22 5HH
tel 0181 829 2400, fax 0181 829 2401

Home Office presenting officers

Rooms 501–515, 19–29 Woburn Place
London WC1H 0JQ
tel 0171 273 8700, fax 0171 278 5472

6th floor, Blythswood House
200 West Regent Street
Glasgow G2 4DJ
tel 0141 221 7171, fax 0141 221 7172

3rd and 4th floors, 21–47 High Street
Feltham Green TW13 4ND
tel 0181 844 2507, fax 0181 957 3259

3rd floor, Portcullis House
Seymour Grove, Old Trafford
Manchester M16 0NE
tel 0161 886 4128, fax 0161 877 6323

10th floor, Dudley House
133 Albion Street, Leeds LS2 8PN
tel 0113 243 2457, fax 0113 246 0717

2nd floor front suite, Virginia House
56 Warwick Road, Olton
Birmingham B92 7HX
tel 0121 706 9741, fax 0121 706 4495

2nd floor, 654 Lordship Lane
London N22 5HQ
tel 0181 829 2456/7, fax 0181 829 2452

Passport Agency offices

Clive House, Petty France
London SW1H 9HD
tel 0171 799 2290
(recorded message 0171 271 8808)

Hampton House, 47–53 High Street
Belfast BT1 2QS
tel 01232 232371

3 Northgate, 96 Milton Street
Cowcaddens, Glasgow G4 0BT
tel 0141 332 0271

5th floor, India Buildings
Water Street
Liverpool L2 0QZ
tel 0151 237 3010

Olympia House, Upper Dock Street
Newport, Gwent NP9 1XA
tel 01633 244500/244292

Aragon Court, Northminster Road
Peterborough PE1 1QG
tel 01733 895555, recorded message
01733 555688

Some other government departments

Aliens Registration Office
10 Lamb's Conduit Street
London WC1X 3MX
tel 0171 230 1208

Department for Education and Employment
Overseas Labour Service
Porter Brook House, W5 Moorfoot
Sheffield S1 4PQ
tel 0114 259 4074, fax 0114 275 3275
Work permit application forms sent out
from 01937 840224

Department of Social Security
Benefits Agency Overseas Branch
Tyneview Park, Whitley Road
Newcastle-upon-Tyne NE98 1YX
tel 0191 213 5000

Foreign and Commonwealth Office
Migration and Visa Division
1 Palace Street, London SW1H 5HE
tel 0171 270 3000, 0171 238 4633
fax 0171 238 4646 (policy)
    0171 238 4660 (operations)
    0171 238 4651 (Correspondence Unit)
    0171 270 3735 (application form requests)

Home Office (Minister's private office)
Queen Anne's Gate
London SW1H 9AT
tel 0171 273 4604

Training and Employment Agency
Work Permits Section
Room 304, Clarendon House
9–21 Adelaide Street, Belfast BT2 8DJ
tel 01232 541713, fax 541746

Treasury Solicitor
Queen Anne's Chambers, 28 Broadway
London SW1H 9JS
tel 0171 210 3000, fax 0171 222 6006

Members of Parliament

Write to them at the House of Commons
London SW1A 0AA, tel 0171 219 3000
or House of Lords
London SW1A 0PW, tel 0171 219 3000

Some British high commissions and embassies abroad

Bangladesh
British High Commission
Immigration Section
United Nations Road
P.O. Box 6079
Baridhara, Dhaka 12
tel 882705
fax 883437, 883666 (immigration)
office hours GMT 01.30–08.00

Barbados
British High Commission
Lower Collymore Rock, P.O. Box 676
Bridgetown
tel 436 6694, fax 809 426 7916
office hours GMT 12.00–20.00.

For Anguilla, Antigua and Barbuda, British Virgin Islands, Dominica, Grenada Montserrat, St Christopher and Nevis St Lucia, St Vincent and the Grenadines: all apply at Barbados.

China
British Embassy
11 Guang Hua Lu, Jian Guo Men Wai
Beijing
tel 8610 6532 1961/4
fax 8610 6532 1937/9

Cyprus
British High Commission
Alexander Pallis Street, P.O. Box 1978
Nicosia
tel 357 2 473131/7, fax 357 2 477758
office hours GMT 05.30–12.00
except Tuesdays, 05.30–11.00 and
12.00–15.30

France
British Consulate-General
16 rue Dranjou
75008 Paris
tel 331 42 66 38 10, fax 331 40 07 05 77

Ghana
British High Commission, Osu Link
off Gamel Abdul Nasser Avenue
P.O. Box 296, Accra
tel 221665, 221715, 221738, fax 664652
office hours GMT 07.45–14.45

Guyana
British High Commission
44 Main Street, P.O. Box 10849
Georgetown
tel 65881/2/3/4, fax 592 253555
office hours GMT 11.30–18.30

Hong Kong
Immigration Department
7 Gloucester Road, Wanchai
tel 852 28293283, fax 852 28241133

British Trade Commission
9th floor, Bank of America Tower
12 Harcourt Road, Central
Hong Kong P.O. Box 528
tel 852 2523 0176, fax 852 2845 2870
office hours GMT 00.30–09.15

India
British High Commission
Immigration Section, Chanakyapuri
New Delhi 1100–21
tel 687 2161, fax 91 11 6872882
office hours GMT 03.30–07.30 and
  09.30–11.30

British Deputy High Commission
Maker Chambers IV
222 Jamnalal Bajaj Road
P.O. Box 11714, Nariman Point
Bombay 400 021
tel 91 22 2830517/2832330
fax 91 22 2027940
office hours GMT 02.30–07.30 and
  08.30–10.30

British Deputy High Commission
1 Ho Chi Minh Sarani, Calcutta 700 071
tel 242 5171, fax 242 3435

British Deputy High Commission
III floor, Kakani Towers
15 Khader Nawaz Khan Road
Madras 600 006
tel 827 0658, fax 91 44 827 5130
office hours GMT 03.00–07.30 and
  08.00–10.30

Jamaica
British High Commission
P.O. Box 575, Trafalgar Road
Kingston 10
tel 926 9050, fax 1 809 92 97869
office hours GMT 13.30–18.00 and
 19.00–21.30

Jordan
British Embassy, P.O. Box 87
Abdoun, Amman
tel 962 6823100, fax 962 6813759

Kenya
British High Commission
P.O. Box 30465, Bruce House
Standard Street, Nairobi
tel 335944, fax 254 2333196
office hours GMT 04.45–09.30 and
 10.30–13.30

Malawi
British High Commission
Lingadzi House, P.O. Box 30042
Lilongwe 3
tel 782400, fax 265 782657
office hours GMT 05.30–10.00 and
 11.30–14.30

Morocco
British Consulate-General
60 boulevard d'Anfa
BP 13762 Casablanca
tel 2122 221741, fax 265779

Nigeria
British High Commission
Private Mail Box 12136, 11 Eleke Crescent
Victoria Island, Lagos
tel 234 1261 9531/9537/9541/9566
fax 234 1261 4021
office hours GMT 07.00–14.00

Visa Section, Wema Towers
54 Marina, Lagos
tel 1266 7061/6413/6128/2903/3893
fax 234 1266 6909

Pakistan
British High Commission
Diplomatic Enclave, Ramna 5
P.O. Box 1122, Islamabad
tel 822131/5, fax 92 51 823439/822131
British Deputy High Commission
Shahrah-e-Iran, Clifton, Karachi 75400
tel 9221 5872431, fax 5874014
office hours GMT
 Sun–Wed 03.30–10.30
 Thurs 03.30–08.30

Philippines
British Embassy
15–17 Floor, L. V. Locsin Building
6752 Ayala Corner, Makati
Metro Manila 3116
P.O. Box 2927 MCPO
tel 632 816 7116, fax 632 819 7206
office hours GMT 00.00–05.30

Sierra Leone
British High Commission
Spur Road, Freetown
tel 232 22223961/5, fax 871 1447733

Sri Lanka
British High Commission
190 Galle Road, Kollupitiya
P.O. Box 1433
Colombo 3
tel 437336/43, fax 941 430308
office hours GMT 02.30–11.00
 Visa Office 02.00–05.30

Tanzania
British High Commission
Hifadhi House, Samora Avenue
P.O. Box 9200, Dar-es-Salaam
tel 117660, fax 255 51 117586

Thailand
British Embassy Visa Section
1031 Wireless Road, Bangkok 10330
tel 662 253 0191, fax 662 254 9579

Trinidad and Tobago
British High Commission
19 St Clair Avenue, St Clair
P. O. Box 778
Port of Spain, Trinidad
tel 809 622 8960, fax 809 622 4555

Turkey
British Consulate-General
Mesrutiyet Caddesi no. 34
Tepebasi, Beyoglu
PK 33, Istanbul
tel 90 212 293 7540, fax 245 6354
office hours GMT
 summer 05.30–10.00, 10.45–13.45
 winter 06.30–11.00 and 11.45–14.45

Zambia
British High Commission
Independence Avenue, P.O. Box 50050
Lusaka
tel 251133, fax 2601 253798
office hours GMT 06.00–10.30 and
 12.00–14.30

Some agencies working on immigration and nationality matters

Joint Council for the Welfare of Immigrants
115 Old Street, London EC1V 9JR
tel 0171 251 8708, fax 0171 251 8707

AIRE Centre (Advice on Individual Rights in Europe)
74 Eurolink Business Centre
49 Effra Road, London SW2 1BZ
tel 0171 924 0927, fax 0171 733 6786

African Churches Council for Immigration and Social Justice (ACCIS)
Unit 6–7, 321 Essex Road
London N1 3PS
tel and fax 0171 704 2331

Amnesty International UK
99–119 Rosebery Avenue
London EC1R 4RE
tel 0171 814 6200, fax 0171 833 1510

Anglo-Philippines Association for Real Togetherness (APART)
c/o Ken Strudwick, 46 Hayley Road
Lancing, West Sussex
tel 01903 763949

Association of Visitors to Immigration Detainees
c/o Mrs A. Atter, 53 Western Road
Winchester, Hants SO22 5AH
tel 01962 863317

Asylum Aid, 244A Upper Street
London N1 1RU
tel 0171 359 4026, fax 0171 354 9187

Asylum Rights Campaign
46 Francis Street, London SW1P 1QN
tel 0171 798 9008, fax 0171 798 9010

British Agencies for Adoption and Fostering (BAAF)
Skyline House, 200 Union Street
London SE1 0LY
tel 0171 593 2000, fax 0171 593 2001

Campaign to Close Campsfield
c/o 111 Magdalen Road, Oxford OX4 1RQ
tel 01865 724452/726804
Campsfield Visitors' Group 01865 205108

Cellmark Diagnostics
P.O. Box 265, Blacklands Way
Abingdon Business Park
Abingdon, Oxon, OX14 1DY
tel 01235 528609, fax 01235 528141

Children's Legal Centre
University of Essex
Wivenhoe Park, Colchester CO4 3SQ
tel 01206 873820/872466
fax 01206 874026

Christian Action for Justice in Immigration Law
c/o Iona Community, Pearce Institute
Govan, Glasgow G51 3UU

Commission for Racial Equality
Elliot House, 10–12 Allington Street
London SW1E 5EH
tel 0171 828 7022, fax 0171 630 7605

Detention Advice Service
244A Upper Street
London N1 1RU
tel 0171 704 8954, fax 0171 354 9187

Educational Grants Advisory Service
501–505 Kingsland Road
London E8 2DY

Electronic Immigration Network
c/o Rochdale REC, tel 01706 352374
fax 01796 711259
Internet ein-admin@mcr1.poptel.org.uk

European Commission London office
8 Storey's Gate, London SW1P 3AT
tel 0171 973 1992, fax 0171 973 1900

European Commission and Court of Human Rights
Maison de l'Europe, BP 431
R6, 67075 Strasbourg Cedex, France
tel 8861 4961, fax 8837 3265

Free Representation Unit
Room 140, 1st floor, 49–51 Bedford Row
London WC1R 4LR
tel 0171 831 0692

Greater Manchester Immigration Aid Unit
400 Cheetham Hill Road
Manchester M8 7EL
tel 0161 740 7722, fax 0161 740 5172

Human Rights Watch
2nd floor, 33 Islington High Street
London N1 9LH
tel 0171 713 1995, fax 0171 713 1800

Immigration Advisory Service
County House, 190 Great Dover Street
London SE1 4YB
tel 0171 357 6917, fax 0171 378 0665
admin 0171 357 7511

Immigration Advisory Service, continued
also Ports and Detention Unit
24 hour helpline 0171 378 9191
freephone 0800 435427
fax 0171 378 9300
3rd floor, Federation House
2309 Coventry Road
Birmingham B26 3PG
tel 0121 742 1221, fax 0121 742 1331
211A City Road, Roath
Cardiff CF2 3JD
tel 01222 496662, fax 01222 496602
Room 3049, Gatwick Village
Gatwick Airport
West Sussex RH6 0NN
tel 01293 533385, fax 01293 568831
115 Bath Street, Glasgow G2 4LE
tel 0141 248 2956, fax 0141 221 5388
71 Grove Road, Hounslow
Middlesex TW3 3PR
tel 0181 814 1115, fax 0181 814 1116/1578
Matthew Murray House
97 Water Lane, Leeds LS11 5QN
tel 0113 244 2460, fax 0113 243 1006
Suite 7B, 7th floor, Blackfriars House
Parsonage Street, Manchester M3 5JA
tel 0161 834 9942, fax 0161 832 9322
Immigration Law Practitioners' Association
Lindsey House, 40/42 Charterhouse Street
London EC1M 6JH
tel 0171 251 8383, fax 0171 251 8384
Independent Immigration Support Agency
3rd floor, Ladywell House, Hurst Street
Birmingham B5 4BN
tel 0121 622 7353
Institute of Race Relations
2-6 Leeke Street
London WC1X 8HS
tel 0171 837 0041, fax 0171 278 0623
Interights
33 Islington High Street
London N1 9LH
tel 0171 278 3230, fax 0171 278 4334
International Social Service of Great Britain
Cranmer House, 39 Brixton Road
London SW9 6DD
tel 0171 735 8941, fax 0171 582 0696

Justice
59 Carter Lane
London EC4V 5AQ
tel 0171 329 5100, fax 0171 329 5055
Kalayaan
c/o Commission for Filipino Migrant Workers
St Francis Centre, Pottery Lane
London W11 4NQ
tel 0171 243 2942, fax 0171 792 3060
Law Centres Federation
Duchess House, 18-19 Warren Street
London W1P 5DB
tel 0171 387 8570, fax 0171 387 8368
Legal Action Group
242-244 Pentonville Road
London N1 9UN
tel 0171 833 2931, fax 0171 837 6094
Liberty-NCCL
21 Tabard Street, London SE1 4LA
tel 0171 403 3888, fax 0171 407 5354
London Interpreting Project
The Print House, Ashwin Street
London E8 3DL
tel 0171 923 3437
Medical Foundation for the Care of Victims of Torture
96-98 Grafton Road
London NW5 3EJ
tel 0171 813 7777, fax 0171 813 0011
Merseyside Immigration Advice Unit
34 Princes Road
Liverpool L8 1TH
tel 0151 709 8360, fax 0151 709 4996
Minority Rights Group
379 Brixton Road, London SW9 7DE
tel 0171 978 9498, fax 0171 738 6265
National Association of Citizens' Advice Bureaux
Myddleton House
115-123 Pentonville Road
London N1 9LZ
tel 0171 833 2181, fax 0171 833 4371
National Coalition of Anti-Deportation Campaigns
22 Berners Street, Birmingham B19 2DR
tel 0121 554 6947, fax 0121 507 1567
National Union of Students
461 Holloway Road, London N7 6LJ
tel 0171 272 8900, fax 0171 263 5713

North of England Refugee Service
1st floor, 19 Bigg Market
Newcastle-upon-Tyne
Tyne and Wear NE1 1UN
tel 0191 222 0406, fax 0191 222 0239

Refugee Arrivals Project
Room 2005, 2nd floor, Queen's Building
Heathrow Airport TW6 1DL
tel 0181 759 5740, fax 0181 759 7058

Refugee Council
Bondway House, 3–9 Bondway
London SW8 1SJ
tel 0171 582 6922/1162
fax 0171 582 9929

Unaccompanied child asylum-seekers panel
tel 0171 582 4947

RASU (Refugee Advisers' Support Unit
0171 582 9927

Refugee Legal Centre
Sussex House, 39–45 Bermondsey Street
London SE1 3XF
tel 0171 827 9090 (admin)
0171 378 6242 (advice)
0171 378 6243 (detention)
0831 598057 (emergencies)
fax 0171 378 1979

Refugee Legal Group
c/o North Islington Law Centre
161 Hornsey Road
London N7 6DU
tel 0171 607 2461, fax 0171 700 0072

Royal College of Nursing
   Immigration Advisory Service
1–7 Harley Street
London W1N 1DA
tel 0171 637 1828, fax 0171 636 8789

Runnymede Trust
133 Aldersgate Street, London EC1A 4JA
tel 0171 600 9666, fax 0171 600 8529

Scottish Refugee Council
43 Broughton Street, Edinburgh EH1 3JU
tel 0131 557 8083, fax 0131 556 7617
98 West George Street, Glasgow G2 1PJ
tel 0141 333 1850, fax 0141 333 1860

Southall Black Sisters
52 Norwood Road
Southall, Middlesex UB2 4DW
tel 0181 571 9595, fax 0181 574 6781

Stonewall Immigration Group
16 Clerkenwell Close, London EC1R 0AA
tel 0171 336 8860, fax 0171 336 8864

UKCOSA, the Council for International
   Education
9–17 St Alban's Place, London N1 0NX
tel 0171 226 3762, fax 0171 226 3373

United Nations High Commission for
   Refugees
21st floor, Millbank Tower
21–24 Millbank, London SW1P 1QP
tel 0171 828 9191, fax 0171 630 5349

University Diagnostics
South Bank Technopark
90 London Road, London SE1 6LN
tel 0171 401 9898, fax 0171 928 9297

Waltham Forest Immigration Aid Centre
William Morris Community Centre
Greenleaf Road, London E17 6QQ
tel/fax 0181 503 6628

World University Service
20 Dufferin Street, London EC1Y 8PD
tel 0171 426 5800, fax 0171 251 1314

SECTION 11: USEFUL INFORMATION

Glossary

Adjudicator: The person who hears and decides an immigration appeal at first instance. Adjudicators hear cases on their own, in centres around the country. In most cases it is possible to apply for leave to appeal to the Immigration Appeal Tribunal against an adjudicator's decision.

Association Agreement: A treaty signed between the European Community and another country, which gives the nationals of the other country preferential access to the countries of the EEA, mainly as self-employed or business people. There are such agreements with Bulgaria, the Czech Republic, Poland, Romania and Slovakia. An Agreement with Hungary gives access to business people only and with Turkey gives extra rights to Turks who have been employed in the EEA for more than a year. Agreements with Estonia, Latvia, Lithuania and Slovenia are currently being ratified.

Asylum: Allowing a person to stay in the UK because of the danger he or she would face if returned. Often used as another word for *refugee* status (see below).

Asylum Screening Unit: The Home Office department which registers people applying for asylum after entering the UK, and carries out fingerprinting and identity checks.

Asylum-seeker: A person requesting *asylum* or *refugee* status in the UK, whose application has not yet been decided.

Benefits Agency: The administrative branch of the Department of Social Security (DSS), which makes benefits payments.

British citizens

There are two kinds of British citizens: British citizens **otherwise than by descent** and British citizens **by descent**. The difference is that the first group can pass British citizenship on automatically to their children born outside the UK and the second cannot.

British citizens otherwise than by descent are people who acquired their citizenship in the UK, either because they were born in the UK, or because they registered or naturalised in the UK, or because they are people who were British nationals because of their connection to a British colony or ex-colony but had been settled and had spent more than five years in the UK before 1983.

British citizens by descent are people born outside the UK who became British automatically at birth because their father, or in some circumstances their paternal grandfather, or (if they were born on or after 1 January 1983) their mother or father was a British citizen. A British citizen by descent can never change his or her status to become a British citizen otherwise than by descent.

British Dependent Territories citizens: These are people who are British because of their connection with a place that is still a British *colony*. They may have been born, adopted, registered or naturalised in that colony and can retain British Dependent Territories

Glossary • 357

citizenship as long as the colony continues. When the colony gains independence or ceases to exist, people from that territory lose British Dependent Territories citizenship as the dependent territory no longer exists.

British Nationals (Overseas): This status was created for British Dependent Territories citizens from Hong Kong who will be able to keep this British nationality status when Hong Kong reverts to China on 1 July 1997.

British Overseas citizens: These are people who were born in a place that used to be a British colony but who did not qualify for citizenship under the law of the new independent country or of any other country and therefore retained their British nationality.

British protected persons: These are people who are from a country which used to be a British protectorate, protected state or trust territory rather than a colony, but who did not gain the citizenship of the new independent country or of any other country.

British subjects: These are people who are from a country which used to be a British colony, who never became citizens of the UK and Colonies under the British Nationality Act 1948 and who did not gain citizenship of the new independent country or of any other country. Before 1983, the term 'British subject' meant exactly the same as 'Commonwealth citizen' but it is now only used for this small group of people.

Carriers' Liability Act: The 1987 legislation which allows the Home Office to fine airlines and shipping companies £2000 for each person they bring to the UK who does not have valid entry documents.

Certified case: Under the Asylum and Immigration Act 1996 the Home Secretary may 'certify' some asylum applications. The effect of this is that if the application is refused either the person only has a *fast-track appeal* right in the UK or no appeal until after being returned to a third country.

Colony: A territory which is ruled by another country and is not yet independent. The largest British colony is Hong Kong, which will return to China on 1 July 1997. The others are Anguilla, Bermuda, British Antarctica, British Indian Ocean Territory, Cayman Islands, Falkland Islands, Gibraltar, Montserrat, Pitcairn Island, St Helena, Turks and Caicos Islands, Virgin Islands, Cyprus sovereign base areas.

Commissioner's decisions: Decisions made on social security appeals, at an equivalent level to the Immigration Appeal Tribunal. They are cited as CIS/reference number/year.

Common Travel Area: The UK, Republic of Ireland, Isle of Man and the Channel Islands. There are no immigration controls at the borders between them and people's passports are not stamped with leave to enter.

Commonwealth citizens: Most ex-British colonies when they gained independence decided to join this loose group of countries, headed by the British monarch, to retain contacts, trade preferences etc. Commonwealth citizens still retain some immigration-law advantage over others.

All kinds of British nationals, except British protected persons, are Commonwealth citizens. So are citizens of the following countries, with their dates of independence or joining in brackets: Antigua and Barbuda (1 November 1981), Australia (1 January 1901), Bahamas (10 July 1973), Bangladesh (26 March 1971, as East Pakistan 15 August 1947), Barbados (30 November 1966), Belize (21 September 1981), Botswana (30 September 1966), Cameroon (joined 1 November 1995), Canada (1 July 1867), Cyprus (16 August 1960, joined 13 March 1961), Dominica (3 November 1978), Gambia (18 February 1965), Ghana (6 March 1957), Grenada (7 February 1974), Guyana (26 May 1966), India (15 August 1947), Jamaica (6 August 1962), Kenya (12 December 1963), Kiribati (12 July 1979), Lesotho (4 October 1966), Malawi (6 July 1964), Malaysia (31 August 1957), Malta

(21 September 1964), Mauritius (12 March 1968), Mozambique (joined 14 November 1995), Namibia (joined 21 March 1990), Nauru (31 January 1968, joined 31 January 1980), Nevis (19 September 1983), New Zealand (26 September 1907), Nigeria (1 October 1960), Pakistan (15 August 1947), Papua New Guinea (16 September 1975), St Kitts (19 September 1983), St Lucia (22 February 1979), St Vincent and the Grenadines (27 October 1979), Seychelles (29 June 1976), Sierra Leone (27 April 1961), Singapore (3 June 1959, was part of Malaysia from 16 September 1963 until 8 August 1965), Solomon Islands (7 July 1978), South Africa (rejoined 31 May 1994), Sri Lanka (4 February 1948), Swaziland (6 September 1968), Tanzania (9 December 1961), Tonga (4 June 1970), Trinidad and Tobago (31 August 1962), Tuvalu (1 October 1978), Uganda (9 October 1962), Vanuatu (30 July 1980), Western Samoa (1 January 1962, joined 28 August 1970), Zambia (24 October 1964), Zimbabwe (18 April 1980).

Deportation means sending a person out of the UK under an order signed by the Home Secretary, after the person has remained in the UK without permission, or broken another condition of stay, or has been convicted of a serious criminal offence, or because the Home Secretary has decided on public policy or national security grounds that the person's presence is 'not conducive to the public good'. The person cannot return unless the order has first been revoked.

Document Reception Centre: a department of the Home Office set up solely to decide whether applications for variation of leave made on the new forms are valid and to return those considered invalid as soon as possible.

Domicile means the country to which people feel they belong and in which they intend to spend the rest of their life. Normally people are considered to have a 'domicile of origin', usually the country in which they were born and grew up. This can only be changed by a conscious decision to settle and stay in another country and thus acquire a 'domicile of choice'. Questions asked to determine the domicile of people who have left their countries of origin often include where they hope to die and be buried/cremated. Domicile is important in deciding which countries' laws affect a particular person, for example in deciding whether a person is capable of contracting a polygamous marriage, or of adopting a child in a particular country. People's immigration status has no direct connection with their domicile.

ECHR: European Convention on Human Rights, an international instrument agreed by the Council of Europe, a wider grouping than the EEA. Individuals who believe that the British government has contravened their rights under this Convention can complain to the European Commission of Human Rights. If the Commission finds the case 'admissible', and the parties cannot arrive at a 'friendly settlement', the case is referred to the European Court of Human Rights for a decision. Both the Commission and the Court are based in Strasbourg.

EEA: The European Economic Area, which covers the countries of the European Union (EU, previously the European Community) and three other European countries, Iceland, Liechtenstein and Norway. The countries of the EU are Austria, Belgium, Denmark, Finland, France, Germany, Greece, Ireland, Italy, Luxembourg, the Netherlands, Portugal, Spain, Sweden and the UK. (Austria. Finland and Sweden joined from 1 January 1995). Nationals of all these countries have free movement in all 18 countries.

Entry clearance officers: Officials at British posts overseas who deal with immigration applications there. In a visa country, they may be known as visa officers, in a non-visa Commonwealth country as entry certificate officers.

EU: European Union, *see* EEA.

Exceptional leave to enter or remain: People who apply for refugee status in the UK and are refused, but the Home Office does not think it is safe for them to return for the time being, may be granted exceptional leave to enter or remain in the UK. The Home Office may also grant exceptional leave to other people who have strong compassionate reasons for needing to remain. It is entirely outside the immigration rules, at the discretion of the Home Office.

Fast-track appeal: Appeal against refusal of asylum, where the Home Office has *certified* the asylum claim to be one which will only have this type of appeal, with shortened time limits. People can appeal to a special adjudicator, but if the case is dismissed there is no right to apply for leave to appeal to the Tribunal.

Green books: The popular name for the Immigration Appeals Reports (Imm AR).

Green form legal aid: The system under which solicitors are paid through the Legal Aid Board for legal advice and assistance they give on matters of English law (pink form in Scotland), when the client qualifies under a strict means test. It is available for dealing with the immigration authorities and for appeal preparation, but not for representation at immigration or asylum appeals.

Habitual residence: A term used in social security law in order to exclude some people from eligibility for income support, housing benefit and council tax benefit and from council housing. As well as the history of a person's residence here, it also takes into account their employment record and their intentions. See also *ordinary residence*.

Illegal entrant means a person who immigration officers believe has entered the UK illegally, either by bypassing immigration control altogether, or by deception as to his or her identity or reasons for coming to the UK, or by entering in breach of a current deportation order.

IM2: The application forms, obtainable from British posts overseas, to apply for entry clearance to the UK. The basic form, filled in by all who apply for entry clearance, is IM2A. It is available in English, French, German, Russian, Spanish and Turkish. Many applicants must also fill in another form; those applying for settlement for the first time also fill in IM2B; those coming for work or business IM2C; those who have the right of abode, IM2D; those who have previously been refused entry clearance or entry, IM2E and those previously required to leave the UK, IM2F.

Imm AR: The Immigration Appeals Reports, published quarterly, but with page numbers continuing throughout a year. They contain selected decisions of the High Court, Court of Appeal, Scottish Court of Session, House of Lords and of the Immigration Appeal Tribunal. They are also known as the 'green books'. Cases are usually cited by their name, year of publication and page, for example, *Wirdestedt*, (1990 Imm AR 20).

Immigration Appeal Tribunal: The second tier of the immigration appeals system. The Tribunal will grant leave to appeal from the decision of an *adjudicator* if it decides there is an arguable point of law in a case, or other arguments which should be heard. It is a three-person body. It is possible to apply for leave to move for judicial review against its decision not to hear a case and to the Court of Appeal after it has heard and dismissed a case. All cases have their own reference number.

Immigration officer: An official at a British port of entry dealing with immigration applications who decides on granting and refusing leave to enter, and what conditions should be attached to any leave granted.

Immigration rules: The rules of practice, published by the Home Office, on how immigration officials should implement the immigration and asylum laws. They have the force of law and are interpreted by the Home Office and through decisions of the Immigration Appeal Tribunal. If they are published while Parliament is sitting, they are called House of Commons papers, such as HC 395; if in a Parliamentary recess, they are Command papers, such as Cm 3365.

Indefinite leave: Leave to enter or remain in the UK without any time limit. If there is no time limit, no other immigration conditions can be put on the person's stay either. A person who has indefinite leave to enter or remain is *settled* (see below) in the UK.

Judicial review: A means of asking the High Court to rule on the legal validity of decision-making by a public body. It may be the only way of contesting an immigration refusal when there is no right of appeal, or an asylum refusal when there is no Tribunal appeal or it has refused leave to appeal.

K4 Committee: This committee is set up under the Justice and Home Affairs pillar of the Maastricht Treaty on European Union. It consists of senior officials of the member states' governments, and carries out work in relation to justice and home affairs matters, which includes third-country migration.

Leave to enter/remain: Permission given by immigration officials to people to enter or remain in the UK. It may be indefinite or limited.

Limited leave: Permission to enter or remain in the UK which has a time limit, and may have other conditions attached to it.

Naturalisation: A process of applying for British nationality. The application is at the discretion of the Home Office and can be made on the basis of residence in the UK, marriage to a British partner or Crown service. Naturalisation and *registration* (see below) are both ways of gaining British citizenship; the citizenship obtained is the same whichever process is used.

Ordinary residence: This is defined in the case of *Shah* (sometimes called *Akbarali*) in the House of Lords (1983 2 AC 309), as the place where someone is normally living for the time being. Lord Scarman held that it means 'the person must be normally and habitually resident here, apart from temporary or occasional absences of long or short duration...a man's abode in a particular place or country which he has adopted voluntarily and for settled purposes as part of the regular order of his life for the time being, whether of short or long duration.' If a person is not legally in a country, that period does not count as ordinary residence. Reasons for residence can include 'education, business or profession, employment, health, family or merely love of the place'.

People can be ordinarily resident in the UK without being settled here – for example, students, work permit holders and au pairs. It is not an immigration status and has no direct connection to this; the term is also used in other areas of law, including the National Health Service and some benefits regulations. Ordinary residence may change; the Home Office could argue that several months' residence abroad, particularly if the person had taken a job or given up a home in the UK, had broken ordinary residence in the UK. However, it is possible to be ordinarily resident in more than one country at a time, so such decisions can be challenged.

Overstayer means a person who was allowed in to the UK for a limited period but who has remained longer than the time allowed without permission from the Home Office.

Patriality is another word for *right of abode*. It was first used in the Immigration Act 1971 but was replaced by the term 'right of abode' in the British Nationality Act 1981.

Permanent stay: Another phrase meaning *settled* (see below).

Permit-free employment: A list of jobs which people may come to the UK to do without the employers needing to get work permits from the Department for Education and Employment. Permission is obtained direct from the Home Office or through the British post in the worker's country of origin.

Person from abroad: A term first used by the Department of Social Security Benefits Agency meaning a person who is not eligible to claim income support at the normal rate. It has now been extended to other benefits, including housing benefit and council tax benefit.

Pillars: One way of explaining the significance of the Maastricht Treaty on European Union is to consider the Union as the roof of a building, supported by three pillars. One pillar is the European Community (which includes economic policy and the free movement of EEA nationals), the second is the Common Foreign and Security Policy (CFSP) and the third Justice and Home Affairs matters (which includes third-country-national migration).

Police registration certificate: The certificate provided by the police to those non-Commonwealth, non-EEA citizens who are required to register their personal details with them.

Political asylum: Another word used for *refugee* status (see below).

Public funds: Public funds for immigration purposes are attendance allowance, child benefit, council tax benefit, disability living allowance, disability working allowance, family credit, housing benefit, income-based jobseeker's allowance, income support, invalid care allowance and severe disablement allowance, and housing under Part II or Part III of the Housing Act 1985, Part I or Part II of the Housing (Scotland) Act 1987 or Part II of the Housing (Northern Ireland) Order 1988 (all council housing provisions).

Quota voucher *see* Special quota voucher.

Re-entry visa: These no longer exist: they were abolished from 16 May 1991. Visa nationals visiting the UK who want to travel in and out must either obtain multiple-entry visas initially or apply for new visas when they are outside the UK.

Refugee: The United Nations Convention relating to the Status of Refugees defines a refugee as a person who, 'owing to a well-founded fear of being persecuted for reasons of race, religion, nationality, membership of a particular social group or political opinion is outside the country of his nationality and is unable, or owing to such fear, is unwilling to avail himself of the protection of that country; or who, not having a nationality and being outside the country of his former habitual residence... is unable or, owing to such a fear, is unwilling to return to it.' When the Home Office recognises people as refugees, it grants them asylum in the UK, and normally gives them leave to remain for four years initially.

Registration: There are three distinct immigration/nationality law uses of this term.
1 A process of applying for British nationality. The word is now used for any child applying for British nationality and for a person who holds any other kind of British nationality applying to become a British citizen. Registration and *naturalisation* (see above) are both ways of gaining British nationality; the nationality obtained through either process is the same.
2 Registering the birth of a child at a British post overseas. A child born outside the UK to a British citizen parent who was not him- or herself born in the UK may be registered within one year of birth to become a British citizen by descent.
3 Registering with the police. People who are not Commonwealth or EEA citizens, who are over 16 and who have been allowed to remain in the UK for more than six months but are not settled may be required to register with the police. This means going to the local police station, or the Aliens Registration Office in London, with the passport, two passport-sized photos and details of address and occupation, registering these details with the police and paying a fee (see appendix).

Removal means the procedure for sending a person refused entry, or a person being treated as an illegal entrant, away from the UK. People have no right of appeal against removal until they have left the UK. There is no formal order made against them so they are able to apply to return, but will have to fit into the immigration rules.

Residence permit: A document issued by the Home Office to EEA nationals to confirm their right to live in the UK.

Returning residents are people who are *settled* in the UK and are returning to the UK within two years of departure. They should be admitted for an indefinite period, provided the immigration officers are satisfied that they intend to return to stay permanently.

Right of abode means being free of immigration control and able to enter the UK freely at any time, after no matter how long an absence. It is more than simply having the right to live in the UK, or the right to stay indefinitely. All British citizens have the right of abode. So do some Commonwealth citizens – people who were born before 1 January 1983 and had a parent born in the UK (when the parent is the father, he must have been married to the mother) and women who were Commonwealth citizens before 1 January 1983 and were married before that date to a man who was born, registered or naturalised in the UK, or who is a Commonwealth citizen with a parent born in the UK, as above.

Right of readmission: The right of British nationals who are not British citizens but who have been given *indefinite leave* to enter or remain in the UK to return for settlement after any length of absence.

Schengen group: This comprises all EU countries except the UK, Ireland and Denmark. The group has planned since 1988 to establish a common immigration policy and common border controls, with no internal border checks. The agreement came into effect on 26 March 1995 for seven countries. It is expected to come fully into effect for all Europe in 2004.

Settled means someone who is legally in the UK, without any conditions (for example, they have no limit on the time they can remain, and no restrictions on working or the sort of work they can do while in the UK). Other terms used for this are *'permanent stay'* or *'indefinite leave'*. People who have lived in the UK for a long time, or who came with their parents are likely to be settled (as long as they are in the country legally). Most (but not all) settled people have a stamp in their passports saying that they have 'indefinite leave to remain in the UK'.

Special adjudicator: Adjudicator who hears asylum appeals. In December 1996 there were 29 full-time and 97 part-time special adjudicators.

Special quota voucher: The permission granted to certain British nationals, who are not British citizens, to come to settle in the UK. The system was set up in 1968, after the Commonwealth Immigrants Act 1968 removed the rights of British people without a connection by birth or descent with Britain itself to come to Britain. In order to qualify under the scheme, people must have no other nationality but British, be 'heads of households', have some connection with East Africa and be under pressure to leave the country in which they are currently living.

Sponsorship: The act of supporting financially people who are applying to come to the UK. Sponsors may be requested to sign a formal *undertaking* (see below).

Standard acknowledgement letter (SAL): A letter issued by the Home Office or immigration service to people seeking asylum. People who applied for asylum on entry to the UK have a document called SAL1 and people who applied after entry have SAL2s. SALs may be used as identity documents in establishing entitlement to benefits and other purposes.

Temporary admission: A kind of limbo state, used as an alternative to detention. While immigration officers are considering whether to allow someone in at a port of entry, or after refusal of entry and before removal, or when a person is being treated as an illegal entrant, he or she may either be detained or released on temporary admission. If released, the person has not been granted formal leave to enter the UK, and can be recalled and detained at any time. *Asylum-seekers* may be on temporary admission for long periods.

Third country: This is used in two distinct senses.

1. A country which is not a member of the EEA. A Jamaican settled in the UK or a Moroccan living in France might be called a 'third country national'.
2. A country through which an asylum-seeker has travelled before reaching the country where he or she seeks asylum. A Somali whose flight from Somalia touched down for some hours in Rome before continuing to the UK could be refused asylum here on the grounds she had travelled through a third country, Italy, and be removed there to claim asylum.

Transit visas: People of certain nationalities always need visas, even when in transit through the UK for up to 48 hours. These countries are Afghanistan, China, Eritrea, Ethiopia, Ghana, Iran, Iraq, Libya, Nigeria, Somalia, Sri Lanka, Turkey, Uganda and Zaire.

Undertaking: A formal statement signed by a person living in the UK that he or she will support another person, usually a relative, who is applying to come to or to remain in the UK. It means that the person about whom it was signed is not eligible to claim income support, housing benefit or council tax benefit for five years after it was signed, or after the person was given leave to enter or remain in the UK on this basis, whichever is the later, unless the signer of the undertaking dies.

Visa nationals: People who always need to get entry clearance in advance of travelling to the UK, for whatever purpose, unless they are *returning residents* or are returning within a period of earlier leave granted for more than six months. Countries whose citizens are visa nationals in January 1997 are: Afghanistan, Albania, Algeria, Angola, Armenia, Azerbaijhan, Bahrain, Bangladesh, Belarus, Benin, Bhutan, Bosnia-Herzegovina, Bulgaria, Burkina Faso, Burma, Burundi, Cambodia, Cameroon, Cape Verde, Central African Republic, Chad, China, Comoros, Congo, Cuba, Djibouti, Dominican Republic, Egypt, Equatorial Guinea, Eritrea, Ethiopia, Fiji, Gabon, Gambia, Georgia, Ghana, Guinea, Guinea-Bissau, Guyana, Haiti, India, Indonesia, Iran, Iraq, Ivory Coast, Jordan, Kazakhstan, Kenya, Kyrgyzstan, Korea (North), Kuwait, Laos, Lebanon, Liberia, Libya, Macedonia, Madagascar, the Maldives, Mali, Mauritania, Mauritius, Moldova, Mongolia, Montenegro, Morocco, Mozambique, Nepal, Niger, Nigeria, Oman, Pakistan, Papua New Guinea, Peru, Philippines, Qatar, Romania, Russia, Rwanda, Sao Tome e Principe, Saudi Arabia, Senegal, Serbia, Sierra Leone, Somalia, Sri Lanka, Sudan, Surinam, Syria, Taiwan, Tajikistan, Tanzania, Thailand, Togo, Tunisia, Turkey, Turkmenistan, Uganda, Ukraine, United Arab Emirates, Uzbekistan, Vietnam, Yemen, Zaire, Zambia.

'Without foundation' case: Under the Asylum and Immigration Appeals Act 1993, when the Home Office believed an asylum application 'does not raise any issue as to the UK's obligations under the Convention or is otherwise frivolous or vexatious' it could be certified 'without foundation', and the person would then only have a fast-track appeal against refusal. The most common example was a person who had travelled through a third country on the way to the UK. Under the Asylum and Immigration Act 1996, the concept was widened and they are now known as '*certified*' cases.

Work permits: The permission gained by employers to employ a worker from overseas who does not otherwise qualify to come to live in the UK. The Department for Education and Employment issues permits to employers, not to workers, to employ a named person in a specific job. Any change of job means the new employers must apply for a new permit.

SECTION 11: USEFUL INFORMATION

Appendices

1 RELEVANT ACTS AND RULES

Immigration Act 1971	Asylum and Immigration Appeals Act 1993
British Nationality Act 1981	Immigration (European Economic Area) Order 1994
Immigration (Carriers' Liability) Act 1987	Asylum and Immigration Act 1996
	Immigration Appeals (Procedure) Rules 1984
Immigration Act 1988	Asylum Appeals (Procedure) Rules 1996

Immigration rules in force at January 1997

HC 395	Statement of changes in immigration rules, 23 May 1994, in effect from 1 October 1994. The main rules, as referred to in the text.
Cm 2663, 20 September 1994	Introduced visas for Ivory Coast and Sierra Leone
HC 797, 26 October 1995	Introduced visas for the Gambia
Cmnd 3073, 4 January 1996	Introduced visas for Tanzania
HC 274, 7 March 1996	Introduced visas for Kenya
HC 329, 2 April 1996	Added disability benefits to the definition of 'public funds' for immigration purposes; provided for compulsory immigration application forms; introduced visas for Bahrain, the Dominican Republic, Fiji, Guyana, Kuwait, the Maldives, Mauritius, Niger, Papua New Guinea, Peru, Qatar, Surinam, the United Arab Emirates and Zambia
Cmnd 3365, 30 August 1996	Amended the rules on asylum-seekers and on family deportation in line with the provisions of the Asylum and Immigration Act 1996; provided that a formal condition requiring people to maintain and accommodate themselves without recourse to public funds could be imposed on their stay
HC 31, 31 October 1996	Added child benefit, all council housing and income-based jobseeker's allowance to the public funds definition; imposed a requirement to maintain and accommodate themselves without recourse to public funds on more categories of people

2 DELAYS

Entry clearance applications

In July 1996 the waiting times for interviews for settlement entry clearance, at selected posts, were: Philippines, 10 weeks; Ghana, 13 working days; Jamaica, 7 weeks; Thailand, 5 weeks; Nigeria: Lagos, 38 days, Abuja, same day.

In the countries of the Indian subcontinent there are separate queues. In July 1996 the delays (in months) were:

	Q1	Q2	Q3	Q4
Islamabad	6	6	6	12
Dhaka	3	7	5	8
New Delhi	0	3.5	5.75	10.5
Bombay	0	2.5	2.5	6
Madras	1.5	1.5	1.5	1.5

Q1 People with a claim to the right of abode, dependent relatives over 70 years old, special compassionate cases (not defined further)

Q2 All spouses, and all children under 18

Q3 Fiance(é)s and other relatives applying for the first time

Q4 Reapplicants

Applications for citizenship

Applications for naturalisation completed in December 1996 had taken 12–15 months on average. Applications for registration of adults and children completed in December 1996 had taken 6–9 months on average.

3 SELECTED FEES, as at January 1997

The Home Office or Foreign and Commonwealth Office may raise fees at very short notice. It is rare for these rises to receive much publicity unless they are unusually steep.

Applying for entry clearance

All entry clearance fees are non-refundable. The Foreign Office raised fees in December 1994 and August 1996 and stated that there would be another rise to bring fees up to a level to cover costs by mid-1997.

Visitor (including a transit visitor who will be entering the UK), student, prospective student, working holidaymaker, au pair, employment or self-employment for less than six months, returning resident
 single-entry £33
 six-month multiple entry £45
 one-year multiple entry £55
 two-year multiple entry £65
 five-year multiple entry £130

Transit visa (not entering UK) £25

Work permit or permit-free employment or self-employed or sole representative, over 6 months £50

Business or independent means £50

Family members of any of these people accompanying them or coming to join them pay the same fee as their sponsor.

Commonwealth citizens with UK-born grandparent £50

Settlement (to accompany or join a relative already settled in the UK) £210

Certificate of entitlement (from abroad) £210

Other fees in the UK

Fee for a police registration certificate £34

Fee for DNA testing through Cellmark Diagnostics £145 plus VAT per sample of blood tested, £2 plus VAT for transport of each sample to the UK

Fee for DNA testing through University Diagnostics £381 plus VAT for up to 3 samples tested, £100 plus VAT for each additional sample

Fees continued

Fee for a certificate of entitlement to the right of abode from the Home Office £20

British passport (standard) £18

British passport (jumbo) £27

Home Office travel document,
refugees £18
people granted exceptional leave, stateless people £67

Applying for British citizenship

Registration (for children under 18 and other kinds of British nationals applying for British citizenship) £120

Naturalisation on the grounds of marriage to a British citizen £120

Naturalisation on the grounds of residence in the UK £150

Renunciation of British citizenship £20

Resumption of British citizenship after renunciation £20

4 DESIGNATED POSTS

The Foreign and Commonwealth Office designates some British high commissions and embassies abroad to offer a full entry clearance service and some only a partial service, mainly for refugee family reunion and official visits. This list was current at December 1996.

Posts which offer a full entry clearance service

Country	Post	Country	Post
Angola	Luanda	Canada	Ottawa
Argentina	Buenos Aires	Chile	Santiago
Australia	Canberra	China	Peking
Austria	Vienna	Colombia	Bogota
Bahamas	Nassau	Costa Rica	San José
Bahrain	Bahrain	Croatia	Zagreb
Bangladesh	Dhaka	Cuba	Havana
Barbados	Bridgetown	Cyprus	Nicosia
(also deals with applications from Anguilla, Antigua and Barbuda, British Virgin Islands, Dominica, Grenada, Montserrat, St Kitts and Nevis, St Lucia, St Vincent and the Grenadines, by visiting the islands periodically)		Czech Republic	Prague
		Denmark	Copenhagen
		Ecuador	Quito
		Egypt	Cairo
		El Salvador	San Salvador
Belarus	Minsk	Ethiopia	Addis Ababa
Belgium	Brussels	Falkland Islands	Stanley
Belize	Belmopan	Fiji	Suva
Bermuda	Hamilton	Finland	Helsinki
Bolivia	La Paz	France	Paris
Botswana	Gaborone	The Gambia	Banjul
Brazil	Rio de Janeiro	Germany	Düsseldorf
Brunei	Bandar Seri Begawan	Ghana	Accra
Bulgaria	Sofia	Gibraltar	Gibraltar
Burma (Myanmar)	Rangoon	Greece	Athens
Cambodia	Phnom Penh	Guatemala	Guatemala City
(applications considered at Bangkok)		Guyana	Georgetown
Cameroon	Yaoundé	Honduras	Tegucigalpa

Country	Post	Country	Post
Hong Kong	Hong Kong British Trade Commission	Portugal	Lisbon
		Qatar	Doha
Hungary	Budapest	Romania	Bucharest
Iceland	Reykjavik	Russian Federation	Moscow, St Petersburg
India	Bombay, Calcutta, Madras, New Delhi	Saudi Arabia	Jedda, Riyadh
Indonesia	Jakarta	Senegal	Dakar
Irish Republic	Dublin	Seychelles	Victoria
Israel	Tel Aviv	Sierra Leone	Freetown
Italy	Rome	Singapore	Singapore
Ivory Coast	Abidjan	Slovak Republic	Bratislava
Jamaica	Kingston	Solomon Islands	Honiara
Japan	Tokyo	South Africa	Pretoria
Jordan	Amman	Spain	Madrid
Kenya	Nairobi	Sri Lanka	Colombo
Korea (South)	Seoul	Sudan	Khartoum
Kuwait	Kuwait	Swaziland	Mbabane
Lebanon	Beirut	Sweden	Stockholm
Lesotho	Maseru	Switzerland	Geneva
Luxembourg	Luxembourg	Syria	Damascus
Madagascar	Antananarivo	Tanzania	Dar es Salaam
Malawi	Lilongwe	Thailand	Bangkok
Malaysia	Kuala Lumpur	Tonga	Nuku'alofa
Malta	Valletta	Trinidad and Tobago	Port of Spain
Mauritius	Port Louis		
Mexico	Mexico City	Tunisia	Tunis
Mongolia	Ulaanbaatar	Turkey	Istanbul
Morocco	Casablanca	Uganda	Kampala
Mozambique	Maputo	Ukraine	Kiev
Namibia	Windhoek	United Arab Emirates	Abu Dhabi, Dubai
Nepal	Kathmandu		
Netherlands	Amsterdam	United States	Chicago, Houston, Los Angeles, New York, Washington
New Zealand	Wellington		
Nicaragua	Managua	Uruguay	Montevideo
Nigeria	Lagos, Abuja	Vanuatu	Port Vila
Norway	Oslo	Venezuela	Caracas
Oman	Muscat	Vietnam	Hanoi, Ho Chi Minh City
Pakistan	Islamabad, Karachi		
Panama	Panama City	Yemen	Sana'a
Papua New Guinea	Port Moresby	Former Yugoslavia	Belgrade
Peru	Lima	Zaire	Kinshasa
Philippines	Manila	Zambia	Lusaka
Poland	Warsaw	Zimbabwe	Harare

Limited service

The following posts accept applications for diplomatic/official, medical and business visits and refugee family reunion only. The posts in the countries of the former USSR normally accept applications only from residents of the country. People applying for ordinary visit visas may apply at any designated post in another country.

Country	Post	Country	Post
Algeria	Algiers	Latvia	Riga
Others should apply at Tunis or Paris.		Libya	Tripoli
Armenia	Yerevan	Others should apply at Valletta.	
Azerbaijhan	Baku	Lithuania	Vilnius
Dominican Republic	Santo Domingo	Macedonia	Skopje
Others should apply at Kingston.		Others should apply at Belgrade or Sofia.	
Estonia	Tallinn	Taiwan	
Iran	Tehran	British Trade and Cultural Office in Taipei deals with visit, student and business visa applications only.	
Others should apply at Istanbul, Karachi or Nicosia.			
Kazakhstan	Almaty	Uzbekistan	Tashkent
Also deals with residents of Kyrgyzstan.		Also deals with residents of Tajikistan.	

Countries where there is no full entry clearance service

Applicants for visit visas may apply at any designated post. Others should apply at the post listed.

Country	Apply at	Country	Apply at
Albania	Rome	Guinea	Dakar
Andorra	Madrid	Guinea-Bissau	Dakar
Benin	Lagos	Haiti	Kingston
Bhutan	Calcutta	Kiribati	Suva
Bosnia-Herzegovina	Zagreb	Korea (North)	Peking
Burkina Faso	Abidjan	Kyrgyzstan	Almaty
Burundi	most accessible post	Laos	Bangkok
Cape Verde	Dakar	Liberia	Abidjan
Cayman Islands	Kingston	Liechtenstein	Geneva
Central African Republic	Yaoundé	Macao	Hong Kong
Chad	Lagos or Abuja	Maldives	Colombo
Comoros	Antananarivo	Mali	Dakar
Congo	Kinshasa	Marshall Islands	Suva
Djibouti	Addis Ababa	Mauritania	Casablanca
Equatorial Guinea	Yaoundé, or most accessible post	Micronesia	Suva
		Moldöva	Moscow
Eritrea	Addis Ababa	Monaco	Paris
Estonia	Moscow	Nauru	Suva
Gabon	Yaoundé, or most accessible post	Netherlands Antilles	Caracas or Amsterdam
		Niger	Abidjan
Georgia	Moscow	Palau	most accessible post

Appendices • 369

Country	Apply at	Country	Apply at
Paraguay	Rio de Janeiro	Suriname	Georgetown
Rwanda	most accessible post	Tajikistan	Tashkent
San Marino	Rome	Togo	Accra
Sao Tomé e Principe	Luanda	Turks and Caicos Islands	Nassau
Sikkim	Calcutta	Tuvalu	Suva
Slovak Republic	Prague	Western Samoa	Wellington
Slovenia	Zagreb		

Three posts were temporarily closed: Kabul, Baghdad and Mogadishu. People from those countries applying for visit visas may apply at any designated post. Other applicants from Afghanistan should apply at Islamabad, from Iraq at Amman and from Somalia at Nairobi or Addis Ababa.

5 STANDARD FORMS AND LETTERS

Pages 370–73	Entry clearance application form IM2A
Page 374	Undertaking of support, from application form SET(F)
Page 375	Grant of temporary admission, IS 96
Pages 376–77	Letter granting one year's leave to remain as a spouse, RON 124
Page 378	Letter granting indefinite leave to remain, RON 60
Pages 379–80	Letter granting exceptional leave to remain, GEN 19
Page 381	Refusal of leave to remain, with right of appeal, APP 101A
Page 382	Standard letter sent after appeal has been dismissed, RON 67
Pages 383–84	Decision to make a deportation order, APP 104
Pages 385–91	Application form SET(M)

ENTRY CLEARANCE APPLICATION FORM — IM2A/page 1

THIS FORM IS SUPPLIED FREE OF CHARGE

IM2A (revised 10/96)

Application for United Kingdom entry clearance

Reference:

- ☞ Please complete the form in black ink and tick the boxes which apply.
- ☞ Short stay applicants must complete all the questions on this form.
- ☞ Long stay applicants must complete questions 1–22 and any additional forms stated below.

Please send with this form :-
- ☞ the correct fee (*entry clearance fees will not be refunded*)
- ☞ two passport-sized photographs (*not more than six months old*) and
- ☞ your current passport.

A separate form should be completed by every person intending to travel *unless* you are a dependant under 16 included on your parent's Passport.

⇨ All applicants must sign this form on page 4

RECENT PHOTOGRAPHS TO BE ATTACHED HERE

1 Reason for travelling to the UK *(please tick appropriate boxes)* *(please specify)*
Short stay: Visitor Private ☐ Official ☐ Business ☐ Student ☐ Other ☐

Type of entry clearance required   Transit ☐   Single entry ☐   Multiple entry ☐

Settlement as: spouse/fiancé(e)/other relative ☐   *Please also complete form IM2B*
Long stay: Permit free employment/Retired Person of Independent Means/ Investor/ Working Holidaymaker/Work permit holder or to establish a business ☐   *Please also complete form IM2C*
Certificate of entitlement, UK ancestry ☐   *Please also complete form IM2D*
Dependant of any applicant in long stay categories ☐
Returning resident ☐

2 Are you applying as a non-EEA dependant of an EEA national?   Yes ☐ No ☐
If 'Yes', are you travelling with EEA national/joining EEA national?   Yes ☐ No ☐

3 Full name   *(as written in your passport, please write in both styles if two scripts have been used)*

4 Other names used now or in the past   *(eg name before marriage)*

5 Date of birth   day month year   **6** Sex M ☐ F ☐   **7** Town and country of birth

8 Your father's full name

9 Your mother's full name

10 Passport or travel document details   Issuing government/authority   Number   Nationality as shown in passport

Document type *(eg ordinary passport)*   Place of issue   Date of issue day month year   Valid until day month year

If you are not travelling on your own passport give the following details:
Name of passport holder   Your relationship to passport holder

Is this your first passport?
If not please provide details of previous passport(s)   No ☐   Yes ☐
Number   Date and Place of Issue   Number   Date and Place of Issue

Only complete this section if dependants included on your passport are travelling with you.
Full name of dependant	Place of birth	Date of birth	Relationship to yourself	Nationality

for bar code

Page 1   Stock Nº CPS 040

Appendices • 371

ENTRY CLEARANCE APPLICATION FORM — IM2A/page 2

11 What is your present job?

12 Where do you work? *(Give details of company/organisation)*
Tel N° — Fax N°
What date did you start this job? *day month year*
What is your annual income?

13 What is your present home address?
Tel N° — Fax N°

14 Please give your permanent address if different from above
Tel N° — Fax N°

15 Are you? Married ☐ Single ☐ Divorced ☐ Widowed ☐ Separated ☐

16 If married, please give details of spouse: Full name of spouse — Date of birth *day month year*
Nationality of spouse — Where is your spouse now? — Where is your spouse normally resident?

17 How many children under 18 years old do you have? — Please give their ages

18 Have you applied to go to the UK before? ☐ No ☐ Yes — If 'Yes', please give dates and places of application

19 Have you visited the UK before? ☐ No ☐ Yes — If 'Yes', please give dates and lengths of each stay

20
a Have you ever been refused a visa/entry clearance at a UK diplomatic mission or Post? ☐ No ☐ Yes — If 'Yes' complete form IM2E
b Have you ever been refused leave to enter on arrival in the UK? ☐ No ☐ Yes — If 'Yes' complete form IM2E
c Have you ever been deported, removed or otherwise required to leave the UK? ☐ No ☐ Yes
d Have you ever been refused a visa for another country? ☐ No ☐ Yes — If 'Yes' name country
e Have you ever been deported from another country? ☐ No ☐ Yes — If 'Yes' name country
f Do you have any criminal convictions in UK or elsewhere? ☐ No ☐ Yes
g Have you ever been a charge on public funds in the UK? ☐ No ☐ Yes

21 Country of normal residence — Residence Permit n° *(if any)* — Date of issue *day month year* — Valid until *day month year*

22 How long do you intend to stay in the UK?

23 What is your proposed date of arrival in the UK? *day month year*

24 Have you bought your ticket? Yes — If 'Yes' what kind of ticket do you have? Single ☐ Open dated ☐ Return confirmed ☐
No — If 'No' what kind of ticket do you intend to buy?

25 (a) Flight no./vessel (if known) — (b) Who is paying/has paid for the ticket?

26 How much money is available to you during your stay? *(evidence of this may be required)* (a) from your own resources — (b) from other sources

27 Do you have any relatives or friends in the UK? ☐ No ☐ Yes

Page 2

ENTRY CLEARANCE APPLICATION FORM — IM2A/page 3

28 Where will you stay in the UK? *Please give details of host/sponsor/contact address.*
☞ If you are staying in a hotel give its name and address
(It is not enough to say c/o Embassy or High Commission)

Full name of sponsor/contact address/hotel

Nationality of sponsor

Address

Telephone number   Resident in UK since   Occupation   Relationship to you

29 Is your visit for business or official reasons? ☐ No ☐ Yes   If 'Yes', give name of UK company/organisation to be visited

30 Are you travelling to another country BEFORE the UK? ☐ No ☐ Yes   If 'Yes', give name of country

Do you have a visa OR residence permit for that country?   *If so, please give details:* Number   Valid until day month year   Issuing Authority

31 To which country are you travelling AFTER the UK?   Name of country

Do you have a visa OR residence permit for that country?   *If so, please give details:* Number   Valid until day month year   Issuing Authority

☞ *This section to be answered by students only*

32 Please give name and address of school/university at which you will study

33 What technical or educational certificates do you hold?   *Any relevant diplomas or certificates should be submitted.*

34 Describe fully the course you wish to follow   *Please submit evidence of acceptance for a course of study, ie degree, 'A' levels etc, and evidence of accommodation.*

35 Who will pay for the course?

36 How many hours of organised study will you do per week?

☞ *This section must be read and signed by all applicants*

☞ An entry clearance can be a Visa or an Entry Certificate.
☞ Even if you hold a valid entry clearance you can still be refused entry into the United Kingdom by an Immigration Officer if he is satisfied that:
  (a) your entry clearance was obtained by false representations or by concealment of relevant facts, whether or not you knew of these actions; or
  (b) a change in circumstances between the date of your application and your arrival in the UK invalidates your entry clearance; or a refusal is justified on the grounds of restricted returnability, medical grounds, criminal record, because you are subject to a deportation order, or your exclusion would be conducive to the public good.
☞ An Immigration Officer can ask anyone to be medically examined on arrival in the UK, if he considers it necessary. You may be required to have a medical examination before your entry clearance is issued.

Drugs Warning: the UK has severe penalties against drug smuggling. Drug traffickers may try to bribe travellers. If you are travelling to the UK avoid any involvement with drugs.

DECLARATION ☞ I have read and understood the notes above.
☞ I declare that the information given in this application is correct to the best of my knowledge and belief.

Information you give will be treated in confidence, but may be disclosed to government departments and agencies to enable them to carry out their functions.

Applicant's Signature   Date

ENTRY CLEARANCE APPLICATION FORM — IM2A/page 4

For office use only

CASH REGISTER DETAILS

CASH REGISTER DETAILS (optional space)

| Fee — Taken/Gratis *(amount)* | Check 1 | Check 2 |

Documents seen:

| Tier 2 Interview *(date)* | Tier 3 Interview *(date)* | Tier 4 Interview *(date)* |

Refer to | Date

Issue/Refuse: Category | Type | Endorsement

Tier | ECO time elapsed *(minutes)*

Authorising ECO | EC number | Issued *(date)*

Page 4

UNDERTAKING OF SUPPORT attached to Home Office application form SET(F)

SPONSORSHIP DECLARATION

Completion of this declaration by the applicant's sponsor is not compulsory but an application will normally be refused if the sponsor refuses to do so. This form should only be completed if the sponsor is resident in the UK.

1. I, ... (name), of
(full postal address - see **Note 4** below) ....
.... (house number and street)
.... (post town)
.... (county)
.... (postcode)
hereby declare that my date of birth is ....
and that I am employed as .... (occupation)
at (full work address) ....
.... (company name and street)
.... (post town)
.... (county)
.... (post code).

My National Insurance number is ....

2. I hereby undertake that if .... (name of sponsored person) who was born in .... on
.... (place and date of birth of sponsored person) is granted leave to enter or remain in the UK I shall be responsible for his/her maintenance and accommodation in the UK throughout the period of leave and any variation of it.

3. During his/her stay in the UK, the sponsored person will reside at: (full postal address) ....
.... (house number and street)
.... (post town)
.... (county)
.... (postcode)

4. I understand that this undertaking shall be made available to the Department of Social Security in the UK who will take appropriate steps to recover from me the cost of any public funds paid to or in respect of the person who is the subject of this undertaking.

Signed:
Date:

FOR OFFICIAL USE ONLY

Certificate

I certify that this document, apart from this certificate, is an undertaking given in pursuance of the Immigration Rules within the meaning of the Immigration Act 1971.

Signed by .... , being a person authorised to make this certificate on behalf of the Secretary of State.

Signature:

Personalised date stamp:

Note 4: The sponsor/principal wage earner should provide evidence that he/she lives at the address claimed. This should be in the form of a certified copy of the deeds or a letter from the Building Society/Bank which holds the mortgage (if the house is privately owned) or a housing association/council rent book or letter from the council certifying that the sponsor lives at the address (if the house is rented from a housing association or the local authority). If the house is privately rented, correspondence addressed to the sponsor at the address should be provided from at least 3 of the following sources:

    (i) Local authority: notification of council tax
    (ii) Utility Company (Gas, water, etc)
    (iii) Local Health Authority
    (iv) Department of Social Service
    (v) Inland Revenue
    (vi) Any other government department.

GRANT OF TEMPORARY ADMISSION IS96

HOME OFFICE
ind
IMMIGRATION SERVICE

Port Reference: IS 96
Home Office Reference:

HM IMMIGRATION OFFICE

Telephone:

IMMIGRATION ACT 1971 – NOTIFICATION OF TEMPORARY ADMISSION TO A PERSON WHO IS LIABLE TO BE DETAINED

To ....

LIABILITY TO DETENTION   A. You are a person who is liable to be detained*

TEMPORARY ADMISSION/ RESTRICTIONS   B. I hereby authorise your (further) temporary admission to the United Kingdom subject to the following restrictions**:

- You must reside at:– ....
  ....
  .... Telephone: ....

- You may not enter employment, paid or unpaid, or engage in any business or profession.

- You must report to:

Tick ☑ as appropriate
- ☐ an Immigration Officer ⎱ at ....
- ☐ the Police   ⎰ ....
- ☐ on .... 19......, at .... hrs.
- ☐ each .... day at .... hrs. until further notice.
- ☐ on a date and at a time to be notified to you in writing
  ....

ANY CHANGE OF RESTRICTION   If these restrictions are to be changed, an Immigration Officer will write to you.

- Although you have been temporarily admitted, you remain liable to be detained
- You have NOT been given leave to enter the United Kingdom within the meaning of the Immigration Act 1971

Date   Immigration Officer

* Paragraph 16 of Schedule 2 to the Act
** Paragraph 21 of Schedule 2 to the Act

(IS 96 Temporary Admission)

LETTER GRANTING ONE YEAR'S LEAVE TO REMAIN AS A SPOUSE — RON 124

Immigration and Nationality Directorate

HOME OFFICE
ind

Lunar House 40 Wellesley Road
Croydon CR9 2BY
Tel 0181-760-
Fax 0181-760-

Your Reference

Our Reference

Date

Dear Mr.

I am writing about your application to remain in the United Kingdom following your marriage.

A person who marries someone settled in this country may be allowed to stay here for an initial period of up to 12 months, provided that the requirements of the Immigration Rules are met. You may now stay in the United Kingdom until   and may set up a business or take employment without a work permit.

During this period you will be expected not to rely on public funds to support yourself, although there is no objection to your spouse receiving any assistance to which he or she is entitled in his or her own right. Public funds means housing under Part III of the Housing Act 1985 and income support, family credit, council tax benefit and housing benefit under Part VII of the Social Security Contributions and Benefits Act 1992 (and, where relevant, equivalent provisions applying in Scotland and Northern Ireland).

You may apply for the time limit attached to your stay to be removed shortly before your stay expires. You should note that this section will not be able to deal with any such application to remove the time limit. <u>Any enquiries about future applications</u> should be made through our Telephone Enquiry Bureau on 0181-686-0688 or by letter to the address above. If you wish to call at the Public Enquiry Office to make an application in person we suggest that you do so <u>during the month before your stay is due to expire</u> as applications made too far in advance of the completion of the 12 month period may need to be taken in for consideration nearer the completion of the 12 month period. You should enclose with any such application your passport and the birth certificate or passport of your spouse for identification purposes.

For the application to be granted, we will need to be satisfied that your marriage has not ended and that you and your spouse both still intend living permanently with each other as husband and wife. If you provide a statement to this effect, signed by you both, this will assist us in considering your application.

We shall also need to ask if you have received any of the public funds described above since the date of this letter, and any information you can provide about this could again save further enquiry on our part. Short term assistance from public funds in an emergency will not lead to a refusal of your application, but if you have received substantial help from public funds, and in particular it is clear that you are unable to

LETTER GRANTING ONE YEAR'S LEAVE TO REMAIN AS A SPOUSE page 2

maintain and accommodate yourself without further help, your application may be refused under the general considerations in paragraph 322 of the Immigration Rules.

If, when you make your further application, you are no longer living with your spouse, your continued stay in this country (including the question of continuing in employment or in business) will normally be subject to your qualifying for further leave in some other capacity under the Immigration Rules. You should therefore explain your current circumstances and make an application accordingly.

The requirements of the Immigration Rules covering those who wish to stay in this country on the basis of their marriage to someone permanently resident here are set out in full in the 'Statement of Changes in Immigration Rules', House of Commons Paper 395 which came into effect on 1 October 1994. This also sets out the requirements for those who wish to stay here in other categories. Copies are available from Her Majesty's Stationery Office or through booksellers.

If you have any questions about this letter, please write to us at the above address, quoting our reference number.

As from 25th November 1996 application forms will be compulsory for all applications for leave to remain and settlement (except applications for asylum, Work Permit holders, certain right of abode categories, and applications under EC law). Should you wish to apply for further leave to remain or settlement you may be required to do so on an application form. If you wish to check whether an application form is required you may wish to call the Telephone Enquiry Bureau on 0181 686 0688. Application forms are available from the Application Forms Unit on 0181 760 2233.

Yours sincerely

Note

The Home Office supplied this letter to JCWI in February 1997. Readers will note that its list of the benefits defined as 'public funds' for immigration purposes is out of date, it does not refer people to all the current immigration rules on marriage and it leaves room for serious confusion about whether an application form will be necessary when the person applies for settlement. JCWI drew this to the Home Office's attention and we hope that the letter will be amended urgently.

LETTER GRANTING INDEFINITE LEAVE TO REMAIN — RON 60

Immigration and Nationality Directorate

HOME OFFICE
ind

Lunar House 40 Wellesley Road
Croydon CR9 2BY
Tel 0181-760-
Fax 0181-760-

Your Reference

Our Reference

Date

Dear   RON 60

I am writing to say that there are no longer any restrictions on the period for which you may remain in the UK. Your passport, which is enclosed, has been endorsed with vignette number ....

You can now remain indefinitely in the UK. You do not need permission from a Government Department to take or to change employment and you may engage in business or a profession as long as you comply with any general regulations for the business or professional activity.

If you are thinking of going to live or work in the Isle of Man or one of the Channel Islands, you should first consult the Immigration authorities of the Island concerned.

If you leave the UK, you will normally be readmitted for settlement as a returning resident provided that you did not receive assistance from public funds towards the cost of leaving this country; that you had indefinite leave to enter or remain here when you last left; that you have not been away for longer than 2 years; and that you are returning for the purpose of settlement. In order to be considered as settled here, you will have to be able to show that you are habitually and normally resident in this country, and that any absences have been of a temporary or occasional nature. You will not be readmitted as a returning resident if you are resident overseas and only return here for short periods.

If your absence from the UK is for longer than 2 years, but you can still demonstrate that you had indefinite leave to enter or remain here when you last left, and you are returning for the purpose of settlement, you may still qualify for admission as a returning resident if, for example, you have maintained strong connections with this country.

You do not require a visa to return to the UK provided you are returning for settlement after an absence of 2 years or less. However, if you are returning for settlement to the UK after an absence of over 2 years you are advised to apply for an entry clearance at the nearest British Diplomatic Post in the country in which you are living as this will facilitate your re-admission to the UK.

If you obtain a new passport, you may ask us to stamp it to show your immigration status before you travel. You should send or bring it to this Directorate at the address at the top of this letter, or take it to one of our local Public Enquiry Offices. You should also bring or send the enclosed passport and this letter. If you send your passport by post, you should do so at least 2 months before you intend to travel.

If you do not have your passport stamped before you travel, when you return to the UK you will have to satisfy the immigration officer that you had indefinite leave to remain when you left. To do this, you will need to produce either the enclosed passport or other documentary evidence such as bank statements, notices of income tax coding, school or employment records etc relating to the earlier years of your residence in the UK. It may also be helpful to carry this letter with you.

A child born to you in the UK since 1 January 1983 who is not a British citizen may now be entitled to be registered as such a citizen and any child born to you while you remain settled here may be a British citizen automatically at birth. However, you should note that where the parents of a child have never been married to each other British Citizenship can only be derived from the mother. More information about all aspects of British Citizenship including by birth in the UK, and an application form for registration, are available from the Nationality Directorate of the Home Office, 3rd floor, India Buildings, Water Street, Liverpool L2 0QN, telephone 0151 237 5200.

Yours sincerely

LETTER GRANTING EXCEPTIONAL LEAVE TO REMAIN GEN 19

Immigration and
Nationality Directorate

HOME OFFICE
ind

Lunar House 40 Wellesley Road
Croydon CR9 2BY
Tel 0181-760-
Fax 0181-760-

Your Reference

Our Reference

Date

Dear

Your application for refugee status in the United Kingdom has been carefully considered but I have to tell you that it has been refused. It has been decided, however, that although you do not qualify for refugee status it would be right because of the particular circumstances of your case to give you exceptional leave to remain in the United Kingdom until
....

You should, however, fully understand that if during your stay in the United Kingdom you take part in activities involving, for example, the support or encouragement of violence, or conspiracy to cause violence, whether in the United Kingdom or abroad, the Secretary of State may curtail your stay or deport you.

POLICE REGISTRATION

* You must now register with the police: please take this letter to your local police station as soon as possible.

* I enclose your police registration certificate which has been suitably endorsed.

* Please send (or take) your police registration certificate, your **passport** and this letter to your local police registration officer so that the certificate can be endorsed.

If you change your address or any other details of your registration you should tell your local police registration officer (either in person or by letter) within 7 days. Ask at your local police station if you do not know how to contact your police registration officer.

EMPLOYMENT

You do not need the permission of the Department of Employment or the Home Office before taking a job. The Employment Service can help you find a job or train for work - any job centre or unemployment benefit office will be able to help you and you can apply for a place on a government-sponsored training scheme if you meet the normal conditions for these schemes. You are free to set up in business or any

LETTER GRANTING EXCEPTIONAL LEAVE TO REMAIN GEN 19/page 2

professional activity within the general regulations that apply to that business or profession.

If you want to live or work in the Isle of Man or one of the Channel Islands you must ask the Island's immigration authorities.

HEALTH AND SOCIAL SERVICES

You are free to use the National Health Service and the social services and other help provided by local authorities as you need them. You will be able to get social security benefit (including income support) if you meet the ordinary conditions. If you need any of these services, take this letter with you and show it if there is any question about your entitlement to the service. Your local Social Security Office will give you advice on social security benefits, the British Refugees Council (Bondway House, 3-9 Bondway, London SW8 1SJ; telephone 071-582 6922) can advise you on other welfare services, and your local Citizens Advice Bureau will help you with general questions.

FAMILY REUNION

This grant of exceptional leave to remain does not entitle your spouse or children under 18 to join you. An application for them to do so cannot normally be considered until 4 years from the date of this letter. This is subject to your having received further grants of exceptional leave. The normal requirements of the Immigration Rules regarding support and accommodation of relatives would have to be satisfied. An application for family reunion may be granted at an earlier point if there are compelling compassionate circumstances.

TRAVEL ABROAD

You should be aware that, if you travel abroad, the leave you are now being granted will lapse. Any application to return will be considered as an application for fresh leave.

You should keep your present passport valid. If, however, your national authorities will not renew or replace your passport, or you can show it would be unreasonable to expect you to approach your Embassy or Consulate here, you can apply for a Home Office travel document from the Travel Document Section (telephone 081-760 2345) at the Home Office, Lunar House, Croydon, CR9 2BY.

FURTHER LEAVE TO REMAIN

Your passport is enclosed, endorsed with leave to remain until .... Any application you make for further leave to remain will be carefully considered.

                                        Yours sincerely

* Delete as appropriate
ENC(S)

REFUSAL OF LEAVE TO REMAIN, WITH RIGHT OF APPEAL — APP 101A

Reference: APP 101A

Home Office Immigration and Nationality Directorate

IMMIGRATION ACT 1971 - NOTICE OF REFUSAL TO VARY LEAVE

(Paragraph 289 with reference to 287(ii) and (iii) of HC 395)

To:

The Secretary of State therefore refuses your application.

Under the Immigration (Variation of Leave) Order 1976, your stay has been extended to 28 days after the date of this notice. If you do not wish to appeal, you should leave the United Kingdom by that date.

RIGHT OF APPEAL You are entitled to appeal against this decision under Section 14(1) of the Immigration Act 1971 to the appellate authorities.

HOW TO APPEAL If you wish to appeal you should complete the attached form (APP 1) and return it to the Appeals Section, Home Office, Lunar House, Wellesley Road, Croydon, CR9 2BY. An envelope is provided for this purpose but you will need to affix a postage stamp and you may wish to return it by recorded delivery.

TIME LIMIT FOR APPEALING The completed appeal form must be returned to arrive at Lunar House not later than <u>14 days</u> after the date of this notice.

ASSISTANCE AND ADVICE Please turn over.

[for information about IAS]

Signed:
On behalf of the Secretary of State

Date:

[Home Office IND stamp: 16 JAN 1997 (118)]

STANDARD LETTER AFTER APPEAL HAS BEEN DISMISSED — RON 67

Immigration and
Nationality Directorate

HOME OFFICE
ind

Lunar House 40 Wellesley Road
Croydon CR9 2BY
Tel 0181-760-
Fax 0181-760-

Your Reference

Our Reference

Date

Dear

Your appeal against the Secretary of State's decision of ....
was withdrawn/dismissed by the adjudicator on ....

* and we have no evidence that you have an appeal against the dismissal pending before the Immigration Appeal Tribunal.

* and your application to the Immigration Appeal Tribunal has been refused.

* and the Immigration Appeal Tribunal has dismissed your appeal.

You therefore have no basis of stay in this country and must now leave the United Kingdom immediately.

If you fail to embark, you will be liable to prosecution for an offence under the Immigration Act 1971 (as amended by the Immigration Act 1988). You will also be liable to deportation under administrative powers contained in section 3(5)(a) of the 1971 Act. If you fail to embark, the Secretary of State will consider whether on the basis of facts known to him it would be right to make a deportation order against you.

Yours sincerely

* Delete as appropriate

DECISION TO MAKE A DEPORTATION ORDER APP 104

Reference: APP 104

Home Office Immigration and Nationality Department

**IMMIGRATION ACTS 1971 AND 1988 -
DECISION TO MAKE A DEPORTATION ORDER**

The Secretary of State has therefore decided to make an order by virtue of Section 3(5) of the Immigration Act 1971 requiring you to leave the United Kingdom and prohibiting you from re-entering while the order is in force. He proposes to give directions for your removal to China, the country of which you are a national or which most recently provided you with a travel document.

RIGHT OF APPEAL — You are entitled to appeal against this decision under Section 15(1)(a) of the Immigration Act 1971 (as amended by the Immigration Act 1988) to the appellate authorities and you are entitled under Section 17(3) of the Immigration Act 1971 to object to your removal to the country specified above in your appeal. If you wish to appeal against the direction for removal you must state the name of the country to which you claim you ought to be removed. You should attach to the form a statement of the reasons why you object to removal to the country specified in the direction. You should also produce evidence which demonstrates or tends to show that that country or territory so identified would admit you if removed there. It is for you to satisfy the appellate authorities that the government of the country of your choice will admit you on deportation from the United Kingdom.

HOW TO APPEAL — If you wish to appeal you should complete the attached form (APP 11) and return it to the Appeals Section, Home Office, Lunar House, Wellesley Road, Croydon, CR9 2BY. An envelope is provided for this purpose, but you will need to affix a postage stamp and you may wish to return it by recorded delivery.

LH20 271612.ISE

DECISION TO MAKE A DEPORTATION ORDER — APP 104/page 2

TIME LIMIT FOR APPEALING
The completed appeal form must be returned to arrive at Lunar House not later than <u>14 days</u> after the date of this notice.

ASSISTANCE AND ADVICE
The Immigrants Advisory Service (IAS) and the Refugee Legal Centre (RLC) are both voluntary organisations, independent of the government, who will be able to advise you about the decisions taken against you and whether to exercise your right of appeal. If you decide to appeal they can help you prepare and present your appeal to the appellate authorities. These services are confidential and <u>free of charge</u>.

The London Office of IAS is:

> 2nd Floor
> County House
> 190 Great Dover Street
> London
> SE1 4YB
> (Telephone: (0171) 357-6917)

(IAS also has offices in Birmingham, Cardiff, Gatwick Airport, Glasgow, Hounslow, Leeds and Manchester).

The London Office of RLC is:

> Sussex House
> 39-45 Bermondsey Street
> London
> SE1 3XF
> (Telephone: (0171) 827-9090)

You can also obtain advice from a solicitor or law centre: the names and addresses of solicitors/law centres are listed in telephone directories. (Legal representation is not available under the Legal Aid Scheme for proceedings before either the Immigration Adjudicators or Immigration Appeals Tribunal. However, legal advice and assistance under the Green Form Scheme may be available.)

You may also contact your High Commission or Consul or anyone else you think may be able to help you.

Signed: *[signature]*
On behalf of the Secretary of State

Date: 2 7 MAR 1996

Information you give us will be treated in confidence but may be disclosed to other Government Departments and agencies and local authorities to enable them to carry out their functions.

APPLICATION FORM SET(M) to apply for settlement after a year's leave on marriage grounds has been granted

This form is provided **free of charge**.

SET(M)
Version 3.0

Immigration and Nationality Directorate

HOME OFFICE

ind

APPLICATION FOR INDEFINITE LEAVE TO REMAIN IN THE UNITED KINGDOM (UK) AS THE HUSBAND OR WIFE (SPOUSE) OF A PERSON PRESENT AND SETTLED IN THE UK

- If you wish to make an application on the basis set out above you must complete this form answering all the questions that apply to you. You must also provide all the documents specified in Section 4 of the form or give reasons which the Secretary of State considers satisfactory as to why missing documents cannot be provided and explaining when they will be provided. If you fail to do so your application will be invalid. All documents must be originals, not photocopies.

- The requirements for indefinite leave to remain as the spouse of a person present and settled in the UK include that you must have been admitted to the UK or given an extension of stay for a period of 12 months and have completed a period of 12 months as the spouse of a person present and settled here. You must apply for such an extension of stay on form FLR(M).

- This form is only valid for applications made on or before 14 April 1997. If you need another form please telephone the Application Forms Unit on 0181-760-2233 (calls will be answered in turn - please wait for a reply).

- If you need help to fill in this form, or you are unsure whether you have the right form, please telephone the Telephone Enquiry Bureau on 0181-686-0688 (calls will be answered in turn - please wait for a reply).

- You should fill in this form and send it to us not more than one month before your leave to enter or remain in the UK runs out.

- If you are completing this form by hand please write in BLOCK capitals and black ink.

- Information you give us will be treated in confidence, but may be disclosed to other Government Departments and agencies and local authorities to enable them to carry out their functions.

- The address of IND's internet information service is http://www.open.gov.uk/home_off/ind.htm

- We reserve the right to consider and decide your application on the evidence provided one month after the application has been made.

APPLICATION FORM SET(M)   page 2

SECTION 1 - ABOUT THE APPLICANT

Please tell us your:

1.1 Family name.

1.2 Other names.

1.3 Nationality.

1.4 Date of birth.

1.5 Name at birth if different, and any other names by which you have been known.

1.6 Current full address where you live in the UK and any other addresses where you have lived during the last 12 months. Please continue on a separate sheet if necessary.

Current address:

Postcode:

Previous address:

Postcode:

Previous address:

Postcode:

APPLICATION FORM SET(M)   page 3

SECTION 2 - YOUR CHILDREN

2.1 You must provide the information requested in the table below about all children of your present marriage as well as any children you or your spouse have from previous relationships who are dependent on you or your spouse. If more than six children fall within this description please continue in the same format on a separate sheet and submit it with your application.

	First Child	Second Child	Third Child
Full name			
Date of birth			
Relationship to the applicant			
Relationship to the applicant's spouse			
Do they live with you in the UK?			
Who pays for their support?			

	Fourth Child	Fifth Child	Sixth Child
Full name			
Date of birth			
Relationship to the applicant			
Relationship to the applicant's spouse			
Do they live with you in the UK?			
Who pays for their support?			

APPLICATION FORM SET(M) page 4

2.2 Are any of the children listed in response to question 2.1 applying for indefinite leave to remain in the UK with you ?   Yes ❑ No ❑

If you have answered **yes**, you must provide their names in the table below. If you need space for more than six children please continue in the same format on a separate sheet and submit it with your application.

First child	
Second child	
Third child	
Fourth child	
Fifth child	
Sixth child	

SECTION 3 - YOUR FINANCES

3.1 Are you working in the UK ?   Yes ❑ No ❑

3.2 Is your spouse working in the UK ?   Yes ❑ No ❑

3.3 Are you or your spouse receiving any public funds ? (see **Note 1**)   Yes ❑ No ❑

> **Note 1:**
> **Under the Immigration Rules, "public funds" includes the following:**
>
> Attendance Allowance, Severe Disablement Allowance, Invalid Care Allowance, Disability Living Allowance, Income Support, Family Credit, Council Tax Benefit, Disability Working Allowance, Child Benefit, Job Seekers Allowance and Housing Benefit.

If you have answered **yes** to question 3.3, which of these are you receiving ?

APPLICATION FORM SET(M) page 5

SECTION 4 - DOCUMENTARY EVIDENCE

> You must provide
>
> **EITHER** all the documents listed below
>
> **OR** as many of them as you can together with a document (for example a letter) explaining why the missing ones cannot be provided now or can only be provided as a photocopy, and explaining when the missing documents (or the missing originals of photocopy documents) will be provided.

You should tick the boxes as appropriate to show what you are sending.

- ❏ A recent passport sized photograph of yourself.
- ❏ A recent passport sized photograph of your spouse.
- ❏ A recent passport sized photograph of each dependant child who is applying for indefinite leave to remain in the UK with you.
- ❏ Your unexpired passport or travel document.
- ❏ A full birth certificate for each child of your marriage listed in answer to question 2.1.
- ❏ Unexpired passport(s) or travel document(s) for each dependant child who is applying for indefinite leave to remain in the UK with you (see question 2.2). Please state how many additional passports are enclosed: _____ .
- ❏ Evidence that your spouse is present and settled in the UK (see **Note 2**).

> **Note 2:**
> Evidence that someone is present and settled in the UK is best given by sending us their passport. If your spouse is a British Citizen without a passport, sending his/her full birth certificate (which will show their parents' names) on its own will not prove that he/she is present and settled in the UK. We will also need to see other evidence that proves their identity, for example, one or more of the following documents which will show that your spouse has been resident in the UK for the last three years:
>
>   (i) Notice of income tax coding
>   (ii) Driving Licence
>   (iii) Building Society passbook/ bank statement
>   (iv) National Insurance/ National Health Service registration issued by the Dept of Health, Dept of Social Security, or a local health authority.

APPLICATION FORM SET(M) page 6

Please state which evidence is enclosed.

☐ Your civil marriage certificate.

☐ If you have answered **yes** to question 3.1, your wage slips for the last three months, or for the time you have worked if shorter.

☐ If you have answered **yes** to question 3.2, wage slips for your spouse for the last three months, or for the time worked if shorter.

☐ Evidence that indicates that your marriage subsists (see **Note 3**).

> **Note 3:**
> We must be satisfied that your marriage subsists for indefinite leave to remain to be granted. You should therefore provide evidence that indicates that you and your spouse live together. We may, for example, accept that your marriage subsists if you provide five items of correspondence addressed to you during the past year from the following sources if they clearly show that you and your spouse live at the same address:
>
> (a) British Telecom, or other telecommunications company
> (b) British Gas, or other gas company
> (c) Electricity Company
> (d) Water Company
> (e) Local Authority
> (f) Local Social Services Department
> (g) Local Health Authority
> (h) Department of Health
> (i) Benefits Agency
> (j) Inland Revenue
> (k) Bank / Building Society
> (l) Employment Service
> (m) Credit card statements of account
> (n) Insurance certificates complete with address
> (p) Mortgage agreement / tenancy agreement

APPLICATION FORM SET(M) page 7

SECTION 5 - WHAT TO DO NOW

Please remember that you must complete all the sections of this form that apply to you. If you fail to do so your application will be invalid. You must also provide all the required documents. These documents must be originals, not photocopies. You and your spouse should now read the declarations below and sign them. They must be signed by the applicant and spouse personally and not by a representative or other person acting on their behalf.

By the applicant:

I hereby apply for indefinite leave to remain in the UK on the basis of my marriage to the person who has signed the declaration below. I declare that we are still married, that we are living together as husband and wife and intend to do so permanently. The information I have given is complete and is true to the best of my knowledge. I am aware that it is an offence under the Immigration Act 1971 to make to a person acting in execution of the Act a statement or representation which the maker knows to be false or does not believe to be true. I confirm that if, before this application is decided, there is a material change in my circumstances or new information relevant to this application becomes available I will inform the Home Office.

Signed:_____ Date:_____

By your husband or wife:

I, _____, confirm that I am the husband/wife of the applicant; and I declare that we are still married, that we are living together as husband and wife and intend to do so permanently. I am aware that it is an offence under the Immigration Act 1971 to make to a person acting in execution of the Act a statement or representation which the maker knows to be false or does not believe to be true.

Signed:_____ Date:_____

You should then post this form and all the required documents to:

      The Document Reception Centre
      Room 828
      The Immigration and Nationality Directorate
      Lunar House
      40 Wellesley Road
      Croydon
      CR9 2BY

Alternatively you may take it to the Public Enquiry Office at the address shown above or one of the Regional Public Enquiry Offices

Index

* means subject dealt with in most detail here

A
abode *see* right of abode
academic workers 137–8, 178
access to children 35–6
accommodation 14–15, 108, 150–1, 180, 185–6, 200–3, 219–20
    adequate 14, 181, 201, 219–20
    council 166, 200–3, 219, 361
adjudicator 5, 274, 292, 293, 294–5, 296, 305–6, 356
adoption 43, 46, 58–64*, 323
Adoption (Designation of overseas adoptions) Order 58, 63
agents 86, 90, 266
AIDS 209–10
Akbarali see Shah
Akinde 281
Alexander 272
aliens 4, 6, 317–8
Aliens Act 1905 6
Aliens Registration Office 164, 258–9, 350
Amin 333
Amnesty International 98, 101–2, 353
Anson, Dame Elizabeth 152, 244
Antonissen 116, 189
APART 38, 217, 353
appeals 5, 7, 117–8, 292–316*, 346, 349–50
    abandonment 241, 301, 314
    adjournment 303–4
    against deportation 24, 35, 103, 118, 252, 269–70, 271, 273–4, 288, 293, 296, 308
    against destination 274–5, 288, 296
    against refusal of asylum 79, 81, 99, 100, 103–5, 247, 288, 308–16*
    against refusal of entry clearance 17, 50, 108, 223, 232, 242–3, 293, 295
    against refusal of leave to enter 117–8, 154, 164, 232, 246, 288, 293, 295
    against refusal of leave to remain 21, 145, 156, 186, 241, 293, 295

appeals *continued*
    against refusal to revoke a deportation order 278, 293, 296,
    against removal 247–8, 278, 283, 293, 296
    of EEA nationals 117–8
    'fast-track' 104, 310–3, 359
    'for mention' 302–3
    from abroad 292, 295, 296, 308, 310, 312–3
    hearings 299, 301–4, 305–7, 313–5
    lodging 298–300, 310
    mixed 103, 296, 310
    on the papers 305
    out of time 273, 300–1
    withdrawal 304–5, 314
appellate authorities 81, 300, 302, 304
application forms 9, 17, 18, 19, 20, 28, 29, 44, 46, 49, 70, 75, 106, 133–4, 136, 139, 156, 166–7, 168, 196, 216, 232–4*, 236, 248, 295, 297–8, 385–91
Application Forms Unit 233, 247
approved employment *see* work permits
Armat Ali 231
artists 146–7
Arun Kumar 38, 39–40
Association Agreements 8, 111, 123–4, 128, 146, 198, 199, 356
asylum 3, 35, 79–110*, 274, 309, 347–8, 356
Asylum Appeals (Procedure) Rules 5, 104, 292, 309, 313–4, 364
Asylum and Immigration Act 1996 1, 4, 7, 8, 30, 35, 79, 99, 102, 144–5, 166, 181, 192, 200, 265, 266, 281, 309, 364
Asylum and Immigration Appeals Act 1993 1, 4, 7, 79, 86, 100, 101, 106, 152, 154, 155, 200, 243, 249, 274, 289, 297, 298, 307, 308, 364
Asylum Screening Unit 94, 95–6, 348, 356

Index • 393

asylum-seekers 4, 7, 8, 18, 29–30, 55, 79–110*, 126, 127, 170, 209, 237, 266, 285–6, 289, 314, 356
 and benefits 99–100, 193–5, 198, 200, 201, 206, 212
 and marriage 29–30, 94, 107–8
attendance allowance 180, 199, 361
au pairs 143–4, 237
aunts 51–2, 77
Azem 218

B

backdating of benefit 99, 105, 194–5, 197
Bagdadi 42
bail 102, 252, 284, 288–9, 291
Baker, Nicholas 25, 185
Bastiampillai 74
Benefits Agency 7, 74, 99, 121, 188–9, 194, 195–6, 204–5, 265, 356
 Overseas Branch 205, 350
Berrehab 36, 42, 69, 76
Binbasi 82–3
Bouchereau 118
Bouzagou 225
breach of conditions 25, 144, 192, 224, 235, 266–8
British citizens 1, 2, 4, 123, 318, 320–330*, 337, 356
 by adoption 61, 62, 323, 326
 by birth 1, 44, 67–68, 323–5, 326
 by descent 1, 32, 44, 323, 326–30, 343, 356
 otherwise than by descent 323, 327–8, 329, 330, 356
British dependent territories citizens 1, 123, 318, 320, 321, 322, 327, 330–2, 333, 342, 356–7
British Nationality Act 1948 317, 318, 319
British Nationality Act 1981 1, 2, 6, 10, 318, 319–20, 323, 328, 343, 345, 364
British Nationality (Falkland Islands) Act 1983 2, 318, 320
British Nationality (Hong Kong) Act 1990 171, 336
British nationals (overseas) 1, 2, 263, 318, 320, 330–2, 335–6, 342, 357
British overseas citizens 1, 250, 263, 279, 318, 320, 321, 328, 330–2, 333, 334–6, 342, 346, 357
British protected persons 1, 263, 317–8, 319, 320, 321, 330–2, 333, 342, 357
British subjects 1, 6, 123, 263, 317, 318, 319, 320, 321, 330–2, 333, 342, 357
British Visitor's passport 227
brothers 77

business people 27–8, 53, 115, 117, 123–4, 128, 145–6*, 149, 153–4, 237, 257–8, 346

C

Campsfield House detention centre 102, 288, 291, 349
carers 156–7, 210
Carriers' Liability Act 7, 84–6, 153, 312, 357, 364
Castelli 115, 190
certificate of entitlement 10–11, 44–5, 227, 255, 322, 365, 366
certificate of identity 322, 337
'certified' cases 104, 308, 310–3, 357
Chahal 84, 270, 290–1, 298
Channel Islands 3, 121, 123, 224, 279, 357
Chhinderpal Singh 185
child benefit 49, 166, 180, 199–200, 212, 361
Child Protection Act 43
children 13, 22, 24, 34–6, 37, 42, 43–69*, 71, 133–4, 136, 166–7, 210–1, 217, 234, 235, 272–3, 333–4, 342–4
 adopted 43, 58–64*, 323
 asylum-seekers 94, 101, 348
 born in UK 67–9, 325–6, 342–3
 in care 63, 64–6, 67, 344
 of EEA nationals 45, 118–9, 325
 joining lone parents 50–3
 meaning in immigration rules 46–7
 'over-age' 56–7, 134
 of refugees and people with exceptional leave 55
 'related as claimed' 47–8, 217
 of students 54
 of workers and business people 53–4
 of working holidaymakers 54, 55, 143, 210
Children Act 1989 43–4, 64, 66, 69, 197–8, 204
citizens of the UK and Colonies 317–8, 319–20, 321
common-law relationship 11, 30–1
Common Travel Area 3, 121, 149, 187, 224–5, 279, 357
Commonwealth citizens 2, 4, 6, 10, 116, 142–3, 152, 318, 319, 320, 321, 357–8, 362
Commonwealth Immigrants Act 1962 6, 318, 335
Commonwealth Immigrants Act 1968 318, 332
Community legislation 2, 10, 17, 32, 70, 112, 114, 118, 119–20, 125–6

Community legislation *continued*
  directives 2, 113, 115, 116, 126–7, 175, 190
  regulations 2, 113, 119
composers 146–7
Convention travel document 105, 109
Co-operation Agreements 8, 111, 123–4
council housing 166, 200–3, 219, 361
council tax benefit 74, 99, 180, 183, 196–7, 361
Court of Appeal 253, 307, 316
credibility 81, 87–90, 96–8, 314–5
criminal convictions 82, 83–4, 118, 144–5, 264, 266–70, 277, 285, 340, 345
Crown service 330, 341–2
curtailment of leave 102–3, 184
customary marriage 16, 32–3

D

Dadibhai 74
deception 20, 35, 86, 264, 266, 278, 280–1
Dela Vina Corte 12
delays 15–16, 98, 105, 131, 233, 302, 365
departure stamp 241, 262
deportation 6, 23, 24, 66, 69, 118, 169, 251–3, 262, 264, 266–78*, 290, 296, 347, 358
  decision to deport 21, 35, 101, 103, 144, 169, 239, 270–4, 285, 296, 307–8, 383
  liability to deportation 268–9, 271
  recommendation for deportation 118, 268–70*, 274, 276, 285
deportation order 276, 277, 278, 279–80, 285, 296, 307–8
deprivation of citizenship 345
designated list *see* white list
designated posts 216, 366–9
designated service 330
detention 86, 92, 101–2, 246–7, 251–3, 277, 281, 284–91*
DfEE *see* Education and Employment, Department for
Dhudi Abdi 310
Di Paolo 188
diplomats 139–40, 323
directives 2, 113, 115, 116, 126–7, 175, 190
disability living/working allowance 180, 199, 361
discretion 4, 234–9, 274, 294–5
divorce 11, 12, 16, 30–1, 32–3, 35–6, 37–8, 72, 76, 330, 339
DNA testing 48, 50, 52, 56, 303, 365
Document Reception Centre 232–3, 347, 358

domestic violence 34–5, 83
domestic workers 130, 138–9
domicile 33, 59, 358
DSS *see* Social Security, Department of
dual nationals 90, 119–21
Dublin Convention 87, 93–4, 126
Durojaiye 281

E

EC law *see* Community legislation
EEA 2, 7, 32, 111–27*, 358
EEA family permits 45, 118
EEA nationals 2, 3, 4, 10, 45, 70–1, 114–8, 171, 175–6, 182, 186–7, 189–90, 232, 268, 346
  family members 10, 41–2, 45, 70, 118–21, 171, 172, 325
EEA Order 1994 118, 182, 364
EU 7, 10, 42, 79, 80, 111–27*
EU nationals 111–27*, 171, 172, 325
  UK's definition 122–3
education 66, 210–1
  fees 105, 109, 160, 161, 170–1, 175–6, 211
  grants 105, 109, 161, 170–2, 176
Education and Employment, Department for 124, 138–42, 140–1, 144, 163, 171, 172, 173–5, 210–1, 220, 232, 257, 267
  Overseas Labour Service 124, 138–42, 173, 350
'Efficiency Scrutiny' 7, 170, 171, 210, 211–2, 265
Electronic Immigration Network 99, 353, 404
emotional dependence 74
employers' checks 145, 265, 265–7, 347
employment *see* work
entertainers 129
entry clearance 5, 9, 12, 18, 36, 49, 108, 136, 215–23*, 242–4, 254–5, 278, 292, 309–10, 365, 366–9, 370–3
  for asylum 91, 309–10
  for children 43, 44, 47, 53–4, 59, 60, 63, 133
  for settlement 75, 215, 216–20
  for spouses/fiancé(e)s 11, 12, 15–16, 17, 23, 28, 36–9, 133, 217–20, 254
  for studies 220–1
  for visits 152, 154, 220–1, 242–3
  for work 131, 134–5, 136, 138, 142, 215, 220
  revocation of 154
entry clearance officers 16, 36–9, 53, 74, 154, 216–7, 358
Entry through Ireland Order 225

Index • 395

Environment, Department of the 166, 202–3
environmental health department 219
European Commission 113, 116, 125, 126–7
European Commission/Court of Human Rights 36, 42, 69, 76, 84, 291, 332, 353
European Community *see* EEA/EU
European Convention on Human Rights 3, 8, 36, 69, 83, 84, 86, 198, 277, 291, 311, 316, 358
European Council 2, 113, 116, 127
European Court of Justice 10, 112, 113–4, 116, 121
European Economic Area *see* EEA
European Parliament 113
European Union *see* EU
exceptional leave 9, 29, 55, 79, 83, 91, 106–8, 128, 170, 172, 181, 234, 258, 309, 358–9, 379–80
exclusion clause 83–4, 109
exclusion undesirable 50, 52–3, 59, 136
exempt from control 136, 139–40, 238
explanatory statement 38, 301–2, 303, 304

F
Fadele 69, 76
family credit 180, 198–9, 361
'fast-track' procedures 104, 310–3, 359
fathers 46, 51–2, 326, 328
fiancés and fiancées 9–42*, 237
fingerprinting 87, 92, 94, 96
in re Fleur Matondo 43–4
Flynn, ex parte 125
Foreign and Commonwealth Office 5, 139, 216, 243–4, 350
fostering 64–5, 211
fourteen-year-concession 239
Free Representation Unit 294, 353
freedom of movement 2, 7, 8, 10, 42, 111–2, 114–6, 120, 121, 123, 124–5, 127
full-time studies 160–1

G
Gal 325
gays 9, 31–2, 82–3, 147
general practitioners 209
Getachew 121, 190
Gibraltar 123, 357
Golchin 83
'good character' test 339–40, 341, 343
grandchildren 45, 71, 119
grandfathers 327, 328
grandparents 27, 51–2, 53, 70–6*, 119,

grandparents *continued*
142, 319
'green books' 293, 359
green form 48, 294, 304, 359
grounds of appeal 299–300, 306

H
habeas corpus 290–1
habitual residence 121, 182, 186–9*, 190, 203, 359
Handbook on procedures and criteria for determining refugee status 80, 82, 88, 89–90
Hardial Singh 290
Harmondsworth detention centre 287, 348
Haslar prison 102, 288, 349
Health, Department of 61–2, 63, 174
Health Service *see* National Health Service
Home Office 4, 5, 211, 346–8
 instructions 4, 13, 18, 21–3, 58, 63–4, 65–6, 69, 209–10, 272–3, 285–6
 policy 56, 84–6, 87, 185–6, 211–2, 233, 285–6, 295
 practice 13, 15, 19, 20, 24, 28, 30, 32, 34–5, 51–2, 131, 138–9, 156–7, 185–6, 209–10, 234–41*, 252–3, 260
Home Office presenting officers 303–4, 305, 350
Home Office reference number 260
homelessness 99–100, 180, 184, 186, 200–3, 361
Hong Kong 2, 322, 335–7, 357
Hong Kong Act 1985 2, 318, 320, 335–6
Hong Kong (British Nationality) Orders 1986 and **1993** 2, 335–6
Hoque and Singh 40
housing 99–100, 166, 180, 184, 200–3, 212, 361
Housing Act 1985 180, 200, 219
Housing Act 1996 203, 212, 219
housing benefit 74, 99, 180, 183, 196–7, 361
Howard, Michael 211, 295, 336
Human Rights Watch 98, 353

I
Ibraheem 78
Iftikhar Ahmed 15, 219
illegal entrants 23, 33, 68, 75, 96, 101, 163, 251–3, 278–83*, 285, 289, 290, 293, 296, 345, 359
illegal entry 20, 86, 264, 278–83*, 347
illegible stamps 224

ILPA 98, 354
Immigration Act 1971 1, 2, 3, 4, 6, 64, 101, 283, 309, 318, 364
Immigration Act 1988 1, 2, 6, 32, 35, 103, 113, 117, 118, 182, 228, 271, 273, 294, 364
Immigration Advisory Service (IAS) 236, 294, 299, 304, 353–4
Immigration Appeal Tribunal 5, 39, 118, 289, 292, 293, 296, 306–7, 310, 312, 315–6, 359
immigration appeals *see* appeals
Immigration Appeals (Procedure) Rules 5, 103, 292, 364
Immigration Appeals reports (Imm AR) 293, 359
immigration appellate authorities *see* appellate authorities
Immigration (Carriers' Liability) Act 1987 *see* Carriers' Liability Act
Immigration (Control of entry through Republic of Ireland) Order *see* Entry through Ireland Order
Immigration (European Economic Area) Order *see* EEA Order
immigration officer 4, 5, 85, 150, 162, 223–4, 244–7, 279, 349, 359
immigration rules 4, 235, 250, 359, 364
  on asylum 87–90
  on children 45–6, 50, 58
  on deportation 272
  on other relatives 56, 77
  on parents/grandparents 71
  on returning residents 229–31
  on spouses/fiancé(e)s 4, 11–15, 18–19, 21, 26, 27–8
  on students 4, 159–60, 164–6, 172–3
  on visitors 4, 148–51, 155
  on work 131, 174
Immigration (Variation of Leave) Order *see* Variation of Leave Order
income support 74, 99, 121–2, 180, 183, 184, 191–6*, 361
  urgent cases rate 99, 183, 192–6
indefinite leave *see* settlement
independent means 71, 147, 237, 346
instructions to immigration officials *see* Home Office instructions
intention to leave 149–50, 155, 162, 167–8,
intergovernmental conference 112, 113
internal controls 7, 8, 210–14, 265–6
International Social Service 283, 354
interpreters 97, 217, 299, 303, 305–6, 315
interviews 16, 47, 92, 94–5, 96–8, 101, 217, 339

invalid care allowance 180, 199, 361
investors 147, 237
Iqbal Ali 52
Iram Iqbal 41
Ireland 3, 70, 121, 224–5, 279–80, 357
Irish citizens 3, 4, 10, 70, 116, 119–20
Isle of Man 3, 121, 123, 224, 279, 357

J

Jacques 83
Jonah 90
jobseeker's allowance 121–2, 180, 190, 191–6, 361
judicial review 247, 253, 278, 282, 316, 360
Justice and Home Affairs Council 80

K

K4 Committee 114, 360
Kalayaan 139, 354
Kandiya and Khan 40
Kartar Kaur 72
Kausar 15
'keyworker' 130–1, 132
Khan 290
Khawaja and Khera 280
Khokhar 231
Kirkhope, Timothy 30, 271
Koyazia Kaja 81, 315
Kus 123

L

language assistants 137
language test 339–40, 341
leave to appeal 306–7
leave to enter 153, 163, 223–5, 227–8, 231, 240–1, 244–8, 255–8, 278, 279–80, 325, 360
leave to remain 132, 156, 248–9, 260, 360
legal aid 253, 294, 304, 307
lesbians 9, 31–2, 82
'liable relatives' 74
Lilley, Peter 193
Livingstone 31
Lizarzaburu 31
local authority 65, 67, 100, 184, 197, 198, 201–3, 204, 213, 265, 344
lone parent 43, 49, 50–3, 122
Lord Chancellor's department 5, 292, 309

M

M, R v London Borough of Hammersmith ex parte 100, 198
Maastricht treaty 2, 7, 111, 112, 113, 115, 122
maintain *see* support

'mandatory refusals' 141, 155, 223, 249–50, 297
Manshoora Begum 77
marriage 9, 10, 16, 33, 42, 213–4, 234, 339
marriage breakdown 9, 34–6, 124
medical examination 5, 104, 220, 222, 223
Medical Foundation for the Care of Victims of Torture 98, 354
medical treatment 22, 151, 156, 157, 205–10, 272
Meharban 14
Members of Parliament 238, 247, 249, 251, 252–3, 282, 341, 351
Miller v IAT 90
'minded to refuse' 104
ministers of religion 134–5
Minority Rights Group 98, 354
missionaries 135
Mohammed Saftar 40
monitor of visit visa refusals 152, 244
mothers 51–2, 72, 326–7

N

Naheed Ejaz 345
Naillie 86
Najma Rafique 40
National Assistance Act 1948 100, 197–8, 204
National Health Service 7, 49, 129, 133, 173, 180, 205–9*
 charges 205–9
 exemption from charges 206–7
national insurance 132, 200, 213, 267
'national security' 235, 270, 293, 298
nationality 1–2, 122–3, 317–345, 348
naturalisation 1, 324, 338–41, 360, 365, 366
'non-suspensive' appeals 308, 310, 312–3
nurses 142, 172–3

O

O v IAT and SSHD 82
Office of National Statistics 23–4
Ofori 239
Oladehinde 272
'one-year rule' 17, 20–1, 25–7, 34–5
ordinary residence 170, 172, 198, 205–6, 207, 360
'other relatives' 56–7, 73, 77–8, 119
Overseas Labour Service *see* Education and Employment, Department for
overseas newspaper representatives 136
overstayers 18, 21, 23, 54, 96, 144, 234, 266–8, 279, 307, 338, 360

P

PAQ *see* political asylum questionnaire
parents 46–7, 70–6*, 119, 152, 234, 319, 325
passport 1, 5, 26, 45, 68, 88–9, 104, 106–7, 109–10, 116, 131, 145, 156, 179, 208, 217–8, 220, 239–40, 276–7, 283, 322–3, 326, 337, 341, 344, 350, 366
 checks 211–4
 as proof of identity 23, 89, 95, 211–4, 222–3
 stamps/endorsements 10, 17, 133, 139–40, 143, 153, 155, 169, 178, 181, 221, 223–4, 227, 240–1, 248, 254–63*, 277, 280, 337
Passport Agency 344, 350
patriality 6, 255, 318, 321, 328, 360
Pattuwearachchi 161–2
pensioners 2–3, 73, 115
permanent stay *see* settlement
permit-free employment 134–7, 360
persecution 3, 34, 80–3, 104, 311
'persons from abroad' 121, 185, 189–90, 191–4, 361
pillars 112, 113, 361
Poku 42, 69, 76
police 5, 251, 265–6, 271, 276–7, 282, 284–5
police registration 106, 163–4, 258–9, 267, 361, 365
political asylum *see* asylum
political asylum questionnaire 95, 96
polygamous wives 2, 11–12, 32, 45–6, 47
preliminary issue 250, 298
'pre-sift' process 152
primary purpose rule 11, 12–13, 36–42*, 57, 300
programme refugees 91
prospective students 159–60, 162–3, 164–6, 173, 298
public funds 14–15, 17, 20, 25, 121–2, 133, 142, 166, 180–205*, 224, 267, 361
'public good' 222–3, 225, 270, 279, 345
'public policy' 117, 118, 268
public service employment 116

Q

quota voucher *see* special quota voucher

R

Radiom 270
Raja Zafar Zia 41
Rajendrakumar 314
Ramos 51

Raulin 190
readmission *see* right of readmission
recommendations 274, 285, 294–5
Refugee Arrivals Project 95, 355
Refugee Council 101, 105, 355
Refugee Legal Centre 95, 98, 236, 294, 299, 304, 355
refugees 3, 6, 9, 29, 79–110*, 126, 128, 170, 181, 195, 237, 258, 361
refusal
   of asylum 83, 93, 96, 100, 102–5, 308–16
   of entry clearance 17, 50, 51–2, 108, 141, 152, 222–3, 232, 242–4, 262, 295, 302
   of leave to enter 8, 132, 154, 164, 179, 185, 222–3, 232, 244–8, 262, 284, 290, 295, 301
   of leave to remain 21, 25, 105, 141, 155, 185, 234–5, 262–3, 295, 381
   of naturalisation 341
   to revoke deportation order 293, 296
   without right of appeal 141, 154–5, 249–50, 295–8, 309
register offices 23–4, 213–4
registration 62, 67, 324, 326, 328–30, 331–2, 338, 342–4, 361, 365, 366
registration with police *see* police registration
regulations 2, 113, 119
Rehabilitation of Offenders Act 277–8
Rehal 279
religious orders 135
Remelien 115, 122, 190
removal 23, 101, 247–8, 251–3, 264, 282–3, 296, 361–2
repatriation 231, 283
representatives of overseas firms 136, 346
requirement to leave 115, 122, 189–90
residence order 44
residence permit 116–7, 118, 120, 175, 362
resident domestic workers *see* domestic workers
retired people 147
returning residents 11, 110, 229–32*, 261, 340, 362
revocation of deportation order 275, 277–8
right of abode 2, 4, 6, 10, 32, 44–5, 71, 123, 171, 226–7, 255, 263, 318, 319, 322, 337, 346, 362
right of readmission 263, 331, 362
Rochester prison 102, 288, 291, 349
Rudolph 51, 52
Rush Portuguesa 125

S

'safe third country' 86–7, 91, 93–4, 104, 247, 308, 363
Saghir Ahmed 15
Sahota 120
SAL 92, 94, 95–6, 99, 100, 145, 362
Samateh 290
same-sex relationships 11, 31–2, 78
Sandralingham and Ravichandran 314
Sarwar 190
Schengen 7, 125, 362
scholarships 177
Scott 185, 218–9
seasonal agricultural workers 137, 145, 155
section 3(3)(b) 26, 178, 228–9, 259
self-employment 115, 117, 123–4, 146–7*, 237
Senga 89
servants
   of diplomats 136
   domestic *see* domestic workers
service providers 115, 125–6
settlement 5, 9, 12, 21, 25, 31, 35, 45, 49, 50, 54, 56, 57, 105, 106, 117, 123, 128, 133–4, 171, 181, 186, 224, 230, 234, 237, 238–9, 256, 260–1, 324–5, 338–9, 378
severe disablement allowance 180, 199, 361
Sevince 124
Shah v Brent London Borough Council 207, 360
Shameem Wali 40
Shingara 270
'short courses' 166, 168
short procedure 92–3
Single European Act 2, 7, 112, 115, 124
single parent *see* lone parent
sisters 77
Sivakumaran 81, 315
social group 81, 82–3, 90
Social Security, Department of 74, 99, 121, 166, 182, 191, 350
   Commissioners 105, 121, 187–8
Social Security Contributions and Benefits Act 1992 74, 180, 183
Social Services departments 61, 65, 66, 69, 100, 101
sole responsibility rule 50–3, 136
Somali concession 108, 310
Southall Black Sisters 35, 355
special adjudicator 5, 104, 292, 308, 313–5, 362
special quota voucher 57, 171, 263, 321, 332–5*, 336, 362

sponsor 74, 108, 150–1, 182–6, 204–5
sponsorship 74–5, 182–4, 362
sportspeople 129
spouses 9–42*, 94, 107–8, 119–121, 128, 133–4, 136, 164–6, 237, 333–4, 376–7
standard acknowledgement letter *see* SAL
standard of proof 81, 150, 294, 314–5
state education 49, 66, 133, 180, 210–11
statelessness 107, 325, 331, 344–5
Statement of changes in immigration rules *see* immigration rules
stepfathers/stepmothers 46, 78
Stonewall 31, 209, 355
students 2, 28–9, 54, 64, 66, 115, 137–8, 141, 159–79*, 201, 237, 239, 241, 256–7, 267, 271, 298
  EEA students 115, 171–2, 175–6
  fees and grants 105, 109, 160, 161, 170–2, 175–6
  and marriage 28–9
student nurses 142, 172–3
Sujon Miah 66
Sumeina Masood 40–1
supervised departure 262, 276, 278
support 14–15, 20, 25, 72–3, 76, 108, 150–1, 181, 185–6, 218–9, 333–4
sureties 284, 289
Surinder Singh 10, 41–2, 120
Swaddling 121
Syeda Shah 83

T

T 84
temporary admission 18, 29, 92, 95, 102, 108, 246, 362–3, 375
temporary refuge 91, 106
temporary release 252, 285, 289–90
ten-year-concession 140, 177, 238–9
terrorism 84, 109
'third country cases' 93–4, 104, 363
'third country nationals' 118, 119–21, 125–6, 363
Thong Sum Yee 147
Tinsley House detention centre 102, 287, 349
Tohur Ali 59
torture 86, 98, 104, 312
tourists *see* visitors
Tower Hamlets, R v Secretary of State for the Environment ex parte 184, 201–2
training permit 129, 140–1, 172, 173–5, 232
transfer of asylum 109
Transit Visa Order 1993 85, 153
travel document 88–9, 105, 107, 109, 241,

travel document *continued*
  258, 275, 325, 331, 344–5, 348, 366
Treaty of Rome 2, 112, 126
Treaty on European Union *see* Maastricht Treaty
Tribunal *see* Immigration Appeal Tribunal
Tristan-Garcia 115, 190
TWES 140–1, 172, 173–5, 178
  see also training permit *and* work experience

U

unaccompanied child asylum-seekers 101, 355
uncles 51–2, 59, 77
'under-12 concession' 52–3
undertaking 74–5, 183–4*, 191, 193, 204–5, 235, 363, 374
UKCOSA, the Council for International Education 165, 167, 172, 219–20, 355
Union citizenship 114, 115, 122–3
United Nations Convention against Torture 3, 86, 311
United Nations Convention relating to the status of refugees 3, 79–84*, 86, 88, 89, 90, 93, 109, 198, 258, 310, 311, 314, 361
United Nations High Commission for Refugees 80, 87, 98, 294, 309, 355
unmarried daughters 56–7
urgent cases rate *see* income support

V

validity of applications 75, 232–4
Vander Elst 125
Variation of Leave Order 240
Victoria Hansford 41
visa 4, 5, 7, 8, 16, 55, 84–6, 107–8, 118, 126, 131, 158, 215, 242–4, 365
  multiple-entry 158, 179, 228, 255, 259
  re-entry 158, 228, 361
  single-entry 158, 228, 255
  transit 85, 153, 363
visa exemption 229, 259
visa nationals 5, 12, 26, 45, 85, 118, 132, 148, 157, 160, 163, 176, 225, 228–9, 279, 312, 363
visit 12, 55, 75, 78, 220–1
visitors 54, 71, 148–58*, 163, 177, 227–8, 237, 256, 298
  business 149, 153–4
  family 149–51, 156
  medical 151, 156, 208–9
  transit 85, 153, 256, 279
Vitale 115

VOLO *see* Variation of Leave Order
'voluntary' departure 275, 278, 282
voluntary work 137, 154
Vraciu 83

W

Waddington, David 25, 185
Wardle, Charles 31
Wasfi Mahmod 290
Webb 31
well-founded fear of persecution 80–3
Widdecombe, Ann 211
'white list' countries 104, 311
widows/widowers 72
Wirdestedt 31
withdrawal of applications 240, 242–3, 298
'without foundation' 90, 93, 285, 363
Wolke 115, 122, 190
Wong 119
work 2, 5, 27–8, 29, 37, 53, 100, 109, 114–5, 117, 128–45*, 169, 178–9,

work *continued*
 257–8, 301
 part-time 144, 169, 267
 prohibition on working 144, 151, 153, 163, 165, 169, 224, 256–8, 267
 restriction on working 116, 144, 163, 169, 224, 256–7, 267
 unauthorised 130, 144–5, 169, 265–6, 267
work experience 129, 140, 141, 173–5, 178
work permit 128–34*, 135, 137, 142, 173, 232, 237, 363
work seekers 121
working holidaymakers 54, 128, 130, 142–3, 152, 237
World University Service 105, 355
writers 146–7

Z

Zeghraba 120

JCWI Training

JCWI provides high-quality training in immigration, nationality and refugee law and practice to advisers and practitioners, students and lawyers, individuals and all those interested in working for justice.

Each year we train hundreds of advisers and practitioners, with varying levels of expertise, from experienced solicitors to new volunteers in community groups to local authority staff and academics. Our programme ranges from introductory one or two day sessions to advanced courses and seminars. JCWI's training is based on our practical experience of casework and advice to thousands of people each year, our policy and lobbying work to influence change, and the information used to produce this handbook.

JCWI's courses and seminars include:
- basic nationality and immigration
- refugees and immigration law
- detention, deportation and illegal entry
- implications of the 1996 Asylum and Immigration Act
- immigration status and welfare benefits
- immigration and the European Economic Area

and other areas of the law and practice.

All our courses and seminars are accredited by the Law Society for continuing professional development hours.

Contact Dawn Richards at JCWI, 0171 251 8708 ext. 220, for more details of our training programme.

We also provide in-house training for organisations wanting to train their workers in this way. We can discuss organisations' requirements in detail and tailor courses precisely to their needs. Contact Robert Phillips ext. 223 or Kaltun Hassan ext. 205 for more information.

ALSO FROM JCWI

Other publications from JCWI

JCWI European directory of migrant and ethnic minority organisations

September 1996, £27.50. ISBN 90 75719 03 5

This directory lists over 9100 organisations in all European countries and is a vital resource for all those interested in developing or building links with European groups. It divides them into:
- community and solidarity organisations
- support and service organisations
- anti-racist organisations
- agencies and authorities
- research and documentation centres.

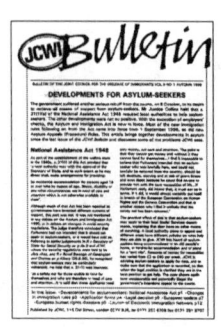

JCWI Bulletin

JCWI's quarterly *Bulletin* is essential reading about developments in the law and practice. It includes:
- articles explaining changes in the law and practice
- details of campaigns and actions
- a digest of important Immigration Appeal Tribunal cases
- updates on developments in European freedom of movement law, human rights and other relevant materials.

Subscribe to the *Bulletin* to be kept up-to-date with changes after the *Handbook* is printed.

JCWI briefings and factsheets

JCWI produces many leaflets about the law and practice. They include clear factual leaflets, explaining a specific part of the law, for example on marriage or on visits. We also write briefings on developments in the law, for MPs, advisers and campaigners to support their work. JCWI plans new editions of factsheets and briefings during 1997.

**Shifting responsibility:
carriers' liability in the member states of
the European Union and North America**
1995, £9.95. ISBN 1 85856 035 7

This book discusses the operation of carriers'
liability legislation in Europe and north America,
concentrating on the UK in most detail. It shows
how it is incompatible with human rights obligations
and refugee protection.

**Women's movement:
women under immigration, nationality
and refugee law**
1994, £12.95. ISBN 1 85856 007 1

Throughout the history of immigration, nationality
and refugee law, women have been treated
differently from men. This book documents that
history and the campaigns to give women
independent status and equal rights, from a feminist
and anti-racist viewpoint.

**Detained without trial:
a survey of Immigration Act detention**
1993, £4.99. ISBN 1 874010 01 3

This book discusses the continuing scandal of
detention under Immigration Act powers – how
people are detained without charge, trial, conviction
or sentence, for indefinite periods, solely for
immigration reasons. The book is vital for all
those concerned about injustice, racism and the
treatment of minorities.

Contact JCWI, using the card at the back of this book,
for details of other publications over the past decades.

Into the future

JCWI continues to advise, represent, inform and train people in all aspects of immigration, nationality and refugee law and practice. But we are also moving into the future, working in partnership with other organisations to introduce electronic services during 1997.
Our email address is jcwi@mcr1.poptel.org.uk.

JCWI is one of the initiators of the **Electronic Immigration Network** (EIN). EIN subscribers will benefit from a range of electronic services of substantial value to practitioners and advisers. These include:

- a database containing the full texts of Immigration Appeal Tribunal determinations and other relevant documents such as Home Office press releases and government statements on immigration and asylum issues
- bulletin boards containing information supplied by many specialist organisations, such as ILPA and RLC as well as JCWI. This will include briefings, articles and details of training courses.
- a facility to 'post' queries to a bulletin board, particularly useful for workers in small agencies working on their own
- a facility for all members to 'publish' information about their activities, for example mobilising a network of campaigners.

EIN also has its own website, accessible to all, with direct links to information providers, up-to-date country reports etc, at
http://www.poptel.org.uk.ein

For more details, contact EIN c/o Rochdale REC
Deen House, Station Road, Rochdale OL11 1DR
tel 01706 352374 fax 01706 711259
ein-admin@mcr1.poptel.org.uk

JCWI will also be developing a service on the Internet, together with the **Centre for Research in Ethnic Relations at the University of Warwick**. This is planned to include extracts from the *Handbook*, information on our publications and briefings and extracts from our *Bulletin*.
Web site   http://www.warwick.ac.uk/fac/soc/CRER_RC.